Linguistic Annotation Workshop 2007

(The LAW)

Held in conjunction with ACL 2007

Prague, Czech Republic
28-29 June 2007

ISBN: 978-1-61738-522-3

Printed from e-media with permission by:

Curran Associates, Inc.
57 Morehouse Lane
Red Hook, NY 12571
www.proceedings.com

Some format issues inherent in the e-media version may also appear in this print version.

Printed by Curran Associates, Inc. (2010)

Association for Computational Linguistics
209 N. Eighth Street
Stroudsburg, Pennsylvania 18360

Phone: 1-570-476-8006
Fax: 1-570-476-0860

acl@aclweb.org

Preface

Welcome to The Linguistic Annotation Workshop (The LAW).

Linguistically annotated corpora play a major role in parsing, information extraction, question answering, machine translation and many other areas of computational linguistics, and provide an empirical testbed for theoretical linguistics research. This has led to a proliferation of annotation systems, frameworks, formats, and schemes. Recognition of the need to harmonize annotation practices and frameworks has become increasingly critical, as witnessed by numerous workshops dealing with different aspects of linguistic annotation over the past few years.

The LAW addresses all aspects of linguistic annotation in a single forum by merging two existing workshop series: NLPXML (Natural Language Processing and XML) and FLAC (Frontiers in Linguistically Annotated Corpora). The goals of the workshop include:

1. The exchange and propagation of research results with respect to the annotation, manipulation and exploitation of corpora, taking into account different applications and theoretical investigations in the field of language technology and research;

2. Working towards harmonization and interoperability from the perspective of the increasingly large number of tools and frameworks that support the creation, instantiation, manipulation, querying, and exploitation of annotated resources;

3. Working towards a consensus on all issues crucial to the advancement of the field of corpus annotation.

These proceedings include 11 long papers, 5 short papers, 4 demo descriptions and 8 posters selected by the program committee from 51 submissions for presentation at the workshop. In addition to these presentations, the workshop includes demonstrations of annotation tools, reports by working groups, and an open discussion session.

We would like to thank the members of the program committee for their timely reviews. We also thank the Workshops Chair and other organizers of ACL-2007 for their support. Finally, we congratulate Adriane Boyd, the winner of the Innovative Student Annotation Award for the paper *Discontinuity Revisited: An Improved Conversion to Context-Free Representations*.

Branimir Boguraev
Nancy Ide
Adam Meyers
Shigeko Nariyama
Manfred Stede
Janyce Wiebe
Graham Wilcock

Organizers

Workshop Chairs

Branimir Boguraev, IBM T. J. Watson Research Center
Nancy Ide, Vassar College
Adam Meyers, New York University
Shigeko Nariyama, University of Melbourne
Manfred Stede, University of Potsdam
Janyce Wiebe, University of Pittsburgh
Graham Wilcock, University of Helsinki

Program Committee

David Ahn, University of Amsterdam
Lars Ahrenberg, Linköping University
Timothy Baldwin, University of Melbourne
Francis Bond, NICT
Kalina Bontcheva, University of Sheffield
Paul Buitelaar, DFKI
Jean Carletta, University of Edinburgh
Key-Sun Choi, KAIST
Christopher Cieri, Linguistic Data Consortium/University of Pennsylvania
Hamish Cunningham, University of Sheffield
David Day, MITRE Corporation
Thierry Declerck, DFKI
Ludovic Denoyer, LIP6 - University of Paris 6
Tomaz Erjavec, Jozef Stefan Institute
David Farwell, New Mexico State University
Alex Chengyu Fang, City University of Hong Kong
Chuck Fillmore, International Computer Science Institute, Berkeley
Anette Frank, DFKI
John Fry, San Jose State University
Claire Grover, University of Edinburgh
Jan Hajic, Charles University
Ed Hovy, University of Southern California
Baden Hughes, University of Melbourne
Emi Izumi, NICT
Tsai Jia-Lin, Tung Nan Institute of Technology
Aravind Joshi, University of Pennsylvania
Ewan Klein, University of Edinburgh
Mounia Lalmas, University of London
Mike Maxwell, University of Maryland
Chieko Nakabasami, Toyo University
Stephan Oepen, University of Oslo
Kyonghee Paik, KLI

Martha Palmer, University of Colorado
Antonio Pareja-Lora, Universidad Complutense de Madrid / OEG - UPM
Manfred Pinkal, Saarland University
James Pustejovsky, Brandeis University
Owen Rambow, Columbia University
Laurent Romary, MPG-INRIA
Henry Thompson, University of Edinburgh
Erik Tjong Kim Sang, University of Amsterdam
Theresa Wilson, University of Edinburgh
Nainwen Xue, University of Colorado

Table of Contents

Workshop Program

Thursday, June 28, 2007

Session 1: Introduction and Long Papers

14:30–14:55 Introduction to the Workshop

14:55–15:20 *GrAF: A Graph-based Format for Linguistic Annotations*
Nancy Ide and Keith Suderman

15:20–15:45 *Efficient Annotation with the Jena ANnotation Environment (JANE)*
Katrin Tomanek, Joachim Wermter and Udo Hahn

15:45–16:15 Break

Session 2: Long Papers

16:15–16:40 *Mining Syntactically Annotated Corpora with XQuery*
Gosse Bouma and Geert Kloosterman

16:40–17:05 *Assocating Facial Displays with Syntactic Constituents for Generation*
Mary Ellen Foster

17:05–17:30 *An Annotation Type System for a Data-Driven NLP Pipeline*
Udo Hahn, Ekaterina Buyko, Katrin Tomanek, Scott Piao, John McNaught, Yoshimasa Tsuruoka and Sophia Ananiadou

Demonstration and Poster Session

17:30–18:30 Demonstrations and Posters
(Listed at end of program)

Friday, June 29, 2007

Session 3: Working Groups

09:30–10:00 Shared Corpora Working Group Report
Adam Meyers, Nancy Ide, Ludovic Denoyer and Yusuke Shinyama

10:00–10:45 Panel Session on Discourse Annotation
Manfred Stede, Eva Hajicova, Brian Reese, Simone Teufel, Bonnie Webber and Theresa Wilson

10:45–11:15 Break

Session 4: Short Papers

11:15–11:30 *Discontinuity Revisited: An Improved Conversion to Context-Free Representations*
Adriane Boyd

11:30–11:45 *Usage of XSL Stylesheets for the Annotation of the Sámi Language Corpora.*
Saara Huhmarniemi, Sjur N. Moshagen and Trond Trosterud

11:45–12:00 *Criteria for the Manual Grouping of Verb Senses*
Cecily Jill Duffield, Jena D. Hwang, Susan Windisch Brown, Dmitriy Dligach, Sarah E. Vieweg, Jenny Davis and Martha Palmer

12:00–12:15 *Semi-Automated Named Entity Annotation*
Kuzman Ganchev, Fernando Pereira, Mark Mandel, Steven Carroll and Peter White

12:15–12:30 *Querying Multimodal Annotation: A Concordancer for GeM*
Martin Thomas

12:30–14:30 Lunch

Friday, June 29, 2007 (continued)

Session 5: Long Papers

14:30–14:55 *Annotating Chinese Collocations with Multi Information*
Ruifeng Xu, Qin Lu, Kam-Fai Wong and Wenjie Li

14:55–15:20 *Computing Translation Units and Quantifying Parallelism in Parallel Dependency Treebanks*
Matthias Buch-Kromann

15:20–15:45 *Adding Semantic Role Annotation to a Corpus of Written Dutch*
Paola Monachesi, Gerwert Stevens and Jantine Trapman

15:45–16:15 Break

Session 6: Long Papers

16:15–16:40 *A Search Tool for Parallel Treebanks*
Martin Volk, Joakim Lundborg and Maël Mettler

16:40–17:05 *Annotating Expressions of Appraisal in English*
Jonathon Read, David Hope and John Carroll

17:05–17:30 *Active Learning for Part-of-Speech Tagging: Accelerating Corpus Annotation*
Eric Ringger, Peter McClanahan, Robbie Haertel, George Busby, Marc Carmen, James Carroll, Kevin Seppi and Deryle Lonsdale

Discussion Session

17:30–18:30 Open Discussion

GrAF: A Graph-based Format for Linguistic Annotations

Nancy Ide
Department of Computer Science
Vassar College
Poughkeepsie, New York USA
ide@cs.vassar.edu

Keith Suderman
Department of Computer Science
Vassar College
Poughkeepsie, New York USA
suderman@cs.vassar.edu

Abstract

In this paper we describe the Graph Annotation Format (GrAF) and show how it is used represent not only independent linguistic annotations, but also sets of merged annotations as a single graph. To demonstrate this, we have automatically transduced several different annotations of the *Wall Street Journal* corpus into GrAF and show how the annotations can then be merged, analyzed, and visualized using standard graph algorithms and tools. We also discuss how, as a standard graph representation, it allows for the application of well-established graph traversal and analysis algorithms to produce information about interactions and commonalities among merged annotations. GrAF is an extension of the Linguistic Annotation Framework (LAF) (Ide and Romary, 2004, 2006) developed within ISO TC37 SC4 and as such, implements state-of-the-art best practice guidelines for representing linguistic annotations.

1 Introduction

Although linguistic annotation of corpora has a long history, over the past several years the need for corpora annotated for a wide variety of phenomena has come to be recognized as critical for the future development of language processing applications. Considerable attention has been devoted to the development of means to represent annotations so that phenomena at different levels can be merged and/or analyzed in combination. A particular focus has been on the development of standards and best practices for representing annotations that can facilitate "annotation interoperability", that is, the use and re-use of annotations produced in different formats and by different groups and to enable easy adaptation to the input requirements of existing annotation tools.

In this paper we describe the Graph Annotation Format (GrAF) and show how it is used represent not only independent linguistic annotations, but also sets of merged annotations as a single graph. We also discuss how, as a standard graph representation, it allows for the application of well-established graph traversal and analysis algorithms to produce information about interactions and commonalities among merged annotations. GrAF is is an extension of the Linguistic Annotation Framework (LAF) (Ide and Romary, 2004, 2006) developed within ISO TC37 SC4[1] and as such, implements state-of-the-art best practice guidelines for representing linguistic annotations.

This paper has several aims: (1) to show the generality of the graph model for representing linguistic annotations; (2) to demonstrate how the graph-based model enables merging and analysis of multi-layered annotations; and (3) to propose as the underlying model for linguistic annotations, due to its generality and the ease with which it is mapped to other formats. To accomplish this, we have automatically transduced several different annotations of the *Wall Street Journal* corpus into GrAF and show how the annotations can then be merged, analyzed, and visualized using standard graph algorithms and tools. Discussion of the

[1] International Standards Organization Technical Committee 37 Sub-Committee 4 for Language Resource Management.

Proceedings of the Linguistic Annotation Workshop, pages 1–8,
Prague, June 2007. ©2007 Association for Computational Linguistics

transduction process brings to light several problems and concerns with current annotation formats and leads to some recommendations for the design of annotation schemes.

2 Overview

Graph theory provides a well-understood model for representing objects that can be viewed as a connected set of more elementary sub-objects, together with a wealth of graph-analytic algorithms for information extraction and analysis. As a result, graphs and graph-analytic algorithms are playing an increasingly important role in language data analysis, including finding related web pages (Kleinberg, 1999; Dean and Henzinger, 1999; Brin, 1998; Grangier and Bengio, 2005), patterns of web access (McEneaney, 2001; Zaki, 2002), and the extraction of semantic information from text (Widdows and Dorow, 2002; Krizhanovsky, 2005; Nastase and Szpakowicz, 2006). Recently, there has been work that treats linguistic annotations as graphs (Cui *et al.*, 2005; Bunescu and Mooney, 2006; Nguyen *et al.*, 2007; Gabrilovich and Markovitch, 2007) in order to identify, for example, measures of semantic similarity based on common subgraphs.

As the need to merge and study linguistic annotations for multiple phenomena becomes increasingly important for language analysis, it is essential to identify a general model that can capture the relevant information and enable efficient and effective analysis. Graphs have long been used to describe linguistic annotations, most familiarly in the form of trees (a graph in which each node has a single parent) for syntactic annotation. Annotation Graphs (Bird and Liberman, 2001) have been widely used to represent layers of annotation, each associated with primary data, although the concept was not extended to allow for annotations linked to other annotations and thus to consider multiple annotations as a single graph. More recently, the Penn Discourse TreeBank released its annotations of the Penn TreeBank as a graph, accompanied by an API that provides a set of standard graph-handling functions for query and access[2]. The graph model therefore seems to be gaining ground as a natural and flexible model for linguistic annotations which, as we demonstrate below, can represent all annotation varieties, even those that were not originally designed with the graph model as a basis.

2.1 LAF

LAF provides a general framework for representing annotations that has been described elsewhere in detail (Ide and Romary, 2004, 2006). Its development has built on common practice and convergence of approach in linguistic annotation over the past 15-20 years. The core of the framework is specification of an abstract model for annotations instantiated by a *pivot format*, into and out of which annotations are mapped for the purposes of exchange.

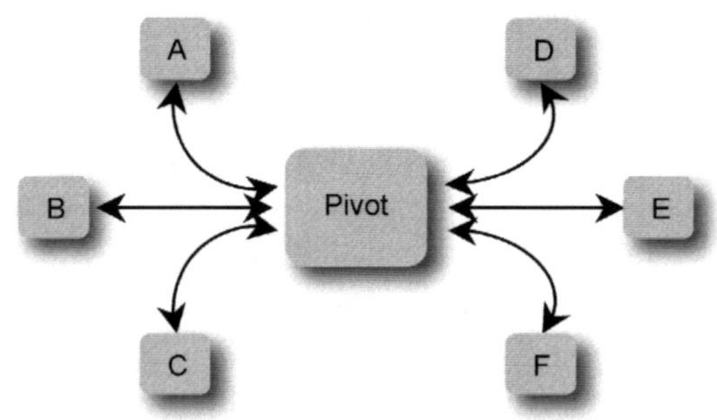

Figure 1: Use of the LAF pivot format

Figure 1 shows the overall idea for six different user annotation formats (labeled A – F), which requires two mappings for each scheme—one into and one out of the pivot format, provided by the scheme designer. The maximum number of mappings among schemes is therefore $2n$, vs. n^2-n mutual mappings without the pivot.

To map to the pivot, an annotation scheme must be (or be rendered via the mapping) isomorphic to the abstract model, which consists of (1) a *referential structure* for associating stand-off annotations with primary data, instantiated as a directed graph; and (2) a *feature structure representation* for annotation content. An annotation thus forms a directed graph referencing n-dimensional regions of primary data as well as other annotations, in which nodes are labeled with feature structures providing the annotation content. Formally, LAF consists of:

- A data model for annotations based on directed graphs defined as follows: A graph of annotations G is a set of vertices $V(G)$ and a set of edges $E(G)$. Vertices and edges may be labeled

2 http://www.seas.upenn.edu/~nikhild/PDTBAPI/

with one or more features. A feature consists of a quadruple (*G', VE, K, V*) where, *G'* is a graph, *VE* is a vertex or edge in *G'*, *K* is the name of the feature and *V* is the feature value.

- A *base segmentation* of primary data that defines edges between virtual nodes located between each "character" in the primary data.[3] The resulting graph *G* is treated as an *edge graph G'* whose nodes are the edges of *G*, and which serve as the leaf ("sink") nodes. These nodes provide the base for an annotation or several layers of annotation. Multiple segmentations can be defined over the primary data, and multiple annotations may refer to the same segmentation.
- Serializations of the data model, one of which is designated as the pivot.
- Methods for manipulating the data model.

Note that LAF does not provide specifications for annotation *content categories* (i.e., the labels describing the associated linguistic phenomena), for which standardization is a much trickier matter. The LAF architecture includes a *Data Category Registry* (DCR) containing pre-defined data elements and schemas that may be used directly in annotations, together with means to specify new categories and modify existing ones (see Ide and Romary, 2004).

2.2 GrAF

GrAF is an XML serialization of the generic graph structure of linguistic annotations described by LAF. A GrAF document represents the referential structure of an annotation with two XML elements: `<node>` and `<edge>`. Both `<node>` and `<edge>` elements may be labeled with associated annotation information. Typically, annotations describing a given object are associated with `<node>` elements. Although some annotations, such as dependency analyses, are traditionally depicted with labeled edges, GrAF converts these to nodes in order to analyze both the annotated objects and the relations of a graph uniformly. Associating annotations with nodes also simplifies the association of an annotation (node) with multiple objects.

According to the LAF specification, an annotation is itself a graph representing a feature structure. In GrAF, feature structures are encoded in XML according to the specifications of ISO TC37 SC4 document 188[4]. The feature structure graph associated with a given node is the corresponding `<node>` element's content. Note that the ISO specifications implement the full power of feature structures and define inheritance, unification, and subsumption mechanisms over the structures, thus enabling the representation of linguistic information at any level of complexity. The specifications also provide a concise format for representing simple feature-value pairs that suffices to represent many annotations, and which, because it is sufficient to represent the vast majority of annotation information, we use in our examples.

`<edge>` elements may also be labeled (i.e., associated with a feature structure), but this information is typically not an annotation *per se*, but rather information concerning the meaning, or role, of the link itself. For example, in PropBank, when there is more than one target of an annotation (i.e., a node containing an annotation has two or more outgoing edges), the targets may be either coreferents or a "split argument" whose constituents are not contiguous, in which case the edges collect an ordered list of constituents. In other case, the outgoing edges may point to a set of alternatives. To differentiate the role of edges in such cases, the edge may be annotated. Unlabeled edges default to pointing to an unordered list of constituents.

A base segmentation contains only `<sink>` elements (i.e., nodes with no outgoing edges), which are a sub-class of `<node>` elements. As noted above, the segmentation is an edge graph created from edges (spans) defined over primary data. The *from* and *to* attributes on `<sink>` elements in the base segmentation identify the start and end points of these edges in the primary data.

Each annotation document declares and associates the elements in its content with a unique namespace. Figure 2 shows several XML fragments in GrAF format.

[3] A character is defined to be a contiguous byte sequence of a specified length .For text, the default is UTF-16.

[4] See ISO TC37 SC4 document N188, Feature Structures-Part 1: Feature Structure Representation (2005-10-01), available at http://www.tc37sc4.org/

Base segmentation:

```
<seg:sink seg:id="42" seg:start="24"
      seg:end="35"/>
```

Annotation over the base segmentation:

```
<msd:node msd:id="16">
   <msd:f name="cat" value="NN"/>
</msd:node>

<msd:edge from="msd:16" to="seg:42"/>
```

Annotation over another annotation:

```
<ptb:node ptb:id="23">
   <ptb:f name="type" value="NP"/>
   <ptb:f name="role" value="-SBJ"/>
</ptb:node>
```

Figure 2: GrAF annotations in XML

3 Transduction

To test the utility of GrAF for representing annotations of different types produced by different groups, we transduced the Penn TreeBank (PTB), PropBank (PB), NomBank (NB), Penn Discourse TreeBank (PDTB), and TimeBank (TB) annotations of the *Wall Street Journal (WSJ)* corpus to conform to the specifications of LAF and GrAF. These annotations are represented in several different formats, including both stand-off and embedded formats. The details of the transduction process, although relatively mundane, show that the process is not always trivial. Furthermore, they reveal several seemingly harmless practices that can cause difficulties for transduction to any other format and, therefore, use by others. Consideration of these details is therefore informative for the development of best practice annotation guidelines.

The Penn TreeBank annotations of the *WSJ* are embedded in the data itself, by bracketing components of syntactic trees. Leaf nodes of the tree are comprised of POS-word pairs; thus, the PTB includes annotations for both morpho-syntax and syntax. To coerce the annotations into LAF/GrAF, it was necessary to

- extract the text in order to create a primary data document;
- provide a primary segmentation reflecting the tokenization implicit in the PTB;
- separate the morpho-syntactic annotation from the syntactic annotation and render each as a stand-off document in GrAF format, with links to the primary segmentation.

NB, PB, and PDTB do not annotate primary data, but rather annotate the PTB syntax trees by providing stand-off documents with references to PTB Tree nodes. The format of the NB and PB stand-off annotations is nearly identical; consider for example the following PB annotation:

```
wsj/00/wsj_0003.mrg 18 18 gold include.01
p---a 14:1,16:1-ARG2 18:0-rel 19:1-ARG1
```

In GrAF, this becomes

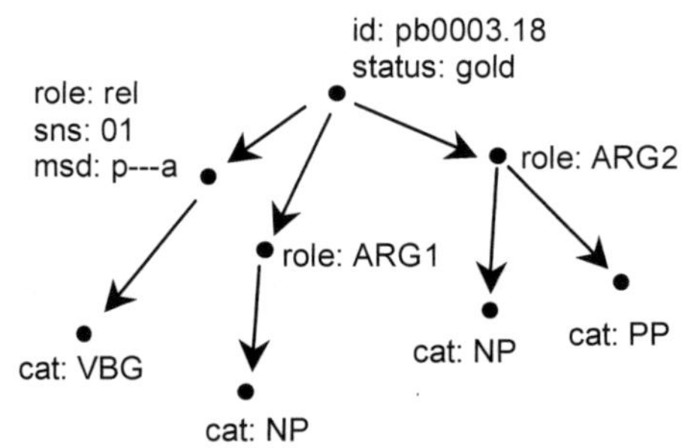

Each line in the PB and NB stand-off files provides a single annotation and therefore interpreted as an annotation node with a unique *id*. Each annotation is associated with a node with an edge to the annotated entity. The PB/NB comma notation (e.g., `14:1,16:1`) denotes reference to more than one node in the PTB tree; in GrAF, a dummy node is created to group them so that if, for example, a NB annotation refers to the same node set, in a merged representation a graph minimization algorithm can collapse the dummy nodes while retaining the annotations from each of PB and NB as separate nodes.

Some interpretation was required for the transduction, for example, we assume that the sense number and morpho-syntactic descriptor are associated with the element annotated as "rel" (vs. the "gold" status that is associated with the entire proposition), an association that is automatically discernible from the structure. Also, because the POS/word pairs in the PTB leaf nodes have been split into separate nodes, we assume the PB/NB annotations should refer to the POS annotation rather than the string in the primary data, but either option is possible.

Given the similarities of the underlying data models for the PDTB and LAF, creating GrAF-compliant structures from the PDTB data is relatively trivial. This task is simplified even further because the PDTB API allows PDTB files to be loaded in a few simple steps, and allows the programmer to set and query features of the node as well as iterate over the children of the node. So, given a node *P* that represents the root node of a PDTB tree, an equivalent graph *G* in GrAF format can be created by traversing the PDTB tree and creating matching nodes and edges in the graph *G*.

Like the PTB, TimeBank annotation is embedded in the primary data by surrounding annotated elements with XML tags. TB also includes sets of "link" tags at the end of each document, specifying relations among annotated elements. The same steps for rendering the PTB into GrAF could be followed for TB; however, this would result in a separate (and possibly different) primary data document. Therefore, it is necessary to first align the text extracted from TB with the primary data derived from PTB, after which the TB XML annotations are rendered in GrAF format and associated with the corresponding nodes in the base segmentation.

Note that in the current GrAF representation, TB's *tlink*, *slink*, and *alink* annotations are applied to edges, since they designate relations among nodes. However, further consideration of the nature and use of the information associated with these links may dictate that associating it with a node is more appropriate and/or useful.

Variations in tokenization exist among the different annotations, most commonly for splitting contractions or compounds ("cannot" split into "can" and "not", "New York-based" split into "New York", "-", and "based", etc.). This can be handled by adding edges to the base segmentation (not necessarily in the same segmentation document) that cover the relevant sub-spans, and pointing to the new edge nodes as necessary. Annotations may now reference the original span, the entire annotation, or any sub-part of the annotation, by pointing to the appropriate node. Alternative segmentations of the same span can be joined by a "dummy" parent node so that when different annotations of the same data are later merged, nodes labeling a sub-graph covering the same span can be combined. For example, in Figure 3, if the PTB segmentation (in gray) is the base segmentation, an alternative segmentation of the same span (in black) is created and associated to the PTB segmentation via a dummy node. When annotations using each of the different segmentations are merged into a single graph, features associated with any node covering the same sub-tree (in bold) are applied to the dummy node (as a result of graph minimization), thus preserving the commonality in the merged graph.

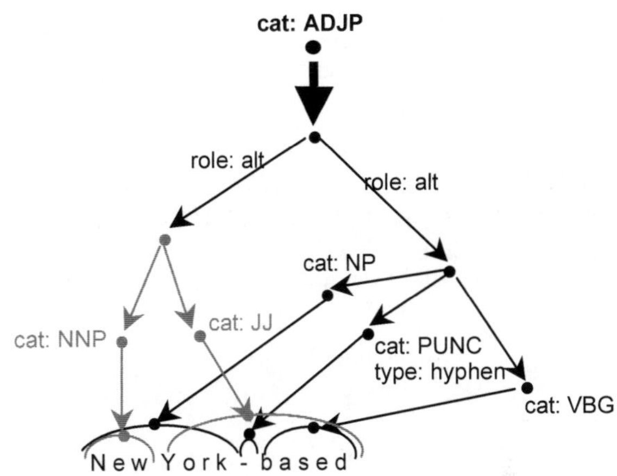

Figure 3: Alternative segmentations

4 Merging Annotations

Once they are in in GrAF format, merging annotations of the same primary data, or annotations referencing annotations of the same primary data, involves simply combining the graphs for each annotation, starting with graph *G* describing the base segmentation and using the algorithm in Figure 4. Once merged, graph minimization, for which efficient algorithms exist (see, e.g., Cardon and Crochemore, 1982; Habib *et al.*, 1999), can be applied to collapse identically-labeled nodes with edges to common subgraphs and eliminate dummy nodes such as the one in Figure 3.

```
Given a graph G :

for each graph of annotations Gp do
  for each vertex vp in Gp do
    if vp is not a leaf in Gp then
      add vp to G
  for each edge (vi, vj) in Gp do
    if vj is a leaf in Gp then
      find corresponding vertex vg ∈ G
        add a new edge (vi, vg) to G
      else
       add edge (vi, vj) to G
```

Figure 4: Graph-merging algorithm

5 Using the Graphs

Because the GrAF format is isomorphic to input to many graph-analytic tools, existing software can be exploited; for example, we have generated graph diagrams directly from a merged graph including PTB, NB, and PB annotations using GraphViz[5], which takes as its input a simple text file representation of a graph. Generating the input files to GraphViz involves simply iterating over the nodes and edges in the graph and printing out a suitable string representation. Figure 5 shows a segment of the GraphViz output generated from the PTB/NB/PB merged annotations (modified slightly for readability).

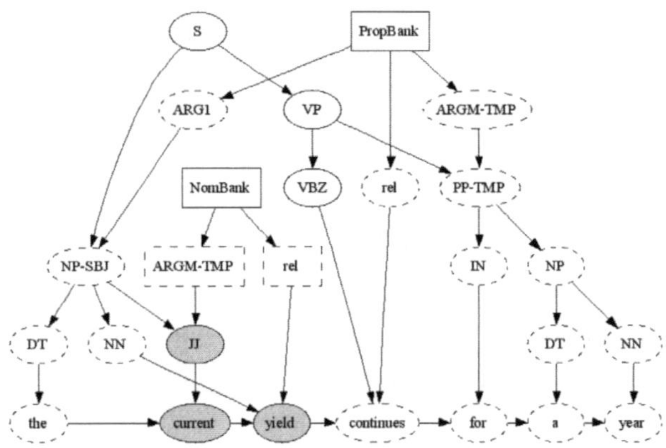

Figure 5: Fragment of GraphViz output

Graph-traversal and graph-coloring algorithms can be used to identify and generate statistics concerning commonly annotated components in the merged graph. For example, we modified the merging algorithm to "color" the annotated nodes as the graphs are constructed to reflect the source of the annotation (e.g., PTB, NB, PB, etc.) and the annotation content itself. Colors are propagated via outgoing edges down to the base segmentation, so that each node in the graph can be identified by the source and type of annotation applied. The colored graph can then be used to identify common subgraphs. So, for example, a graph traversal can identify higher-level nodes in PTB that cover the same spans as TB annotations, which in the merged graph are connected to sink nodes (tokens) only, thus effectively "collapsing" the two annotations.

Traversal of the colored graph can also be used to generate statistics reflecting the interactions among annotations. As a simple example, we generated a list of all nodes annotated as ARG0 by both PB and NB[6], the "related" element (a verb for PB, a nominalization for NB), the PTB annotation, and the set of sink nodes covered by the node, which reveals clusters of verb/nominalization pairs and can be used, for example, to augment semantic lexicons. Similar information generated via graph traversal can obviously provide a wealth of statistics that can in turn be used to study interactions among linguistic phenomena. Other graph-analytic algorithms—including common sub-graph analysis, shortest paths, minimum spanning trees, connectedness, identification of articulation vertices, topological sort, graph partitioning, etc.—may prove to be useful for mining information from a graph of annotations at multiple linguistic levels, possibly revealing relationships and interactions that were previously difficult to observe. We have, for example, generated frequent subgraphs of the PB and NB annotations using the IBM Frequent Subgraph Miner[7] (Inokuchi *et al.*, 2005). We are currently exploring several additional applications of graph algorithms to annotation analysis.

The graph format also enables manipulations that may be desirable in order to add information, modify the graph to reflect additional analysis, correct errors, etc. For example, it may be desirable to delete or move constituents such as punctuation and parenthetical phrases under certain circumstances, conjoin sub-graphs whose sink nodes are joined by a conjunction such as "and", or correct PP attachments based on information in the tree.

6 Discussion

GrAF provides a serialization of annotations that follows the specifications of LAF and is therefore a candidate to serve as the LAF pivot format. The advantages of a pivot format, and, in general, the use of the graph model for linguistic annotations, are numerous. First, transduction of the various formats into GrAF, as described in section 4, demanded substantial programming effort; similar effort would be required to transduce to any other

[5] www.graphviz.org

[6] The gray nodes in Figure 5 are those that have been "colored" by both PB and NB.

[7] http://www.alphaworks.ibm.com/tech/fsm

format, graph-based or not. The role of the LAF pivot format is to reduce this effort across the community by an order of magnitude, as shown in Figure 1. Whether or not GrAF is the pivot, the adoption of the graph *model,* at least for the purposes of exchange, would result in a similar reduction of effort, since graph representations are in general trivially mappable.

In addition to enabling the generation of input to a wide range of graph-handling software, the graph model for annotations is isomorphic to representation formats used by emerging annotation frameworks, in particular, UIMA's Common Analysis System[8]. It is also compatible with tools such as the PDTBAPI, which is easily generalized to handle graphs as well as trees. In addition, the graph model underlies Semantic Web formats such as RDF and OWL, so that any annotation graph is trivially transducable to their serializations (which include not only XML but several others as well), and which, as noted above, has spawned a flurry of research using graph algorithms to extract and analyze semantic information from the web.

A final advantage of the graph model is that it provides a sound basis for devising linguistic annotation schemes. For example, the PB and NB format, although ultimately mappable to a graph representation, was not developed with the graph model as a basis. The format is ambiguous as to the relations among the parts of the annotation, in particular, the relation between the information at the beginning of the line providing the status ("gold"), sense number, and morpho-syntactic description, and the rest of the annotation. Human interpretation can determine that the status (probably) applies to the whole annotation, and the sense number and msd apply to the PTB lexical item being annotated, as reflected in the graph-based representation given in section 3. This somewhat innocuous example demonstrates an all-too-pervasive feature of many annotation schemes: reliance on human interpretation to determine structural relations that are implicit in the *content* of the annotation. Blind automatic transduction of the format to any other format is therefore impossible, and the interpretation, although more or less clear in this example, is prone to human error. If the designers of the PB/NB format had begun with a graph-based model—i.e., had been forced to "draw the circles and lines"—this ambiguity would likely have been avoided.

8 http://www.alphaworks.ibm.com/tech/uima

7 Conclusion

We have argued that a graph model for linguistic annotations provides the generality and flexibility required for representing linguistic annotations of different types, and provides powerful and well-established means to analyze these annotations in ways that have been previously unexploited. We introduce GrAF, an XML serialization of the graph model, and demonstrate how it can be used to represent annotations originally made available in widely varying formats. GrAF is designed to be used in conjunction with the Linguistic Annotation Framework, which defines an overall architecture for representing layers of linguistic annotation. We show how LAF stand-off annotations in GrAF format can be easily merged and analyzed, and discuss the application of graph-analytic algorithms and tools.

Linguistic annotation has a long history, and over the past 15-20 years we have seen increasing attention to the need for standardization as well as continuing development and convergence of best practices to enable annotation interoperability. Dramatic changes in technology, an in particular the development of the World Wide Web, have impacted both the ways in which we represent linguistic annotations and the urgency of the need to develop sophisticated language processing applications that rely on them. LAF and GrAF are not based on brand new ideas, but rather reflect and make explicit what appears to be evolving as common best practice methodology.

References

A. Cardon and Maxime Crochemore, 1982. Partitioning a graph in O(|A| log2 |V|).*Theoretical Computer Science,* 19(1):85–98.

Akihiro Inokuchi, Takashi Washio, and Hiroshi Motoda, 2005. A General Framework for Mining Frequent Subgraphs from Labeled Graphs. *Fundamenta Informaticae,* 66:1-2, 53-82.

Andrew A. Krizhanovsky, 2005. Synonym search in Wikipedia: Synarcher. http://www.citebase.org/abstract?id=oai:arXiv.org:cs/0606097

Dat P.T Nguyen, Yutaka Matsuo, and Mitsuru Ishizuka, 2007. Exploiting Syntactic and Semantic Information for Relation Extraction from Wikipedia. IJCAI *Workshop on Text-Mining & Link-Analysis (TextLink 2007)*.

Dominic Widdows and Beate Dorow, 2002. A graph model for unsupervised lexical acquisition. *Proceedings of the 19th International Conference on Computational Linguistics,* 1093-1099.

Evgeniy Gabrilovich and Shaul Markovitch, 2007. Computing Semantic Relatedness Using Wikipedia-based Explicit Semantic Analysis. *Proceedings of the 20th International Joint Conference on Artificial Intelligence*, Hyderabad, India.

Hang Cui, Renxu Sun, Keya Li, Min-Yen Kan and Tat-Seng Chua, 2005. Question answering passage retrieval using dependency relations. *SIGIR '05: Proceedings of the 28th Annual International ACM SIGIR Conference on Research and Development in Information Retrieval*, 400-407.

Jeffrey Dean, Monika R. Henzinger, 1999. Finding related pages in the World Wide Web. *Computer Networks,* 31(11-16):1467–1479.

John E. McEneaney, 2001. Graphic and numerical methods to assess navigation in hypertext. *International Journal of Human-Computer Studies*, 55, 761-786.

Jon M. Kleinberg, 1999. Authoritative sources in a hyper-linked environment. *Journal of the ACM* 46(5):604-632.

Michel Habib, Christophe Paul, Laurent Viennot, 1999. Partition refinement techniques: An interesting algorithmic tool kit. International Journal of Foundations of Computer Science, 10(2):147–170.

Mohammed J. Zaki, 2002. Efficiently mining trees in a forest. *Proceedings of SIGKDD'02.*

Nancy Ide and Laurent Romary, 2004. A Registry of Standard Data Categories for Linguistic Annotation. *Proceedings of the Fourth Language Resources and Evaluation Conference* (LREC), Lisbon, 135-39.

Nancy Ide and Laurent Romary, 2004. International Standard for a Linguistic Annotation Framework. *Journal of Natural Language Engineering,* 10:3-4, 211-225.

Nancy Ide and Laurent Romary, 2006. Representing Linguistic Corpora and Their Annotations. *Proceedings of the Fifth Language Resources and Evaluation Conference* (LREC), Genoa, Italy.

Razvan C. Bunescu and Raymond J. Mooney, 2007. Extracting relations from text: From word sequences to dependency paths. In Anne Kao and Steve Poteet (eds.), *Text Mining and Natural Language Processing*, Springer, 29-44.

Sergey Brin, 1998. Extracting patterns and relations from the world wide web. *Proceedings of the 1998 International Workshop on the Web and Databases*, 172-183.

Sisay Fissaha Adafre and Maar ten de Rijke, 2005. Discovering missing links in Wikipedia. *Workshop on Link Discovery: Issues, Approaches and Applications.*

Stephen Bird and Mark Liberman, 2001. A formal framework for linguistic annotation. *Speech Communication,* 33:1-2, 23-60.

Vivi Nastase and Stan Szpakowicz, 2006. Matching syntactic-semantic graphs for semantic relation assignment. *Proceedings of TextGraphs: the Second Workshop on Graph Based Methods for Natural Language Processing*, 81-88.

Efficient Annotation with the Jena ANnotation Environment (JANE)

Katrin Tomanek **Joachim Wermter** **Udo Hahn**
Jena University Language & Information Engineering (JULIE) Lab
Fürstengraben 30
D-07743 Jena, Germany
{tomanek|wermter|hahn}@coling-uni-jena.de

Abstract

With ever-increasing demands on the diversity of annotations of language data, the need arises to reduce the amount of efforts involved in generating such value-added language resources. We introduce here the Jena ANnotation Environment (JANE), a platform that supports the complete annotation life-cycle and allows for 'focused' annotation based on active learning. The focus we provide yields significant savings in annotation efforts by presenting only informative items to the annotator. We report on our experience with this approach through simulated and real-world annotations in the domain of immunogenetics for NE annotations.

1 Introduction

The remarkable success of machine-learning methods for NLP has created, for supervised approaches at least, a profound need for annotated language corpora. Annotation of language resources, however, has become a bottleneck since it is performed, with some automatic support (pre-annotation) though, by humans. Hence, annotation is a time-costly and error-prone process.

The demands for annotated language data is increasing at different levels. After the success in syntactic (Penn TreeBank (Marcus et al., 1993)) and propositional encodings (Penn PropBank (Palmer et al., 2005)), more sophisticated semantic data (such as temporal (Pustejovsky et al., 2003) or opinion annotations (Wiebe et al., 2005)) and discourse data (e.g., for anaphora resolution (van Deemter and Kibble, 2000) and rhetorical parsing (Carlson et al., 2003)) are being generated. Once the ubiquitous area of newswire articles is left behind, different domains (e.g., the life sciences (Ohta et al., 2002)) are yet another major concern. Furthermore, any new HLT application (e.g., information extraction, document summarization) makes it necessary to provide appropriate human annotation products. Besides these considerations, the whole field of non-English languages is desperately seeking to enter into enormous annotation efforts, at virtually all encoding levels, to keep track of methodological requirements imposed by such resource-intensive research activities.

Given this enormous need for high-quality annotations at virtually all levels the question turns up how to minimize efforts within an acceptable quality window. Currently, for most tasks several hundreds of thousands of text tokens (ranging between 200,000 to 500,000 text tokens) have to be scrutinized unless valid tagging judgments can be learned. While significant time savings have already been reported on the basis of automatic pre-tagging (e.g., for POS and parse tree taggings in the Penn TreeBank (Marcus et al., 1993), or named entity taggings for the Genia corpus (Ohta et al., 2002)), this kind of pre-processing does not reduce the number of text tokens actually to be considered.

We have developed the Jena ANnotation Environment (JANE) that allows to reduce annotation efforts by means of the *active learning* (AL) approach. Unlike random or sequential sampling of linguistic items to be annotated, AL is an intelligent selective

Proceedings of the Linguistic Annotation Workshop, pages 9–16,
Prague, June 2007.

sampling strategy that helps reduce the amount of data to be annotated substantially at almost no loss in annotation effectiveness. This is achieved by focusing on those items particularly relevant for the learning process.

In Section 2, we review approaches to annotation cost reduction. We turn in Section 3 to the description of JANE, our AL-based annotation system, while in Section 4 we report on the experience we made using the AL component in NE annotations.

2 Related Work

Reduction of efforts for training (semi-) supervised learners on annotated language data has always been an issue of concern. Semi-supervised learning provides methods to bootstrap annotated corpora from a small number of manually labeled examples. However, it has been shown (Pierce and Cardie, 2001) that semi-supervised learning is brittle for NLP tasks where typically large amounts of high quality annotations are needed to train appropriate classifiers.

Another approach to reducing the human labeling effort is *active learning* (AL) where the learner has direct influence on the examples to be manually labeled. In such a setting, those examples are taken for annotation which are assumed to be maximally useful for (classifier) training. AL approaches have already been tried for different NLP tasks (Engelson and Dagan, 1996; Hwa, 2000; Ngai and Yarowsky, 2000), though such studies usually report on simulations rather than on concrete experience with AL for real annotation efforts. In their study on AL for base noun phrase chunking, Ngai and Yarowsky (2000) compare the costs of rule-writing with (AL-driven) annotation to compile a base noun phrase chunker. They conclude that one should rather invest human labor in annotation than in rule writing.

Closer to our concerns is the study by Hachey et al. (2005) who apply AL to named entity (NE) annotation. There are some differences in the actual AL approach they chose, while their main idea, *viz.* to apply committee-based AL to speed up real annotations, is comparable to our work. They report on negative side effects of AL on the annotations and state that AL annotations are cognitively more difficult for the annotators to deal with (because the sentences selected for annotation are more complex). As a consequence, diminished annotation quality and higher per-sentence annotation times arise in their experiments. By and large, however, they conclude that AL selection should still be favored over random selection because the negative implications of AL are easily over-compensated by the significant reduction of sentences to be annotated to yield comparable classifier performance as under random sampling conditions.

Whereas Hatchey *et al.* focus only on one group of entity mentions (*viz.* four entity subclasses of the astrophysics domain), we report on broader experience when applying AL to annotate several groups of entity mentions in biomedical subdomains. We also address practical aspects as to how create the seed set for the first AL round and how one might estimate the efficiency of AL. The immense savings in annotation effort we achieve here (up to 75%) may mainly depend on the sparseness of many entity types in biomedical corpora. Furthermore, we here present a *general* annotation environment which supports AL-driven annotations for most segmentation problems, not just for NE recognition.

In contrast, annotation editors, such as e.g. WordFreak[1], typically offer facilities for supervised correction of automatically annotated text. This, however, is very different from the AL approach.

3 JANE – Jena ANnotation Environment

JANE, the Jena ANnotation Environment, supports the whole annotation life-cycle including the compilation of annotation projects, annotation itself (via an external editor), monitoring, and the deployment of annotated material. In JANE, an *annotation project* consists of a *collection of documents* to be annotated, an associated *annotation schema* – a specification of what has to be annotated in which way, according to the accompanying annotation guidelines – a set of configuration parameters, and an *annotator* assigned to it.

We distinguish two kinds of annotation projects: A *default project*, on the one hand, contains a predefined and fixed collection of naturally occurring documents which the annotator handles independently of each other. In an *active learning project*, on the other hand, the annotator has access to exactly one

[1] `http://wordfreak.sourceforge.net`

(AL-computed pseudo) document at a time. After such a document has completely been annotated, a new one is dynamically constructed which contains those sentences for annotation which are the most informative ones for training a classifier. Besides annotators who actually do the annotation, there are *administrators* who are in charge of (annotation) project management, monitoring the annotation progress, and deployment, i.e., exporting the data to other formats.

JANE consists of one central component, the *annotation repository*, where all annotation and project data is stored centrally, two *user interfaces*, namely one for the annotators and one for the administrator, and the *active learning* component which interactively generates documents to speed up the annotation process. All components communicate with the annotation repository through a network socket – allowing JANE to be run in a distributed environment. JANE is largely platform-independent because all components are implemented in Java. A test version of JANE may be obtained from `http://www.julielab.de`.

3.1 Active Learning Component

One of the most established approaches to active learning is based on the idea to build an ensemble of classifiers from the already annotated examples. Each classifier then makes its prediction on all unlabeled exampels. Examples on which the classifiers in the ensemble disagree most in their predictions are considered informative and are thus requested for labeling. Obviously, we can expect that adding these examples to the training corpus will increase the accuracy of a classifier trained on this data (Seung et al., 1992). A common metric to estimate the disagreement within an ensemble is the so-called *vote entropy*, the entropy of the distribution of labels l_i assigned to an example e by the ensemble of k classifiers (Engelson and Dagan, 1996):

$$D(e) = -\frac{1}{\log k} \sum_{l_i} \frac{V(l_i,e)}{k} \log \frac{V(l_i,e)}{k}$$

Our AL component employs such an ensemble-based approach (Tomanek et al., 2007). The ensemble consists of $k = 3$ classifiers[2]. AL is run on the sentence level because this is a natural unit for many segmentation tasks. In each round, b sentences with the highest disagreement are selected.[3] The pool of (available) unlabeled examples can be very large for many NLP tasks; for NE annotations in the biomedical domain we typically download several hundreds of thousands of abstracts from PUBMED.[4] In order to avoid high selection times, we consider only a (random) subsample of the pool of unlabeled examples in each AL round. Both the selection size b (which we normally set to $b = 30$), the composition of the ensemble, and the subsampling ratio can be configured with the administration component.

AL selects single, non-contiguous sentences from *different* documents. Since the context of these sentences is still crucial for many (semantic) annotation decisions, for each selected sentence its original context is added (but blocked from annotation). When AL selection is finished, a new document is compiled from these sentences (including their contexts) and uploaded to the annotation repository. The annotator can then proceed with annotation.

Although optimized for NE annotations, the AL component may – after minor modifications of the feature sets being used by the classifiers – also be applied to other segmentation problems, such as POS or chunk annotations.

3.2 Administration Component

Administering large-scale annotation projects is a challenging management task for which we supply a GUI (Figure 1) to support the following tasks:

User Management Create accounts for administrators and annotators.

Creation of Projects The creation of an annotation project requires a considerable number of documents and other files (such as annotation schema definitions) to be uploaded to the annotation repository. Furthermore, several parameters, especially for AL projects have to be set appropriately.

Editing a Project The administrator can reset a project (especially when guidelines change, one

[2] Currently, we incorporate as classifiers Naive Bayes, Maximum Entropy, and Conditional Random Fields.

[3] Here, the vote entropy is calculated separately for each token. The sentence-level vote entropy is then the average over the respective token sequence.

[4] `http://www.ncbi.nlm.nih.gov/`

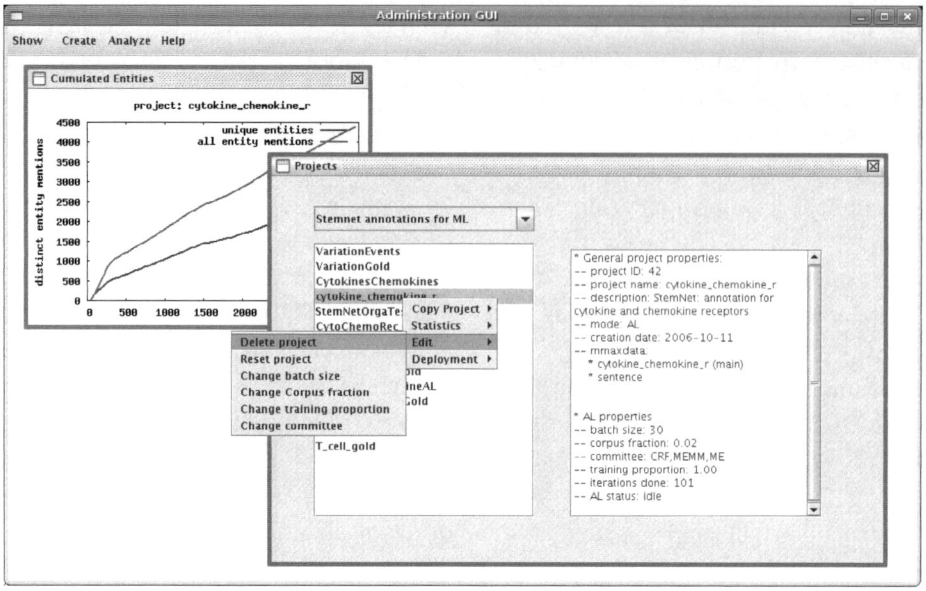

Figure 1: Administration GUI: frame in foreground shows actions that can be performed on an AL project.

might want to start the annotation process anew, i.e., delete all previous annotations but keep the rest of the project unchanged), delete a project, copy a project (which is helpful when several annotators label the same documents to check the applicability of the guidelines by inter-annotator agreement calculation), and change several AL-specific settings.

Monitoring the Annotation Process The administrator can check which documents of an annotation project have already been annotated, how long annotation took on the average, when an annotator logged in last time, etc. Furthermore, the progress of AL projects can be visualized by learning and disagreement curves and an enumeration of the number of (unique) entities found so far.

Inter-Annotator Agreement For related projects (projects sharing the same annotation schema and documents to be annotated) the degree to which several annotators mutually agree in their annotations can be calculated. Such an inter-annotator agreement (IAA) is common to estimate the quality and applicability of particular annotation guidelines (Kim and Tsujii, 2006). Currently, several IAA metrics of different strictness for NE annotations (and other segmentation tasks) are incorporated.

Deployment The annotation repository stores the annotations in a specific XML format (see Section 3.3). For deployment, the annotations may be needed in a different format. Currently, the administration GUI basically supports export into the IOB format. Only documents marked by the annotators as *'completely annotated'* are considered.

3.3 Annotation Component

As the annotators are rather domain experts (in our case graduate students of biology or related life sciences) than computer specialists, we wanted to make life for them as easy as possible. Hence, we provide a separate GUI for the annotators. After log-in the annotator is given an overview of his/her annotation projects along with a short description. Double clicking on a project, the annotators get a list with all documents in this project. Documents have different flags (*raw*, *in progress*, *done*) to indicate the current annotation state as set by each annotator.

Annotation itself is done with MMAX, an external annotation editor (Müller and Strube, 2003), which can be customized with respect to the particular annotation schema. The document to be annotated, the annotations, and the configuration parameters are stored in separate XML files. Our annotation repository reflects this MMAX-specific data structure.

Double clicking on a specific document directly opens MMAX for annotation. During annotation, the annotation GUI is locked to ensure data integrity. When working on an AL project, the annotator can start the AL selection process (which then runs on a separate high-performance machine) after having finished the annotation of the current document. During the AL selection process (it usually takes up to several minutes) the current project is blocked. However, meanwhile the annotator can go on annotating other projects.

3.4 Annotation Repository

The annotation repository is the heart of our annotation environment. All project, user, and annotation relevant data is stored here centrally. This is a crucial design criterion because it lets the administrator access (e.g., for backup or deployment) *all* annotations from one central site. Furthermore, the annotators do not have to care about how to shift the annotated documents to the managerial staff. All state information related to the entire annotation cycle is recorded and kept centrally in this repository.

The repository is realized as a relational database[5] reflecting largely the data structure of MMAX. Both, the GUIs and the AL component, communicate with the repository via the JDBC network driver. Thus, each component can be run on a different machine as long as it has a network connection to the annotation repository. This has two main advantages: First, annotators can work remotely (e.g., from home or from a physically dislocated lab). Second, resource-intensive tasks, e.g., AL selection, can be run on separate machines to which the annotators normally do not have access. The components communicate with each other only through the annotation repository. In particular, there is no direct communication between the annotation GUI and the AL component.

4 Experience with Real-World Annotations

We are currently conducting NE annotations for two large-scale information extraction and semantic retrieval projects. Both tasks cover two non-overlapping biomedical subdomains, *viz.* one in the field of hematopoietic stem cell transplantation (immunogenetics), the other in the area of gene regulation. Entity types of interest are, e.g., cytokines and their receptors, antigens, antibodies, immune cells, variation events, chemicals, blood diseases, etc. In this section, we report on our actual experience and findings in annotating entity mentions (drawing mainly on our work in the immunogenetics subdomain) with JANE, with a focus on methodological issues related to active learning.

In the biomedical domain, there is a vast amount of unlabeled material available for almost any topic of interest. The most prominent source is probably PUBMED, a literature database which currently includes over 16 million citations, mostly abstracts, from MEDLINE and other life science sources. We used MESH terms[6] and publication date ranges[7] to select relevant documents from the immunogenetics subdomain. Thus, we retrieved about 200,000 abstracts ($\approx$ 2,000,000 sentences) as our document pool of unlabeled examples for immunogenetics. Through random subsampling, only about 40,000 sentences are considered for AL selection.

For several of our entity annotations, we did both an active learning (AL) annotation and a gold standard (GS) annotation. The latter is performed in the default project mode on 250 abstracts randomly chosen from the entire document pool. We asked different annotators to annotate the same (subset of the) GS to calculate inter-annotator agreement in order to make sure that our annotation guidelines were non-ambiguous. Furthermore, as the annotation proceeds, we regularly train a classifier on the AL annotations and evaluate it against the GS annotations. From this *learning curve*, we can estimate the potential gain of further AL annotation rounds and decide when to stop AL annotation.

4.1 Reduction of Annotation Effort through AL

In real-world AL annotation projects, the amount of cost reduction is hard to estimate properly. We have thus extensively simulated and tested the gain in the reduction of annotation costs of our AL component on available entity annotations of the biomedical domain (GENIA[8] and PENNBIOIE[9]) and the general-

[5] We chose MYSQL, a fast and reliable open source database with native Java driver support

[6] MESH (`http://www.nlm.nih.gov/mesh/`) is the U.S. National Library of Medicine's controlled vocabulary used for indexing PUBMED articles.

[7] Typically, articles published before 1990 are not considered to contain relevant information for molecular biology.

[8] `http://www-tsujii.is.s.u-tokyo.ac.jp/GENIA/`

[9] `http://bioie.ldc.upenn.edu/`

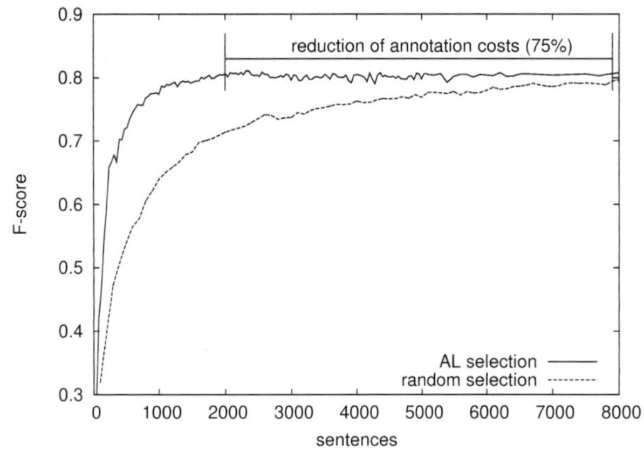

Figure 2: Learning curves for AL and random selection on variation event entity mentions.

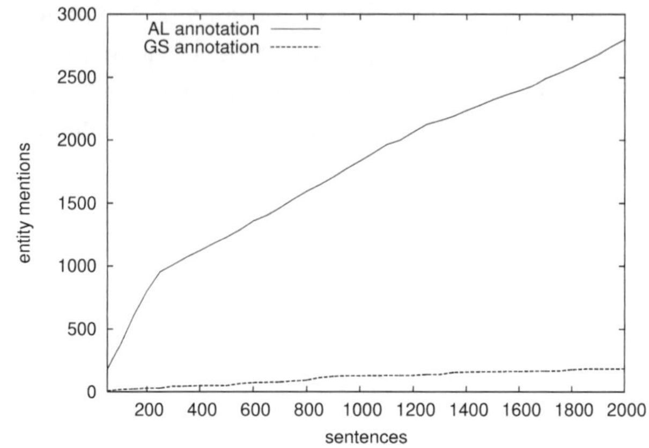

Figure 3: Cumulated entity density on AL and GS annotations of cytokine receptors.

language newspaper domain (English data set of the CoNLL-2003 shared task (Tjong Kim Sang and De Meulder, 2003)). As a metric for annotation costs we here consider the number of sentences to be annotated such that a certain F-score is reached with our NE tagger.[10] We therefore compare the learning curves of AL and random selection. On almost every scenario, we found that AL yields cost savings of about 50%, sometimes even up to 75%.

As an example, we report on our AL simulation on the PENNBIOIE corpus for variation events. These entity mentions include the following six subclasses: type, event, original state, altered state, generic state, and location. The learning curves for AL and random selection are shown in Figure 2. Using random sampling, an F-score of 80% is reached by random selection after $\approx$ 8,000 sentences (200,000 tokens). In contrast, AL selection yields the same F-score after $\approx$ 2,000 sentences (46,000 tokens). This amounts to a reduction of annotation costs on the order of 75%.

Our real-world annotations revealed that AL is especially beneficial when entity mentions are very sparsely distributed in the texts. After an initialization phase needed by AL to take off (which can considerably be accelerated when one carefully selects the sentences of the first AL round, see Section 4.2), AL selects, by and large, only sentences which contain at least one entity mention of the type of interest. In contrast, random selection (or in real annotation projects: sequential annotations of abstracts as in our default project mode), may lead to lots of negative training examples with no entity mentions of interest. When there is no simulation data at hand, the entity density of AL annotations (compared with the respective GS annotation) is a good estimate of the effectiveness of AL.

Figure 3 depicts such a cumulated entity density plot on AL and GS annotations of subtypes of cytokine receptors, really very sparse entity types with one entity mention per PUBMED abstract on the average. The 250 abstracts of the GS annotation only contain 193 cytokine receptor entity mentions. AL annotation of the same number of sentences resulted in 2,800 annotated entity mentions of this type. The entity density in our AL corpus is thus almost 15 times higher than in our GS corpus. Such a dense corpus is certainly much more appropriate for classifier training due to the tremendous increase of positive training instances. We observed comparable effects with other entity types as well, and thus conclude that the sparser entity mentions of a specific type are in texts, the more benefical AL-based annotation actually is.

4.2 Mind the Seed Set

For AL, the sentences to be annotated in the first AL round, the *seed set*, have to be manually selected. As stated above, the proper choice of this set is crucial for efficient AL based annotation. One should definitely refrain from a randomly generated seed set

[10] The named enatity tagger used throughout in this section is based on Conditional Random Fields and similar to the one presented by (Settles, 2004).

– especially, when sparse entity mentions are annotated – because it might take quite a while for AL to take off. If, in the worst case, the seed set contains no entity mentions of interest, AL based annotation resembles (for several rounds in the beginning until incidentally some entity mentions are found) a random selection – which is, as shown in Section 4.1, suboptimal. Figure 4 shows the simulated effect of three different seed sets on variation event annotation (PENNBIOIE). In the tuned seed set, each sentence contains at least one variation entity mention. On this seed, AL performs significantly better than the randomly assembled seed or the seed with no entity mentions at all. Of course, in the long run, the three curves converge. Given this evidence, we stipulate that the sparser an entity type is[11] or the larger the document pool to be selected from is, the later the point of convergence and, thus, the more relevant an effective seed set is.

We developed a useful three-step heuristic to compile effective seed sets without excessive manual work. In the first step, a list is compiled comprised of as many entity mentions (of interest to the current annotation project) as possible. In knowledge- and expert-intensive domains such as molecular biology, this can either be done by consulting a domain expert or by harvesting entity mentions from online resources (such as biological databases).[12] In a second step, the compiled list is matched against each sentence of the document pool. Third, a ranking procedure orders the sentences (in descending order) according to the number of *diverse* matches of entity mentions. This ensures that textual mentions of all items from the list are included in the seed set. Depending on the variety and density of the specific entity types, our seed sets typically consist of 200 to 500 sentences.

4.3 Portability of Corpora

While we are working in the field of immunogenetics, the PENNBIOIE corpus focuses on the subdomain of oncogenetics and provides a sound annota-

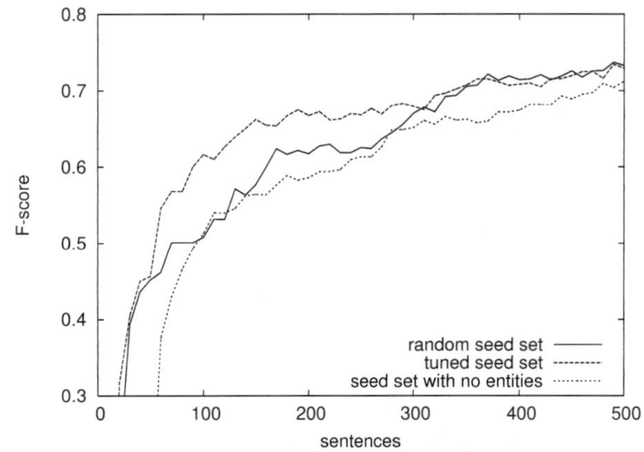

Figure 4: Effect of different seed sets for AL on variation event annotation.

tion of these entity mentions (PBVAR).[13] We did a GS annotation on 250 randomly chosen abstracts ($\approx$ 2,000 sentences/65,000 tokens) from our document pool applying PENNBIOIE's annotation guidelines for variation events to the subdomain of immunogenetics (IMVAR-Gold). We then evaluated how well our entity tagger trained on PBVAR would do on this data. Surprisingly, the performance was dramatically low, *viz.* 31.2% F-score.[14]

Thus, we did further variation event annotations for the immunogenetics domain with AL: We annotated $\approx$ 58,000 tokens (IMVAR-AL). We trained our entity tagger on this data and evaluated the tagger on both IMVAR-Gold and PBVAR. Table 1 summarizes the results. We conclude that porting training corpora, even from one related subdomain into another, is only possible to a very limited extent. This may be because current NE taggers (ours, as well) make extensive use of lexical features. However, the results also reveal that annotations made by AL may be more robust when ported to another domain: a tagger trained on IMVAR-AL still yields about 62.5% F-score on PBVAR, whereas training the tagger on the respective GS annotation (IMVAR-Gold), only about half the performance is yielded (35.8%).

[11]Variation events are not as sparse in PENNBIOIE as, e.g., cytokine receptors in our subdomain. Actually, there is a variation entity in almost every second sentence.

[12]In an additional step, some spelling variations of such entity mentions could automatically be generated.

[13]Although oncogenetics and immunogenetics are different subdomains, they share topical overlaps – in particular, with respect to the types of relevant variation entity mentions (such as '*single nucleotide polymorphism*', '*translocation*', '*in-frame deletion*', '*substitution*', etc.). Hence, at least at this level the two subdomains are related.

[14]Note that in a 10-fold cross-validation on PBVAR our entity tagger yielded about 80% F-score.

training data	evaluation data PBVAR	IMVAR-Gold
PBVAR (≈ 200.000 tokens)	≈ 80%	31.2%
IMVAR-AL (58.251 tokens)	62.5%	70.2%
IMVAR-Gold (63.591 tokens)	35.8%	–

Table 1: Corpus portability: PENNBIOIE's variation entity annotations (PBVAR) *vs.* ours for immunogenetics (IMVAR-AL and -Gold).

5 Conclusion and Future Work

We introduced JANE, an annotation environment which supports the whole annotation life-cycle from annotation project compilation to annotation deployment. As one of its major contributions, JANE allows for focused annotation based on active learning, i.e., it automatically presents sentences for annotation which are of most use for classifier training.

We have shown that porting annotated training corpora, even from one *sub*domain to another and thus related to a good extent, may severely degrade classifier performance. Thus, generating new annotation data will increasingly become important, especially under the prospect that there are more and more real-world information extraction projects for different (sub)domains and languages. We have shown that focused, i.e., AL-driven, annotation is a reasonable choice to significantly reduce the effort needed to create such annotations – up to 75% in a realistic setting. Furthermore, we have highlighted the positive effects of a high-quality seed set for AL and outlined a general heuristic for its compilation.

At the moment, the AL component may be used for most kinds of segmentation problems (e.g. POS tagging, text chunking, entity recognition). Future work will focus on the extension of the AL component for relation encoding as required for coreferences or role and propositional information.

Acknowledgements

We thank Alexander Klaue for implementing the GUIs. This research was funded by the EC within the BOOTStrep project (FP6-028099), and by the German Ministry of Education and Research within the StemNet project (01DS001A to 1C).

References

Lynn Carlson, Daniel Marcu, and Mary E. Okurowski. 2003. Building a discourse-tagged corpus in the framework of Rhetorical Structure Theory. In J. van Kuppevelt and R. Smith, editors, *Current Directions in Discourse and Dialogue*, pp. 85–112. Kluwer.

Sean Engelson and Ido Dagan. 1996. Minimizing manual annotation cost in supervised training from corpora. In *Proc. of ACL 1996*, pp. 319–326.

B. Hachey, B. Alex, and M. Becker. 2005. Investigating the effects of selective sampling on the annotation task. In *Proc. of CoNLL-2005*, pp. 144–151.

Rebecca Hwa. 2000. Sample selection for statistical grammar induction. In *Proc. of EMNLP/VLC-2000*, pp. 45–52.

Jin-Dong Kim and Jun'ichi Tsujii. 2006. Corpora and their annotation. In S. Ananiadou and J. McNaught, editors, *Text Mining for Biology and Biomedicine*, pp. 179–211. Artech.

M. Marcus, B. Santorini, and M. A. Marcinkiewicz. 1993. Building a large annotated corpus of English: The PENN TREEBANK. *Computational Linguistics*, 19(2):313–330.

C. Müller and M. Strube. 2003. Multi-level annotation in MMAX. In *Proc. of the 4th SIGdial Workshop on Discourse and Dialogue*, pp. 198–207.

Grace Ngai and David Yarowsky. 2000. Rule writing or annotation: Cost-efficient resource usage for base noun phrase chunking. In *Proc. of ACL 2000*, pp. 117–125.

Tomoko Ohta, Yuka Tateisi, and Jin-Dong Kim. 2002. The GENIA corpus: An annotated research abstract corpus in molecular biology domain. In *Proc. of HLT 2002*, pp. 82–86.

Martha Palmer, Daniel Gildea, and Paul Kingsbury. 2005. The Proposition Bank: An annotated corpus of semantic roles. *Computational Linguistics*, 31(1):71–106.

David Pierce and Claire Cardie. 2001. Limitations of co-training for natural language learning from large datasets. In *Proc. of EMNLP 2001*, pp. 1–9.

James Pustejovsky, Patrick Hanks, Roser Saurí, Andrew See, Robert Gaizauskas, Andrea Setzer, Dragomir Radev, Beth Sundheim, David Day, Lisa Ferro, and Marcia Lazo. 2003. The TIMEBANK corpus. In *Proc. of the Corpus Linguistics 2003 Conference*, pp. 647–656.

Burr Settles. 2004. Biomedical named entity recognition using conditional random fields and rich feature sets. In *Proc. of JNLPBA 2004*, pp. 107–110.

H. Sebastian Seung, Manfred Opper, and Haim Sompolinsky. 1992. Query by committee. In *Proc. of COLT 1992*, pp. 287–294.

Erik Tjong Kim Sang and Fien De Meulder. 2003. Introduction to the CONLL-2003 shared task: Language-independent named entity recognition. In *Proc. of CoNLL 2003*, pp. 142–147.

Katrin Tomanek, Joachim Wermter, and Udo Hahn. 2007. An approach to downsizing annotation costs and maintaining corpus reusability. In *Proc of EMNLP-CoNLL 2007*.

Kees van Deemter and Rodger Kibble. 2000. On coreferring: Coreference in MUC and related annotation schemes. *Computational Linguistics*, 26(4):629–637.

Janyce Wiebe, Theresa Wilson, and Claire Cardie. 2005. Annotating expressions of opinions and emotions in language. *Language Resources and Evaluation*, 39(2/3):165–210.

Mining Syntactically Annotated Corpora with XQuery

Gosse Bouma and **Geert Kloosterman**
Information Science
University of Groningen
The Netherlands
g.bouma|g.j.kloosterman@rug.nl

Abstract

This paper presents a uniform approach to data extraction from syntactically annotated corpora encoded in XML. XQuery, which incorporates XPath, has been designed as a query language for XML. The combination of XPath and XQuery offers flexibility and expressive power, while corpus specific functions can be added to reduce the complexity of individual extraction tasks. We illustrate our approach using examples from dependency treebanks for Dutch.

1 Introduction

Manually annotated treebanks have played an important role in the development of robust and accurate syntactic analysers. Now that such parsers are available for various languages, there is a growing interest in research that uses automatically annotated corpora. While such corpora are not error-free, the fact that they can be constructed relatively easily, and the fact that they can be an order of magnitude larger than manually corrected treebanks, makes them attractive for several types of research. Syntactically annotated corpora have succesfully been used to acquire lexico-semantic information (Lin and Pantel, 2001; Snow et al., 2005), for relation extraction (Bunescu and Mooney, 2005), in IR (Cui et al., 2005), and in QA (Katz and Lin, 2003; Mollá and Gardiner, 2005).

What these tasks have in common is the fact that they all operate on large amounts of data extracted from syntactically annotated text. Tools to perform this task are often developed with only a single application in mind (mostly corpus linguistics) or are developed in an ad-hoc fashion, as part of a specific application.

We propose a more principled approach, based on two observations:

- XML is widely used to encode syntactic annotation. Syntactic annotation is not more complex that some other types of information that is routinely stored in XML. This suggests that XML technology can be used to process syntactically annotated corpora.
- XQuery is a query language for XML data. As such, it is the obvious choice for mining syntactically annotated corpora.

The remainder of this paper is organised as follows. In the next section, we present the Alpino treebank format, which we use for syntactic annotation. The Alpino parser has been used to annotate large corpora, and the results have been used in a number of research projects.[1]

In section 3, we discuss the existing approaches to data extraction from Alpino corpora. We note that all of these have drawbacks, either because they lack expressive power, or because they require a serious amount of programming overhead.

In section 4, we present our approach, starting from a relatively straightforward corpus linguistics task, that requires little more than XPath, and ending with a more advanced relation extraction task,

[1] See www.let.rug.nl/~vannoord/research.html

Proceedings of the Linguistic Annotation Workshop, pages 17–24,
Prague, June 2007.

that requires XQuery. We demonstrate that much of the complexity of advanced tasks can be avoided by providing users with a corpus specific module, that makes available common concepts and functions.

2 The Alpino Treebank format

As part of the development of the Alpino parser (Bouma et al., 2001), a number of manually annotated dependency treebanks have been created (van der Beek et al., 2002). Annotation guidelines were adopted from the Corpus of Spoken Dutch (Oostdijk, 2000), a large corpus annotation project for Dutch. In addition, large corpora (e.g. the 80M word Dutch CLEF[2] corpus, the 500M word Twente News corpus[3], and Dutch Wikipedia[4]) have been annotated automatically. Both types of treebanks have been used for corpus linguistics (van der Beek, 2005; Villada Moirón, 2005; Bouma et al., 2007). The automatically annoted treebanks have been used for lexical acquisition (van der Plas and Bouma, 2005), and form the core of a Dutch QA system (Bouma et al., 2005).

The format of Alpino dependency trees is illustrated in figure 1. The (somewhat simplified) XML for this tree is in fig. 2. Nodes in the tree are labeled with a dependency relation and a category or POS-tag. Furthermore, the begin and end position of constituents is represented in attributes,[5] and the root and word form of terminal nodes is encoded. Note that heads do not have their dependents as children, as is the case in most dependency tree formats. Instead, the head is a child of the constituent node if which it is the head, and its dependents are siblings of the head. Finally, trees may contain index nodes (indicated by indices in bold in the graphical representation and by the `index` attribute in the XML) to indicate 'secondary' edges. The subject *Alan Turing* in fig. 2 is a subject of the passive auxiliary *word*, but also a direct object of the verb *aan_tref*. Thus, Alpino dependency trees are actually graphs.

A large syntactically annotated corpus tends to

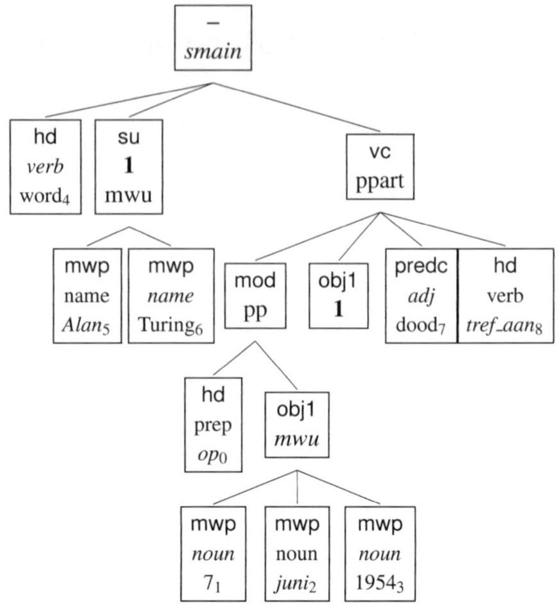

Figure 1: Op 7 juni 1954 werd Alan Turing dood aangetroffen (*On June 7, 1954, Alan Turing was found dead*)

give rise to even larger volumes of XML. To support efficient storage and retrieval of XML data, a set of tools has been developed for compression of XML data (using dictzip[6]) and for efficient visualisation and search of data in compressed XML files. The tools are described in more detail at the Alpino website.[7]

3 Existing approaches to extraction

Users have taken quite different approaches to corpus exploration and data extraction.

- For corpus exploration, Alpino `dtsearch` is the most widely used tool. It allows XPath queries to be matched against trees in a treebank. The result can be a visual display of trees with matching nodes highlighted, but alternative outputs are possible as well. Examples of how XPath can be used for extraction are presented in the next section.

- For relation extraction (i.e. finding symptoms of diseases), the Alpino system itself has been

[2] www.clef-campaign.org

[3] www.vf.utwente.nl/~druid/TwNC/TwNC-main.html

[4] nl.wikipedia.org

[5] Note that constituents may be discontinuous, and thus, the yield of a constituent may not contain every terminal node between `begin` and `end`. See also section 4.2.

[6] www.dict.org

[7] www.let.rug.nl/~vannoord/alp/Alpino/TreebankTools.html

```
<node begin="0" cat="smain" end="9" rel="--">
  <node begin="4" end="5" pos="verb" rel="hd" root="word" word="werd"/>
  <node begin="5" cat="mwu" end="7" index="1" rel="su">
    <node begin="5" end="6" pos="name" rel="mwp" neclass="PER" root="Alan" word="Alan"/>
    <node begin="6" end="7" pos="name" rel="mwp" neclass="PER" root="Turing" word="Turing"/>
  </node>
  <node begin="0" cat="ppart" end="9" rel="vc">
    <node begin="0" cat="pp" end="4" rel="mod">
      <node begin="0" end="1" pos="prep" rel="hd" root="op" word="Op"/>
      <node begin="1" cat="mwu" end="4" rel="obj1">
        <node begin="1" end="2" pos="noun" rel="mwp" root="7" word="7"/>
        <node begin="2" end="3" pos="noun" rel="mwp" root="juni" word="juni"/>
        <node begin="3" end="4" pos="noun" rel="mwp" root="1954" word="1954"/>
      </node>
    </node>
    <node begin="5" end="7" index="1" rel="obj1"/>
    <node begin="7" end="8" pos="adj" rel="predc" root="dood" word="dood"/>
    <node begin="8" end="9" pos="verb" rel="hd" root="tref_aan" word="aangetroffen"/>
  </node>
</node>
```

Figure 2: XML encoding of the Alpino depedency tree in fig. 1

used. It provides functionality for converting dependency trees in XML into a Prolog list of dependency triples. The full functionality of Prolog can then be used to do the actual extraction.

- Alternatively, one can use XSLT to extract data from the XML directly. As XSLT is primarily intended for transformations, this tends to give rise to complex code.
- Alternatively, a general purpose scripting or programming language such as Perl or Python, with suitable XML support, can be used. As in the Alpino/Prolog case, this has the advantage that one has a full programming language available. A disadvantage is that there is no specific support for working with dependency trees or triples.

None of the approaches listed above is optimal. XPath is suitable only for identifying syntactic patterns, and does not offer the possibility of extraction of elements (i.e. it has no *capturing* mechanism). The other three approaches do allow for both matching and extraction, but they all require skills that go considerably beyond conceptual knowledge of the treebank and some basic knowledge of XML.

Another disadvantage of the current situation is that there is little or no sharing of solutions between users. Yet, different applications tend to encounter the same problems. For instance, multiword expressions (such as *Alan Turing* or *7 juni 1954*) are encoded as trees, dominated by a `cat='mwu'` node. An extraction task that requires names to be extracted must thus take into account the fact that names can be both nodes with a label `pos='name'` as well as `cat='mwu'` nodes (dominating a `pos='name'`). The situation is further complicated by the fact that individual parts of a name, such as *Alan* in *Alan Turing*, should normally not be matched. Similar problems arise if one wants to match e.g. finite verbs (there is no single attribute which expresses tense) or NPs (the `cat='np'` attribute is only present on complex NPs, not on single words). A very frequent issue is the proper handling of index nodes. Searching for the object of the verb *tref_aan* in fig. 2 requires that one finds the node in the tree that is coindexed with the `rel='obj1'` node with index **1**. This is a challenge in all approaches listed above, except for Alpino/Prolog, which solves the problem by converting trees to sets of dependency triples.

Some of the problems mentioned above could be solved by introducing more and more fine-grained attributes (i.e. a separate attribute for tense, assigning both a category and a POS-tag to (non-head) terminal-nodes, etc.) or by introducing unary branching nodes. This has the obvious drawback of introducing redundancy in the encoding, would mean another departure from the usual conception of dependency trees (in the case unary branching is introduced), and may still not cover all distinctions that users need to make. Also, finding the content of an index-node cannot be solved in this way.

One might consider moving to a radically different treebank format, such as Tiger XML[8] for instance, in which trees are basically a listing of nodes, with non-terminal nodes dominating a number of edge elements that take (the index of) other nodes as value. Note, however, that most of the problems mentioned above refer to linguistic concepts, and thus are unlikely to be solved by changing the architecture of the underlying XML representation.

4 XQuery and XPath

Two closely related standards for processing XML documents are XSLT[9] and XQuery[10] . Both make use of XPath[11], the XML language for locating parts of XML documents. While XSLT is primarily intended for transformations of documents, XQuery is primarily intended for extraction of information from XML databases. XQuery is in many respects similar to SQL and is rapidly becoming the standard for XML database systems.[12] A distinctive difference between the XSLT and XQuery is the fact that XSLT documents are themselves XML documents, whereas this is not the case for XQuery. This typically makes XQuery more concise and easier to read than XSLT.[13]

These considerations made us experiment with XQuery as a language for data extraction from syntactically annotated corpora. Similar studies were carried out by Cassidy (2002) (for an early version of XQuery) and Mayo et al. (2006), who compare the NITE Query Language and XQuery. Below, we first illustrate a task that requires use of XPath only, and then move on to tasks that require the additional functionality of XQuery.

[8] www.ims.uni-stuttgart.de/projekte/TIGER/

[9] www.w3.org/TR/xslt20

[10] www.w3.org/TR/xquery

[11] www.w3.org/TR/xpath20

[12] e.g. exist.sourceforge.net, monetdb.cwi.nl, www.oracle.com/database/berkeley-db/xml

[13] See Kay (2005) for a thorough comparison.

4.1 Corpus exploration with XPath

As argued in Bouma and Kloosterman (2002), XPath provides a powerful query language for formulating linguistically relevant queries, provided that the XML encoding of the treebank reflects the syntactic structure of the trees.

Inherent reflexive verbs, for instance, are verbal heads with a `rel='se'` dependent. A verb with an inherently reflexive can therefore be found as follows (remember that in Alpino dependency trees, dependents are actually siblings of the head):

```
//node[@pos="verb"
   and @rel="hd"
   and ../node[@rel="se"]
  ]
```

The double slash ('//') ensures that we search for nodes anywhere within the XML document. The material in brackets (`[ ]`) can be used to specify additional constraints that matching nodes have to meet. The `@`-sign is used to refer to attributes of an element. The double dots ('..') locate the parent element of an XML element. Children of an element are located using the single slash ('/') operator. The two can be combined to locate siblings.

Comparison operators are available to compare e.g. attributes that have a numeric value. The following XPath query identifies cases where the reflexive precedes the subject:

```
//node[@pos="verb"
   and @rel="hd"
   and ../node[@rel="se"]/@begin <
         ../node[@rel="su"]/@begin
  ]
```

Note that we can also use the '/' to locate attributes of an element, and that the `begin` attribute encodes the initial string position of a constituent.

Reflexives preceding the subject are a marked option in Dutch. We may contrast matching verbs with verbs matching the following expression:

```
//node[@pos="verb"
    and @rel="hd"
    and ../node[@rel="se"]/@begin >
          ../node[@rel="su"]/@begin
    and not(../node[@rel="su"]/@begin="0")
  ]
```

Here we have simply reversed the comparison operator. As we want to exclude from consideration cases where the subject precedes the finite verb (e.g. is in sentence-initial position), we have added a negative constraint with this effect.

REFL-SU		SU-REFL		verb (*gloss*)
%	#	%	#	
94.3	33	5.7	2	vorm (*to shape*)
91.7	11	8.3	1	ontvouw (*to unfold*)
74.1	234	25.9	82	doe_voor (*to happen*)
73.5	36	26.5	13	teken_af (*to form*)
58.8	10	41.2	7	wreek (*to take revenge*)
57.1	44	42.9	33	voltrek (*to take place*)
56.0	42	44.0	33	verzamel (*to assemble*)
54.6	309	45.4	257	bevind (*to be located*)
50.0	18	50.0	18	dring_op (*to impose*)
48.3	58	51.7	62	dien_aan (*to announce*)

Table 1: Relative frequency of REFL-SU VS SU-REFL word order

Using the two queries above to search one year of newspaper text, we can collect the outcome and compute, for a given verb, the relative frequency of REFL-SU vs. SU-REFL order for non-subject initial sentences in Dutch. A sample of verbs that have a high percentage of REFL-SU occurrences, is given in table 1. The result confirms an observation in Haesereyn et al. (1997), that REFL-SU word order occurs especially with verbs having a somewhat 'bleeched semantics' and expressing that something exists or comes into existence.

It should be noted that XPath offers considerable more possibilities than what is illustrated here. XPath 2.0 in particular is an important step forward for linguistic search, as it includes far more functionality for string processing (i.e. tokenization and regular expressions) than its predecessors. Bird et al. (2006) propose an extension of XPath 1.0 for linguistic queries. The intuitive notation they introduce might be useful for some users. However, the examples they concentrate on (all having to do with linear order) presuppose trees without 'crossing branches'. The introduction of `begin` and `end` attributes in the Alpino format makes it possible to handle such queries for dependency trees (with crossing branches) as well, and furthermore, does not require an extension of XPath.

4.2 Data Extraction with XQuery

The kind of explorative corpus search for which XPath is ideally suited is supported by most other treebank query languages as well, although not all alternatives offer the same expressive power. There are many applications, however, in which it is necessary to extract more than just (root forms of) matching nodes. XQuery offers the functionality that is required to perform arbitrary extraction.

XQuery programs consist of so-called FLWOR expressions (`for, let, where, order by, return`, not all parts are required). The example below illustrates this. Assume we want to extract from a treebank all occurrences of names, along with their named entity class. The following XQuery script covers the base case.

```
for $name in
   collection('ad1994')//node[@pos="name"]

let $nec := string($node/@neclass)

return
  <term nec="{$nec}">
    {string($name/@word)}
  </term>
```

The `for`-statement locates the nodes to be processed. Nodes are located by XPath expressions. The *collection*-predicate defines the directory to be processed. For every document in the collection, nodes with a POS-attribute *name* are processed. We use a `let`-statement to assign the variable `$nec` is assigned the string value of the `neclass`-attibute (which indicates the named entity class of the name). The `return`-statement returns for each matching node an XML element containing the string value of the word attribute of the name, as well as an attribute indicating the named entity class.

The complexity of XQuery scripts can increase considerably, depending on the complexity of the underlying XML data and the task being performed. One of the most interesting features of XQuery is the possibility to define functions. They can be used to enhance the readibility of code. Furthermore, functions can be collected in modules, and thus can be reused across applications.

For Alpino treebanks, for instance, we have implemented a module that covers concepts and tasks that are needed frequently. As pointed out above, names in the Alpino treebank are not just single nodes, but, in case a name consists of two or more words, can also consist of multiple `node[@pos='name']` elements, with a `node[@cat='mwu']` as parent. This motivates the introduction of a `name` and `neclass` function, as shown in fig. 3. Assuming that the `alpino` module has been imported, we can now write a better name extraction script:

```
for $name in
   collection('ad1994')//node

where alpino:name($name)

return
  <term nec="{alpino:neclass($name)}">
    {alpino:yield{$name)}
  </term>
```

As we are matching with non-terminal nodes as well, we need to take into account that it no longer suffices to return the value of `word` to obtain the yield of a node. As this situation arises frequently as well, we added a `yield` function (see fig. 3). It takes a node as argument, collects all descendant `node/@word` attribute values in the variable `$words`, sorted by the `begin` value of their `node` element. The `yield` function returns the string concatenation of the elements in `$words`, separated by blanks. Note that this solution also gives the correct result for discontinuous constituents.

We used a wrapper around the XQuery processor Saxon[14] to execute XQuery scripts directly on compacted corpora. The result is output such as:

```
<term nec="ORG">PvdA</term>
<term nec="LOC">Atlantische Oceaan</term>
```

A more advanced relation extraction example is given in fig. 4. It is a script for extraction of events involving the death of a person from a syntactically annotated corpus (Dutch wikipedia in this case). It will return the name of the person who died, and, if these can be found in the same sentence, the date, location, and cause of death.[15] The script makes heavy use of functions from the `alpino` module that were added to facilitate relation extraction. The `selector-of` function defines the 'semantic head' of a phrase. This is either the sibling marked `rel='hd'`, or (for nodes that are themselves heads) the head of the mother. For appositions and conjuncts, it it the selector of the head. Note that the last case involves a recursive function call. Similarly, the semantic role is normally identical to the value of the `rel`-attribute, but we go up one additional level for heads, appositions and conjuncts. The value of `$resolved` is given by the `resolve-index` function shown in fig. 3, i.e. if a node is just an index (as is the case for the object of *aan_tref* in fig. 1), the 'antecedent' node is returned. In all other cases, the node itself is returned. Date and place are found using functions for locating the date and place dependents of the verb. Finally, relevant events are found using the `die-verb` and `kill-verb` functions.

Some examples of the output of the extraction script are (i.e. John Lennon was killed on December 8, 1980, and Erasmus died in Basel on July, 12, 1536):

```
<died-how place="nil" file="1687-98"
   person="John Lennon" cause="vermoord"
   date="op 8 december 1980"/>
<died-how place="in Bazel" file="20336-37"
   person="Erasmus"  cause="overlijd"
   date="op 12 juli 1536"/>
```

The functions illustrated in the two examples can be used for a range of similar data extraction tasks, whether these are intended for corpus linguistics research or as part of an information extraction system. The definition of corpus specific functions that cover frequently used syntactic and semantic concepts allows the application specific code to be relatively compact and straightforward. In addition, code which builds upon well tested corpus specific functions tends to give more accurate results than code developed from scratch.

5 Conclusions

In this paper, we have presented an approach to mining syntactically corpora that uses standard XML technology. It can be used both for corpus exploration as well as for information extraction tasks. By providing a corpus specific module, the complexity of such tasks can be reduced. By adopting standard XML languages, we can benefit optimally from the fact that these are far more expressive than what is provided in application specific languages or tools. In addition, there is no shortage of tools or platforms supporting these languages. Thus, development of corpus specific tools can be kept at a minimum.

[14] `www.saxonica.com`

[15] Questions about such facts are relatively frequent in Question Answering evaluation tasks.

```
module namespace alpino="alpino.xq" ;

declare function name($constituent as element(node)) as xs:boolean
  { if   ( $constituent[@pos='name'] or
           $constituent[@cat = 'mwu']/node[@neclass='PER'] )
    then fn:true()
    else fn:false()
  };
declare function neclass($constituent as element(node)) as xs:string
  { if   $constituent[@neclass]
    then fn:string($constituent/@neclass)
    else if   $constituent/node[@neclass]
         then fn:string($constituent/node[1]/@neclass)
  };
declare function alpino:yield($constituent as element(node)) as xs:string
  { let $words :=
          for      $leaf in $constituent/descendant-or-self::node[@word]
          order by number($leaf/@begin)
          return   $leaf/@word
    return string-join($words," ")
  };
declare function alpino:resolve-index($constituent as element(node))
        as element(node)
  { if   ( $constituent[@index and not(@pos or @cat)] )
    then $constituent/ancestor::alpino_ds/
              descendant::node
                 [@index = $constituent/@index and (@pos or @cat)]
    else $constituent
  };
```

Figure 3: XQuery module (fragment) for Alpino treebanks

```
for $node in collection('wikipedia')/alpino_ds//node

let $verb      := alpino:selector-of($node)
let $date      := if    ( exists(alpino:date-dependents($verb)) )
                  then alpino:yield(alpino:date-dependents($verb)[1])
                  else 'nil'
let $place     := if ( exists(alpino:location-dependents($verb)) )
                  then alpino:yield(alpino:location-dependents($verb)[1])
                  else 'nil'
let $cause     := if    ( $verb/../node[@rel="pc"]/node[@root="aan"] )
                  then alpino:yield($verb/../node[@rel="pc"])
                  else [[omitted]]
let $role      := alpino:semantic-role($node)
let $resolved := alpino:resolve-index($node)

where      alpino:person-node($resolved)
      and (    ( $role="su"     and alpino:die-verb($verb)   )
           or (  $role="obj1" and alpino:kill-verb($verb)  )
          )

return
<died-how  file="{alpino:file-id($node)}" person="{alpino:root-string($resolved)}"
   cause="{$cause}"  date="{$date}" place = "{$place}" />
```

Figure 4: Extracting circumstances of the death of a person

References

Steven Bird, Yi Chen, Susan B. Davidson, Haejoong Lee, and Yifeng Zheng. Designing and evaluating an XPath dialect for linguistic queries. In *Proceedings of 22nd International Conference on Data Engineering (ICDE)*, 2006.

Gosse Bouma and Geert Kloosterman. Querying dependency treebanks in XML. In *Proceedings of the 3rd conference on Language Resources and Evaluation (LREC)*, Gran Canaria, 2002.

Gosse Bouma, Gertjan van Noord, and Robert Malouf. Alpino: Wide-coverage computational analysis of Dutch. In *Computational Linguistics in The Netherlands 2000*. Rodopi, Amsterdam, 2001.

Gosse Bouma, Ismail Fahmi, Jori Mur, Gertjan van Noord, Lonneke van der Plas, and Jörg Tiedeman. Linguistic knowledge and question answering. *Traitement Automatique des Langues*, 2(46): 15–39, 2005.

Gosse Bouma, Petra Hendriks, and Jack Hoeksema. Focus particles inside prepositional phrases: A comparison of Dutch, English, and German. *Journal of Comparative Germanic Linguistics*, 10(1), 2007.

Razvan Bunescu and Raymond Mooney. A shortest path dependency kernel for relation extraction. In *Proceedings of HLT/EMNLP*, pages 724–731, Vancouver, 2005.

Steve Cassidy. XQuery as an annotation query language: a use case analysis. In *Language Resources and Evaluation Conference (LREC)*, Gran Canaria, 2002.

Hang Cui, Renxu Sun, Keya Li, Min-Yen Kan, and Tat-Seng Chua. Question answering passage retrieval using dependency relations. In *Proceedings of SIGIR 05*, Salvador, Brazil, 2005.

W. Haesereyn, K. Romijn, G. Geerts, J. De Rooy, and M.C. Van den Toorn. *Algemene Nederlandse Spraakkunst*. Martinus Nijhoff Uitgevers Groningen / Wolters Plantyn Deurne, 1997.

Boris Katz and Jimmy Lin. Selectively using relations to improve precision in question answering. In *Proceedings of the workshop on Natural Language Processing for Question Answering (EACL 2003)*, pages 43–50, Budapest, 2003. EACL.

Michael Kay. Comparing XSLT and XQuery. In *Proceedings of XTech 2005*, Amsterdam, 2005. URL `www.idealliance.org/proceedings/xtech05`.

Dekan Lin and Patrick Pantel. Discovery of inference rules for question answering. *Natural Language Engineering*, 7:343–360, 2001.

Neil Mayo, Jonathan Kilgour, and Jean Carletta. Towards an alternative implementation of NXT query language via XQuery. In *Proceedings of the EACL Workshop on Multi-dimensional Markup in NLP*, Trento, 2006.

D. Mollá and M. Gardiner. Answerfinder - question answering by combining lexical, syntactic and semantic information. In *Australasian Language Technology Workshop (ALTW) 2004*, Sydney, 2005.

Nelleke Oostdijk. The Spoken Dutch Corpus: Overview and first evaluation. In *Proceedings of LREC 2000*, pages 887–894, 2000.

Rion Snow, Daniel Jurafsky, and Andrew Y. Ng. Learning syntactic patterns for automatic hypernym discovery. In Lawrence K. Saul, Yair Weiss, and Lon Bottou, editors, *Advances in Neural Information Processing Systems 17*, pages 1297–1304. MIT Press, Cambridge, MA, 2005.

L. van der Beek, G. Bouma, R. Malouf, and G. van Noord. The Alpino dependency treebank. In *Computational Linguistics in the Netherlands (CLIN) 2001*, Twente University, 2002.

Leonoor van der Beek. *Topics in Corpus Based Dutch Syntax*. PhD thesis, University of Groningen, Groningen, 2005.

Lonneke van der Plas and Gosse Bouma. Automatic acquisition of lexico-semantic knowledge for question answering. In *Proceedings of Ontolex 2005 – Ontologies and Lexical Resources*, Jeju Island, South Korea, 2005.

Begoña Villada Moirón. Linguistically enriched corpora for establishing variation in support verb constructions. In *Proceedings of the 6th International Workshop on Linguistically Interpreted Corpora (LINC-2005)*, Jeju Island, Republic of Korea, 2005.

Associating Facial Displays with Syntactic Constituents for Generation

Mary Ellen Foster
Informatik VI: Robotics and Embedded Systems
Technical University of Munich
Boltzmannstraße 3, 85748 Garching, Germany
foster@in.tum.de

Abstract

We present an annotated corpus of conversational facial displays designed to be used for generation. The corpus is based on a recording of a single speaker reading scripted output in the domain of the target generation system. The data in the corpus consists of the syntactic derivation tree of each sentence annotated with the full syntactic and pragmatic context, as well as the eye and eyebrow displays and rigid head motion used by the the speaker. The behaviours of the speaker show several contextual patterns, many of which agree with previous findings on conversational facial displays. The corpus data has been used in several studies exploring different strategies for selecting facial displays for a synthetic talking head.

1 Introduction

An increasing number of systems designed to automatically generate linguistic and multimodal output now make use of corpora to help in decision-making (cf. Belz and Varges, 2005). Some implementations use corpora to help select output that is grammatical or fluent; for example, Langkilde and Knight (1998) and White (2006) both used n-gram language models to guide stochastic surface realisers. In other systems, corpora are used to make decisions based on pragmatic factors such as the reading level of the target user (Williams and Reiter, 2005) or the visual features of an object being described (Cassell et al., 2007). The latter type of domain-specific contextual information is not often included in generally-available corpora. For this reason, developers of generation systems that need this type of information often create and make use of application-specific corpora.

The easiest method of including the necessary pragmatic information in a corpus is to base the corpus on output generated in situations where the contextual factors are known; this eliminates the need to annotate these factors explicitly. Stone et al. (2004), for example, created a multimodal corpus based on the voice and body language of an actor performing scripted output in the domain of the target generation system: an animated instructor character for a snowboarding video game. The contextual information in the corpus scripts included the move that the player attempted in the game and the result of that attempt. Similarly, van Deemter et al. (2006) created a corpus of multimodal referring expressions produced in specific pragmatic contexts and used it to compare several referring-expression generation algorithms to human performance.

In this work, the task is to select facial displays for an animated talking head to use while presenting output in the COMIC multimodal dialogue system (Foster et al., 2005), which generates spoken descriptions and comparisons of bathroom-tile options. The output of the COMIC text planner includes a range of information in addition to the text: the syntactic derivation tree, the user's evaluation of the object being described, the information status (new or old, contrastive) of each fact described, and the predicted speech-synthesiser prosody. All of this contextual information can be used to help select

Proceedings of the Linguistic Annotation Workshop, pages 25–32,
Prague, June 2007.

appropriate facial displays to accompany the spoken presentation; however—as in the other systems mentioned above—this requires a corpus where the full context for every facial display is known. To create such a corpus, we recorded a speaker performing scripted output in the domain of COMIC.

This paper is arranged as follows. In Section 2, we first describe how the scripts for the corpus were created and how the recording was made. Section 3 then presents the annotation scheme and the tool that was used to perform the annotation, while Section 4 describes the measures that were taken to ensure that the annotation was reliable. Section 5 then summarises the high-level patterns that were found in the displays annotated in the corpus and compares them to other findings on conversational facial displays. At the end of the section, we use the corpus data to test two assumptions that were made in the annotation scheme. After that, in Section 6, we describe several experiments in which different methods of using the data in this corpus to select facial displays for a synthetic head have been compared. Finally, in Section 7, we summarise the contributions of this paper and draw some conclusions about the usefulness of this corpus for its intended task.

2 Recording

For this corpus, we recorded a single speaker reading a set of 444 scripted sentences in the domain of the COMIC multimodal dialogue system. The sentences were generated by the full COMIC output-generation process, which uses the OpenCCG surface realiser (White, 2006) to create texts including prosodic specifications for the speech synthesiser and incorporates information from the dialogue history and a model of the user's likes and dislikes.

Every node in the OpenCCG derivation tree for each sentence in the script was initially annotated with all of the available syntactic and pragmatic information from the output planner, including the following features:

- The user-model evaluation of the object being described (positive or negative);
- Whether the fact being presented was previously mentioned in the discourse (*as I said before, ...*) or is new information;

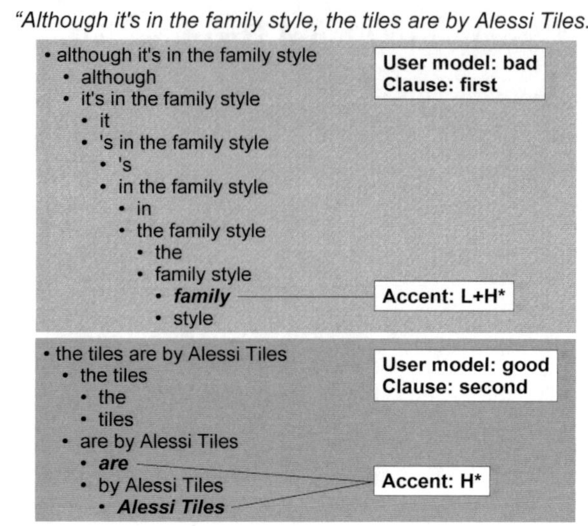

Figure 1: Annotated OpenCCG derivation tree

- Whether the fact is explicitly compared or contrasted with a feature of the previous tile design (*once again ... but here ...*);
- Whether the node is in the first clause of a two-clause sentence, in the second clause, or is an only clause;[1]
- The surface string associated with the node;
- The surface string, with words replaced by semantic classes or stems drawn from the grammar (e.g., *this design is classic* becomes *this [mental-obj] be [style]*); and
- Any pitch accents specified by the text planner.

Figure 1 illustrates the annotated OpenCCG derivation tree for a sample sentence drawn from the recording script. The annotations indicate that every node in the first half of this sentence is associated with a negative user-model evaluation and is in the first clause of a two-clause sentence, while every node in the second half is linked to a positive evaluation and is in the second clause of the sentence. The figure also shows the pitch accents selected by the output planner according to Steedman's (2000) theory of information structure and intonation.

For the recording, the sentences in the script were presented one at a time to the speaker; the presen-

[1]No sentence in the script had more than two clauses.

tation included both the linguistic content (with accented words highlighted) as well as the intended pragmatic context. Each sentence was displayed in a large font on a laptop computer directly in front of the speaker, with the camera positioned directly above the laptop to ensure that the speaker was looking towards the camera at all times. The speaker was instructed to read each sentence out loud as expressively as possible into the camera.

3 Annotation

Once all of the sentences in the script had been recorded as described in the preceding section, the next step was to annotate the facial displays that occurred. We first used Anvil (Kipp, 2004) to split the video into individual clips corresponding to each sentence. This section describes how the facial displays in each of the clips were then annotated.

3.1 Annotation scheme

We annotated the speaker's facial displays by linking each to the span of nodes in the OpenCCG derivation tree with which it was temporally related. Making cross-modal links at this level made it possible to use the annotated information directly in the output-generation process for the experiments described in Section 6.

A display was associated with the full span of words that it coincided with temporally, as follows. If a single node in the derivation tree covered exactly all of the relevant words, then the annotation was placed on that node; if the words spanned by a display did not coincide with a single node, it was attached to the set of nodes that did span the necessary words. For example, in the derivation shown in Figure 1, the sequence *the family style* is associated with a single node, so a motion temporally associated with that sequence would be attached to that node. On the other hand, if there were a motion associated with *the tiles are*, it would be attached to both the *the tiles* node and the *are* node.

The following were the features that were considered; for each feature, we note the corresponding Action Unit (AU) from the well-known Facial Action Coding System (Ekman et al., 2002).

- Eyebrows: up (AU 1+2) or down (AU 4)
- Eye squinting (AU 43)

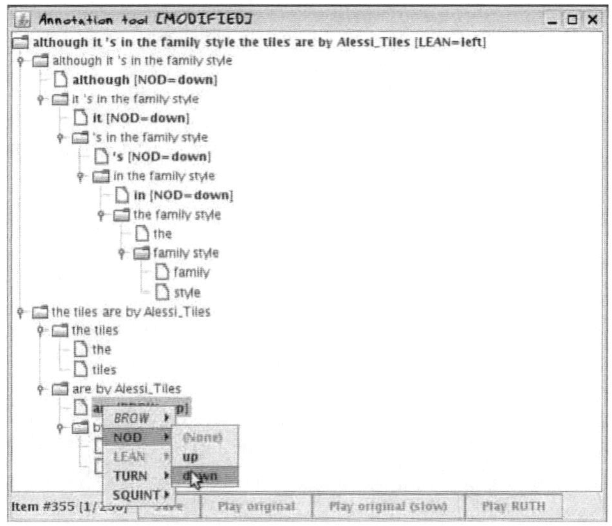

Figure 2: Annotation tool

- Head nodding: up (AU 53) or down (AU 54)
- Head leaning: left (AU 55) or right (AU 56)
- Head turning: left (AU 57) or right (AU 58)

This set of displays was chosen based on a combination of three factors: the emphatic facial displays documented in the literature, the capabilities of the target talking head, and the actual displays of the speaker during the recording session.

3.2 Annotation tool

The tool for the annotation was a custom-written program that allowed the coder to play back a recorded sentence at full speed or slowed down, and to associate any combination of displays with any node or set of nodes in the OpenCCG derivation tree of the sentence. The tool also allowed the coder to play back a proposed annotation sequence on a synthetic talking head to verify that it was as close as possible to the actual motions. Figure 2 shows a screenshot of the annotation tool in use on the sentence from Figure 1. In the screenshot, a left turn is attached to the entire sentence (i.e., the root node), while a series of nods is associated with single leaf nodes in the first half of the sentence. The annotator has already attached a brow raise to the word *are* in the second half and is in the process of adding a nod to the same word.

The output of the annotation tool is an XML document including the original contextually-annotated

```
<node surf="although it 's in the family style the tiles are by Alessi_Tiles" LEAN="left"
    sc="although [pro3n] be in the [style] [abstraction] the [phys-obj] be by [manufacturer]">
  <node surf="although it 's in the family style" um="b" first="y"
      sc="although [pro3n] be in the [style] [abstraction]">
    <node surf="although" um="b" first="y" NOD="down" />
    <node surf="it 's in the family style" um="b" first="y"
        sc="[pro3n] be in the [style] [abstraction]">
      <node surf="it" stem="pro3n" um="b" first="y" NOD="down" />
      <node surf="'s in the family style" um="b" first="y" sc="be in the [style] [abstraction]">
        <node surf="'s" stem="be" um="b" first="y" NOD="down" />
        <node surf="in the family style" um="b" first="y" sc="in the [style] [abstraction]">
          <node surf="in" um="b" first="y" NOD="down" />
          <node surf="the family style" um="b" first="y" sc="the [style] [abstraction]">
            <node surf="the" um="b" first="y" />
            <node surf="family style" um="b" first="y" sc="[style] [abstraction]">
              <node surf="family" sc="[style]" accent="L+H*" um="b" first="y" NOD="down" />
              <node surf="style" sc="[abstraction]" um="b" first="y" />
            </node>
          </node>
        </node>
      </node>
    </node>
  </node>
  <node surf="the tiles are by Alessi_Tiles" um="g" first="n"
      sc="the [phys-obj] be by [manufacturer]">
    <node surf="the tiles" um="g" first="n" sc="the [phys-obj]">
      <node surf="the" um="g" first="n" />
      <node surf="tiles" sc="[phys-obj]" stem="tile" um="g" first="n" />
    </node>
    <node surf="are by Alessi_Tiles" um="g" first="n" sc="be by [manufacturer]">
      <node surf="are" stem="be" accent="H*" um="g" first="n" BROW="up" NOD="down" />
      <node surf="by Alessi_Tiles" um="g" first="n" sc="by [manufacturer]">
        <node surf="by" um="g" first="n" />
        <node surf="Alessi_Tiles" sc="[manufacturer]" accent="H*" um="g" first="n" />
      </node>
    </node>
  </node>
</node>
```

Figure 3: Annotated sentence from the corpus

OpenCCG derivation tree of each sentence, with each node additionally labelled with a (possibly empty) set of facial displays. Figure 3 shows the fully-annotated version of the sentence from Figure 1. This document includes the contextual features from the original tree, indicated by italics: every node in the first subtree has um="b" and first="y", while every node in the second subtree has um="g" and first="n", while the accented items also have an accent feature. Every node also specifies the string generated by the subtree that it spans, both in its surface form (surf) and with semantic-class and stem replacement (sc). This tree also includes the facial displays added by the coder in Figure 2, indicated by underlining: (LEAN="left") attached to the root node), a number of downward nods (NOD="down") on individual words in the first half of the sentence, and a nod accompanied by a brow raise (BROW="up") on *are* near the end.

4 Reliability of the annotation

Several measures were taken to ensure that the annotation process was reliable. As the first step, two independent coders each separately processed the same set of 20 sentences, using an initial annotation scheme. The outputs of these two coders were compared, and the coders discussed the differences and agreed on a revised scheme. One of these coders then used the final scheme to process the entire set of 444 sentences. As a further test of reliability, an additional coder was instructed on the use of the annotation tool and scheme and used them to process 286 sentences (approximately 65% of the corpus).

To assess the degree of agreement between these two coders, we used a version of the β agreement coefficient proposed by Artstein and Poesio (2005). β is designed as a coefficient that is weighted, that applies to multiple coders, and that uses a separate probability distribution for each coder. Weighted coefficients like β permit degrees of agreement to be measured, so that partial agreement is penalised less severely than total disagreement. Like other weighted coefficients, β is based on the ratio between the observed and expected disagreement on the corpus.

To use this coefficient, it is necessary to define a measure that computes the distance between two proposed annotations. In this case, to compute the observed disagreement $D_o(S)$ on a sentence S, we use a measure similar to that proposed by Passonneau (2004) for measuring agreement on set-valued annotations. For each display proposed by each coder on the sentence, we search for a corresponding display proposed by the other coder—one with the same value (e.g., a brow raise) and covering a similar span of nodes. If both proposed exactly the same display, that indicates no disagreement (0); if one display covers a strict subset of the nodes covered by the other, that indicates minor disagreement ($\frac{1}{3}$); if the nodes covered by the two proposals overlap, that is a more major disagreement ($\frac{2}{3}$); and if no corresponding display can be found from the second coder, then that indicates the maximum level of disagreement (1). The total observed disagreement on a sentence is the sum of the disagreement level for each display proposed by each coder.

The expected disagreement $D_e(S)$ for a sentence S depends on the length of that sentence, as follows. We first use the corpus counts to compute the probability of each coder assigning each possible facial display to word spans of all possible lengths. We then use these probabilities to estimate the likelihood of the two coders assigning identical, super/subset, overlapping, or disjoint annotations to the sentence, for each possible display. The total expected disagreement for the sentence is the sum of these probabilities across all displays, using the same weights as the observed disagreement above.

The overall observed disagreement in the corpus D_o is the arithmetic mean of the disagreement on each sentence; similarly, the overall expected disagreement D_e is the mean of the expected disagreement across all of the sentences. To compute the value of β for the output of the two coders, we subtract the ratio of these two values from 1:

$$\beta = 1 - \frac{D_o}{D_e}$$

As Artstein and Poesio (2005) point out, for weighted measures such as β, there is no significance test for agreement, and the actual value is strongly affected by the distance metric that is selected. However, β values can be compared with one another to assess degrees of agreement. The overall β value between the two coders on the full set of 286 sentences processed by both was 0.561, with β values on individual facial displays ranging from a high of 0.661 on nodding to a low of 0.285 on squinting (a very rare motion). To put these values into context, we computed β on the set of 20 sentences processed by the final coder as part of the training process (which are not included in the set of 286). The overall β value for these sentences is 0.231, with negative values for some of the individual displays. This demonstrates that the training process had a positive effect on agreement.

5 Patterns in the corpus

We investigated the contextual features to see which had the most significant effect on the facial displays occurring on a node. To determine this, we used multinomial logit regression to select the factors and factor interactions that had the most significant effects on the distribution of each display; this form of regression is appropriate when, as in this case, the response variable is categorical. In this section, we list the most significant factors and give a qualitative description of the impact of each.

The single most influential contextual factor was the user-model evaluation, which had an effect on all of the facial displays. In positive user-model contexts, eyebrow raising and turning to the right were relatively more frequent (Figure 4(a)); in negative contexts, on the other hand, the rates of eyebrow lowering, squinting, and leaning to the left were all higher (Figure 4(b)). Other factors also affected the

(a) Positive

(b) Negative

Figure 4: Characteristic facial displays for different user-model evaluations

distribution of facial displays. In the first half of two-clause sentences, brow lowering was also more frequent, as was upward nodding, while downward nodding and right turns showed up more often in the second clause of two-clause sentences. Nodding and brow raising were both more frequent on nodes with any sort of predicted pitch accent.

Several of these factors agree with previous findings on conversational body language. The increased frequency of nodding and brow raising on accented words agrees with many previous studies: Ekman (1979), Cavé et al. (1996), Graf et al. (2002), Keating et al. (2003), Krahmer and Swerts (2004), and Flecha-García (2006) all noted similar displays on prosodically accented parts of the sentence. The speaker's tendency to move right on positive descriptions and left on negative descriptions is also consistent with other findings. According to the work of Davidson and colleagues (Davidson and Irwin, 1999), emotion and affect processing are asymmetrically organised in the human brain. The right hemisphere is associated with negative affect (and withdrawal behaviours), and the left with positive affect (and approach behaviours). Because both perceptual and motor systems are contra-laterally organised, this means that higher levels of right hemisphere activity are associated with attention being oriented towards the left, while higher levels of left hemisphere activity are associated with attention being oriented to the right; this fits with our speaker's pattern of movements.

The annotation scheme described here allowed a display to be associated with any contiguous span of words in the sentence. Annotators were encouraged to use syntactic constituents wherever possible, but also had the option to select multiple nodes where a display did not correspond with a single constituent in the derivation tree. Earlier versions of the annotation scheme did not support this degree of flexibility, so we used the patterns in the corpus to test whether the modifications to the scheme were useful.

In a previous study using the same video recordings but a different, simpler scheme (Foster and Oberlander, 2006), facial displays could only be associated with single leaf nodes (i.e., words); that is, in the terminology of Ekman (1979), all motions were considered to be *batons* rather than *underliners*. Based on the data in the current corpus, that restriction was clearly unrealistic: the mean number of nodes spanned by a display in the full corpus was 1.95, with a maximum of 15 and a standard deviation of 2. The results were similar in the sub-corpus produced by the final coder, in which the mean number of nodes spanned by a display was 2.25.

The annotation rules for this study did not initially permit displays to be associated with more than nodes in the derivation tree. This capability was added following inter-coder discussions after the initial test annotation to deal with cases where the speaker's displays did not correspond to syntactic constituents—for example, if the speaker raised his eyebrows on *the tiles are* or some other such non-standard constituent. The data in the annotated corpus supports this modification. Approximately 6% of the annotations in the main corpus—165 of 2826—were attached to more than one node in the derivation tree; for the final coder, 4.5% of annotations were on multiple nodes.

6 Generation experiments

The primary reason for creating this corpus of facial displays was to use the resulting data to select facial displays for the artificial talking head in the COMIC multimodal dialogue system. Several different strategies have been implemented to use the corpus data for this task, and a number of automated and human evaluations have been carried out comparing the different implementations.

As described in the preceding section, the factor with the largest influence on the displays of the recorded speaker was the user-model evaluation. Two studies (Foster, 2007b) were carried out to test the generality of the characteristic positive and negative displays (Figure 4). In the first study, users were asked to identify the intended user-model polarity of a description presented by the talking head based only on the facial displays. The participants were generally able to recognise the characteristic positive and negative facial displays; they also identified the displays intended to be neutral (nodding alone) as positive, and tended to judge videos with no facial displays to be negative. In the second study, users' subjective preferences were gathered between videos in which the user model evaluation expressed in speech was either consistent or inconsistent with the facial displays. In this study, the participants generally preferred the videos that showed consistent content on the two output channels.

In another study (Foster and Oberlander, 2007), two different data-driven strategies were implemented that used the corpus data to select facial displays to accompany speech. One strategy always selected the highest-probability option in all contexts, while the other made a stochastic choice among all of the options weighted by the corpus probabilities. These two strategies were compared against each other using both automated and human evaluation methods: the majority strategy scored more highly on the automated cross-validation, while the weighted strategy was strongly preferred by human judges. The judges also preferred resynthesised versions of the original facial displays from the corpus to the output of either of the generation strategies.

Two further human evaluation studies compared the weighted data-driven generation strategy from the preceding study to a rule-based strategy that selected the most characteristic displays based only on the user-model evaluation (Foster, 2007a). When users' subjective judgements were gathered as above, they had a mild preference for the output of the weighted strategy over that of the rule-based strategy. In a second study, videos generated by the weighted strategy significantly decreased participants' ability to select descriptions that were correctly tailored to a given set of user preferences, while videos generated by the rule-based strategy had no such impact.

7 Conclusions

We have described the collection and annotation of an application-specific corpus of conversational facial displays. The designs of both the corpus and the annotation scheme were driven by the needs of a specific generation system, which makes use of a range of pragmatic information while creating output. To use this information to make corpus-based decisions, it is necessary that the full context of every utterance and facial display in the corpus be available. Rather than adding this information to an existing corpus, we chose—like Stone et al. (2004) and van Deemter et al. (2006), for example—to create a corpus based on known contexts so that the full information for every sentence was known before the fact.

The final annotation scheme required each facial display to be linked to the set of nodes in the syntactic derivation tree of the sentence that exactly covered the words temporally associated with the display. Two coders separately processed the sentences in the corpus; on the sentences processed by both coders (about 65% of the corpus), the agreement as measured by β was 0.561.

A number of contextual factors had an influence on the displays used by the recorded speaker. The single most influential factor was the user-model evaluation of the object being described. The speaker's characteristic side-to-side motions on these sentences agree with findings on the relationship between brain hemispheres and affect. In addition, in user studies, human judges were reliably able to identify the intended affect based on resynthesised versions of these characteristic displays. Other patterns in the data also agree with existing findings on facial displays: for example, the speaker tended to nod and raise his eyebrows more frequently on words with prosodic accents.

Several experiments have been performed in which the annotated data from this corpus was used to select the facial displays to accompany the output of an animated talking head. These studies have found interesting results on both the relationship between automated and human judgements of output quality and the relative utility of rule-based and data-driven approaches for selecting conversational facial displays.

Acknowledgements

This research was supported by the EU projects COMIC (IST-2001-32311) and JAST (FP6-003747-IP). Thanks to Amy Isard, Ron Petrick, and Tom Segler for annotation assistance, and to Jon Oberlander and the LAW reviewers for useful comments.

References

R. Artstein and M. Poesio. 2005. Kappa^3 = alpha (or beta). Technical Report CSM-437, University of Essex Department of Computer Science.

A. Belz and S. Varges, editors. 2005. *Corpus Linguistics 2005 Workshop on Using Corpora for Natural Language Generation*. http://www.itri.brighton.ac.uk/ucnlg/ucnlg05/.

J. Cassell, S. Kopp, P. Tepper, K. Ferriman, and K. Striegnitz. 2007. Trading spaces: How humans and humanoids use speech and gesture to give directions. In T. Nishida, editor, *Engineering Approaches to Conversational Informatics*. Wiley. In press.

C. Cavé, I. Guaïtella, R. Bertrand, S. Santi, F. Harlay, and R. Espesser. 1996. About the relationship between eyebrow movements and F_0 variations. In *Proceedings of the 4th International Conference on Spoken Language Processing (ICSLP 1996)*.

R. J. Davidson and W. Irwin. 1999. The functional neuroanatomy of emotion and affective style. *Trends in Cognitive Sciences*, 3(1):11–21. doi:10.1016/S1364-6613(98)01265-0.

K. van Deemter, I. van der Sluis, and A. Gatt. 2006. Building a semantically transparent corpus for the generation of referring expressions. In *Proceedings of the Fourth International Natural Language Generation Conference*, pages 130–132. Sydney, Australia. ACL Anthology W06-1420.

P. Ekman. 1979. About brows: Emotional and conversational signals. In M. von Cranach, K. Foppa, W. Lepenies, and D. Ploog, editors, *Human Ethology: Claims and limits of a new discipline*. Cambridge University Press.

P. Ekman, W. V. Friesen, and J. C. Hager. 2002. *Facial Action Coding System*. A Human Face, Salt Lake City.

M. L. Flecha-García. 2006. *Eyebrow raising in dialogue: Discourse structure, utterance function, and pitch accents*. Ph.D. thesis, Department of Theoretical and Applied Linguistics, University of Edinburgh.

M. E. Foster. 2007a. Comparing rule-based and data-driven selection of facial displays. In *Proceedings of the ACL 2007 Workshop on Embodied Language Processing*.

M. E. Foster. 2007b. Generating embodied descriptions tailored to user preferences. In submission.

M. E. Foster and J. Oberlander. 2006. Data-driven generation of emphatic facial displays. In *Proceedings of the 11th Conference of the European Chapter of the Association for Computational Linguistics (EACL 2006)*, pages 353–360. Trento, Italy. ACL Anthology E06-1045.

M. E. Foster and J. Oberlander. 2007. Corpus-based generation of conversational facial displays. In submission.

M. E. Foster, M. White, A. Setzer, and R. Catizone. 2005. Multimodal generation in the COMIC dialogue system. In *Proceedings of the ACL 2005 Demo Session*. ACL Anthology W06-1403.

H. Graf, E. Cosatto, V. Strom, and F. Huang. 2002. Visual prosody: Facial movements accompanying speech. In *Proceedings of the 5th IEEE International Conference on Automatic Face and Gesture Recognition (FG 2002)*, pages 397–401. doi:10.1109/AFGR.2002.1004186.

P. Keating, M. Baroni, S. Mattys, R. Scarborough, and A. Alwan. 2003. Optical phonetics and visual perception of lexical and phrasal stress in English. In *Proceedings of the 15th International Congress of Phonetic Sciences (ICPhS)*, pages 2071–2074.

M. Kipp. 2004. *Gesture Generation by Imitation - From Human Behavior to Computer Character Animation*. Dissertation.com.

E. Krahmer and M. Swerts. 2004. More about brows: A cross-linguistic study via analysis-by-synthesis. In C. Pelachaud and Z. Ruttkay, editors, *From Brows to Trust: Evaluating Embodied Conversational Agents*, pages 191–216. Kluwer. doi:10.1007/1-4020-2730-3_7.

I. Langkilde and K. Knight. 1998. The practical value of *n*-grams in generation. In *Proceedings of the 9th International Natural Language Generation Workshop (INLG 1998)*. ACL Anthology W98-1426.

R. J. Passonneau. 2004. Computing reliability for coreference annotation. In *Proceedings, Fourth International Conference on Language Resources and Evaluation (LREC 2004)*, volume 4, pages 1503–1506. Lisbon.

M. Steedman. 2000. Information structure and the syntax-phonology interface. *Linguistic Inquiry*, 31(4):649–689. doi:10.1162/002438900554505.

M. Stone, D. DeCarlo, I. Oh, C. Rodriguez, A. Lees, A. Stere, and C. Bregler. 2004. Speaking with hands: Creating animated conversational characters from recordings of human performance. *ACM Transactions on Graphics (TOG)*, 23(3):506–513. doi:10.1145/1015706.1015753.

M. White. 2006. Efficient realization of coordinate structures in Combinatory Categorial Grammar. *Research on Language and Computation*, 4(1):39–75. doi:10.1007/s11168-006-9010-2.

S. Williams and E. Reiter. 2005. Deriving content selection rules from a corpus of non-naturally occurring documents for a novel NLG application. In Belz and Varges (2005).

An Annotation Type System for a Data-Driven NLP Pipeline

Udo Hahn **Ekaterina Buyko** **Katrin Tomanek**
Jena University Language & Information Engineering (JULIE) Lab
Fürstengraben 30, 07743 Jena, Germany
{hahn|buyko|tomanek}@coling-uni-jena.de

Scott Piao **John McNaught** **Yoshimasa Tsuruoka** **Sophia Ananiadou**
NaCTeM and School of Computer Science
University of Manchester
{scott.piao|john.mcnaught|yoshimasa.tsuruoka|sophia.ananiadou}@manchester.ac.uk

Abstract

We introduce an annotation type system for a data-driven NLP core system. The specifications cover formal document structure and document meta information, as well as the linguistic levels of morphology, syntax and semantics. The type system is embedded in the framework of the Unstructured Information Management Architecture (UIMA).

1 Introduction

With the maturation of language technology, software engineering issues such as re-usability, interoperability, or portability are getting more and more attention. As dozens of stand-alone components such as tokenizers, stemmers, lemmatizers, chunkers, parsers, etc. are made accessible in various NLP software libraries and repositories the idea sounds intriguing to (re-)use them on an 'as is' basis and thus save expenditure and manpower when one configures a composite NLP pipeline.

As a consequence, two questions arise. First, how can we abstract away from the specific code level of those single modules which serve, by and large, the same functionality? Second, how can we build NLP systems by composing them, at the abstract level of functional specification, from these already existing component building blocks disregarding concrete implementation matters? Yet another burning issue relates to the increasing availability of multiple metadata annotations both in corpora and language processors. If alternative annotation tag sets are chosen for the same functional task a 'data conversion' problem is created which should be solved at the abstract specification level as well (Ide et al., 2003).

Software engineering methodology points out that these requirements are best met by properly identifying input/output capabilities of constituent components and by specifying a general data model (e.g., based on UML (Rumbaugh et al., 1999)) in order to get rid of the low-level implementation (i.e., coding) layer. A particularly promising proposal along this line of thought is the *Unstructured Information Management Architecture* (UIMA) (Ferrucci and Lally, 2004) originating from IBM research activities.[1] UIMA is but the latest attempt in a series of proposals concerned with more generic NLP engines such as ATLAS (Laprun et al., 2002) or GATE (Cunningham, 2002). These frameworks have in common a data-driven architecture and a data model based on annotation graphs as an adaptation of the TIPSTER architecture (Grishman, 1997). They suffer, however, from a lack of standards for data exchange and abstraction mechanisms at the level of specification languages.

This can be achieved by the definition of a common annotation scheme. We propose an UIMA schema which accounts for a significant part of the complete NLP cycle – from the collection of documents and their internal formal structure, via sentence splitting, tokenization, POS tagging, and parsing, up until the semantic layer (still excluding discourse) – and which aims at the implementation-independent specification of a core NLP system.

[1]Though designed for any sort of unstructured data (text, audio and video data), we here focus on special requirements for the analysis of written documents.

Proceedings of the Linguistic Annotation Workshop, pages 33–40,
Prague, June 2007.

2 Related work

Efforts towards the design of annotation schemata for language resources and their standardization have a long-standing tradition in the NLP community. In the very beginning, this work often focused exclusively on subdomains of text analysis such as document structure meta-information, syntactic or semantic analysis. The *Text Encoding Initiative* (TEI)[2] provided schemata for the exchange of documents of various genres. The *Dublin Core Metadata Initiative*[3] established a de facto standard for the Semantic Web.[4] For (computational) linguistics proper, syntactic annotation schemes, such as the one from the Penn Treebank (Marcus et al., 1993), or semantic annotations, such as the one underlying ACE (Doddington et al., 2004), are increasingly being used in a quasi standard way.

In recent years, however, the NLP community is trying to combine and merge different kinds of annotations for single linguistic layers. XML formats play a central role here. An XML-based encoding standard for linguistic corpora XCES (Ide et al., 2000) is based on CES (Corpus Encoding Standard) as part of the EAGLES Guidelines.[5] Work on TIGER (Brants and Hansen, 2002) is an example for the liaison of dependency- and constituent-based syntactic annotations. New standardization efforts such as the *Syntactic Annotation Framework* (SYNAF) (Declerck, 2006) aim to combine different proposals and create standards for syntactic annotation.

We also encounter a tendency towards multiple annotations for a single corpus. Major bio-medical corpora, such as GENIA (Ohta et al., 2002) or PennBioIE,[6] combine several layers of linguistic information in terms of morpho-syntactic, syntactic and semantic annotations (named entities and events). In the meantime, the *Annotation Compatibility Working Group* (Meyers, 2006) began to concentrate its activities on the mutual compatibility of annotation schemata for, e.g., POS tagging, treebanking, role labeling, time annotation, etc.

The goal of these initiatives, however, has never been to design an annotation scheme for a complete NLP pipeline as needed, e.g., for information extraction or text mining tasks (Hahn and Wermter, 2006). This lack is mainly due to missing standards for specifying comprehensive NLP software architectures. The MEANING format (Pianta et al., 2006) is designed to integrate different levels of morphosyntactic annotations. The HEART OF GOLD middleware (Schäfer, 2006) combines multidimensional mark-up produced by several NLP components. An XML-based NLP tool suite for analyzing and annotating medical language in an NLP pipeline was also proposed by (Grover et al., 2002). All these proposals share their explicit linkage to a specific NLP tool suite or NLP system and thus lack a generic annotation framework that can be re-used in other developmental environments.

Buitelaar et al. developed in the context of an information extraction project an XML-based multilayered annotation scheme that covers morphosyntactic, shallow parsing and semantic annotation (Buitelaar et al., 2003). Their scheme borrows concepts from object-oriented programming (e.g., abstract types, polymorphism). The object-oriented perspective already allows the development of a domain-independent schema and extensions of core types without affecting the base schema. This schema is comprehensive indeed and covers a significant part of advanced NLP pipelines but it is also not connected to a generic framework.

It is our intention to come full circle within a general annotation framework. Accordingly, we cover a significant part of the NLP pipeline from document meta information and formal document structure, morpho-syntactic and syntactic analysis up to semantic processing. The scheme we propose is intended to be compatible with on-going work in standardization efforts from task-specific annotations and to adhere to object-oriented principles.

3 Data-Driven NLP Architecture

As the framework for our specification efforts, we adopted the *Unstructured Information Management Architecture* (UIMA) (Ferrucci and Lally, 2004). It provides a formal specification layer based on UML, as well as a run-time environment for the interpretation and use of these specifications. This dualism is going to attract more and more researchers as a basis

[2] `http://www.tei-c.org`
[3] `http://dublincore.org`
[4] `http://www.w3.org/2001/sw`
[5] `http://www.ilc.cnr.it/EAGLES96/`
[6] `http://bioie.ldc.upenn.edu`

for proper NLP system engineering.

3.1 UIMA-based Tool Suite

UIMA provides a platfrom for the integration of NLP components (ANALYSIS ENGINES in the UIMA jargon) and the deployment of complex NLP pipelines. It is more powerful than other prominent software systems for language engineering (e.g., GATE, ATLAS) as far as its pre- and post-processing facilities are concerned — so-called COLLECTION READERS can be developed to handle any kind of input format (e.g., WWW documents, conference proceedings), while CONSUMERS, on other hand, deal with the subsequent manipulation of the NLP core results (e.g., automatic indexing). Therefore, UIMA is a particularly suitable architecture for advanced text analysis applications such as text mining or information extraction.

We currently provide ANALYSIS ENGINES for sentence splitting, tokenization, POS tagging, shallow and full parsing, acronym detection, named entity recognition, and mapping from named entities to database term identifiers (the latter is motivated by our biological application context). As we mainly deal with documents taken from the biomedical domain, our collection readers process documents from PUBMED,[7] the most important literature resource for researchers in the life sciences. PUBMED currently provides more than 16 million bibliographic references to bio medical articles. The outcomes of ANALYSIS ENGINES are input for various CONSUMERS such as semantic search engines or text mining tools.

3.2 Common Analysis System

UIMA is based on a data-driven architecture. This means that UIMA components do not exchange or share code, they rather exchange data only. The components operate on common data referred to as COMMON ANALYSIS SYSTEM (CAS)(Götz and Suhre, 2004). The CAS contains the subject of analysis (document) and provides meta data in the form of annotations. Analysis engines receive annotations through a CAS and add new annotations to the CAS. An annotation in the CAS then associates meta data with a region the subject of the analysis occupies (e.g., the start and end positions in a document).

UIMA defines CAS interfaces for indexing, accessing and updating the CAS. CASes are modelled independently from particular programming languages. However, JCAS, an object-oriented interface to the CAS, was developed for JAVA. CASes are crucial for the development and deployment of complex NLP pipelines. All components to be integrated in UIMA are characterized by abstract input/output specifications, so-called *capabilities*. These specifications are declared in terms of *descriptors*. The components can be integrated by wrappers conforming with the descriptors. For the integration task, we define in advance what kind of data each component may manipulate. This is achieved via the UIMA *annotation type system*. This type system follows the object-oriented paradigm. There are only two kinds of data, *viz.* types and features. *Features* specify slots within a type, which either have primitive values such as integers or strings, or have references to instances of types in the CAS. *Types*, often called feature structures, are arranged in an inheritance hierarchy.

In the following section, we propose an ANNOTATION TYPE SYSTEM designed and implemented for an UIMA Tool Suite that will become the backbone for our text mining applications. We distinguish between the design and implementation levels, talking about the ANNOTATION SCHEME and the TYPE SYSTEM, respectively.

4 Annotation Type System

The ANNOTATION SCHEME we propose currently consists of five layers: *Document Meta, Document Structure & Style, Morpho-Syntax, Syntax* and *Semantics*. Accordingly, annotation types fall into five corresponding categories. *Document Meta* and *Document Structure & Style* contain annotations about each document's bibliography, organisation and layout. *Morpho-Syntax* and *Syntax* describe the results of morpho-syntactic and syntactic analysis of texts. The results of lemmatisation, stemming and decomposition of words can be represented at this layer, as well. The annotations from shallow and full parsing are represented at the *Syntax* layer. The appropriate types permit the representation of dependency- and constituency-based parsing results. *Semantics*

[7] `http://www.pubmed.gov`

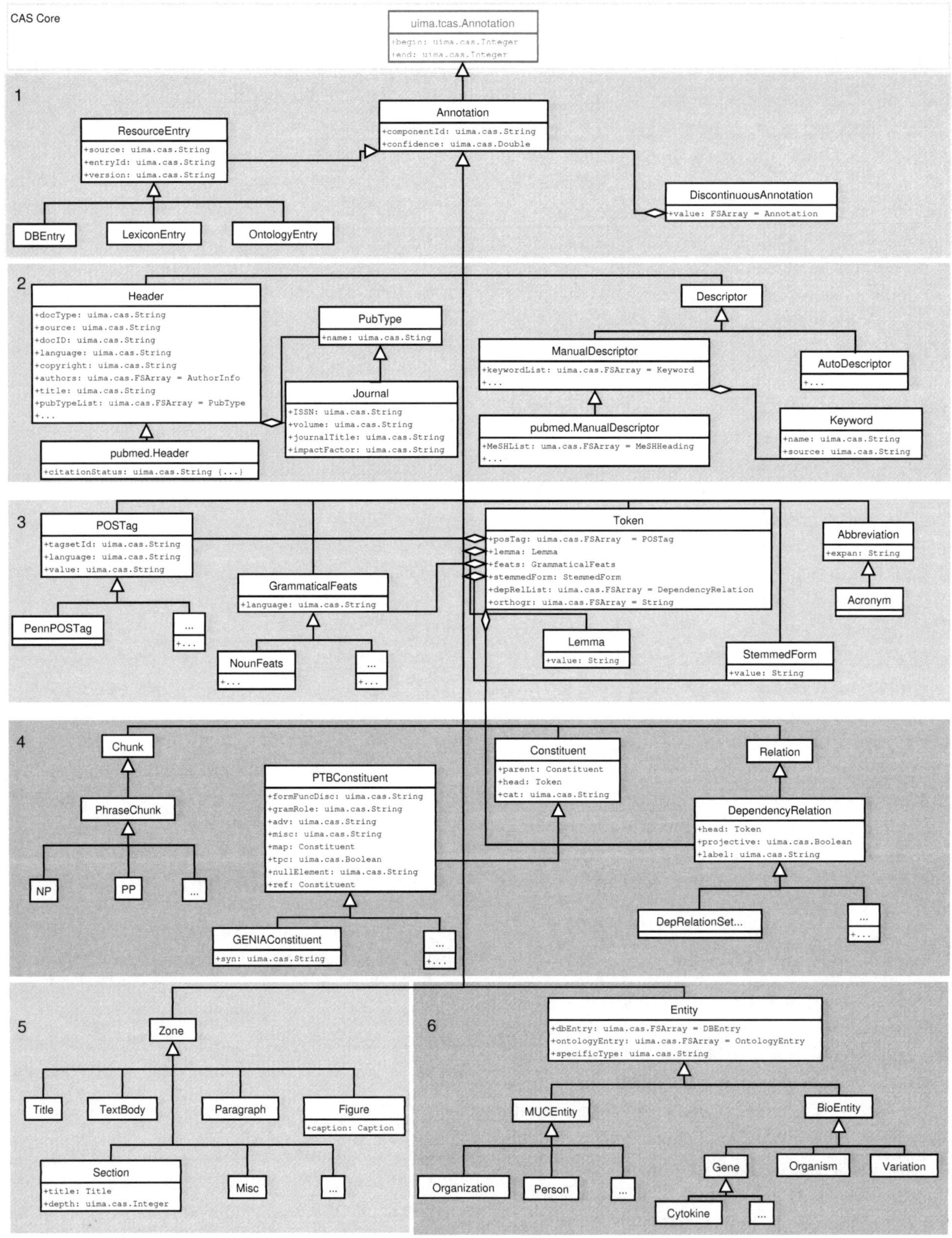

Figure 1: Multi-Layered UIMA Annotation Scheme in UML Representation. 1: Basic Feature Structure and Resource Linking. 2: Document Meta Information. 3: Morpho-Syntax. 4: Syntax. 5: Document Structure & Style. 6: Semantics.

currently covers information about named entities, events and relations between named entities.

4.1 Basic Feature Structure

All types referring to different linguistic layers derive from the basic type `Annotation`, the root type in the scheme (cf. Figure 1-1). The `Annotation` type itself derives information from the default UIMA annotation type `uima.tcas.Annotation` and, thus, inherits the basic annotation features, *viz. begin* and *end* (marking spans of annotations in the subject of analysis). `Annotation` extends this default feature structure with additional features. The *componentId* marks which NLP component actually computed this annotation. This attribute allows to manage multiple annotations of the same type The unique linkage between an analysis component and an annotation item is particularly relevant in cases of parallel annotations. The component from which the annotation originated also assigns a specific confidence score to its *confidence* feature. Each type in the scheme is at least supplied with these four slots inherited from their common root type.

4.2 Document Meta Information

The *Document Meta* layer (cf. Figure 1-2) describes the bibliographical and content information of a document. The bibliographical information, often retrieved from the header of the analyzed document, is represented in the type `Header`. The *source* and *docID* attributes yield a unique identifier for each document. We then adopted some Dublin Core elements, e.g., *language, title, docType*. We distinguish between domain-independent information such as language, title, document type and domain-dependent information as relevant for text mining in the bio-medical domain. Accordingly, the type `pubmed.Header` was especially created for the representation of PUBMED document information. A more detailed description of the document's publication data is available from types which specialize `PubType` such as `Journal`. The latter contains standard journal-specific attributes, e.g., *ISSN, volume, journalTitle*.

The description of the document's content often comes with a list of keywords, information assigned to the `Descriptor` type. We clearly distinguish between content descriptors manually provided by an author, indexer or curator, and items automatically generated by text analysis components after document processing. While the first kind of information will be stored in the `ManualDescriptor`, the second one will be represented in the `AutoDescriptor`. The generation of domain-dependent descriptors is also possible; currently the scheme contains the `pubmed.ManualDescriptor` which allows to assign attributes such as chemicals and genes.

4.3 Document Structure & Style

The *Document Structure & Style* layer (cf. Figure 1-5) contains information about the organization and layout of the analyzed documents. This layer enables the marking-up of document structures such as paragraphs, rhetorical zones, figures and tables, as well as typographical information, such as italics and special fonts. The focus of modeling this layer is on the annotation of scientific documents, especially in the life sciences. We adopted here the SCIXML[8] annotation schema, which was especially developed for marking-up scientific publications. The `Zone` type refers to a distinct division of text and is the parent type for various subtypes such as `TextBody`, `Title` etc. While it seems impossible to predict all of the potential formal text segments, we first looked at types of text zones frequently occurring in scientific documents. The type `Section`, e.g., represents a straightforward and fairly standard division of scientific texts into introduction, methods and results sections. The divisions not covered by current types can be annotated with `Misc`. The annotation of tables and figures with corresponding types enables to link text and additional non-textual information, an issue which is gaining more and more attention in the text mining field.

4.4 Morpho-Syntax

The *Morpho-Syntax* layer (cf. Figure 1-3) represents the results of morpho-syntactic analysis such as tokenization, stemming, POS tagging. The smallest annotation unit is `Token` which consists of five attributes, including its part-of-speech information

[8] `http://www.cl.cam.ac.uk/~aac10/escience/sciborg.html`

(*posTag*), *stemmedForm*, *lemma*, grammatical features (*feats*), and orthographical information (*orthogr*).

With respect to already available POS tagsets, the scheme allows corresponding extensions of the supertype `POSTag` to, e.g., `PennPOSTag` (for the Penn Tag Set (Marcus et al., 1993)) or `GeniaPOSTag` (for the GENIA Tag Set (Ohta et al., 2002)). The attribute *tagsetId* serves as a unique identifier of the corresponding tagset. The value of the POS tag (e.g., NN, VVD, CC) can be stored in the attribute *value*. The potential values for the instantiation of this attribute are always restricted to the tags of the associated tagset. These constraints enforce formal control on annotation processes.

As for morphologically normalized lexical items, the `Lemma` type stores the canonical form of a lexical token which can be retrieved from a lexicon once it is computed by a lemmatizer. The lemma *value*, e.g., for the verb *'activates'* would be *'activate'*. The `StemmedForm` represents a base form of a text token as produced by stemmers (e.g., *'activat-'* for the noun *'activation'*).

Due to their excessive use in life science documents, abbreviations, acronyms and their expanded forms have to be considered in terms of appropriate types, as well. Accordingly, `Abbreviation` and `Acronym` are defined, the latter one being a child type of the first one. The expanded form of a short one can easily be accessed from the attribute *expan*.

Grammatical features of tokens are represented in those types which specialize the supertype `GrammaticalFeats`. Its child types, *viz.* `NounFeats`, `VerbFeats`, `AdjectiveFeats`, `PronounFeats` (omitted from Figure 1-3) cover the most important word categories. Attributes of these types obviously reflect the properties of particular grammatical categories. While `NounFeats` comes with *gender*, *case* and *number* only, `PronounFeats` must be enhanced with *person*. A more complex feature structure is associated with `VerbFeats` which requires attributes such as *tense*, *person*, *number*, *voice* and *aspect*. We adapted here specifications from the TEI to allow compatibility with other annotation schemata.

The type `LexiconEntry` (cf. Figure 1-1) enables a link to the lexicon of choice. By designing this type we achieve much needed flexibility in linking text snaps (e.g., tokens, simplex forms, multiword terms) to external resources. The attributes *entryId* and *source* yield, in combination, a unique identifier of the current lexicon entry. Resource version control is enabled through an attribute *version*.

Text annotations often mark disrupted text spans, so-called *discontinuous annotations*. In coordinated structures such as *'T and B cell'*, the annotator should mark two named entities, *viz.* *'T cell'* and *'B cell'*, where the first one results from the combination of the disjoint parts *'T'* and *'cell'*. In order to represent such discontinous annotations, we introduced the type `DiscontinuousAnnotation` (cf. Figure 1-1) which links through its attribute *value* spans of annotations to an annotation unit.

4.5 Syntax

This layer of the scheme provides the types and attributes for the representation of syntactic structures of sentences (cf. Figure 1-4). The results from shallow and full parsing can be stored here.

Shallow parsing (chunking) aims at dividing the flow of text into phrases (chunks) in a non-overlapping and non-recursive manner. The type `Chunk` accounts for different chunk tag sets by subtyping. Currently, the scheme supports `PhraseChunks` with subtypes such as NP, VP, PP, or ADJP (Marcus et al., 1993).

The scheme also reflects the most popular full parsing approaches in NLP, *viz.* constituent-based and dependency-based approaches. The results from constituent-based parsing are represented in a parse tree and can be stored as single nodes in the `Constituent` type. The tree structure can be reconstructed through links in the attribute *parent* which stores the *id* of the parent constituent. Besides the attribute *parent*, `Constituent` holds the attributes *cat* which stores the complex syntactic category of the current constituent (e.g., NP, VP), and *head* which links to the head word of the constituent. In order to account for multiple annotations in the constituent-based approach, we introduced corresponding constituent types which specialize `Constituent`. This parallels our approach which we advocate for alternatives in POS tagging and the management of alternative chunking results.

Currently, the scheme supports three different constituent types, *viz.* `PTBConstituent`,

GENIAConstituent (Miyao and Tsujii, 2005) and PennBIoIEConstituent. The attributes of the type PTBConstituent cover the complete repertoire of annotation items contained in the Penn Treebank, such as functional tags for form/function dicrepancies (*formFuncDisc*), grammatical role (*gramRole*), adverbials (*adv*) and miscellaneous tags (*misc*). The representation of null elements, topicalized elements and gaps with corresponding references to the lexicalized elements in a tree is reflected in attributes *nullElement*, *tpc*, *map* and *ref*, respectively. GENIAConstituent and PennBIoIEConstituent inherit from PTB-Constituent all listed attributes and provide, in the case of GENIAConstituent , an additional attribute *syn* to specify the syntactic idiosyncrasy (coordination) of constituents.

Dependency parsing results are directly linked to the token level and are thus referenced in the Token type. The DependencyRelation type inherits from the general Relation type and introduces additional features which are necessary for describing a syntactic dependency. The attribute *label* characterizes the type of the analyzed dependency relation. The attribute *head* indicates the head of the dependency relation attributed to the analyzed token. The attribute *projective* relates to the property of the dependency relation whether it is projective or not. As different dependency relation sets can be used for parsing, we propose subtyping similar to the constituency-based parsing approaches. In order to account for alternative dependency relation sets, we aggregate all possible annotations in the Token type as a list (*depRelList*).

4.6 Semantics

The *Semantics* layer comprises currently the representation of named entities, particularly for the bio-medical domain. The entity types are hierarchically organized. The supertype Entity (cf. Figure 1-6) links annotated (named) entities to the ontologies and databases through appropriate attributes, *viz. ontologyEntry* and s*dbEntry*. The attribute *specificType* specifies the analyzed entity in a more detailed way (e.g., Organism can be specified through the species values 'human', 'mouse', 'rat', etc.) The subtypes are currently being developed in the bio-medical domain and cover, e.g., genes, proteins, organisms, diseases, variations. This hierarchy can easily be extended or supplemented with entities from other domains. For illustration purposes, we extended it here by MUC (Grishman and Sundheim, 1996) entity types such as Person, Organization, etc.

This scheme is still under construction and will soon also incorporate the representation of relationships between entities and domain-specific events. The general type Relation will then be extended with specific conceptual relations such as location, part-of, etc. The representation of events will be covered by a type which aggregates pre-defined relations between entities and the event mention. An event type such as InhibitionEvent would link the text spans in the sentence *'protein A inhibits protein B'* in attributes *agent* (*'protein A'*), *patient* (*'protein B'*), *mention* (*'inhibits'*).

5 Conclusion and Future work

In this paper, we introduced an UIMA annotation type system which covers the core functionality of morphological, syntactic and semantic analysis components of a generic NLP system. It also includes type specifications which relate to the formal document format and document style. Hence, the design of this scheme allows the annotation of the entire cycle of (sentence-level) NLP analysis (discourse phenomena still have to be covered).

The annotation scheme consists mostly of core types which are designed in a domain-independent way. Nevertheless, it can easily be extended with types which fit other needs. The current scheme supplies an extension for the bio-medical domain at the document meta and structure level, as well as on the semantic level. The morpho-syntactic and syntactic levels provide types needed for the analysis of the English language. Changes of attributes or attribute value sets will lead to adaptations to other natural languages.

We implemented the scheme as an UIMA type system. The formal specifications are implemented using the UIMA run-time environment. This direct link of formal and implementational issues is a major asset using UIMA unmatched by any previous specification approach. Furthermore, all annotation results can be converted to the XMI format within the UIMA framework. XMI, the XML Metadata Interchange format, is an OMG[9] standard for the XML representation of object graphs.

The scheme also eases the representation of annotation results for the same task with alternative and often competitive components. The identification of the component which provided specific annotations can be retrieved from the attribute *componentId*. Furthermore, the annotation with alternative and multiple tag sets is supported as well. We have designed for each tag set a type representing the corresponding annotation parameters. The inheritance trees at almost all annotation layers support the parallelism in annotation process (e.g., tagging may proceed with different POS tagsets).

The user of the scheme can restrict the potential values of the types or attributes. The current scheme makes use of the customization capability for POS tagsets, for all attributes of constituents and chunks. This yields additional flexibility in the design and, once specified, an increased potential for automatic control for annotations.

The scheme also enables a straightforward connection to external resources such as ontologies, lexicons, and databases as evidenced by the corresponding subtypes of `ResourceEntry` (cf. Figure 1-1). These types support the specification of a relation between a concrete text span and the unique item addressed in any of these resources.

With these considerations in mind, we strive for the elaboration of a common standard UIMA type system for NLP engines. The advantages of such a standard include an easy exchange and integration of different NLP analysis engines, the facilitation of sophisticated evaluation studies (where, e.g., alternative components for NLP tasks can be plugged in and out at the spec level), and the reusability of single NLP components developed in various labs.

Acknowledgments. This research was funded by the EC's 6th Framework Programme (4th call) within the BOOTStrep project under grant FP6-028099.

References

S. Brants and S. Hansen. 2002. Developments in the TIGER annotation scheme and their realization in the corpus. In *Proc. of the 3rd LREC Conference*, pages 1643–1649.

P. Buitelaar, T. Declerck, B. Sacaleanu, Š. Vintar, D. Raileanu, and C. Crispi. 2003. A multi-layered, XML-based approach to the integration of linguistic and semantic annotations. In *Proc. of EACL 2003 Workshop NLPXML-03*.

H. Cunningham. 2002. GATE, a general architecture for text engineering. *Computers and the Humanities*, 36:223–254.

T. Declerck. 2006. SYNAF: Towards a standard for syntactic annotation. In *Proc. of the 5th LREC Conference*.

G. Doddington, A. Mitchell, M. Przybocki, L. Ramshaw, S. Strassel, and R. Weischedel. 2004. The Automatic Content Extraction (ACE) Program. In *Proc. of the 4th LREC Conference*, pages 837–840.

D. Ferrucci and A. Lally. 2004. UIMA: an architectural approach to unstructured information processing in the corporate research environment. *Natural Language Engineering*, 10(3-4):327–348.

T. Götz and O. Suhre. 2004. Design and implementation of the UIMA Common Analysis System. *IBM Systems Journal*, 43(3):476–489.

R. Grishman and B. Sundheim. 1996. Message Understanding Conference – 6: A brief history. In *Proc. of the 16th COLING*, pages 466–471.

R. Grishman. 1997. Tipster architecture design document, version 2.3. Technical report, Defense Advanced Research Projects Agency (DARPA), U.S. Departement of Defense.

C. Grover, E. Klein, M. Lapata, and A. Lascarides. 2002. XML-based NLP tools for analysing and annotating medical language. In *Proc. of the 2nd Workshop NLPXML-2002*, pages 1–8.

U. Hahn and J. Wermter. 2006. Levels of natural language processing for text mining. In S. Ananiadou and J. McNaught, editors, *Text Mining for Biology and Biomedicine*, pages 13–41. Artech House.

N. Ide, P. Bonhomme, and L. Romary. 2000. XCES: An XML-based standard for linguistic corpora. In *Proc. of the 2nd LREC Conference*, pages 825–830.

N. Ide, L. Romary, and E. de la Clergerie. 2003. International standard for a linguistic annotation framework. In *Proc. of the HLT-NAACL 2003 SEALTS Workshop*, pages 25–30.

C. Laprun, J. Fiscus, J. Garofolo, and S. Pajot. 2002. A practical introduction to ATLAS. In *Proc. of the 3rd LREC Conference*, pages 1928–1932.

M. Marcus, B. Santorini, and M.A. Marcinkiewicz. 1993. Building a large annotated corpus of English: The PENN TREEBANK. *Computational Linguistics*, 19(2):313–330.

A. Meyers. 2006. Annotation compatibility working group report. In *Proc. of the COLING-ACL 2006 Workshop FLAC 2006'*, pages 38–53.

Y. Miyao and J. Tsujii. 2005. Probabilistic disambiguation models for wide-coverage HPSG parsing. In *Proc. of the ACL 2005*, pages 83 – 90.

T. Ohta, Y. Tateisi, and J.-D. Kim. 2002. The GENIA corpus: An annotated research abstract corpus in molecular biology domain. In *Proc. of the 2nd HLT*, pages 82–86.

E. Pianta, L. Bentivogli, C. Girardi, and B. Magnini. 2006. Representing and accessing multilevel linguistic annotation using the MEANING format. In *Proc. of the 5th EACL-2006 Workshop NLPXML-2006*, pages 77–80.

J. Rumbaugh, I. Jacobson, and G. Booch. 1999. *The Unified Modeling Language Reference Manual*. Addison-Wesley.

U. Schäfer. 2006. Middleware for creating and combining multi-dimensional NLP markup. In *Proc. of the 5th EACL-2006 Workshop NLPXML-2006*, pages 81–84.

[9] `http://www.omg.org`

Discontinuity Revisited: An Improved Conversion to Context-Free Representations

Adriane Boyd
Department of Linguistics
The Ohio State University
1712 Neil Ave.
Columbus, OH 43210
adriane@ling.osu.edu

Abstract

This paper introduces a new, reversible method for converting syntactic structures with discontinuous constituents into traditional syntax trees. The method is applied to the Tiger Corpus of German and results for PCFG parsing requiring such context-free trees are provided. A labeled dependency evaluation shows that the new conversion method leads to better results by preserving local relationships and introducing fewer inconsistencies into the training data.

1 Introduction

Unlike traditional treebanks, the Negra and Tiger Corpora (Brants et al., 2002) allow crossing branches in the syntactic annotation to handle certain features of German. In order to use the Negra or Tiger Corpus data to train a PCFG parser, it is necessary to convert the syntactic annotation into context-free syntax trees. In previous work (see section 3.1), a non-reversible method has been used that raises nodes in the tree to eliminate discontinuities. This method effectively introduces inconsistencies into the data and disrupts the grammatical dependency annotation in the trees. This paper presents a new, reversible method for converting Negra and Tiger syntactic structures into context-free syntax trees appropriate for training a PCFG parser. A reversible conversion allows the original grammatical dependency relations to be reconstructed from the PCFG parser output. This paper focuses on the newer, larger Tiger Corpus, but methods and results are very similar for the Negra Corpus.

2 Tiger Corpus

The Tiger Corpus was a joint project between Saarland University, the University of Stuttgart, and University of Potsdam. The Tiger Corpus Version 2 contains 50,474 sentences of newspaper text. The Tiger annotation combines features from phrase structure grammar and dependency grammar using a tree-like syntactic structure with grammatical functions labeled on the edges of the tree (Brants et al., 2002). Flat sentence structures are used in many places to avoid attachment ambiguities and non-branching phrases are not allowed. The annotation scheme emphasizes the use of the tree structure to encode all grammatical relations in local trees regardless of whether a grammatical dependency is local within in the sentence. This leads to the use of discontinuous constituents to handle flexible word order, extraposition, partial constituent fronting, and other phenomena. An example of a Tiger tree with discontinuous constituents (both VPs) is shown in Figure 1.

3 Conversion to Context-Free Syntax Trees

For research involving PCFG parsing models trained on Tiger Corpus data, it is necessary to convert the syntax graphs with crossing branches into traditional syntax trees in order to extract context-free grammar rules from the data. Approximately 30% of sentences in Tiger contain at least one discontinuous constituent.

3.1 Existing Tiger Corpus Conversion

In previous research, crossing branches have been resolved by raising non-head nodes out of discon-

Proceedings of the Linguistic Annotation Workshop, pages 41–44,
Prague, June 2007. ©2007 Association for Computational Linguistics

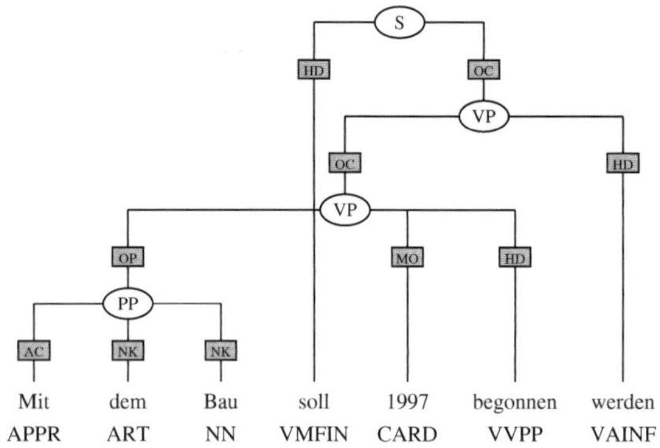

'Construction should start in 1997.'
(lit. *with the construction should 1997 begun be*)

Figure 1: Discontinuous Tiger tree

tinuous constituents until no more branches cross. The converted sentence from Figure 1 is shown in Figure 2. In any sentence, multiple nodes could each be raised one or more times, so it is difficult to automatically reconstruct the original sentence. Previous work on PCFG parsing using Negra or Tiger has either used the provided Penn Treebank-style versions of the corpora included with Negra and Tiger Version 1 (Dubey and Keller, 2003; Dubey, 2004) or used a program provided with the Negra/Tiger *Annotate* software (Plaehn and Brants, 2000) which performs the raising algorithm (Kübler, 2005; Kübler et al., 2006). This conversion will be referred to as the "raising method".

3.2 A New Approach to Eliminating Discontinuities

The raising method has the advantages of preserving the number of nodes in the tree, but it is not easily reversible and disrupts local trees. Raising non-head nodes is not an ideal way of eliminating discontinuities because it does not preserve the relationship between a head and a dependent that is represented in a local tree in the Tiger annotation. After raising one or more nodes in 30% of the sentences in the corpus, local trees are no longer consistent across the treebank. Some VPs may contain all their objects while others do not. For example, in Figure 2 the PP object *Mit dem Bau* is no longer in the local tree with its head *begonnen*. The PCFG has lessened chance of capturing generalizations from the resulting inconsistent training data.

Preferable to the raising method is a conversion that is reversible and that preserves local trees as

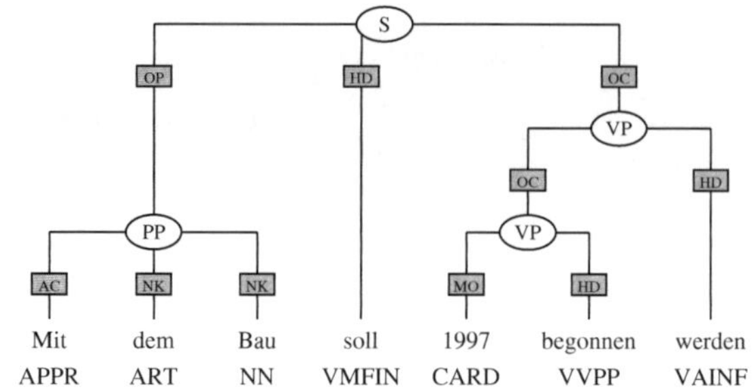

Figure 2: Result of conversion by raising

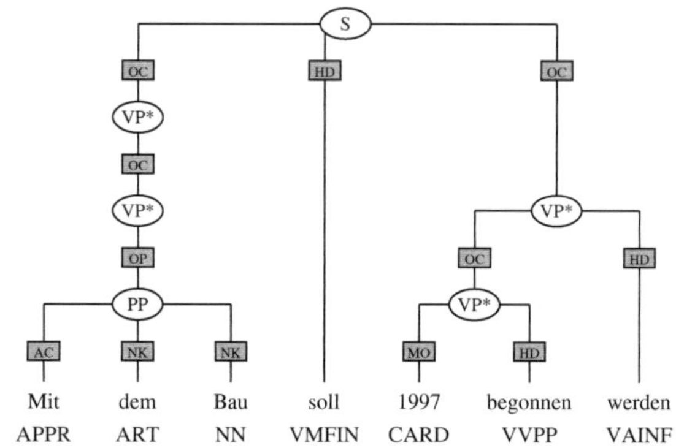

Figure 3: Result of conversion by splitting

much as possible. The new approach to the conversion involves splitting discontinuous nodes into smaller "partial nodes". Each subset of the original children with a continuous terminal yield becomes a partial node. In this way, it is possible to remove crossing branches while preserving the parent relationships from the original tree. Because partial nodes retain their original parents, the reverse conversion is greatly simplified.

In order to make the conversion easily reversible, the partial nodes need to be marked in some way so that they can be identified in the reverse conversion. A simple method is to use a single mark (*) on all partial nodes.[1] For example, a discontinuous VP with the children NN-OA (noun acc. obj.) and VVINF-HD (infinitive) would be converted into a VP* with an NN-OA child and a VP* with a VVINF-HD child. The method of creating partial nodes with a single mark will be called the "splitting method". It is completely reversible unless there are two discontinuous sisters with the same label. While it is not unusual for a Tiger tree to have multiple dis-

[1]This approach was inspired by Joakim Nivre's paper *Pseudo-Projective Dependency Parsing* (Nivre, 2005), in which non-projective dependency structures are converted to easier-to-parse projective dependency structures in a way that limits the number of new labels introduced, but is mostly reconstructible.

continuous nodes with same label (as in Figure 1), two nodes with the same label are never sisters so the conversion is reversible for all sentences. Each tree is converted with the following algorithm, which is a postorder traversal that starts at the root node of the tree. The postorder traversal guarantees that every child of a node is continuous before the node itself is evaluated, so splitting the node under consideration into partial nodes will resolve the discontinuity.

```
SPLIT-DISC-NODES(Node)
 for each Child of Node
    SPLIT-DISC-NODES(Child)
 if Node's terminal yield is discontinuous
    Children := immediate children of Node
    ContSets := divide Children into subsets
                    with continuous terminal yields
    for each ChildSubset in ContSets
       PNode := new node
       PNode's label := Node's label with mark (*)
       PNode's parent := Node's parent
       for each Child in ChildSubset
         Child's parent := PNode
    remove Node from tree
```

The splitting conversion of the sentence from Figure 1 can be seen in Figure 3. To convert the split version back to the original version, the tree is examined top-down, rejoining any marked sister nodes with the same label.

4 Results

All parsing was performed using the unlexicalized parsing model from the left corner parser LoPar Schmid (2000). The input data was labeled with perfect tags from the corpus to prevent errors in tagging from affecting the parsing results.

4.1 Data Preparation

For the following experiments, the Tiger Corpus Version 2 was divided into training, development, and testing sections. Following the data split from Dubey (2004), 90% of the corpus was used as training data, 5% as development data, and 5% as test data. In preprocessing, all punctuation was removed because it is not attached within the sentence. 6.5% of sentences are excluded because they contain no annotation beyond the word level or because they contain multiple root nodes. After preprocessing, there are 42,612 sentences in the training set. For evaluation, only sentences with 40 words or fewer are used, leaving 2,312 test sentences. The raised version is created using the *Annotate* software and the split version is created using the method described in section 3.2. For the split version, partial nodes are rejoined before evaluation.

In the Penn Treebank-style versions of the corpus appropriate for training a PCFG parser, each edge label has been joined with the phrase or POS label on the phrase or word immediately below it. Because of this, the edge labels for single-word arguments (e.g., pronoun subjects) are attached to the POS tag of the word, which provides the parser with the perfect grammatical function label when perfect lexical tags are provided. This amounts to providing the perfect grammatical function labels for approximately one-third of arguments in Tiger, so to avoid this problem, non-branching phrase nodes are introduced for single-word arguments. Phrase nodes are introduced above all single-word subjects, accusative objects, dative objects, and genitive objects. The category of the inserted phrase depends on the POS tag on the word (NP, VP, or AP as appropriate).

4.2 Experiment 1: Reversibility of Splitting Conversion

All sentences in the test set were converted into syntax trees by splitting discontinuous nodes according to the algorithm in section 3.2. All 2,312 sentences in the test set can be converted back to their original versions with no errors. The most frequently split nodes are VP (~55%) and NP (~20%).

4.3 Experiment 2: Labeled Dependency Evaluation

A labeled dependency evaluation is chosen instead of a typical PARSEVAL evaluation for two reasons: 1) PARSEVAL is unable to evaluate trees with discontinuous constituents; 2) a bracketing evaluation examines all types of brackets in the sentence and may not reflect how accurately significant grammatical dependencies have been identified.

It is useful to look at an evaluation on grammatical functions that are important for determining the functor-argument structure of the sentence. In this evaluation, subjects, accusative objects, prepo-

	Raised			Split		
GF	P	R	F	P	R	F
Subj	74.8	71.6	73.2	74.7	73.5	74.1
AccObj	46.3	48.9	47.4	49.2	53.7	51.4
PPObj	20.4	10.7	15.6	31.9	15.6	23.8
DatObj	20.1	11.5	15.8	25.5	14.3	19.9

Table 1: Labeled Dependency Evaluation

sitional objects, and dative objects are considered as part of labeled dependency triples consisting of the lexical head verb, the grammatical function label, and the dependent phrase bearing the grammatical function label. The internal structure of the dependent phrase is not considered.

In Tiger annotation, the head of an argument is the sister marked with the grammatical function label HD. HD labels are found with an f-score of 99% by the parser, so this evaluation mainly reflects how well the arguments in the dependency triple are identified. This evaluation uses lexical heads, so if the sister with the label HD is a phrase, then a recursive search for heads within that phrase finds the lexical head. For 5.7% of arguments in the gold standard, it is not possible to find a lexical head. Further methods could be applied to find the remaining heads heuristically, but the additional parameters this introduces for the evaluation are avoided by ignoring these cases.

The results for a labeled dependency evaluation on important grammatical function labels are shown in Table 4.3. Grammatical functions are listed in order of decreasing frequency. The results for subjects remain similar between the raised and split version, as expected, and the results for all other types of arguments improve 4-8% for the split version.

Subjects are rarely affected by the raising method because S nodes are rarely discontinuous, so it is not surprising that the results for subjects are similar for both methods. However, VPs are by far the most frequently discontinuous nodes, and since the raising method can move an object away from its head, the difference between the two conversion methods is most evident in the object relations. Data sparsity plays a role in the lower scores for the objects, since there are approximately twice as many subjects as accusative objects and twelve times as many subjects as dative objects.

5 Future Work

Further research will extend the dependency evaluation presented in this paper to include more or all of the grammatical functions. There is significant work on a dependency conversion for Negra by the Partial Parsing Project (Daum et al., 2004) that could be adapted for this purpose.

6 Conclusion

By using an improved conversion method to remove crossing branches from the Negra/Tiger corpora, it is possible to generate trees without crossing branches that can be converted back to the original format with no errors. This is a significant improvement over the previously used conversion by raising, which was not reversible and had the effect of introducing inconsistencies into the corpus. The new splitting conversion method shows a 4-8% improvement in a labeled dependency evaluation on accusative, prepositional, and dative objects.

References

Sabine Brants, Stefanie Dipper, Silvia Hansen, Wolfgang Lezius and George Smith, 2002. The TIGER Treebank. In *Proceedings of TLT 2002*.

Michael Daum, Kilian Foth and Wolfgang Menzel, 2004. Automatic transformation of phrase treebanks to dependency trees. In *Proceedings of LREC 2004*.

Amit Dubey, 2004. Statistical Parsing for German: Modeling Syntactic Properties and Annotation Differences. Ph.D. thesis, Universität des Saarlandes.

Amit Dubey and Frank Keller, 2003. Probabilistic Parsing Using Sister-Head Dependencies. In *Proceedings of ACL 2006*.

Sandra Kübler, 2005. How do treebank annotation schemes influence parsing results? Or how not to compare apples and oranges. In *Proceedings of RANLP 2005*.

Sandra Kübler, Erhard W. Hinrichs and Wolfgang Maier, 2006. Is it really that difficult to parse German? In *Proceedings of EMNLP 2006*.

Joakim Nivre, 2005. Pseudo-Projective Dependency Parsing. In *Proceedings of ACL 2005*.

Oliver Plaehn and Thorsten Brants, 2000. Annotate – An Efficient Interactive Annotation Tool. In *Proceedings of ANLP 2000*.

Helmut Schmid, 2000. *LoPar: Design and Implementation*. Technical report, Universität Stuttgart.

Usage of XSL Stylesheets for the annotation of the Sámi language corpora

Saara Huhmarniemi
University of Tromsø
saara.huhmarniemi@helsinki.fi

Sjur N. Moshagen
Norwegian Sámi Parliament
sjur.moshagen@samediggi.no

Trond Trosterud
University of Tromsø
trond.trosterud@hum.uit.no

Abstract

This paper describes an annotation system for Sámi language corpora, which consists of structured, running texts. The annotation of the texts is fully automatic, starting from the original documents in different formats. The texts are first extracted from the original documents preserving the original structural markup. The markup is enhanced by a document-specific XSLT script which contains document-specific formatting instructions. The overall maintenance is achieved by system-wide XSLT scripts.

1 Introduction

Corpus building for a specific language is considered to require much human effort and time. To overcome this difficulty, there is a recent development of applications for automatic corpus building using often the Web as a resource e.g. (Baroni and Bernardini eds., 2006; Sharoff, 2006). For minority languages, the resources for building a text corpus are often limited. Automatic tools for building corpus database specifically for the minority languages are developed e.g. by (Ghani et al., 2005; Scannell, 2004).

The requirement to have the corpus building process automatized as much as possible was also central in the Sámi language corpora project. However, the collection of texts is done in a "traditional" manner: the files are gathered and classified manually. For North Sámi, there are texts available in electronic form which can be exploited in a corpus database, mainly administrative and newspaper texts. The small amount of those texts forced us to take into account a wide variety of sources and formats, and also to include texts that were of low technical quality. That introduced problems for the automatic processing of the texts. The solution to this problem was the document-specific processing instructions that were implemented in XSLT.

2 The Project

The corpus described here is the first structurally annotated text corpus for any Sámi language. The corpus database was developed in parallel with the spell checker and the syntactic analyzer projects for North and Lule Sámi[1]. The new texts became test material for these two applications as soon as they were added to the corpus database. The requirements for the markup were constantly being re-evaluated during the project. The infrastructure was designed flexible so that it would accomodate to the different needs of the two projects in different phases of the application development.

At the moment, the corpus database consists of almost 6 million words for North Sámi and some 240 000 for Lule Sámi. Even though the system was primarily designed for the Sámi languages, there are no strictly language-dependent sections in the system; it has already been tested with Norwegian and Finnish, among others.

One of the main applications of the text corpus database is the syntactically annotated and fully disambiguated corpus database for Sámi languages. The syntactic annotation is done automatically us-

[1] http://www.divvun.no/, http://giellatekno.uit.no/

Proceedings of the Linguistic Annotation Workshop, pages 45–48,
Prague, June 2007.

ing the tools developed in the syntactic analyzer project, but the process is out of the scope of this paper. There is also some parallel texts with Norwegian, and plans for extending parallel text corpora to different Sámi languages and Finnish and Swedish. The corpus database is freely available for research purposes. There will be a web-based corpus interface for the syntactically annotated corpus and a restricted access to the system for examining the corpus data directly.

3 XSLT and corpus maintenace

Flexibility and reusability are in general the design requirements of annotated text corpora. XML has become the standard annotation system in physical storage representation. XML Transformation Language (XSLT) (Clark ed., 1999) provides an easy data transformation between different formats and applications. XSLT is commonly used in the contemporary corpus development. The power of XSLT mainly comes from its sublanguage XPath (Clark and DeRose eds., 1999). XPath provides an access to the XML structure, elements, attributes and text through concise path expressions.

In the Sámi language corpora, XSLT is used in corpus establishment and maintenance. The raw structural format is produced by text extraction tools and coverted to a preliminary XML-format using XSLT. The markup is further enhanced by document specific information and a system-wide processing instruction, both implemented in XSLT.

4 The Sámi corpus database

4.1 Overall architecture

The corpus database is organized so that the original text resources, which are the documents in various formats (Word, PDF, HTML, text) form the source base. The text is extracted from the original documents using various freely available text extraction tools, such as *antiword* and *HTML Tidy*. They already provide a preliminary structural markup: antiword produces DocBook and HTML Tidy provides output in XHTML. There are XSLT scripts for converting the different preliminary formats the to an intermediate document format.

The intermediate format is further processed to the desired XML-format using XSLT-scripts. The result is the final XML-document with structural markup, see Fig. 1.

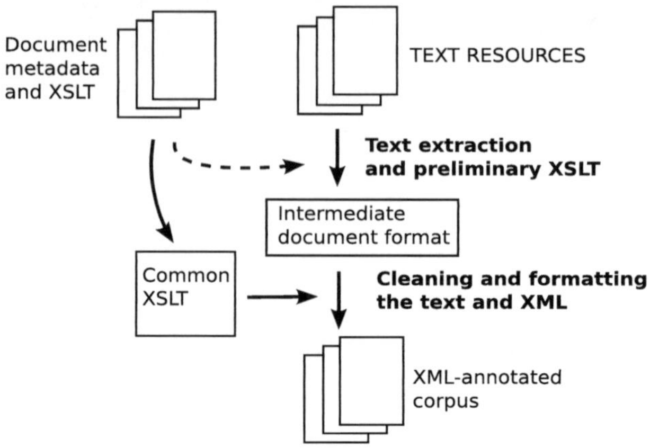

Figure 1: The overall architecture of the conversion process.

The conversion of a document always starts from the original file, which makes it possible to adapt for the latest versions of the text extraction tools and other tools used in the process as well as the changes in XML-markup.

The annotation process is fully automatic and can be rerun at will. Some documents may contain errors or formatting that are not taken into account by the automatic tools. On the other hand, the automatized annotation process does not allow manual correction of the texts, nor manual XML-markup. Those exceptions can be taken into account by document-specific processing instructions, which are implemented using XSLT. The script can be used for adding XML-annotation for specific parts of the document, fixing smaller errors in the document, or even to rescue a corrupted file that would be otherwise unusable. This is a useful feature when building a corpus for a minority language with diverse and often limited text resources.

4.2 XML-annotation

In the Sámi language corpora, markup of running text is simple, containing no more structural information than what is generally available in the original text. The body text can contain sections and paragraphs and each section can contain sections and paragraphs. There are four paragraph types: title, text, table and list. The paragraphs are classified whenever the information is available in the original document. Lists and especially tables contain incomplete sentences and in many cases numeric data. When conducting e.g. syntactic analysis, it might be better to leave tables and even lists or titles out, whereas for e.g. terminological work the tables are highly relevant. Tagging for paragraph type makes it possible to include or exclude the relevant paragraph types at will.

Inside a paragraph, there is a possibility to add emphasis markup and other span information, such as quotes. The sentence-level and word-level markup is not included in the text corpus. The markup is added when the text corpus is moved to the syntactically annotated corpus database.

The XML-annotation does not follow any standardized XML-format, but it is, in essence, a subset of the XCES (Ide et al., 2000) format. Furthermore, the system is designed so that changing the XML-annotation and moving to a standardized format is a straightforward process.

4.3 XSLT processing

Each original document in the corpus database is paired with an XSLT script. The document-specific XSLT script contains processing instructions that are applied to the document during the conversion from the preliminary document format to the final XML-format (see Fig. 1.). The XPath expressions are powerful tools for accessing portions of text in a document and modifying the XML-markup without editing the XML-file itself. The usage of the XPath expressions entails that the XML-structure of a document does not change, which poses some restrictions to the intermediate format of the document.

The XSLT script contains the document metadata and status information, among other relevant data. The document metadata is stored in variables in the document-specific XSLT script, and the system-wide XSLT scripts access these variables and convert them to the required format.

The system-wide XSLT script contains functions and templates that can be called from the document-specific XSLT script. There is for example a string-replacement function for correcting errors that are of technical origin, such as wrongly converted Sámi characters that were missed by the automatic detection of wrongly encoded characters.

Another example of a template that can be called from the document-specific XSLT script is the string-replacement, that can be used for marking spelling errors in the text. Due to the variety of conventions of writing Sámi, the texts tend to contain lot of strings that are classified as spelling errors. The errors disturb the testing of the analyzer, but are on the other hand interesting from the point of view of the spell checker project. When a spelling error is discovered in the text, the erroneous strings and their corrections are added to the document-specific metafile from where they are picked by the conversion process. The errors are thus preserved in the XML-format but with a correction which can be used instead of the erroneous string. This is achieved by a special markup:

```
<error correct="text">tetx</error>
```

In this way the original documents stay intact and the information is preserved also when the file is reconverted. If the error is not just a single word but involves more context, it is possible to add the context to the error string.

In addition, the document-specific XSLT script contains variables that may be used already in the text extraction phase. An example would be the text alignment information of a pdf-file.

4.4 Language identification

Most documents in the Sámi corpus database contain sections of text that are not in the document's main language. Those sections are marked at paragraph level, using the attribute *xml:lang*.

The language identification is done using the *TextCat* tool (van Noord, 1997). Since the different Sámi languages and the close relative Finnish resemble each other significantly (the same is true for the Scandinavian languages), the search space was reduced at the document level. The information of the document languages was stored to the document-specific XSLT script.

Since the Sámi texts contain lot of quotations from other languages, especially from the majority language (Norwegian, Swedish or Finnish), the quoted text fragments are analysed separately using *TextCat* and marked with a corresponding *xml:lang* attribute. For example:

```
<span type="quote" xml:lang="nob">
"Arbeidet med fylkesplanene"
</span>
(bargu fylkkaplánaiguin).
```

When a sentence that contains a quotation in a foreign language is given to the syntactic analyzer, the quotation can be considered as a syntactic unit and that way carried through the analysis.

4.5 Other processing

Character set conversion may be a central task when a corpus is built for minority languages, due to a large repertoire of non-standardized 8-bit character sets, e.g. (McEnery et al., 2000; Trosterud, 1996). In the Sámi corpus database, the text extraction tools often produced wrongly-utf8 -encoded output, due to erroneous codepage IDs and font specifications. There is a specific module for guessing the documents' original code-page, and for fixing errouneous utf8-conversion.

There are a couple of other scripts that are applied to the final XML-documents. For example, real hyphenation marks in the document are preserved for testing of the hyphenator. The hyphen-tags are marked automatically, taking into account some language specific cues and information of e.g list context.

5 Conclusion

The system is flexible and reusable since the central XSLT processing allows for changes in the XML-structure as well as the introduction of new structural information. The intermediate XML-formats which are produced by the text extraction tools are straightforward to convert to a format that conforms to the project's DTD using XSLT processing. Instead of trying to predict the future uses of the corpus database in the beginning of the project, the infrastructure was set up so that it evolves throughout the project.

The main problem in the heavy usage of XSLT is that the syntax of the XSLT is quite restricted although XSLT/XPath 2 brings some improvements. The lack of regular expressions is one of the restrictions, so some of the string-replacement functions had to be implemented by other means. In the future, these could probably be replaced with XPath 2 functions.

Fully-automated, XSL/XML-based conversion has made it possible to build a corpus of decent size for small languages. After the initial infrastructure is created, adding new documents does not require much resources. The system does not involve any strictly language-dependent processing, so it is portable to other languages. The result is a clean, classified and XML-annotated corpus which can be used in research and different language technology applications.

References

Marco Baroni and Silvia Bernardini (eds.). 2006. *Wacky! Working papers on the Web as Corpus.* http://wacky.sslmit.unibo.it/.

James Clark (ed.). 1999. *XSL Transformations (XSLT) 1.0.* W3C Recommendation. http://www.w3.org/TR/xslt.

James Clark and Steve DeRose (eds.). 1999. *XML Path Language (XPath) 1.0.* W3C Recommendation. http://www.w3.org/TR/xpath.

Rayid Ghani, Rosie Jones, and Dunja Mladenic. 2005. *Building Minority Language Corpora by Learning to Generate Web Search Queries. Knowledge and Information Systems*, 7(1):56–83.

Nancy Ide, Patrice Bonhomme, and Laurent Romary. 2000. *XCES: An XML-based Encoding Standard for Linguistic Corpora. Proceedings of the Second Language Resources and Evaluation Conference (LREC)* 825–830.

Anthony McEnery, Paul Baker, Rob Gaizauskas, Hamish Cunningham. 2000 *EMILLE: Building a corpus of South Asian languages. Vivek, A Quarterly in. Artificial Intelligence*, 13(3): 23–32.

Kevin P. Scannell. 2004. *Corpus Building for Minority Languages.* http://borel.slu.edu/crubadan/.

Serge Sharoff. 2006. *Open-source corpora: using the net to fish for linguistic data International Journal of Corpus Linguistics*, 11(4): 435-462.

Trond Trosterud. 1996 *Funny characters on the net. How information technology may (or may not) do support minority languages. Arbete människa miljö & Nordisk Ergonomi*, 3:114–125.

Gertjan van Noord. 1997. *TextCat Language Guesser.* http://www.let.rug.nl/~vannoord/TextCat/.

Criteria for the Manual Grouping of Verb Senses

Cecily Jill Duffield, Jena D. Hwang, Susan Windisch Brown, Dmitriy Dligach, Sarah E.Vieweg, Jenny Davis, Martha Palmer
Departments of Linguistics and Computer Science
University of Colorado
Boulder, C0 80039-0295, USA
{cecily.duffield, hwangd, susan.brown, dmitry.dligach, sarah.vieweg, jennifer.davis, martha.palmer}@colorado.edu

Abstract

In this paper, we argue that clustering WordNet senses into more coarse-grained groupings results in higher inter-annotator agreement and increased system performance. Clustering of verb senses involves examining syntactic and semantic features of verbs and arguments on a case-by-case basis rather than applying a strict methodology. Determining appropriate criteria for clustering is based primarily on the needs of annotators.

1 Credits

We gratefully acknowledge the support of the National Science Foundation Grant NSF-0415923, Word Sense Disambiguation, and the GALE program of the Defense Advanced Research Projects Agency, Contract No. HR0011-06-C-0022, a subcontract from the BBN-AGILE Team.

2 Introduction

Word sense ambiguity poses significant obstacles to accurate and efficient information extraction and automatic translation. Successful disambiguation of polysemous words in NLP applications depends on determining an appropriate level of granularity of sense distinctions, perhaps more so for distinguishing between multiple senses of verbs than for any other grammatical category. WordNet, an important and widely used lexical resource, uses fine-grained distinctions that provide subtle information about the particular usages of various lexical items (Felbaum, 1998). When used as a resource for annotation of various genres of text, this fine level of granularity has not been conducive to high rates of inter-annotator agreement (ITA) or high automatic tagging performance. Annotation of verb senses as described by coarse-grained Proposition Bank framesets may result in higher ITA scores, but the blurring of distinctions between verb senses with similar argument structures may fail to alleviate the problems posed by ambiguity. Our goal in this project is to create verb sense distinctions at a middle level of granularity that allow us to capture as much information as possible from a lexical item while still attaining high ITA scores and high system performance in automatic sense disambiguation. We have demonstrated that clear sense distinctions improve annotator productivity and accuracy. System performance typically lags around 10% behind ITA rates. ITA scores of at least 90% for a majority of our sense-groupings result in the expected corresponding improvement in system performance. Training on this new data, Chen et al., (2006) report 86.7% accuracy for verbs using a smoothed maximum entropy model and rich linguistic features. (Also Semeval07[1]) They also report state-of-the-art performance on fine-grained senses, but the results are more than 16% lower. We begin by describing the overall process.

3 The Grouping and Annotation Process

The process for building our database with the appropriate level of verb sense distinctions

[1] Task 17, http://nlp.cs.swarthmore.edu/semeval/.

Proceedings of the Linguistic Annotation Workshop, pages 49–52,
Prague, June 2007.

involves two steps: sense grouping and annotation (Figure 1). During our sense grouping process, linguists (henceforth, "groupers") cluster fine-grained sense distinctions listed in WordNet 2.1 into more coarse-grained groupings. These rough clusters of WordNet entries are based on speaker intuition. Other resources, including PropBank, VerbNet (based on Levin's verb classes (Levin, 1993)), and online dictionaries are consulted in further refining the distinctions between senses (Palmer, et. al., 2005, Kipper et al., 2006). To aid annotators in understanding the distinctions, sense groupings are ordered according to saliency and frequency. Detailed information, including syntactic frames and semantic features, is provided as commentary for the groupings. We also provide the annotators with simple example sentences from WordNet as well as syntactically complex and ambiguous attested usages from Google search results. These examples are intended to guide annotators faced with similar challenges in the data to be tagged.

Completed verb sense groupings are sent through sample-annotation and tagged by two annotators. Groupings that receive an ITA score of 90% or above are then used to annotate all instances of that verb in our corpora in actual-annotation. Groupings that receive less than 90% ITA scores are regrouped (Hovy et al., 2006). Revisions are made based on a second grouper's evaluation of the original grouping, as well as patterns of annotator disagreement. Verb groupings receiving ITA scores of 85% or above are sent through actual-annotation. Verbs scoring below 85% are regrouped by a third grouper, and in some cases, by the entire grouping team. It is sometimes impossible to get ITA scores over 85% for high frequency verbs that also have high entropy. These have to be carefully adjudicated to produce a gold standard. Revised verbs are then evaluated and either deemed ready for actual-annotation or are sent for a third and final round of sample-annotation. Verbs subject to the re-annotation process are tagged by different annotators. Data from actual-annotation is examined by an adjudicator who resolves remaining disagreements between annotators. The adjudicated data is then used as the gold standard for automatic annotation. The final versions of the sense groupings are mapped to VerbNet and FrameNet and linked to the Omega Ontology (Philpot et al., 2005).

Verbs are selected based on frequency of appearance in the WSJ corpus. As the most frequent verbs are also the most polysemous, the number of sense distinctions per verb as well as the number of instances to be tagged decreases as the project continues. The 740 most frequent verbs in the WSJ corpus were grouped in order of frequency. They have an average polysemy of 7 senses in WordNet; our sense groups have reduced the polysemy to 3.75 senses. Of these, 307 verb groupings have undergone regrouping to some extent. A total of 670 verbs have completed actual-annotation and adjudication. The next 660 verbs have been divided into rough semantic domains based on VerbNet classes, and grouping will proceed according to these semantic domains rather than by verb frequency. As groupers create sense groupings for new verbs, old verb sense groupings in the same semantic domain are consulted. This organization allows for more consistent grouping methodologies, as well as more efficiency in integrating our sense groupings into the Ontology.

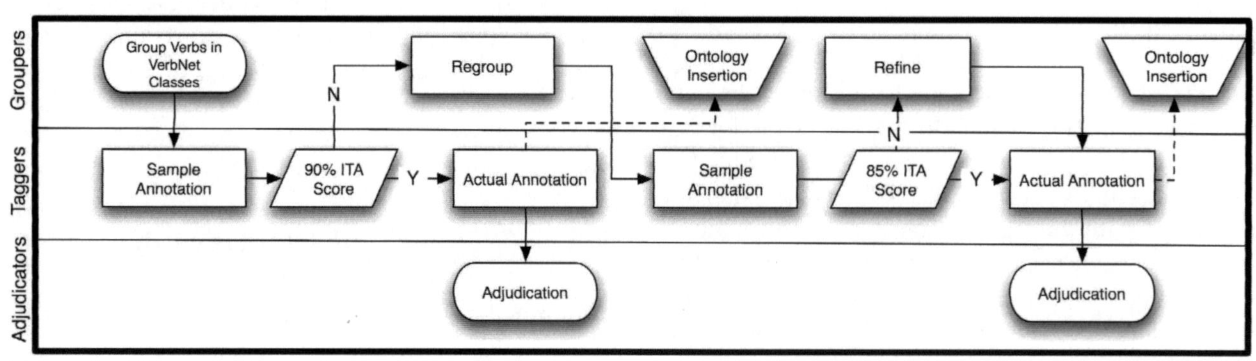

Figure 1: The grouping and annotation process.

4 Grouping Methodology

Various criteria are considered when disambiguating senses and creating sense groupings for the verbs, including frequent lexical usages and collocations, syntactic features and alternations, and semantic features, similarly to Senseval2 (Palmer, et. al. 2006). Because these criteria do not apply uniformly to every verb, groupers take various approaches when creating sense groupings. Groupers recognize that there are many alternate ways to cluster senses at this level of granularity; each grouping represents only one possible clustering as a middle ground between PropBank and WordNet senses for each verb. Our highest priority is to then create clear distinctions among sense groupings that will be easily understood by the annotators and consequently result in high ITA scores. Initial clustering is based on groupers' intuitions of the most salient categories. Many verb groupings, such as that for the verb *kill*, provide little detailed syntactic or semantic analysis and yet have received high ITA scores. The success of these intuitive sense groupings is not due to lack of polysemy; *kill* has 15 WordNet senses and 2 multi-word expressions clustered into 9 sense groupings, yet it received 94% ITA in first round sample-annotation.

While annotators have little trouble tagging text with verb senses that fall neatly into intuitive categories, many verbs have fine-grained WordNet senses that fall on a continuum between two distinct lexical usages. In such cases, syntactic and semantic aspects of the verb and its arguments help groupers cluster senses in such a way that annotators can make consistent decisions in tagging the text.

Syntactic criteria: Annotators have found syntactic frames, such as those defining VerbNet classes, to be useful in understanding boundaries between sense groupings. For example, *split* was originally grouped with consideration for the units resulting from a *splitting* event (i.e. whether a whole unit had been split into incomplete portions of the whole, or into smaller, but complete, individual units.) This grouping proved difficult for annotators to distinguish, with an ITA of 42%. Using the causative/inchoative alternation for verbs in the "break-45.1" class to regroup resulted in higher consistency among annotators, increasing the ITA score to 95%.

Semantic criteria: When senses of a verb have similar syntactic frames, and usages fall along a continuum between these senses, semantic features of the arguments, or less often, of the verb itself, can clarify these senses and help groupers draw clear distinctions between them. Argument features that are considered when creating sense groupings include [+/-attribute], [+/-patient], and [+/-locative]. It is most common for groupers to mark these features on nominal arguments, but a prepositional phrase may also be described in semantic terms. Semantic features of the verb that are considered include aspectual features, as illustrated by the use of [+/-punctual] in sense groupings for *make* (Figure 2). However, it may be argued that this feature is unnecessary for annotators to be able to distinguish between the sense groupings, as the prepositional phrase in sense 9 is a more salient feature for annotators.

Other features of the verb that were used earlier in the project include concrete/abstract, continuative, stative, and others. However, these features proved less useful than those

Sense group	Description and Commentary	WordNet 2.1 senses	Examples
8	Attain or reach something desired NP1[+agent] MAKE[+punctual] NP2[desired goal, destination, state] This sense implies the goal has been met. Includes: MAKE IT	make 13, 22, 38	- He made the basketball team. - We barely made the plane. - I made the opening act in plenty of time. - Can you believe it? We made it!
9	Move toward or away from a location NP1[+agent] MAKE[-punctual] (pronoun+way) PP/INFP	make 30, 37 make off 1 make way 1	- As the enemy approached our town, we made for the hills. - He made his way carefully across the icy parking lot. - They made off with the jewels.

Figure 2: Sense groupings 8 and 9 for "make." Senses are distinguished in part by aspectual features marked on the verb.

described above, and annotators not familiar with linguistic theory found them to be confusing. Therefore, they are now rarely used to label sense groupings. Such concepts, when used, are more likely to be described in prose commentary for the sake of the annotators.

Certain compositional features of verbs have also proven to be confusing for annotators. In several cases, attempts to distinguish sense groupings based on *manner* and *path* have resulted in increased annotator disagreement. In the first attempt at grouping *roll*, syntactic and semantic information, as well as prose commentary, was presented to help annotators distinguish the manner and path sense groupings. Despite this, the admissibility of certain prepositions in both senses ("The baby rolled over," vs "She rolled over to the wall,") may have blurred the distinction. In two rounds of sample-annotation, the greatest number of disagreements occurred with respect to these two senses for *roll*, which were then merged in the final version of the sense groupings.

5 Conclusion

Building on results in grouping fine-grained WordNet senses into more coarse-grained senses that led to improved inter-annotator agreement (ITA) and system performance (Palmer et al., 2004; Palmer et al., 2007), we have developed a process for rapid sense inventory creation and annotation of verbs that also provides critical links between the grouped word senses and the ontology (Philpot et al., 2005). This process is based on recognizing that sense distinctions can be represented by linguists in a hierarchical structure, that is rooted in very coarse-grained distinctions which become increasingly fine-grained until reaching WordNet (or similar) senses at the leaves. Sets of senses under specific nodes of the tree are grouped together into single entries, along with the syntactic and semantic criteria for their groupings, to be presented to the annotators. Criteria are applied on a case-by-case basis, considering syntactic and semantic features as consistently as possible when grouping verbs in similar semantic domains as defined by VerbNet. By using this approach when creating sense groupings, we are able to provide annotators with clear and reliable descriptions of senses, resulting in improved accuracy and performance.

References

Chen, J., A. Schein, L. Ungar and M. Palmer. 2006. An Empirical Study of the Behavior of Word Sense Disambiguation. *Proceedings of HLT-NAACL 2006.* New York, NY.

Fellbaum, C. (ed.) 1998. *WordNet: An On-line Lexical Database and Some of its Applications.* MIT Press, Cambridge, MA.

Kipper, K., A. Korhonen, N. Ryant, and M. Palmer. 2006. Extensive Classifications of English Verbs. *Proceedings of the 12th EURALEX International Congress.* Turin, Italy.

Levin, B. 1993. *English Verb Classes and Alternations.* The University of Chicago Press, Chicago, IL.

OntoNotes, 2006. Hovy, E.H., M. Marcus, M. Palmer, S. Pradhan, L. Ramshaw, and R. Weischedel. 2006. OntoNotes: The 90% Solution. Short paper. *Proceedings of HLT-NAACL 2006.* New York, NY.

Palmer, M., O. Babko-Malaya, and H.T. Dang. 2004. Different Sense Granularities for Different Applications. *Proceedings of the 2nd Workshop on Scalable Natural Language Understanding Systems (HLT-NAACL 2004).* Boston, MA.

Palmer, M., Dang, H.T., and Fellbaum, C., Making Fine-grained and Coarse-grained sense distinctions, both manually and automatically, *Journal of Natural Language Engineering* (to appear, 2007).

Palmer, M., Gildea, D., Kingsbury, P., The Proposition Bank: A Corpus Annotated with Semantic Roles, *Computational Linguistics Journal*, 31:1, 2005.

Philpot, A., E.H. Hovy, and P. Pantel. 2005. The Omega Ontology. *Proceedings of the ONTOLEX Workshop at the International Conference on Natural Language Processing (IJCNLP).* Jeju Island, Korea.

Semi-Automated Named Entity Annotation

Kuzman Ganchev and **Fernando Pereira**
Computer and Information Science,
University of Pennsylvania,
Philadelphia PA
{ kuzman and pereira } @cis.upenn.edu

Mark Mandel
Linguistic Data Consortium,
University of Pennsylvania, Philadelphia PA
mamandel@ldc.upenn.edu

Steven Carroll and **Peter White**
Division of Oncology, Children's Hospital of Philadelphia Philadelphia PA
{ carroll and white }@genome.chop.edu

Abstract

We investigate a way to partially automate corpus annotation for named entity recognition, by requiring only binary decisions from an annotator. Our approach is based on a linear sequence model trained using a k-best MIRA learning algorithm. We ask an annotator to decide whether each mention produced by a high recall tagger is a true mention or a false positive. We conclude that our approach can reduce the effort of extending a seed training corpus by up to 58%.

1 Introduction

Semi-automated text annotation has been the subject of several previous studies. Typically, a human annotator corrects the output of an automatic system.

The idea behind our approach is to start annotation manually and to partially automate the process in the later stages. We assume that some data has already been manually tagged and use it to train a tagger specifically for high recall. We then run this tagger on the rest of our corpus and ask an annotator to filter the list of suggested gene names.

The rest of this paper is organized as follows. Section 2 describes the model and learning algorithm. Section 3 relates our approach to previous work. Section 4 describes our experiments and Section 5 concludes the paper.

2 Methods

Throughout this work, we use a linear sequence model. This class of models includes popular tagging models for named entities such as conditional random fields, maximum entropy Markov models and max-margin Markov networks. Linear sequence models score possible tag sequences for a given input as the dot product between a learned weight vector and a feature vector derived from the input and proposed tas sequence. Linear sequence models differ principally on how the weight vector is learned. Our experiments use the MIRA algorithm (Crammer et al., 2006; McDonald et al., 2005) to learn the weight vector.

2.1 Notation

In what follows, x denotes the generic input sentence, $Y(x)$ the set of possible labelings of x, and $Y^+(x)$ the set of correct labelings of x. There is also a distinguished "gold" labeling $y(x) \in Y^+(x)$. For each pair of a sentence x and labeling $y \in Y(x)$, we compute a vector-valued feature representation $f(x, y)$. Given a weight vector w, the score $w \cdot f(x, y)$ ranks possible labelings of x, and we denote by $Y_{k,w}(x)$ the set of k top scoring labelings for x.

We use the standard `B,I,O` encoding for named entities (Ramshaw and Marcus, 1995). Thus $Y(x)$ for x of length n is the set of all sequences of length n matching the regular expression $(\texttt{O}|(\texttt{BI}*))*$. In a linear sequence model, for suitable feature functions f, $Y_{k,w}(x)$ can be computed efficiently with Viterbi decoding.

2.2 k-best MIRA and Loss Functions

The learning portion of our method finds a weight vector w that scores the correct labelings of the test data higher than incorrect labelings. We used a k-

Proceedings of the Linguistic Annotation Workshop, pages 53–56,
Prague, June 2007.

best version of the MIRA algorithm (Crammer et al., 2006; McDonald et al., 2005). This is an online learning algorithm that starts with a zero weight vector and for each training sentence makes the smallest possible update that would score the correct label higher than the old top k labels. That is, for each training sentence x we update the weight vector w according to the rule:

$$\begin{aligned} & w_{\text{new}} = \arg\min_w \|w - w_{\text{old}}\| \\ & \text{s. t. } w \cdot f(x, y(x)) - w \cdot f(x, y) \geq L(Y^+(x), y) \\ & \quad \forall y \in Y_{k, w_{\text{old}}}(x) \end{aligned}$$

where $L(Y^+(x), y)$ is the *loss*, which measures the errors in labeling y relative to the set of correct labelings $Y^+(x)$.

An advantage of the MIRA algorithm (over many other learning algorithms such as conditional random fields) is that it allows the use of arbitrary loss functions. For our experiments, the loss of a labeling is a weighted combination of the number of false positive mentions and the number of false negative mentions in that labeling.

2.3 Semi-Automated Tagging

For our semi-automated annotation experiments, we imagine the following scenario: We have already annotated half of our training corpus and want to annotate the remaining half. The goal is to save annotator effort by using a semi-automated approach instead of annotating the rest entirely manually.

In particular we investigate the following method: train a high-recall named entity tagger on the annotated data and use that to tag the remaining corpus. Now ask a human annotator to filter the resulting mentions. The mentions rejected by the annotator are simply dropped from the annotation, leaving the remaining mentions.

3 Relation to Previous Work

This section relates our approach to previous work on semi-automated approaches. First we discuss how semi-automated annotation is different from active learning and then discuss some previous semi-automated annotation work.

3.1 Semi-Automated versus Active Learning

It is important not to confuse semi-automated annotation with active learning. While they both attempt to alleviate the burden of creating an annotated corpus, they do so in a completely orthogonal manner. Active learning tries to select which instances should be labeled in order to make the most impact on learning. Semi-automated annotation tries to make the annotation of each instance faster or easier. In particular, it is possible to combine active learning and semi-automated annotation by using an active learning method to select which sentences to label and then using a semi-automated labeling method.

3.2 Previous work on semi-automated annotation

The most common approach to semi-automatic annotation is to automatically tag an instance and then ask an annotator to correct the results. We restrict our discussion to this paradigm due to space constraints. Marcus et al. (1994), Chiou et al. (2001) and Xue et al. (2002) apply this approach with some minor modifications to part of speech tagging and phrase structure parsing. The automatic system of Marcus et al. only produces partial parses that are then assembled by the annotators, while Chiou et al. modified their automatic parser specifically for use in annotation. Chou et al. (2006) use this tag and correct approach to create a corpus of predicate argument structures in the biomedical domain. Culota et al. (2006) use a refinement of the tag and correct approach to extract addressbook information from e-mail messages. They modify the system's best guess as the user makes corrections, resulting in less annotation actions.

4 Experiments

We now evaluate to what extent our semi-automated annotation framework can be useful, and how much effort it requires. For both questions we compare semi-automatic to fully manual annotation. In our first set of experiments, we measured the usefulness of semi-automatically annotated corpora for training a gene mention tagger. In the second set of experiments, we measured the annotation effort for gene mentions with the standard fully manual method and with the semi-automated methods.

4.1 Measuring Effectiveness

The experiments in this section use the training data from the the Biocreative II competition (Tanabe et

Sentence	Expression of SREBP-1a stimulated StAR promoter activity in the context of COS-1 cells
gold label	Expression of SREBP-1a stimulated StAR promoter activity in ...
alternative	Expression of SREBP-1a stimulated StAR promoter activity in ...
alternative	Expression of SREBP-1a stimulated StAR promoter activity in ...

Figure 1: An example sentence and its annotation in Biocreative II. The evaluation metric would give full credit for guessing one of the alternative labels rather than the "gold" label.

al., 2005). The data is supplied as a set of sentences chosen randomly from MEDLINE and annotated for gene mentions.

Each sentence in the corpus is provided as a list of "gold" gene mentions as well as a set of alternatives for each mention. The alternatives are generated by the annotators and count as true positives. Figure 1 shows an example sentence with its gold and alternative mentions. The evaluation metric for these experiments is F-score augmented with the possibility of alternatives (Yeh et al., 2005).

We used 5992 sentences as the data that has already been annotated manually (set **Data-1**), and simulated different ways of annotating the remaining 5982 sentences (set **Data-2**). We compare the quality of annotation by testing taggers trained using these corpora on a 1493 sentence test set.

We trained a high-recall tagger (recall of 89.6%) on **Data-1**, and ran it on **Data-2**. Since we have labels available for **Data-2**, we simulated an annotator filtering these proposed mentions by accepting them only if they exactly match a "gold" or alternative mention. This gave us an F-score of 94.7% on **Data-2** and required 9981 binary decisions.

Figure 2 shows F_1 score as a function of the number of extra sentences annotated. Without any additional data, the F-measure of the tagger is 81.0%. The two curves correspond to annotation with and without alternatives. The horizontal line at 82.8% shows the level achieved by the semi-automatic method (when using all of **Data-2**).

From the figure, we can see that to get comparable performance to the semi-automatic approach, we need to fully manually annotate roughly a third as much data with alternatives, or about two thirds as much data without alternatives. The following section examines what this means in terms of annotator time by providing timing results for semi-automatic and fully-manual annotation without alternatives.

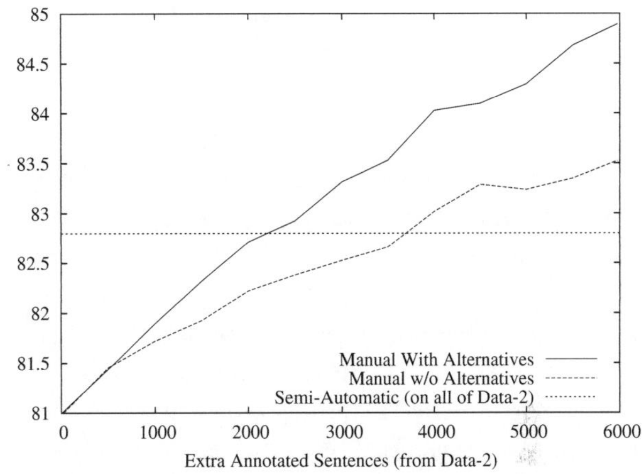

Figure 2: Effect of the number of annotated instances on F_1 score. In all cases the original 5992 instances were used; the curves show manual annotation while the level line is the semi-automatic method. The curves are averages over 3 trials.

4.2 Measuring Effort

The second set of experiments compares annotator effort between fully manual and semi-automatic annotation. Because we did not have access to an experienced annotator from the Biocreative project, and gene mention annotations vary subtly among annotation efforts, we evaluated annotator effort on on the PennBioIE named entity corpus.[1] Furthermore, we have not yet annotated enough data locally to perform both effectiveness and effort experiments on the local corpus alone. However, both corpora annotate gene mentions in MEDLINE abstracts, so we expect that the timing results will not be significantly different.

We asked an experienced annotator to tag 194 MEDLINE abstracts: 96 manually and 98 using the semi-automated method. Manual annotation was done using annotation software familiar to the annotator. Semi-automatic annotation was done with a

[1]Available from http://bioie.ldc.upenn.edu/

Web-based tool developed for the task. The new tool highlights potential gene mentions in the text and allows the annotator to filter them with a mouse click. The annotator had been involved in the creation of the local manually annotated corpus, and had a lot of experience annotating named entities. The abstracts for annotation were selected randomly so that they did not contain any abstracts tagged earlier. Therefore, we did not expect the annotator to have seen any of them before the experiment.

To generate potential gene mentions for the semi-automated annotation, we ran two taggers on the data: a high recall tagger trained on the local corpus and a high recall tagger trained on the Biocreative corpus. At decode time, we took the gene mentions from the top two predictions of each of these taggers whenever there were any gene mentions predicted. As a result, the annotator had to make more binary decisions per sentence than they would have for either training corpus alone. For the semi-automated annotation, the annotator had to examine 682 sentences and took on average 10 seconds per sentence. For the fully-manual annotation, they examined 667 sentences and took 40 seconds per sentence on average. We did not ask the annotator to tag alternatives because they did not have any experience with tagging alternatives and we do not have a tool that makes the annotation of alternatives easy. Consequently, effort totals for annotation with alternatives would have been skewed in our favor. The four-fold speedup should be compared to the lower curve in Figure 2.

5 Discussion and Further Work

We can use the effort results to estimate the relative effort of annotating without alternatives and of semi-automated annotation. To obtain the same improvement in F-score, we need to semi-automatically annotate roughly a factor of 1.67 more data than using the fully manual approach. Multiplying that by the 0.25 factor reduction in annotation time, we get that the time required for a comparable improvement in F-score is 0.42 times as long – a 58% reduction in annotator time.

We do not have any experiments on annotating alternatives, but the main difference between semi-automated and fully-manual annotation is that the former does not require the annotator to decide on boundaries. Consequently, we expect that annotation with alternatives will be considerably more expensive than without alternatives, since more boundaries have to be outlined.

In future work, it would be interesting to compare this approach to the traditional approach of manually correcting output of a system. Due to constraints on annotator time, it was not possible to do these experiments as part of the current work.

References

Fu-Dong Chiou, David Chiang, and Martha Palmer. 2001. Facilitating treebank annotation using a statistical parser. In *HLT '01*. ACL.

Wen-Chi Chou, Richard Tzong-Han Tsai, Ying-Shan Su, Wei Ku, Ting-Yi Sung, and Wen-Lian Hsu. 2006. A semi-automatic method for annotating a biomedical proposition bank. In *FLAC'06*. ACL.

Koby Crammer, Ofer Dekel, Joseph Keshet, Shai Shalev-Shwartz, and Yoram Singer. 2006. Online passive-aggressive algorithms. *JMLR*, 7.

Aron Culota, Trausti Kristjansson, Andrew McCallum, and Paul Viola. 2006. Corrective feedback and persistent learning for information extraction. *Artificial Intelligence*, 170:1101–1122.

Mitchell P. Marcus, Beatrice Santorini, and Mary Ann Marcinkiewicz. 1994. Building a large annotated corpus of english: The penn treebank. *Computational Linguistics*, 19(2):313–330.

Ryan McDonald, Koby Crammer, and Fernando Pereira. 2005. Online large-margin training of dependency parsers. In *ACL'05*. ACL.

Lance Ramshaw and Mitch Marcus. 1995. Text chunking using transformation-based learning. In David Yarovsky and Kenneth Church, editors, *Proceedings of the Third Workshop on Very Large Corpora*. ACL.

Lorraine Tanabe, Natalie Xie, Lynne H. Thom, Wayne Matten, and W. John Wilbur. 2005. GENETAG: a tagged corpus for gene/protein named entity recognition. *BMC Bioinformatics*, 6(Suppl. 1).

Nianwen Xue, Fu-Dong Chiou, and Martha Palmer. 2002. Building a large-scale annotated chinese corpus. In *Proceedings of the 19th international conference on Computational linguistics*. ACL.

Alexander Yeh, Alexander Morgan, Marc Colosimo, and Lynette Hirschman. 2005. BioCreAtIvE Task 1A: gene mention finding evaluation . *BMC Bioinformatics*, 6(Suppl. 1).

Querying multimodal annotation: A concordancer for GeM

Martin Thomas
Centre for Translation Studies
University of Leeds
UK, LS2 9JT
m.thomas@leeds.ac.uk

Abstract

This paper presents a multimodal corpus of comparable pack messages and the concordancer that has been built to query it. The design of the corpus and its annotation is introduced. This is followed by a description of the concordancer's interface, implementation and concordance display. Finally, some ideas for future work are outlined.

1 Introduction

This paper introduces a multimodal concordancer[1] that has been developed to investigate variation between messages on fast-moving consumer goods packaging from China, Taiwan and the UK. The need to develop such a concordancer arises from the fact that these *pack messages* are themselves multimodal. While they communicate through what Twyman (1985) calls the *visual channel*, messages are realized using a combination of three modes (*verbal*, *schematic*, *pictorial*). Moreover, the verbal components of visual messages are modulated and segmented through typography (Waller, 1987).

It is assumed that this multimodality will have complex implications for cross-linguistic variation within the genre of pack messages. The specific nature of these implications is not yet known, but variation in the construal of textual meaning and cohesion would seem to offer a good starting point for investigation. However, using purely linguistic annotation and a monomodal concordancer to analyze such material could reveal only part of the picture.

An existing annotation scheme, developed by the Genre and Multimodality (GeM) project[2], is well-suited to my needs. In addition to information about their verbal and visual realization, the scheme provides a mechanism for encoding the rhetorical relations between message components.

However, existing tools for multimodal analysis do not support simultaneous investigation of verbal, visual and rhetorical phenomena. While Baldry's (2004) multimodal concordancer supports multilayered analysis of video data, his approach does not support the segmentation of still visual layouts, let alone consideration of specific typographical realizations. From an altogether different perspective, the database developed as part of the Typographic Design for Children[3] project does allow access to such typographic information, but does not relate this directly to the linguistic realization of messages.

Their multimodal realization makes pack messages a rich testing ground for the new concordancer and Chinese and English offer great potential for looking at multimodal cross-linguistic variation. Typographic resources are constrained by the writing system of a given language: Chinese offers variety in reading directions and a consistent footprint for each character; English offers a range of case distinctions and a predictable reading direction.

2 Corpus design

I take each pack as a text: through the messages by which it is realized, it 'functions as a unity with respect to its environment' (Halliday and Hasan,

[1] http://corpus.leeds.ac.uk/~martin/

[2] http://www.purl.org/net/gem/

[3] http://www.kidstype.org/

Proceedings of the Linguistic Annotation Workshop, pages 57–60,
Prague, June 2007. ©2007 Association for Computational Linguistics

1976). In the corpus, each text constitutes a record. Each record consists of a set of files. These include the transcribed and annotated pack messages, and photographs of each pack face. In the future, pack metadata will be added to describe the product category to which the pack belongs, the product name, brand owner, variety and so on. I will also record the location and date of purchase of each sample. This will support query constraints at the level of the record (e.g. packs of a certain size) and will facilitate comparisons across time as well as across *locales*, or markets.

Packs are represented in the corpus in an unopened state. As far as possible, every message on each face of the pack which is visible in this state is recorded. There are good reasons for this. Sinclair (1991) makes the point that the differences across specific parts of a text may constitute regularity within a genre. In the context of investigation into cross-linguistic variation within a single genre, this observation seems particularly apt.

The selection of packs for inclusion in the corpus will be made in cooperation with an industrial partner. Packs will be selected from product categories in which the partner is active, or seeks to participate, in all three locales. A combination of popular local brands as well as locally established global brands will be selected. Thus the packs will be comparable commercially as well as in terms of the communicative functions that they perform.

3 Corpus annotation

The GeM scheme is described comprehensively by Henschel (2003). It implements stand-off annotation in four XML layers. The *base* layer segments the document. The resulting *base units* are cross-referenced by layers which describe *layout*, *rhetorical structure* and *navigation*.

Within the layout layer, there are three main sections: layout *segmentation* (each *layout unit* contains one or more base units), *realization* information and a description of the *layout structure* of the document. These components allow a comprehensive picture of the typographic realization of the messages to be built, from details such as font family and colour to information about the composition of each pack and the location, spacing and framing of *chunks* of layout units.

Rhetorical relations between annotated units are expressed in terms of Rhetorical Structure Theory (Mann and Thompson, 1987). In the GeM implementation, RST has been extended to accommodate the graphical elements found in multimodal texts. RST annotation provides a way to identify patterns in the construction of messages and to make comparisons across the corpus. It might be that more RST relations of a specific type, e.g. *elaboration*, are found in messages from a particular locale. Such observations might support or contest claims, such as that packs from developing markets conventionally carry more information about how to use the product. In combination with the layout layer it will also be possible to look for patterns in the choice of semiotic mode used to realize messages involving specific types of relation, such as *evidence*.

In sum, the aim of the annotation is not to support low-level lexicogrammatical analysis, but rather to facilitate the uncovering of patterns in the linguistic and typographical realization of pack messages and to relate these to semantic values expressed in terms of RST relations. Such patterns may reflect local design conventions and language-dependent strategies for ensuring textual cohesion.

So far annotation has begun with several UK and Taiwan packs. All annotation has been performed manually and has proved costly in terms of time. In future it is hoped that at least some annotations may be generated through the conversion of digital copies of designs obtained directly from brand owners.

The pilot annotations have identified a number of ways in which the GeM scheme will need to be extended to accommodate the genre of pack messages and important aspects of Chinese typography: the lists of colours and font families enumerated in the DTD are not sufficiently extensive or delicate and there is no mechanism in the layout annotation layer to record the orientation and reading direction of text.

4 The prototype concordancer

4.1 Design aims and system overview

The concordancer is an established tool for linguistic analysis. Concordance lines, which show instances of a key word in their immediate contexts,

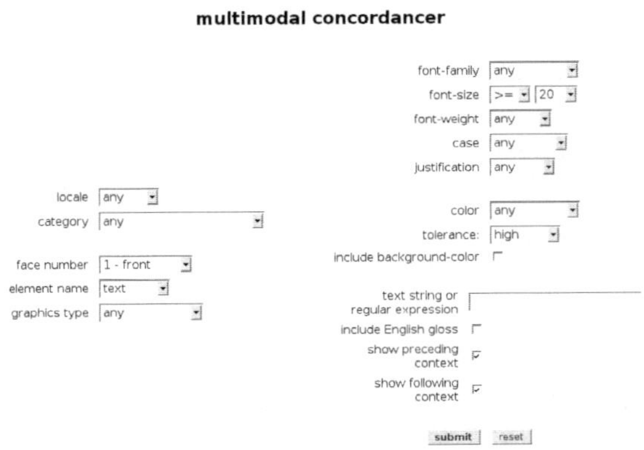

Figure 1: Multimodal concordancer interface

have proved useful in uncovering patterns of usage and variation that may not be apparent either from reading individual texts or from consulting reference resources, such as dictionaries and grammars.

My aim was to develop a similar tool to support multimodal analysis. Such a tool should be able to combine questions relating to the verbal components of messages with those relating to the typographic resources through which they are realized. It should do this in such a way that queries can easily be built and modified. To this end, a user interface is needed. Finally, the concordancer should be usable without the need for local installation of specialist client software.

In order to meet these requirements, I adopted a web-based client-server model. The user interface is shown in Figure 1. The concordancer is implemented in Perl as a CGI script. XPath expressions are used to identify matches from among the XML-annotated packs and to handle cross-references across annotation layers.

Using the concordancer interface to build a query is a process of moving from the general to the specific. By default, all constraints are relaxed: submitting a query with these selections will return every annotated message in the corpus. More usefully, selections can be made to constrain the set of records searched and the linguistic, typographic, and pictorial realization properties of messages to match.

4.2 Search criteria

The search criteria are grouped into high- and low-level selections. I will introduce the high-level selections first.

Locale and category selections control the set of records to be processed.

Given the notion of generic regularity in the differences between different parts of texts, it seemed sensible to allow queries to be constrained by pack face. Looking at the front of a shampoo bottle might be seen as akin to looking at the abstract of an academic paper. This is a step towards implementing more specific constraints about the on-pack position of messages. The pack face constraint, as with most of the remaining selections, is implemented in an XPath expression. The remaining high-level selections constrain the type of encoded element to include in the search.

The first group of low-level selections relate to specific font properties.

The colours used to realize messages are described in the corpus using hexadecimal RGB triplets. While this affords precision in annotation, it also means that some calculation is required to support searching. The current approach is to take any colour selected by the user from the menu and calculate the distance between this and the RGB value for each candidate match. If this distance falls within the tolerance specified by the user, the colour is considered to match. Thus a search for *green* may match RGB values representing various hues.

Finally, all matching layout units are cross-referenced with the base units that they realize. If the user specified a pattern to match (a string or regular expression), this is tested against the string value of the base unit.

4.3 Concordance display

The final options on the interface control the display of the resulting concordance. In the pilot annotations, an English gloss for each Chinese pack message is recorded as an XML comment. These glosses may be reproduced in the concordance. The other display options control whether to display the base unit preceding and/or following the match.

Figure 2 shows the results of a query generated from the selections shown in Figure 1. This is a search for verbal messages on the front of packs which are realized in a large font. Unsurprisingly, in each case, this returns the product name which is conventionally salient.

Details about the search query are given above the

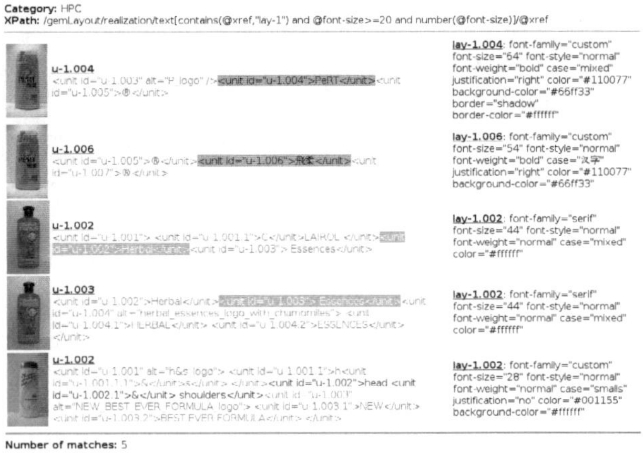

Figure 2: Multimodal concordance example

concordance. Depending on the specific query, this may include selections for locale and product category, the XPath expression which identifies candidate layout realization units, the colour selection and the search string or regular expression.

Information relating to each match is then displayed. As in a traditional concordancer, matches are presented together with the context in which they are found. Optionally, this context includes the preceding and following base units. Moreover, the notion of context is extended to include the visual environment in which each match is found. The colour used on-pack to realize the matching message is reused in the presentation of the match. A thumbnail image of the pack face on which the match is found is also presented, as is information about the typographic realization of the match, taken from the layout annotation. Links are provided to high resolution photographs and to each annotation layer for the pack from which the match is retrieved.

The display of the thumbnail is a step towards a more specific indication of the position of each match on the pack. In the future, I hope to use information from the layout annotation to generate a visual representation of the layout chunk in which each match is found.

The number of matches found is given below the concordance.

5 Conclusions and future work

The prototype concordancer is rather slow: it takes just under a minute to process and print every unit in the pilot corpus and the time taken will increase as more packs are added. But it works. It has also been tested with files taken from the original GeM corpus. Once they have been renamed, following the conventions used by the concordancer, the legacy files integrate seamlessly into the new corpus.

As noted above, there is scope for further development in a number of areas. The pilot corpus needs to be populated with more packs. The GeM annotation scheme requires modification in certain details. It might also be useful to add an annotation layer to record translations of the string values of base units rather than using XML comments for this.

As for the concordancer, support for queries based on the rhetorical relations between message components is the next major step. Other planned functionality includes the generation of typographically realized layout chunks which contain query matches and the calculation of collocation statistics which may be compared across sets of records.

Finally, more work is needed to see whether the concordancer is useful for the kind of analytical work it has been developed to support.

References

Anthony P. Baldry. 2004. Phase and transition, type and instance: patterns in media texts seen through a multimodal concordancer. In Kay O'Halloran, editor, *Multimodal discourse analysis: Systemic-functional perspectives*. Continuum, London.

M.A.K. Halliday and Ruqaiya Hasan. 1976. *Cohesion in English*. Longman, London.

Renate Henschel, 2003. *GeM Annotation Manual Version 2*. GeM Project.

William Mann and Sandra Annear Thompson. 1987. Rhetorical structure theory: A theory of text organization. Technical report, Information Sciences Institute, Los Angeles.

John Sinclair. 1991. *Corpus, concordance, collocation*. Oxford University Press, Oxford.

Michael Twyman. 1985. Using pictorial language: A discussion of the dimensions of the problem. In Thomas Walker and Robert Duffy, editors, *Designing Usable Texts*, chapter 11. Academic Press, Orlando, Florida.

Robert Waller. 1987. *The Typographic Contribution to Language*. Ph.D. thesis, University of Reading.

Annotating Chinese Collocations with Multi Information

Ruifeng Xu[1], **Qin Lu**[1], **Kam-Fai Wong**[2], **Wenjie Li**[1]

[1] Department of Computing,
The Hong Kong Polytechnic University,
Kowloon, Hong Kong

[2] Department of Systems Engineering and Engineering Management
The Chinese University of Hong Kong,
N.T., Hong Kong

{csrfxu,csluqin,cswjli}@comp.polyu.edu.hk kfwong@se.cuhk.edu.hk

Abstract

This paper presents the design and construction of an annotated Chinese collocation bank as the resource to support systematic research on Chinese collocations. With the help of computational tools, the *bi*-gram and *n*-gram collocations corresponding to 3,643 headwords are manually identified. Furthermore, annotations for *bi*-gram collocations include dependency relation, chunking relation and classification of collocation types. Currently, the collocation bank annotated 23,581 *bi*-gram collocations and 2,752 *n*-gram collocations extracted from a 5-million-word corpus. Through statistical analysis on the collocation bank, some characteristics of Chinese *bi*-gram collocations are examined which is essential to collocation research, especially for Chinese.

1 Introduction

Collocation is a lexical phenomenon in which two or more words are habitually combined and commonly used in a language to express certain semantic meaning. For example, in Chinese, people will say *历史-包袱* (*historical baggage*) rather than *历史 -行李* (*historical luggage*) even though *包袱* (*baggage*) and *行李*(*luggage*) are synonymous. However, no one can argue why *历史* must collocate with *包袱*. Briefly speaking, collocations are frequently used word combinations. The collocated words always have syntactic or semantic relations but they cannot be generated directly by syntactic or semantic rules. Collocation can bring out different meanings a word can carry and it plays an indispensable role in expressing the most appropriate meaning in a given context. Consequently, collocation knowledge is widely employed in natural language processing tasks such as word sense disambiguation, machine translation, information retrieval and natural language generation (Manning et al. 1999).

Although the importance of collocation is well known, it is difficult to compile a complete collocation dictionary. There are some existing corpus linguistic researches on automatic extraction of collocations from electronic text (Smadja 1993; Lin 1998; Xu and Lu 2006). These techniques are mainly based on statistical techniques and syntactic analysis. However, the performances of automatic collocation extraction systems are not satisfactory (Pecina 2005). A problem is that collocations are word combinations that co-occur within a short context, but not all such co-occurrences are true collocations. Further examinations is needed to filter out pseudo-collocations once co-occurred word pairs are identified. A collocation bank with true collocations annotated is naturally an indispensable resource for collocation research. (Kosho et al. 2000) presented their works of collocation annotation on Japanese text. Also, the Turkish treebank, (Bedin 2003) included collocation annotation as one step in its annotation. These two collocation banks provided collocation identification and co-occurrence verification information. (Tutin 2005) used shallow analysis based on finite state transducers and lexicon-grammar to identify and annotate collocations in a French corpus. This collocation bank further provided the lexical functions of the collocations. However to this day, there is no reported Chinese collocation bank available.

Proceedings of the Linguistic Annotation Workshop, pages 61–68,
Prague, June 2007. ©2007 Association for Computational Linguistics

In this paper, we present the design and construction of a Chinese collocation bank (acronymed *CCB*). This is the first attempt to build a large-scale Chinese collocation bank as a Chinese NLP resource with multiple linguistic information for each collocation including: (1) annotating the collocated words for each given headword; (2) distinguishing *n*-gram and *bi*-gram collocations for the headword; (3) for *bi*-gram collocations, *CCB* provides their syntactic dependencies, chunking relation and classification of collocation types which is proposed by (Xu and Lu 2006). In addition, we introduce the quality assurance mechanism used for *CCB*. *CCB* currently contains for 3,643 common headwords taken from "*The Dictionary of Modern Chinese Collocations*" (Mei 1999) with 23,581 unique *bi*-gram collocations and 2,752 unique *n*-gram collocations extracted from a five-million-word segmented and chunked Chinese corpus (Xu and Lu, 2005).

The rest of this paper is organized as follows. Section 2 presents some basic concepts. Section 3 describes the annotation guideline. Section 4 describes the practical issues in the annotation process including corpus preparation, headword preparation, annotation flow, and the quality assurance mechanism. Section 5 gives current status of *CCB* and characteristics analysis of the annotated collocations. Section 6 concludes this paper.

2 Basic Concepts

Although collocations are habitual expressions in natural language use and they can be easily understood by people, a precise definition of collocation is still far-reaching (Manning et al. 1999). In this study, we define a *collocation* as *a recurrent and conventional expression of two or more content words that holds syntactic and semantic relation*. Content words in Chinese include noun, verb, adjective, adverb, determiner, directional word, and gerund. Collocations with only two words are called *bi*-gram collocations and others are called *n*-gram collocations.

From a linguistic view point, collocations have a number of characteristics. Firstly, collocations are *recurrent* as they are of habitual use. Collocations occur frequently in similar contexts and they appear in certain fixed patterns. However, they cannot be described by the same set of syntactic or semantic rules. Secondly, free word combinations which can be generated by linguistic rules are normally considered compositional. In contrast, collocations should be *limited compositional* (Manning et al. 1999) and they usually carry additional meanings when used as a collocation. Thirdly, collocations are also *limited substitutable* and *limited modifiable*. Limited substitutable here means that a word cannot be freely substituted by other words with similar linguistic functions in the same context such as synonyms. Also, many collocations cannot be modified freely by adding modifiers or through grammatical transformations. Lastly, collocations are *domain-dependent* (Smadja 1993) and language-dependent.

3 Annotation Guideline Design

The guideline firstly determines the annotation strategy.

(1) The annotation of *CCB* follows the headword-driven strategy. The annotation uses selected headwords as the starting point. In each circle, the collocations corresponding to one headword are annotated. Headword-driven strategy makes a more efficient annotation as it is helpful to estimate and compare the relevant collocations.

(2) *CCB* is manually annotated with the help of automatic estimation of computational features, i.e. semi-automatic software tools are used to generate parsing and chunking candidates and to estimate the classification features. These data are present to the annotators for determination. The use of assistive tools is helpful to produce accurate annotations with efficiency.

The guideline also specifies the information to be annotated and the labels used in the annotation.

For a given headword, *CCB* annotates both *bi*-gram collocations and *n*-gram collocations. Considering the fact that *n*-gram collocations consisting of continuous significant *bi*-grams as a whole and, the *n*-gram annotation is based on the identification and verification of *bi*-gram word combinations and is prior to the annotation of *bi*-gram collocations.

For *bi*-gram annotation, which is the major interest in collocation research, three kinds of information are annotated. The first one is the syntactic dependency of the headword and its co-word in a *bi*-gram collocation . A syntactic dependency normally consists of one word as the governor (or *head*), a dependency type and another word serves as dependent (or *modifier*) (Lin 1998).Totally, 10 types of dependencies are annotated in *CCB*. They are listed in Table 1 below.

	Dependency Description	Example
ADA	Adjective and its adverbial modifier	极其/d 惨痛/a *greatly painful*
ADV	Predicate and its adverbial modifier in which the predicate serves as head	沉重/ad 打击/v *heavily strike*
AN	Noun and its adjective modifier	合法/a 收入/n *lawful incoming*
CMP	Predicate and its complement in which the predicate serves as head	医治/v 无效/v *ineffectively treat*
NJX	Juxtaposition structure	公正/a 合理/a *fair and reasonable*
NN	Noun and its nominal modifier	人身/n 安全/n *personal safety*
SBV	Predicate and its subject	财产/n 转移/v *property transfer*
VO	Predicate and its object in which the predicate serves as head	转换/v 机制/n *change mechanism*
VV	Serial verb constructions which indicates that there are serial actions	跟踪/v 报导/v *trace and report*
OT	Others	

Table 1. The dependency categories

The second one is the syntactic chunking information (a chunk is defined as a minimum non-nesting or non-overlapping phrase) (Xu and Lu, 2005). Chunking information identifies all the words for a collocation within the context of an enclosed chunk. Thus, it is a way to identify its proper context at the most immediate syntactic structure. 11 types of syntactic chunking categories given in (Xu and 2006) are used as listed in Table 2.

	Description	Examples
BNP	Base noun phrase	[市场/n 经济/n]NP *market economy*
BAP	Base adjective phrase	[公正/a 合理/a]BAP *fair and reasonable*
BVP	Base verb phrase	[顺利/a 启动/v]BVP *successfully start*
BDP	Base adverb phrase	[已/d 不再/d]BDP *no longer*
BQP	Base quantifier phrase	[数千/m 名/q]BQP 士兵/n *several thousand soldiers*
BTP	Base time phrase	[早上/t 8 时/t]BTP *8:00 in the morning*
BFP	Base position phrase	[蒙古/ns 东北部/f]BFP *Northeast of Mongolia*
BNT	Name of an organization	[烟台/ns 大学/n]BNT *Yantai University*
BNS	Name of a place	[江苏/ns 铜山/ns]BNS *Tongshan, Jiangsu Province*
BNZ	Other proper noun phrase	[诺贝尔/nr 奖/n]BNZ *The Nobel Prize*
BSV	S-V structure	[领土/n 完整/a]BSV *territorial integrity*

Table 2. The chunking categories

The third one is the classification of collocation types. Collocations cover a wide spectrum of habitual word combinations ranging from idioms to free word combinations. Some collocations are very rigid and some are more flexible. (Xu and Lu 2006) proposed a scheme to classify collocations into four types according to the internal association of collocations including compositionality, non-substitutability, non-modifiability, and statistical significance. They are,

Type 0: *Idiomatic Collocation*

Type 0 collocations are fully non-compositional as its meaning cannot be predicted from the meanings of its components such as *缘木求鱼* (*climbing a tree to catch a fish, which is a metaphor for a fruitless endeavour*). Some terminologies are also Type 0 collocations such as *蓝 牙*(*Blue-tooth*) which refers to a wireless communication protocol. Type 0 collocations must have fixed forms. Their components are non-substitutable and non-modifiable allowing no syntactic transformation and no internal lexical variation. This type of collocations has very strong internal associations and co-occurrence statistics is not important.

Type 1: *Fixed Collocation*

Type 1 collocations are very limited compositional with fixed forms which are non-substitutable and non-modifiable. However, this type can be compositional. None of the words in a Type 1 collocation can be substituted by any other words to retain the same meaning such as in *外交/n 豁免权 /n* (*diplomatic immunity*). Finally, Type 1 collocations normally have strong co-occurrence statistics to support them.

Type 2: *Strong Collocation*

Type 2 collocations are limitedly compositional. They allow very limited substitutability. In other words, their components can only be substituted by few synonyms and the newly generated word combinations have similar meaning, e.g., *缔结/v 同盟 /n* (*alliance formation*) and *缔结/v 联盟/n* (*alliance formation*). Furthermore, Type 2 collocations allow limited modifier insertion and the order of components must be maintained. Type2 collocations normally have strong statistical support.

Type 3: *Loose Collocation*

Type 3 collocations have loose restrictions. They are nearly compositional. Their components may be substituted by some of their synonyms and the newly generated word combinations usually have very similar meanings. Type 3 collocations are modifiable meaning that they allow modifier insertions. Type 3 collocations have weak internal associations and they must have statistically significant co-occurrence.

The classification represents the strength of internal associations of collocated words. The annotation of these three kinds of information is essential to all-rounded characteristic analysis of collocations.

4 Annotation of *CCB*

4.1 Data Preparation

CCB is based on the PolyU chunk bank (Xu and Lu, 2005) which contains chunking information on the People's Daily corpus with both segmentation and part-of-speech tags. The accuracies of word segmentation and POS tagging are claimed to be higher than 99.9% and 99.5%, respectively (Yu et al. 2001). The use of this popular and accurate raw resource helped to reduce the cost of annotation significantly, and ensured maximal sharing of our output.

The set of 3, 643 headwords are selected from "*The Dictionary of Modern Chinese Collocation*" (Mei 1999) among about 6,000 headwords in the dictionary. The selection was based both on the judgment by linguistic experts as well as the statistical information that they are commonly used.

4.2 Corpus Preprocessing

The *CCB* annotations are represented in XML. Since collocations are practical word combinations and word is the basic unit in collocation research, a preprocessing module is devised to transfer the chunked sentences in the PolyU chunk bank to word sequences with the appropriate labels to indicate the corresponding chunking information. This preprocessing module indexes the words and chunks in the sentences and encodes the chunking information of each word in two steps. Consider the following sample sentence extracted from the PolyU chunk bank:

确保/v[人民/n 群众/n]BNP 的/u[生命/n 财产/n 安全/an]BNP

(*ensure life and property safety of the people*)

The first step in preprocessing is to index each word and the chunk in the sentence by giving incremental word ids and chunk ids from left to right. That is,,

[W1] 确保/v [W2]人民/n [W3] 群众/n [W4] 的/u
[W5]生命/n [W6]财产/n [W7]安全/an [C1]BNP [C2]BNP

where, [*W1*] to [*W7*] are the words and [*C1*] to [*C2*] are chunks although chunking positions are not included in this step. One Chinese word may occur in a sentence for more than one times, the unique word ids are helpful to avoid ambiguities in the collocation annotation on these words.

The second step is to represent the chunking information of each word. Chunking boundary information is labeled by following initial/final representation scheme. Four labels, *O/B/I/E*, are used to mark the isolated words outsides any chunks, chunk-initial words, words in the middle of chunks, and chunk-final words, respectively. Finally, a label *H* is used to mark the identified head of chunks and *N* to mark the non-head words.

The above sample sentence is then transferred to a sequence of words with labels as shown below,

<labeled> [W1][O_O_N][O] 确保/v [W2][B_BNP_N][C1] 人民/n [W3][E_BNP_H][C1] 群众/n [W4][O_O_N][O] 的/u [W5][B_BNP_N][C2] 生命/n [W6][I_BNP_N][C2] 财产/n [W7][E_BNP_N][C2] 安全/an </labeled>

For each word, the first label is the word ID. The second one is a hybrid tag for describing its chunking status. The hybrid tags are ordinal with respect to the chunking status of boundary, syntactic category and head, For example, *B_BNP_N* indicates that current word is the beginning or a *BNP* and this word is not the head of this chunk. The third one is the chunk ID if applicable. For the word out of any chunks, a fixed chunk ID *O* is given.

4.3 Collocation Annotation

Collocation annotation is conducted on one headword at a time. For a given headword, an annotators examines its context to determine if its co-occurred word(s) forms a collocation with it and if so, also annotate the collocation's dependency, chunking and classification information. The annotation procedure, requires three passes. We use a headword *安全/an* (*safe*), as an illustrative example.

Pass 1. Concordance and dependency identification

In the first pass, the concordance of the given headword is performed. Sentences containing the headwords are obtained, e.g.

S1: *遵循/v [确保/v 安全/an]BVP 的/u 原则/n*
(follow the principles for ensuring the safety)
S2: *确保/v [人民/n 群众/n]BNP 的/u[生命/n 财产/n 安全/an]BNP*
(ensure life and property safety of people)
S3: *确保/v 长江/ns [安全/an 度汛/v]BVP*
(ensure the flood pass through Yangzi River safely)

With the help of an automatic dependency parser, the annotator determines all syntactically and semantically dependent words in the chunking context of the observing headword. The annotation output of ***S1*** is given below in which XML tags are used for the dependency annotation.

S1:*<sentence>遵循/v [确保/v 安全/an]BVP 的/u 原则/n*

<labeled> [W1][O_O_N][O]遵循/v [W2][B_BVP_H][C1] 确保/v [W3][E_BNP_N][C1]安全/an [W4][O_O_N][O]的 /u [W5][O_O_N][O]原则/n </labeled>
<dependency no="1" observing="安全/an" head="确保 /v" head_wordid="W2" head_chunk ="B_BVP_H" head_chunkid="C1" modifier="安全/an" modifier_wordid="W3" modifier _chunk="E_BVP_N" modifer_chunkid="C1" relation="VO" > </dependency>
</sentence>

Dependency of word combination is annotated with the tag <dependency> which includes the following attributes:

-<dependency> indicates an identified dependency

-no is the id of identified dependency within current sentence according to ordinal sequence

-observing indicates the current observing headword

-head indicates the head of the identified word dependency

-head_wordid is the *word id* of the head

-head_chunk is the hybrid tags for labeling the chunking information of the head

-head_chunkid is the *chunk id* of the head

-modifier indicates the modifier of the identified dependency

-modifier_wordid is the *word id* of the modifier

-modifier_chunk is the hybrid tags for labeling chunking information of the modifier

-modifier_chunkid is the *chunk id* of the modifier

-relation gives the syntactic dependency relations labeled according to the dependency labels listed in Table 1.

In ***S1*** and ***S2***, the word combination *确保/v 安全/an* has direct dependency, and in ***S3***, such a dependency does not exist as *确保/v* only determines *度汛/v* and *安全/an* depends on *度汛/v*. The quality of *CCB* highly depends on the accuracy of dependency annotation. This is very important for effective characteristics analysis of collocations and for the collocation extraction algorithms.

Pass 2. *N*-gram collocations annotation

It is relatively easy to identify *n*-gram collocations since an *n*-gram collocation is of habitual and recurrent use of a series of *bi*-grams. This means that *n*-gram collocations can be identified by finding consecutive occurrence of significant *bi*-grams in certain position. In the second pass, the annotators focus on the sentences where the headword has more than one dependency. The percentage of all appearances of each dependent word at each position around the headword is estimated with the help of a program (Xu and Lu, 2006). Finally, word dependencies frequently co-occurring in consecutive positions in a fixed order are extracted as *n*-gram collocations.

For the headword, an *n*-gram collocation *生命/n 财产/n 安全/an* is identified since the co-occurrence percentage of dependency *生命/-NN-安全/an* and dependency *财产/n-NN-安全/an* is 0.74 is greater than a empirical threshold suggest in (Xu and Lu, 2006). This *n*-gram is annotated in **S2** as follows:

<ncolloc observing="安全/an" w1="生命/n" w2="财产/n" w3="安全/an" start_wordid="5"> </ncolloc>

where,

-<ncolloc> indicates an *n*-gram collocation

-w1, w2,..wn give the components of the *n*-gram collocation according to the ordinal sequence.

-start_wordid indicates the word id of the first component of the *n*-gram collocation.

Since *n*-gram collocation is regarded as a whole, its internal dependencies are ignored in the output file of pass 2. That is, if the dependencies of several components are associated with an *n*-gram collocation in one sentence, the *n*-gram collocation is annotated and these dependencies are filtered out so as not to disturb the bi-gram dependencies.

Pass 3. *Bi*-gram collocations annotation

In this pass, all the word dependencies are examined to identify *bi*-gram collocations. Furthermore, if a dependent word combination is regarded as a collocation by the annotators, it will be further labeled based on the type determined. The identification is based on expert knowledge combined with the use of several computational features as discussed in (Xu and Lu, 2006).

An assistive tool is developed to estimate the computational features. We use the program to obtain feature data based on two sets of data. The first data set is the annotated dependencies in the 5-million-word corpus which is obtained through **Pass 1** and **Pass 2** annotations. Because the dependent word combinations are manually identified and annotated in the first pass, the statistical significance is helpful to identify whether the word combination is a collocation and to determine its type. However, data sparseness problem must be considered since 5-million-word is not large enough. Thus, another set of statistical data are collected from a 100-million segmented and tagged corpus (Xu and Lu, 2006). With this large corpus, data sparseness is no longer a serious problem. But, the collected statistics are quite noisy since they are directly retrieved from text without any verification. By analyzing the statistical features from both sets, the annotator can use his/her professional judgment to determine whether a *bi*-gram is a collocation and its collocation type.

In the example sentences, two collocations are identified. Firstly, *安全/an 度汛/v* is classified as a Type 1 collocation as they have only one peak co-occurrence, very low substitution ratio and their co-occurrence order nearly never altered. Secondly, *确保/v 安全/an* is identified as a collocation. They have frequent co-occurrences and they are always co-occurred in fixed order among the verified dependencies. However, their co-occurrences are distributed evenly and they have two peak co-occurrences. Therefore, *确保/v 安全/an* is classified as a Type 3 collocation. These *bi*-gram collocations are annotated as illustrated below,

<bcolloc observing="安全/an" col="度汛/v" head="度汛/v" type= "1" relation="ADV">
<dependency no="1" observing="安全/an" head="度汛/v" head_wordid="W4" head_chunk ="E_BVP_H" head_chunkid="C1" modifier=" 安 全 /an" modifier_wordid="W3" modifier _chunk="B_BVP_N" modifer_chunkid="C1" relation="ADV" ></dependency></bcolloc>

where,

-**<bcolloc>** indicates a *bi*-gram collocation.

-**col** is for the collocated word.

-**head** indicates the head of an identified collocation

-**type** is the classified collocation type.

-**relation** gives the syntactic dependency relations of this *bi*-gram collocation.

Note that the dependency annotations within the *bi*-gram collocations are reserved.

4.4 Quality Assurance

The annotators of *CCB* are three post-graduate students majoring in linguistics. In the first annotation stage, 20% headwords of the whole set was annotated in duplicates by all three of them. Their outputs were checked by a program. Annotated collocation including classified dependencies and types accepted by at least two annotators are reserved in the final data as the *Golden Standard* while the others are considered incorrect. The inconsistencies between different annotators were discussed to clarify any misunderstanding in order to come up with the most appropriate annotations. In the second annotation stage, 80% of the whole annotations were then divided into three parts and separately distributed to the annotators with 5% duplicate headwords were distributed blindly. The duplicate annotation data were used to estimate the annotation consistency between annotators.

5 Collocation Characteristic Analysis

5.1 Progress and Quality of *CCB*

Up to now, the first version of *CCB* is completed. We have obtained 23,581 unique *bi*-gram collocations and 2,752 unique *n*-gram collocations corresponding to the 3,643 observing headwords. Meanwhile, their occurrences in the corpus are annotated and verified. With the help of a computer program, the annotators manually classified *bi*-gram collocations into three types. The numbers of Type 0/1, Type 2 and Type 3 collocations are 152, 3,982 and 19,447, respectively.

For the 3,643 headwords in The Dictionary of Modern Chinese Collocations (Mei 1999) with 35,742 bi-gram collocations, 20,035 collocations appear in the corpus. We call this collection as Mei's Collocation Collection (MCC). There are 19,967 common entries in MCC and CCB, which means 99.7% collocations in MCC appear in CCB indicating a good linguistic consistency. Furthermore, 3,614 additional collocations are found in CCB which enriches the static collocation dictionary.

5.2 Dependencies Numbers Statistics of Collocations

Firstly, we study the statistics of how many types of dependencies a *bi*-gram collocation may have. The numbers of dependency types with respect to different collocation types are listed in Table 3.

Collocations	1 type	2 types	>2 types	Total
Type 0/1	152	0	0	152
Type 2	3970	12	0	3982
Type 3	17282	2130	35	19447
Total	21404	2142	35	23581

Table 3. Collocation classification versus number of dependency types

It is observed that about 90% *bi*-gram collocations have only one dependency type. This indicates that a collocation normally has only one fixed syntactic dependency. It is also observed that about 10% *bi*-gram collocations have more than one dependency type, especially Type 3 collocations. For example, two types of dependencies are identified in the *bi*-gram collocation *安全/an-国家/n*. They are *安全/an-AN-国家/n* (*a safe nation*) which indicates the dependency of a noun and its nominal modifier where *国家/n* serves as the head, and *国家/n-NN-安全/an* (*national security*) which indicates the dependency of a noun and its nominal modifier where 安全/an serves as the head. It is attributed to the fact that the use of Chinese words is flexible. A Chinese word may support different part-of-speech. A collocation with different dependencies results in different distribution trends and most of these collocations are classified as Type 3. On the other hand, Type 0/1 and Type 2 collocations seldom have more than one dependency type.

5.3 Syntactic Dependency Statistics of Collocations

The statistics of the 10 types of syntactic dependencies with respect to different types of *bi*-gram collocations are shown in Table 4. *No.* is the number of collocations with a given dependency type *D* and a given collocation type *T*. The percentage of *No.* among all collocations with the same collocation type *T* is labeled as *P_T*, and the percentage of *No.* among all of the collocations with the same dependency *D* is labeled as *P_D*.

	Type 0/1			Type 2			Type 3			Total	
	No.	*P_T*	*P_D*	*No.*	*P_T*	*P_D*	*No.*	*P_T*	*P_D*	*No.*	*P_T*
ADA	1	0.7	0.1	212	5.3	11.5	1637	7.6	88.5	1850	7.2
ADV	9	5.9	0.3	322	8.1	11.2	2555	11.8	88.5	2886	11.2
AN	20	13.2	0.4	871	21.8	15.4	4771	22.0	84.3	5662	22.0
CMP	12	7.9	2.2	144	3.6	26.9	379	1.8	70.8	535	2.1
NJX	8	5.3	3.2	42	1.1	16.9	198	0.9	79.8	248	1.0
NN	44	28.9	0.9	1036	25.9	21.6	3722	17.2	77.5	4802	18.6
SBV	4	2.6	0.2	285	7.1	11.1	2279	10.5	88.7	2568	10.0
VO	26	17.1	0.5	652	16.3	12.5	4545	21.0	87.0	5223	20.2
VV	3	2.0	0.2	227	5.7	13.4	1464	6.8	86.4	1694	6.6
OT	25	16.4	7.7	203	5.1	62.5	97	0.4	29.8	325	1.3
Total	152	100.0	0.6	3994	100.0	15.5	21647	100.0	83.9	25793	100.0

Table 4. The statistics of collocations with different collocation type and dependency

Corresponding to 23,581 *bi*-gram collocations, 25,793 types of dependencies are identified (some collocations have more than one types of dependency). In which, about 82% belongs to five major dependency types. They are *AN*, *VO*, *NN*, *ADV* and *SBV*. It is note-worthy that the percentage of *NN* collocation is much higher than that in English. This is because nouns are more often used in parallel to serve as one syntactic component in Chinese sentences than in English.

The percentages of Type 0/1, Type 2 and Type 3 collocations in *CCB* are 0.6%, 16.9% and 82.5%, respectively. However, the collocations with different types of dependencies have shown their own characteristics with respect to different collocation types. The collocations with *CMP*, *NJX* and *NN* dependencies on average have higher percentage to be classified into Type 0/1 and Type 2 collocations. This indicates that *CMP*, NJX and *NN* collocations in Chinese are always used in fixed patterns and these kinds of collocations are not freely modifiable and substitutable. In the contrary, many *ADV* and *AN* collocations are classified as Type 3. This is partially due to the special usage of auxiliary words in Chinese. Many *AN* Chinese collocations can be inserted by a meaningless auxiliary word 的/u and many *ADV* Chinese collocations can be inserted by an auxiliary word 地/u. This means that many *AN* and *ADV* collocations can be modified and thus, they always have two peak co-occurrences. Therefore, they are classified as Type 3 collocations. 7.7% and 62.5% of the collocations with dependency *OT* are classified as Type 0/1 and Type2 collocations, respectively. Such percentages are much higher than the average. This is attributed by the fact that some Type 0/1 and Type 2 collocations have strong semantic relations rather than syntactic relations and thus their dependencies are difficult to label.

5.4 Chunking Statistics of Collocations

The chunking characteristic for the collocations with different types and different dependencies are examined. In most cases, Type 0/1/2 collocations co-occur within one chunk or between neighboring chunks. Therefore, their chunking characteristics are not discussed in detail. The percentage of the occurrences of Type 3 collocations with different chunking distances are given in Table 5. If a collocation co-occurs within one chunk, the chunking distance is 0. If a collocation co-occurs between neighboring chunks, or between neighboring words, or between a word and a neighboring chunk, the chunking distance is 1, and so on.

	ADA	ADV	AN	CMP	NJX	NN	SBV	VO	VV	OT
0 chunk	56.8	53.1	65.7	48.5	70.2	62.4	46.5	41.1	47.2	86.4
1 chunk	38.2	43.7	28.5	37.2	15.4	27.9	41.2	35.7	41.1	13.5
2 chunks	5.0	3.2	3.7	14.2	14.4	9.7	11.0	17.6	9.6	0.1
>2chunks	0.0	0.0	2.1	0.1	0.0	0.0	1.3	5.6	2.1	0.0

Table 5. Chunking distances of Type 3 collocations

It is shown that the co-occurrence of collocations decreases with increased chunking distance. Yet, the behavior for decrease is different for collocations with different dependencies. Generally speaking, the *ADA*, *ADV*, *CMP*, *NJX*, *NN* and *OT* collocations seldom co-occur cross two words or two chunks. Furthermore, the occurrences of *AN*, *NJX* and *OT* collocations quickly drops when the chunking distance is greater than 0, i.e. these collocations tends to co-occur within the same chunk. In the contrary, the co-occurrences of *ADA*, *ADV*, *CMP*, *SBV* and *VV* collocations corresponding to chunking distance equals 0 and 1 decrease steadily. It means that these four kinds of collocations are more evenly distributed within the same chunk or between neighboring words or chunks. The occurrences of *VO* collocations corresponding to chunking distance from 0 to 3 with a much flatter reduction. This indicates that a verb may govern its object in a long range.

6 Conclusions

This paper describes the design and construction of a manually annotated Chinese collocation bank. Following a set of well-designed annotation guideline, the collocations corresponding to 3,643 headwords are identified from a chunked five-million word corpus. 2,752 unique *n*-gram collocations and 23,581 unique *bi*-gram collocations are annotated. Furthermore, each *bi*-gram collocation is annotated with its syntactic dependency information, classification information and chunking information. Based on *CCB*, characteristics of collocations with different types and different dependencies are examined. The obtained result is essential for improving research related to Chinese collocation. Also, *CCB* may be used as a standard answer set for evaluating the performance of different collocation extraction algorithms. In the future, collocations of all unvisited headwords will be annotated to produce a complete 5-million-word Chinese collocation bank.

Acknowledgement

This research is supported by The Hong Kong Polytechnic University (A-P203), CERG Grant (5087/01E) and Chinese University of Hong Kong under the Direct Grant Scheme project (2050330) and Strategic Grant Scheme project (4410001).

References

Bedin N. et al. 2003. The Annotation Process in the Turkish Treebank. In *Proc. 11th Conference of the EACL-4th Linguistically Interpreted Corpora Workshop- LINC.*

Kosho S. et al. 2000. Collocations as Word Co-occurrence Restriction Data - An Application to Japanese Word Processor. In *Proc. Second International Conference on Language Resources and Evaluation*

Lin D.K. 1998. Extracting collocations from text corpora. In *Proc. First Workshop on Computational Terminology*, Montreal

Manning, C.D., Schütze, H. 1999: *Foundations of Statistical Natural Language Processing*, MIT Press

Mei J.J. 1999. *Dictionary of Modern Chinese Collocations*, Hanyu Dictionary Press

Pecina P. 2005. An Extensive Empirical Study of Collocation Extraction Methods. In *Proc. 2005 ACL Student Research Workshop*. 13-18

Smadja. F. 1993. Retrieving collocations from text: Xtract, *Computational Linguistics*. 19. 1. 143-177

Tutin A. 2005. Annotating Lexical Functions in Corpora: Showing Collocations in Context. In *Proc. 2nd International Conference on the Meaning – Text Theory*

Xu R. F. and Lu Q. 2005. Improving Collocation Extraction by Using Syntactic Patterns, In *Proc. IEEE International Conference on Natural Language Processing and Knowledge Engineering*. 52-57

Xu, R.F. and Lu, Q. 2006. A Multi-stage Chinese Collocation Extraction System. *Lecture Notes in Computer Science, Vol. 3930*, Springer-Verlag. 740-749

Yu S.W. et al. 2001. *Guideline of People's Daily Corpus Annotation*, Technical Report, Peking University

Computing translation units and quantifying parallelism in parallel dependency treebanks

Matthias Buch-Kromann
ISV Computational Linguistics Group
Copenhagen Business School
mbk.isv@cbs.dk

Abstract

The linguistic quality of a parallel treebank depends crucially on the parallelism between the source and target language annotations. We propose a linguistic notion of translation units and a quantitative measure of parallelism for parallel dependency treebanks, and demonstrate how the proposed translation units and parallelism measure can be used to compute transfer rules, spot annotation errors, and compare different annotation schemes with respect to each other. The proposal is evaluated on the 100,000 word Copenhagen Danish-English Dependency Treebank.

1 Introduction

Parallel treebanks are increasingly seen as a valuable resource for many different tasks, including machine translation, word alignment, translation studies and contrastive linguistics (Čmejrek et al., 2004; Cyrus, 2006; Hansen-Schirra et al., 2006). However, the usefulness of a parallel treebank for these purposes is directly correlated with the degree of syntactic parallelism in the treebank. Some non-parallelism is inevitable because two languages always differ with respect to their syntactic structure. But non-parallelism can also be the result of differences in the linguistic analyses of the source text and target text, eg, with respect to whether noun phrases are headed by nouns or determiners, whether conjunctions are headed by the first conjunct or the coordinator, whether prepositions are analyzed as heads or adjuncts in prepositional phrases, etc.

In this paper, we focus on parallel dependency treebanks that consist of source texts and translations annotated with dependency analyses and word-alignments. These requirements are directly satisfied by the analytical layer of the Prague Czech-English Dependency Treebank (Čmejrek et al., 2004) and by the dependency layer of the Copenhagen Danish-English Dependency Treebank (Buch-Kromann et al., 2007). The requirements are also indirectly satisifed by parallel treebanks with a constituent layer and a word alignment, eg (Han et al., 2002; Cyrus, 2006; Hansen-Schirra et al., 2006; Samuelsson and Volk, 2006), since it is possible to transform constituent structures into dependency structures — a procedure used in the CoNLL shared tasks in 2006 and 2007 (Buchholz and Marsi, 2006). Finally, it is worth pointing out that the requirements are also met by any corpus equipped with two different dependency annotations since a text is always trivially word-aligned with itself. The methods proposed in the paper therefore apply to a wide range of parallel treebanks, as well as to comparing two monolingual treebank annotations with each other.

The paper is structured as follows. In section 2, we define our notions of word alignments and dependencies. In section 3, we define our notion of translation units and state an algorithm for computing the translation units in a parallel dependency treebank. Finally, in sections 4, 5 and 6, we demonstrate how translation units can be used to compute transfer rules, quantify parallelism, spot annotation errors, and compare monolingual and bilingual annotation schemes with respect to each other.

Proceedings of the Linguistic Annotation Workshop, pages 69–76,
Prague, June 2007.

Complement roles		Adjunct roles	
aobj	adjectival object	**appa**	parenthetical apposition
avobj	adverbial object	**appr**	restrictive apposition
conj	conjunct of coordinator	**coord**	coordination
dobj	direct object	**list**	unanalyzed sequence
expl	expletive subject	**mod**	modifier
iobj	indirect object	**modo**	dobj-oriented modifier
lobj	locative-directional obj.	**modp**	parenthetical modifier
nobj	nominal object	**modr**	restrictive modifier
numa	additive numeral	**mods**	subject-oriented mod.
numm	multiplicative numeral	**name**	additional proper name
part	verbal particle	**namef**	additional first name
pobj	prepositional object	**namel**	additional last name
possd	possessed in genitives	**pnct**	punctuation modifier
pred	subject/object predicate	**rel**	relative clause
qobj	quotation object	**title**	title of person
subj	subject	**xpl**	explification (colon)
vobj	verbal object		

Figure 1: The main dependency roles in the dependency framework Discontinuous Grammar.

2 Word alignments and dependencies

In our linguistic analyses, we will assume that a word alignment $W \leftrightarrow W'$ encodes a translational correspondence between the word clusters W and W' in the source text and target text, ie, the word alignment expresses the human intuition that the subset W of words in the source text corresponds roughly in meaning or function to the subset W' of words in the target text. The translations may contain additions or deletions, ie, W and W' may be empty.

We also assume that a dependency edge $g \xrightarrow{r} d$ encodes a complement or adjunct relation between a word g (the *governor*) and a complement or adjunct phrase headed by the word d (the *dependent*), where the edge label r specifies the complement or adjunct dependency role.[1] As an illustration of how complement and adjunct relations can be encoded by means of dependency roles, the most important dependency roles used in the dependency framework Discontinuous Grammar (Buch-Kromann, 2006) are shown in Figure 1. Finally, we will assume that the dependencies form a tree (or a forest). The tree may be non-projective, ie, it may contain crossing branches (technically, a dependency $g \xrightarrow{r} d$ is projective if and only if g is a transitive governor of all the words between g and d).

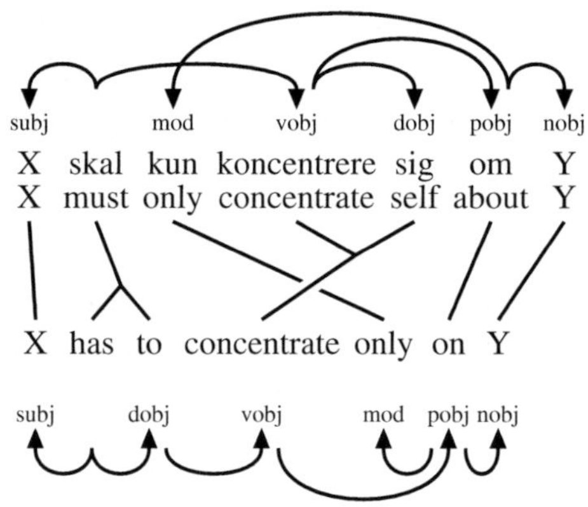

Figure 2: Parallel dependency treebank analysis with word alignment and two monolingual dependency analyses.

Figure 2 shows an example of this kind of analysis, based on the annotation conventions used in Discontinuous Grammar and the associated Copenhagen Danish-English Dependency Treebank (Buch-Kromann et al., 2007). In the example, word alignments are indicated by lines connecting Danish word clusters with English word clusters, and dependencies are indicated by means of arrows that point from the governor to the dependent, with the dependency role written at the arrow tip. For example, the Danish word cluster "koncentrere sig" ("concentrate self") has been aligned with the English word "concentrate", and the English phrase

[1] Following standard dependency theoretic assumptions, we will assume the following differences between complement and adjunct relations: (a) complements are lexically licensed by their governor, whereas adjuncts license their adjunct governor; (b) in the functor-argument structure, complements act as arguments of their governor, whereas adjuncts act as modifiers of their governor; (c) a governor can have several adjuncts with the same adjunct role, whereas no two complements of the same governor can have the same complement role.

headed by "on" is analyzed as a prepositional object of the verb "concentrate." In the Danish dependency analysis, the dependency between the adverbial "kun" ("only") and its prepositional governor "om" ("about") is non-projective because "om" does not dominate the words "koncentrere" ("concentrate") and "selv" ("self").

Dependency analyses differ from phrase-structure analyses in that phrases are a derived notion: in a dependency tree, each word has a derived phrase that consists of all the words that can be reached from the word by following the arrows. For example, the English word "concentrate" heads the phrase "concentrate only on Y," and the Danish word "om" heads the discontinuous phrase "kun ... om Y."

If a parallel dependency analysis is well-formed, in a sense to be made clear in the following section, each alignment edge corresponds to what we will call a translation unit. Intuitively, given an aligment edge $W \leftrightarrow W'$, we can create the corresponding translation unit by taking the source and target subtrees headed by the words in W and W', deleting all parallel adjuncts of $W \leftrightarrow W'$, and replacing all remaining parallel dependents of $W \leftrightarrow W'$ with variables $x_1, \ldots, x_n$ and $x'_1, \ldots, x'_n$. The resulting translation unit will be denoted by $T(x_1, \ldots, x_n) \leftrightarrow T'(x'_1, \ldots, x'_n)$, where T and T' denote the source and target dependency trees in the translation unit. For convenience, we will sometimes use vector notation and write $T(\mathbf{x}) \leftrightarrow T'(\mathbf{x}')$ instead of $T(x_1, \ldots, x_n) \leftrightarrow T'(x'_1, \ldots, x'_n)$. Dependencies are usually defined as relations between words, but by an abuse of terminology, we will say that a word d is a *dependent* of an alignment edge $W \leftrightarrow W'$ provided d is a dependent of some word in $W \cup W'$ and d is not itself contained in $W \cup W'$.

Figure 3 shows the six translation units that can be derived from the parallel dependency analysis in Figure 2, by means of the procedure outlined above. Each translation unit can be interpreted as a bidirectional translation rules: eg, the second translation unit in Figure 3 can be interpreted as a translation rule stating that a Danish dependency tree with terminals "x_1 skal x_2" can be translated into an English dependency tree with terminals "x'_1 has to x'_2" where the English phrases x'_1, x'_2 are translations of the Danish phrases x_1, x_2, and vice versa.

In the following section, we will go deeper into

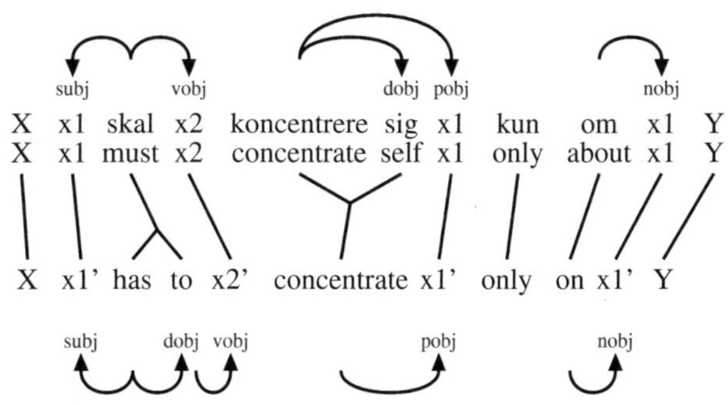

Figure 3: The six translation units derived from the parallel dependency analysis in Figure 2.

the definition and interpretation of these rules. In particular, unlike the essentially context-free translation rules used in frameworks such as (Quirk et al., 2005; Ding, 2006; Chiang, 2007), we will not assume that the words in the translation rules are ordered, and that the translation rules can only be used in a way that leads to projective dependency trees.

3 Translation units within a simple dependency-based translation model

In many parallel treebanks, word alignments and syntactic annotations are created independently of each other, and there is therefore no guarantee that the word or phrase alignments coincide with any meaningful notion of translation units. To rectify this problem, we need to define a notion of translation units that links the word alignments and the source and target dependency analysis in a meaningful way, and we need to specify a procedure for constructing a meaningful set of word alignments from the actual treebank annotation.

Statistical machine translation models often embody an explicit notion of translation units. However, many of these models are not applicable to parallel treebanks because they assume translation units where either the source text, the target text or both are represented as word sequences without any syntactic structure (Galley et al., 2004; Marcu et al., 2006; Koehn et al., 2003). Other SMT models assume translation units where the source and target language annotation is based on either context-free grammar (Yamada and Knight, 2001; Chiang, 2007) or context-free dependency grammar (Quirk et al., 2005; Ding, 2006). However, since nonprojectivity is not directly compatible with context-free grammar, and parallel dependency treebanks tend to encode non-projective dependencies directly, the context-free SMT models are not directly applicable to parallel dependency treebanks in general. But the context-free SMT models are an important inspiration for the simple dependency-based translation model and notion of translation units that we will present below.

In our translation model, we will for simplicity assume that both the source dependency analysis and the target dependency analysis are unordered trees, ie, dependency transfer and word ordering are modelled as two separate processes. In this paper, we only look at the dependency transfer and ignore the word ordering, as well as the probabilistic modelling of the rules for transfer and word ordering. There are three kinds of translation rules in the model:

A. Complement rules have the form $T(\mathbf{x}) \leftrightarrow T'(\mathbf{x}')$ where $T(\mathbf{x})$ is a source dependency tree with variables $\mathbf{x} = (x_1, \ldots, x_n)$, $T'(\mathbf{x}')$ is a target dependency tree with variables $\mathbf{x}' = (x'_1, \ldots, x'_n)$, the words in T are aligned to the words in T', and the variables x_k, x'_k denote parallel source and target subtrees. The rule states that a source tree $T(\mathbf{x})$ can be transferred into a target tree $T'(\mathbf{x}')$ by transferring the source subtrees in $\mathbf{x}$ into the target subtrees in $\mathbf{x}'$.

B. Adjunct rules have the form $(x \xleftarrow{a} T(\mathbf{y})) \leftrightarrow (x' \xleftarrow{a'} T'(\mathbf{y}'))$ where $T(\mathbf{y})$ is a source dependency tree, $T'(\mathbf{y}')$ is a target dependency tree, and x, x' are variables that denote parallel adjunct subtrees with adjunct roles a, a', respectively. The rule states that given a translation unit $T(\mathbf{y}) \leftrightarrow T(\mathbf{y}')$, an a-adjunct of any word in T can be translated into an a'-adjunct of any word in T'.[2]

C. Addition/deletion rules have the form $T(\mathbf{y}) \leftrightarrow (x' \xleftarrow{a'} T'(\mathbf{y}'))$ and $(x \xleftarrow{a} T(\mathbf{y})) \leftrightarrow T'(\mathbf{y}')$ where x, x' are variables that denote adjunct subtrees, and a, a' are adjunct relations. The addition rule states that an adjunct subtree x' can be introduced into the target tree T' in a translation unit $T(\mathbf{y}) \leftrightarrow T(\mathbf{y}')$ without any corresponding adjunct in the source tree T. Similarly, the deletion rule states that the adjunct subtree

[2]In the form stated here, adjunct rules obviously overgenerate because they do not place any restrictions on the words in T' that the target adjunct can attach to. In a full-fledged translation model, the adjunct rules must be augmented with a probabilistic model that can keep track of these restrictions.

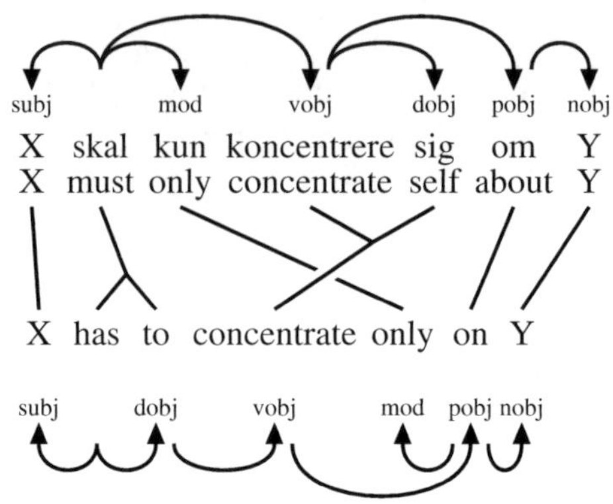

Figure 4: Parallel dependency analysis that is incompatible with our translation model.

x in the source tree T does not have to correspond to any adjunct in the target tree T'.[3]

The translation model places severe restrictions on the parallel dependency annotations. For example, the annotation in Figure 4 is incompatible with our proposed translation model with respect to the adjunct "only', since "only" attaches to the verb "skal/must" in the Danish analysis, but attaches to the preposition "on" in the English analysis — ie, it does not satisfy a requirement that follows implicitly from the adjunct rule: that corresponding source and target adjunct governors must belong to the same translation unit. In our example, there are two ways of rectifying the problem: we can (a) correct the dependency analysis as shown in Figure 2, or (b) correct the word alignment as shown in Figure 5.

It can be shown that our translation model translates into the following four requirements on parallel analyses — ie, the requirements are necessary and sufficient for ensuring that the linguistic annotations are compatible with our translation model. In the following, two words are said to be *coaligned* if they belong to the same alignment edge. A dependency edge $d \xleftarrow{r} g$ is called *internal* if d and g are coaligned, and *external* otherwise. A word w is called *singular* if it fails to be coaligned with at least one word in the other language.

Requirement I. The internal dependencies within a translation unit must form two connected trees. Ie,

[3]As with adjunct rules, addition/deletion rules obviously overgenerate, and must be augmented with probabilistic models that keep track of the precise characteristics of the adjunct subtrees that are added to or deleted from the parallel analyses.

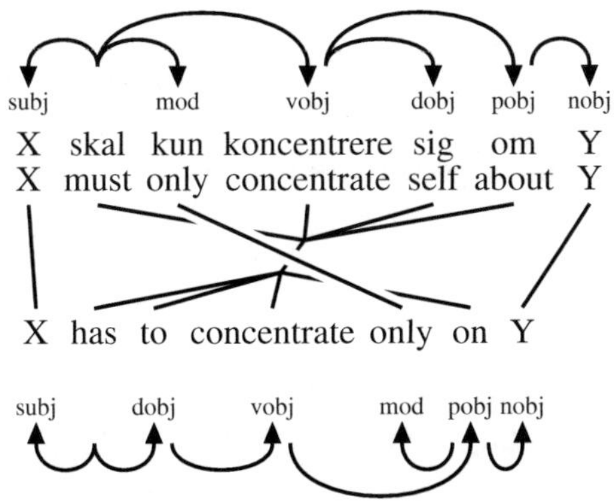

Figure 5: Making the analysis from Figure 4 compatible with our translation model by changing the alignment edges.

in an alignment $W \leftrightarrow W'$, the internal dependencies within W must form a connected source tree, and similarly for W'.

Requirement II. The external dependencies between translation units must form an acyclic graph. Ie, in an alignment $W \leftrightarrow W'$, no word $w \in W$ can be coaligned with an external transitive dependent of any word in W', and vice versa.

Requirement III. Parallel external governors must be aligned to each other. Ie, if two nodes n, n' are coaligned with external governor edges $n \xleftarrow{r} g$ and $n' \xleftarrow{r'} g'$, then g and g' must be coaligned.

Requirement IV. The graph contains no singular external complements. If the source word c is a complement of governor g and c is not coaligned to any target word, then c and g must be coaligned to each other; and similarly for target complements.

A graph that satisfies all four requirements is said to be *well-formed* with respect to our translation model. It can be shown that we can always transform an ill-formed graph G into a well-formed graph G' by merging alignment edges; G' is then called a *reduction* of G, and a reduction with a minimal number of mergings is called a *minimal reduction* of G. In a well-formed graph, we will refer to an alignment edge and its associated source and target dependency tree as a *translation unit*.

It can be shown that minimal reductions can be computed by means of the algorithm shown in Figure 6.[4] The body of the for-loop in Figure 6 ensures

procedure minimal-reduction(graph G)
  merge each alignment edge in G with itself
    (ie, ensure int. connectedness & ext. acyclicity)
  for *each* $W \leftrightarrow W'$ *in bottom-up order* **do**
    merge $W \leftrightarrow W'$ *with all of its external singular complements*
    merge all external governors of $W \leftrightarrow W'$
  return *the modified graph G*

Figure 6: Algorithm for computing the minimal reduction of a graph G.

Requirements III (coaligned external governors) and IV (no singular complements), and the merging operation is designed so that it ensures Requirements I (internal connectedness) and II (acyclicity).[5]

The ill-formed analysis in Figure 4 has the minimal reduction shown in Figure 2, whereas the analyses in Figure 2 and 5 are well-formed, ie, they are their own minimal reductions. In the remainder of the paper, we will describe how minimal reductions and translation units can be used for extracting transfer rules, detecting annotation errors, and comparing different annotation schemes with each other.

4 Extracting transfer rules and quantifying parallelism

The complement, adjunct, and addition/deletion rules in our simple dependency transfer model can be read off directly from the minimal reductions. Figure 7 shows the three complement rules induced from Figure 4 via the minimal reduction in Figure 5. Figure 8 (repeated from Figure 3) shows the six complement rules induced from the alternative analysis in Figure 2.

We have tested the extraction procedure on a large scale by applying it to the 100,000 word Copenhagen Danish-English Dependency Treebank (Buch-Kromann et al., 2007). Figure 9 shows the percentage of translation units with size at least n

[4]In the algorithm, G is viewed as a directed graph that contains the source and target dependencies, and alignment edges $W \leftrightarrow W'$ are viewed as short-hands for the set of all bidirectional edges that link two distinct nodes in $W \cup W'$.

[5]The merging operation performs three steps: (a) replace two alignment edges $W_1 \leftrightarrow W_1'$ and $W_2 \leftrightarrow W_2'$ with their union $W \leftrightarrow W'$ where $W = W_1 \cup W_2$ and $W' = W_1' \cup W_2'$; (b) merge $W \leftrightarrow W'$ with the smallest set of nodes that turns W and W' into connected dependency trees; (c) merge $W \leftrightarrow W'$ with all nodes on cycles that involve at least one node from $W \leftrightarrow W'$.

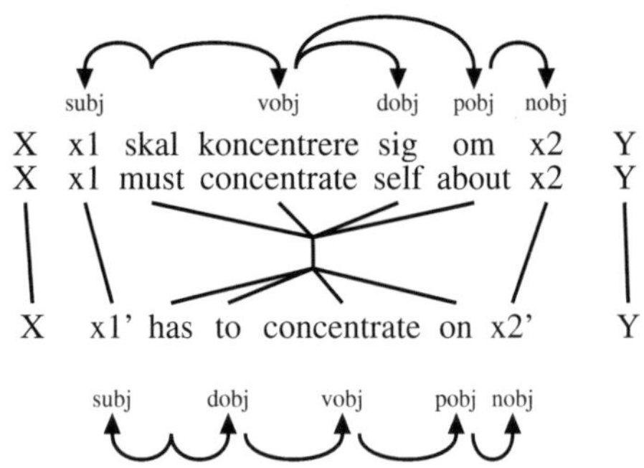

Figure 7: The three complement rules induced from Figure 4 via the minimal reduction in Figure 5.

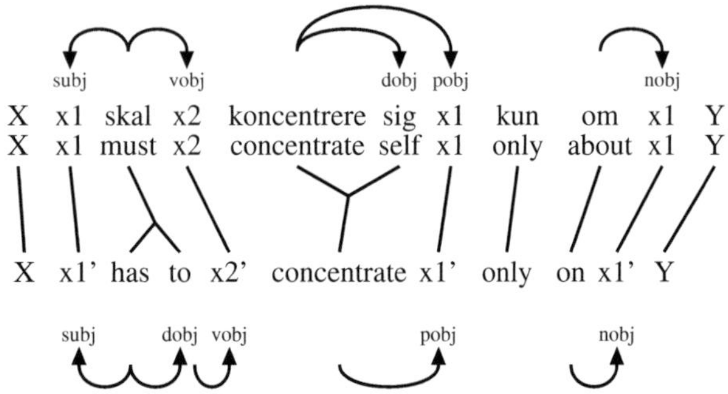

Figure 8: The six complement rules induced from the minimal reduction in Figure 2 (repeated from Figure 3).

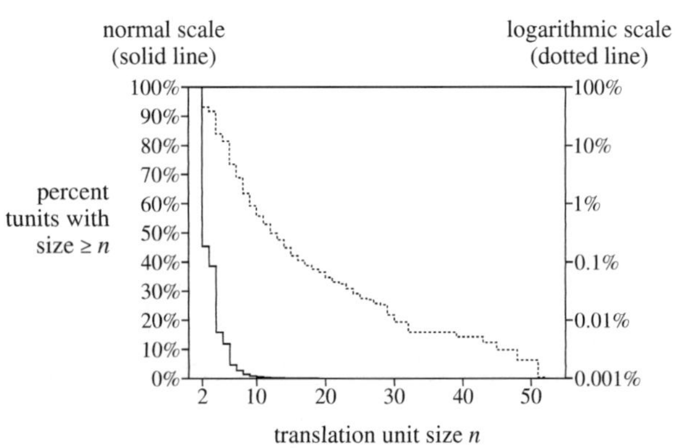

Figure 9: The percentage of translation units in the Copenhagen Danish-English Dependency Treebank with size at least n, plotted on normal and logarithmic scales.

in the parallel treebank, where the size of a translation unit is measured as the number of nodes in the associated complement transfer rule. The extracted transfer rules are useful for many purposes, including machine translation, lexicography, contrastive linguistics, and translation studies, but describing these applications is outside the scope of this paper.

5 Spotting annotation errors

To the human annotator who must check the word-aligned dependency analyses in a parallel dependency treebank, the analyses in Figure 2 and Figure 4 look almost identical. However, from the induced translation units and the associated complement rules shown above, it would have been immediately obvious to the annotator that the analysis in Figure 2 is significantly better than the analysis in Figure 4. This suggests that we can increase the quality of the human annotation in parallel treebank projects by designing annotation tools that continuously compute the induced translation units and present them visibly to the human annotator.

From a linguistic point of view, it can be expected that errors in the dependency annotation will often show up as non-parallelism that results in a large induced translation unit. So in a parallel dependency treebank, we can identify the most egregious examples of non-parallelism errors automatically by computing the induced translation units, and sorting them with respect to their size; the largest translation units will then have a high probability of being the result of annotation errors.

To confirm our linguistic expectation that large translation units are often caused by annotation errors, we have selected a sample of 75 translation units from the Copenhagen Danish-English Dependency Treebank, distributed more or less uniformly with respect to translation unit size in order to ensure that all translation unit sizes are sampled evenly. We have then hand-checked each translation unit carefully in order to determine whether the translation unit contains any annotation errors or not, giving us a data set of the form (C,N) where N is the size of the translation unit and C indicates whether the translation unit is correct ($C = 1$) or not ($C = 0$). Figure 10 shows our maximum likelihood estimate of the conditional probability $P(C = 1|N = n)$ that a translation unit with size n is correct.[6] From the

[6] In order to estimate the conditional probability $p(n) = P(C = 1|S = n)$ that a translation unit with size n is correct, we have fitted $p(n)$ to the parametric family $p(n) = \alpha^{n^\beta}$ by means of conditional maximum likelihood estimation with conditional likelihood $L = \prod_{i=1}^{75} p(n_i)^{c_i}(1-p(n_i))^{1-c_i}$. The resulting esti-

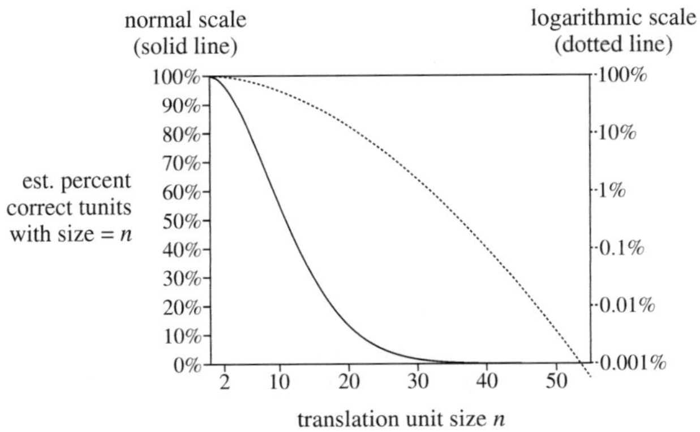

Figure 10: The estimated percentage of translation units with size n that are correct, plotted on normal and logarithmic scales.

graph, we see that the correctness rate decreases quickly with n. For example, only 55% of all translation units with size 10 are correct, and only 13% of all translation units with size 20 are correct. Thus, the statistics confirm that large translation units are often caused by annotation errors in the treebank, so focusing the effort on large translation units can make the postediting more cost-efficient. This also suggests that when developing algorithms for automatic annotation of parallel dependency treebanks, the algorithms can improve their accuracy by penalizing large translation units.

6 Comparing annotation schemes

Translation units can also be used to compare different annotation schemes. This is relevant in parallel treebank projects where there are several possible annotation schemes for one of the languages — eg, because there is more than one treebank or rule-based parser for that language. In this situation, we have the freedom of choosing the annotation schemes for the source and target languages so that they maximize the parallelism between the source and target language annotations. To make an informed choice, we can create a small pilot parallel treebank for each annotation scheme, and compare the treebank annotations qualitatively by looking at their induced translation units, and quantitatively by looking at their average translation unit size. The best choice of annotation schemes is then the combination that leads to the smallest and most sensible translation units.

Since texts are always trivially word-aligned with themselves, the same procedure applies to monolingual corpora where we want to compare two different dependency annotations with each other. In this setup, structural differences between the two monolingual annotation schemes will show up as large translation units. While these structural differences between annotation schemes could have been revealed by careful manual inspection, the automatic computation of translation units speeds up the process of identifying the differences. The method also suggests that the conversion from one annotation scheme to another can be viewed as a machine translation problem — that is, if we can create a machine translation algorithm that learns to translate from one language to another on the basis of a parallel dependency treebank, then this algorithm can also be used to convert from one dependency annotation scheme to another, given a training corpus that has been annotated with both annotation schemes.

7 Conclusion

In this paper, we have addressed the problem that the linguistic annotations in parallel treebanks often fail to correspond to meaningful translation units, because of internal incompatibilities between the dependency analyses and the word alignment. We have defined a meaningful notion of translation units and provided an algorithm for computing these translation units from any parallel dependency treebank. Finally, we have sketched how our notion of translation units can be used to aid the creation of parallel dependency treebanks by using the translation units as a visual aid for the human annotator, by using translation unit sizes to identify likely annotation errors, and by allowing a quantitative and qualitative comparison of different annotation schemes, both for parallel and monolingual treebanks.

mates are $\hat{\alpha} = 0.99$ and $\hat{\beta} = 1.77$ with confidence value 0.87, ie, if a data set D with the same translation unit sizes is generated randomly from the distribution $\hat{p}(n) = \hat{\alpha}^{n^{\hat{\beta}}}$, then the conditional likelihood of D will be larger than the likelihood of our observed data set in 87% of the cases. This means that a two-sided test does not reject that the data are generated from the estimated distribution $\hat{p}(n)$.

8 Acknowledgments

The work was supported by two grants from the Danish Research Council for the Humanities. Thanks to the anonymous reviewers for their helpful comments.

References

Matthias Buch-Kromann, Jürgen Wedekind, and Jakob Elming. 2007. The Copenhagen Danish-English Dependency Treebank. http://www.id.cbs.dk/~mbk/ddt-en.

Matthias Buch-Kromann. 2006. Discontinuous Grammar. A dependency-based model of human parsing and language learning. Dr.ling.merc. dissertation, Copenhagen Business School. http://www.id.cbs.dk/~mbk/thesis.

Sabine Buchholz and Erwin Marsi. 2006. CoNLL-X shared task on Multilingual Dependency Parsing. In *Proc. CoNLL-2006*.

A. Cahill, M. Burke, R. O'Donovan, J. van Genabith, and A. Way. 2004. Long-distance dependency resolution in automatically acquired wide-coverage PCFG-based LFG approximations. In *Proc. of ACL-2004*.

David Chiang. 2007. Hierarchical phrase-based translation. *Computational Linguistics*, 33(2).

Martin Čmejrek, Jan Cuřín, Jiří Havelka, Jan Hajič, and Vladislav Kuboň. 2004. Prague Czech-English Dependency Treebank. Syntactically annotated resources for machine translation. In *Proc. LREC-2004*.

Lea Cyrus. 2006. Building a resource for studying translation shifts. In *Proc. LREC-2006*.

Yuan Ding and Martha Palmer. 2005. Machine translation using Probabilistic Synchronous Dependency Insertion Grammars. In *Proc. ACL-2005*.

Yuan Ding. 2006. *Machine translation using Probabilistic Synchronous Dependency Insertion Grammars*. Ph.D. thesis, Univ. of Pennsylvania.

Michel Galley, Mark Hopkins, Kevin Knight, and Daniel Marcu. 2004. What's in a translation rule? In *Proc. HLT/NAACL-2004*.

Chung-hye Han, Na-Rae Han, Eon-Suk Ko, and Martha Palmer. 2002. Development and evaluation of a Korean treebank and its application to NLP. In *Proc. LREC-2002*.

Silvia Hansen-Schirra, Stella Neumann, and Mihaela Vela. 2006. Multi-dimensional annotation and alignment in an English-German translation corpus. In *Proc. NLPXML-2006*.

Philipp Koehn, Franz Josef Och, and Daniel Marcu. 2003. Statistical phrase-based translation. In *Proc. HLT/NAACL-2003*.

Daniel Marcu, Wei Wang, Abdessamad Echihabi, and Kevin Knight. 2006. SPMT: Statistical machine translation with syntactified target language phrases. In *Proc. EMNLP-2006*.

Franz Josef Och and Hermann Ney. 2003. A systematic comparison of various statistical alignment models. *Computational Linguistics*, 29(1):19–51.

Chris Quirk, Arul Menezes, and Colin Cherry. 2005. Dependency treelet translation: Syntactically informed phrasal SMT. In *Proc. ACL-2005*.

Yvonne Samuelsson and Martin Volk. 2006. Phrase alignment in parallel treebanks. In *Proc. TLT-2006*.

K. Uchimoto, Y. Zhang, K. Sudo, M. Murata, S. Sekine, and H. Isahara. 2004. Multilingual aligned parallel treebank corpus reflecting contextual information and its applications. In *Proc. MLR-2004*.

Kenji Yamada and Kevin Knight. 2001. A syntax-based statistical translation model. In *Proc. ACL-2001*.

Adding semantic role annotation to a corpus of written Dutch

Paola Monachesi, Gerwert Stevens and Jantine Trapman
Utrecht University, Uil-OTS, Trans 10, 3512 JK Utrecht, The Netherlands
{Paola.Monachesi, Gerwert.Stevens, Jantine.Trapman}@let.uu.nl

Abstract

We present an approach to automatic semantic role labeling (SRL) carried out in the context of the Dutch Language Corpus Initiative (D-Coi) project. Adapting earlier research which has mainly focused on English to the Dutch situation poses an interesting challenge especially because there is no semantically annotated Dutch corpus available that can be used as training data. Our automatic SRL approach consists of three steps: bootstrapping from a syntactically annotated corpus by means of a rule-based tagger developed for this purpose, manual correction on the basis of the PropBank guidelines which have been adapted to Dutch and training a machine learning system on the manually corrected data.

1 Introduction

The creation of semantically annotated corpora has lagged dramatically behind. As a result, the need for such resources has now become urgent. Several initiatives have been launched at the international level in the last years, however, they have focused almost entirely on English and not much attention has been dedicated to the creation of semantically annotated Dutch corpora.

Within the *Dutch Language Corpus Initiative* (D-Coi)[1], a recently completed Dutch project, guidelines have been developed for the annotation of a Dutch written corpus. In particular, a pilot corpus has been compiled, parts of which have been enriched with (verified) linguistic annotations.

One of the innovative aspects of the D-Coi project with respect to previous initiatives, such as the Spoken Dutch Corpus (CGN - Corpus Gesproken Nederlands) (Oostdijk, 2002), was the development of a protocol for a semantic annotation layer. In particular, two types of semantic annotation have been addressed, that is semantic role assignment and temporal and spatial semantics (Schuurman and Monachesi, 2006). The reason for this choice lies in the fact that semantic role assignment (i.e. the semantic relationships identified between items in the text such as the agents or patients of particular actions), is one of the most attested and feasible types of semantic annotation within corpora. On the other hand, temporal and spatial annotation was chosen because there is a clear need for such a layer of annotation in applications like information retrieval or question answering.

The focus of this paper is on semantic role annotation. We analyze the choices we have made in selecting an appropriate annotation protocol by taking into consideration existing initiatives such as FrameNet (Johnson et al., 2002) and PropBank (Kingsbury et al., 2002) (cf. also the Chinese and Arabic PropBank). We motivate our choice for the PropBank annotation scheme on the basis of the promising results with respect to automatic semantic role labeling (SRL) which have been obtained for English. Furthermore, we discuss how the SRL research could be adapted to the Dutch situation given that no semantically annotated corpus was available that could be used as training data.

[1] http://lands.let.ru.nl/projects/d-coi/

Proceedings of the Linguistic Annotation Workshop, pages 77–84,
Prague, June 2007.

2 Existing projects

During the last few years, corpora enriched with semantic role information have received much attention, since they offer rich data both for empirical investigations in lexical semantics and large-scale lexical acquisition for NLP and Semantic Web applications. Several initiatives are emerging at the international level to develop annotation systems of argument structure. Within our project we have tried to exploit existing results as much as possible and to set the basis for a common standard. We want to profit from earlier experiences and contribute to existing work by making it more complete with our own (language specific) contribution given that most resources have been developed for English.

The PropBank and FrameNet projects have been evaluated in order to assess whether the approach and the methodology they have developed for the annotation of semantic roles could be adopted for our purposes. Given the results they have achieved, we have taken their insights and experiences as our starting point.

FrameNet reaches a level of granularity in the specification of the semantic roles which might be desirable for certain applications (i.e. Question Answering). Moreover, the predicates are linked to an underlying frame ontology that classifies the verbs within a semantic hierarchy. On the other hand, despite the relevant work of Gildea and Jurafsky (2002), it is still an open issue whether FrameNet classes and frame elements can be obtained and used automatically because of the richness of the semantic structures employed (Dzikovska et al., 2004). Furthermore, the FrameNet approach might raise problems with respect to uniformity of role labeling even if human annotators are involved. Incompleteness, however, constitutes the biggest problem, i.e. several frames and relations among frames are missing mainly because FrameNet is still under development. Adopting the FrameNet lexicon for semantic annotation means contributing to its development with the addition of (language specific) and missing frames.

In our study, we have assumed that the FrameNet classification even though it is based on English could be applicable to Dutch as well. This assumption is supported by the fact that the German project *Saarbrücken Lexical Semantics Annotation and analysis* (SALSA) (K. Erk and Pinkal, 2003) has adopted FrameNet with good results. Although Dutch and English are quite similar, there are differences on both sides. For example, in the case of the Spanish FrameNet it turned out that frames may differ in their number of elements across languages (cf. (Subirats and Sato, 2004)).

The other alternative was to employ the PropBank approach which has the advantage of providing clear role labels and thus a transparent annotation for both annotators and users. Furthermore, there are promising results with respect to automatic semantic role labeling for English thus the annotation process could be at least semi-automatic. A disadvantage of this approach is that we would have to give up the classification of frames in an ontology, as is the case in FrameNet, which could be very useful for certain applications, especially those related to the Semantic Web. However, in (Monachesi and Trapman, 2006) suggestions are given on how the two approaches could be reconciled.

The prospect of semi-automatic annotation was the decisive factor in the decision to adopt the PropBank approach for the annotation of semantic roles within the D-Coi project.

3 Automatic SRL: bootstrapping a corpus with semantic roles

Ever since the pioneering article of Gildea and Jurafsky (2002), there has been an increasing interest in automatic semantic role labeling (SRL). However, previous research has focused mainly on English. Adapting earlier research to the Dutch situation poses an interesting challenge especially because there is no semantically annotated Dutch corpus available that can be used as training data. Furthermore, no PropBank frame files for Dutch exist.

To solve the problem of the unavailability of training data, we have developed a rule-based tagger to bootstrap a syntactically annotated corpus with semantic roles. After manual correction, this corpus was used as training data for a machine learning SRL system. The input data for our SRL approach consists of Dutch sentences, syntactically annotated by the Dutch dependency parser Alpino (Bouma et al., 2000).

Syntactic annotation of our corpus is based on the Spoken Dutch Corpus (CGN) dependency graphs (Moortgat et al., 2000). A CGN dependency graph is a tree-structured directed acyclic graph in which nodes and edges are labeled with respectively c-labels (category-labels) and d-labels (dependency labels). C-labels of nodes denote phrasal categories, such as NP (noun phrase) and PP, c-labels of leafs denote POS tags. D-Labels describe the grammatical (dependency) relation between the node and its head. Examples of such relations are SU (subject), OBJ (direct object) and MOD (modifier).

Intuitively, dependency structures are a great resource for a rule-based semantic tagger, for they directly encode the argument structure of lexical units, e.g. the relation between constituents. Our goal was to make optimal use of this information in an automatic SRL system. In order to achieve this, we first defined a basic mapping between nodes in a dependency graph and PropBank roles. This mapping forms the basis of our rule-based SRL system (Stevens, 2006).

Mapping subject and object complements to PropBank arguments is straightforward: subjects are mapped to ARG0 (proto-typical agent), direct objects to ARG1 (proto-typical patient) and indirect objects to ARG2. An exception is made for ergatives and passives, for which the subject is labeled with ARG1.

Devising a consistent mapping for higher numbered arguments is more difficult, since their labeling depends in general on the frame entry of the corresponding predicate. Since we could not use frame information, we used a heuristic method. This heuristic strategy entails that after numbering subject/object complements with the rules stated above, other complements are labeled in a left-to-right order, starting with the first available argument number. For example, if the subject is labeled with ARG0 and there are no object complements, the first available argument number is ARG1.

Finally, a mapping for several types of modifiers was defined. We refrained from the disambiguation task, and concentrated on those modifiers that can be mapped consistently. These modifiers are:

- **ArgM-NEG** - Negation markers.
- **ArgM-REC** - Reflexives and reciprocals.
- **ArgM-PRD** - Markers of secondary predication: modifiers with the dependency label PREDM
- **ArgM-PNC** - Purpose clauses: modifiers that start with *om te* . These modifiers are marked by Alpino with the c-label OTI.
- **ArgM-LOC** - Locative modifiers: modifiers with the dependency label LD, the LD label is used by Alpino to mark modifiers that indicate a location of direction.

4 XARA: a rule based SRL tagger

With the help of the mappings discussed above, we developed a rule-based semantic role tagger, which is able to bootstrap an unannotated corpus with semantic roles. We used this rule-based tagger to reduce the manual annotation effort. After all, starting manual annotation from scratch is time consuming and therefore expensive. A possible solution is to start from a (partially) automatically annotated corpus.

The system we developed for this purpose is called XARA (XML-based Automatic Role-labeler for Alpino-trees) (Stevens, 2006). [2] XARA is written in Java, the cornerstone of its rule-based approach is formed by XPath expressions; XPath (Clark and DeRose, 1999) is a powerful query language for the XML format.

The corpus format we used in our experiments is the Alpino XML format. This format is designed to support a range of linguistic queries on the dependency trees in XPath directly (Bouma and Kloosterman, 2002). The structure of Alpino XML documents directly corresponds to the structure of the dependency tree: dependency nodes are represented by NODE elements, attributes of the node elements are the properties of the corresponding dependency node, e.g. c-label, d-label, pos-tag, lemma, etc.

A rule in XARA consist of an XPath expression that addresses a node in the dependency tree, and a target label for that node, i.e. a rule is a *(path,label)* pair. For example, a rule that selects direct object nodes and labels them with ARG1 can be formulated as:

```
(//node[@rel='obj1'], 1)
```

[2] The system is available at: http://www.let.uu.nl/~Paola.Monachesi/personal/dcoi/index.html

In this example, a numeric label is used to label a numbered argument. For ARGMs, string value can be used as target label.

After their definition, rules can be applied to local dependency domains, i.e. subtrees of a dependency tree. The local dependency domain to which a rule is applied, is called the rule's context. A context is defined by an XPath expression that selects a group of nodes. Contexts for which we defined rules in XARA are verbal domains, that is, local dependency structures with a verb as head.

Table 1 shows the performance of XARA on our treebank.

Table 1: Results of SRL with XARA

Label	Precision	Recall	$F_{\beta=1}$
Overall	65,11%	45,83%	53,80
Arg0	98.97%	94.95%	96.92
Arg1	70.08%	64.83%	67.35
Arg2	47.41%	36.07%	40.97
Arg3	13.89%	6.85%	9.17
Arg4	1.56%	1.35%	1.45
ArgM-LOC	83.49%	13.75%	23.61
ArgM-NEG	72.79%	58.79%	65.05
ArgM-PNC	91.94%	39.31%	55.07
ArgM-PRD	63.64%	26.25%	37.17
ArgM-REC	85.19%	69.70%	76.67

Notice XARA's performance on highered numbered arguments, especially ARG4. Manual inspection of the manual labeling reveals that ARG4 arguments often occur in propositions without ARG2 and ARG3 arguments. Since our current heuristic labeling method always chooses the first available argument number, this method will have to be modified in order achieve a better score for ARG4 arguments.

5 Manual correction

The annotation by XARA of our tree bank, was manually corrected by one human annotator, however, in order to deal with a Dutch corpus, the PropBank annotation guidelines needed to be revised.

Notice that both PropBank and D-Coi share the assumption that consistent argument labels should be provided across different realizations of the same verb and that modifiers of the verb should be assigned functional tags. However, they adopt a different approach with respect to the treatment of traces since PropBank creates co-reference chains for empty categories while within D-coi, empty categories are almost non existent and in those few cases in which they are attested, a coindexation has been established already at the syntactic level. Furthermore, D-coi assumes dependency structures for the syntactic representation of its sentences while PropBank employs phrase structure trees. In addition, Dutch behaves differently from English with respect to certain constructions and these differences should be spelled out.

In order to annotate our corpus, the PropBank guidelines needed a revision because they have been developed for English and to add a semantic layer to the Penn TreeBank. Besides the adaption (and extension) of the guidelines to Dutch (Trapman and Monachesi, 2006), we also have to consider a Dutch version of the PropBank frameindex. In PropBank, frame files provide a verb specific description of all possible semantic roles and illustrate these roles by examples. The lack of example sentences makes consistent annotation difficult. Since defining a set of frame files from scratch is very time consuming, we decided to attempt an alternative approach, in which we annotated Dutch verbs with the same argument structure as their English counterparts, thus use English frame files instead of creating Dutch ones. Although this causes some problems, for example, not all Dutch verbs can be translated to a 100% equivalent English counterpart, such problems proved to be relatively rare. In most cases applying the PropBank argument structure to Dutch verbs was straightforward. If translation was not possible, an ad hoc decision was made on how to label the verb.

In order to verify the correctness of the annotation carried out automatically by XARA, we have proceeded in the following way:

1. localize the verb and translate it to English; only the argument structure of *verbs* is considered in our annotation while that of NPs, PPs and other constituents has been neglected for the moment.

2. check the verb's frames file in PropBank; the appropriate roles for each

verb could be identified in PropBank (http://verbs.colorado.edu/framesets/).

3. localize the arguments of the verb; arguments are usually NPs, PPs and sentential complements.

4. localize the modifiers; in addition to the arguments of a verb, modifiers of place, time, manner etc. are marked as well.

An appropriate tool has been selected to carry out the manual correction. We have made an investigation to evaluate three different tools for this purpose: *CLaRK*[3], *Salto*[4] and *TrEd*[5]. On the basis of our main requirements, that is whether the tool is able to handle the xml-structure we have adopted and whether it provides a user-friendly graphical interface and we have come to the conclusion that the *TrEd* tool was the most appropriate for our needs.

During the manual correction process, some problems have emerged, as for example the fact that we have encountered some phenomena, such as the interpretation of modifiers, for which linguistic research doesn't provide a standard solution yet, we have discarded these cases for the moment but it would be desirable to address them in the future.

Furthermore, the interaction among levels should be taken more into consideration. Even though the Alpino parser has an accuracy on our corpus of 81%–90% (van Noord, 2006) and the syntactic corpus which has been employed for the annotation of the semantic roles had been manually corrected, we have encountered examples in which the annotation provided by the syntactic parser was not appropriate. This is the case of a PP which was labeled as modifier by the syntactic parser but which should be labeled as argument according to the PropBank guidelines. There should thus be an agreement in these cases so that the syntactic structure can be corrected. Furthermore, we have encountered problems with respect to PP attachment, that is the syntactic representation gives us correct and incorrect structures and at the semantic level we are able to disambiguate. More research is necessary about how to deal with the incorrect representations.

[3]http://www.bultreebank.org/clark/index.html

[4]http://www.coli.uni-saarland.de/projects/salsa/

[5]http://ufal.mff.cuni.cz/ pajas/tred/

6 The TiMBL classification system

The manually corrected sentences have been used as training and test data for an SRL classification system. For this learning system we have employed a Memory Based Learning (MBL) approach, implemented in the Tilburg Memory based learner (TiMBL) (Daelemans et al., 2004).

TiMBL assigns class labels to training instances on the basis of features and the feature set plays an important role in the performance of a classifier. In choosing the feature set for our system, we mainly looked at previous research, especially systems that participated in the 2004 and 2005 CoNLL shared tasks on semantic role labeling (Carreras and Màrquez, 2005).

It is worth noting that none of the systems in the CoNLL shared tasks used features extracted from dependency structures. However, we encountered one system (Hacioglu, 2004) that did not participate in the CoNLL-shared task but did use the same data and was based on dependency structures. The main difference with our system is that Hacioglu did not use a dependency parser to create the dependency trees, instead existing constituent trees were converted to dependency structures. Furthermore, the system was trained and tested on English sentences.

From features used in previous systems and some experimentation with TiMBL, we derived the following feature set. The first group of features describes the predicate (verb):

(1) Predicate stem - The verb stem, provided by Alpino.

(2) Predicate voice - A binary feature indicating the voice of the predicate (passive/active).

The second group of features describes the candidate argument:

(3) Argument c-label - The category label (phrasal tag) of the node, e.g. NP or PP.

(4) Argument d-label - The dependency label of the node, e.g. MOD or SU.

(5) Argument POS-tag - POS tag of the node if the node is a leaf node, null otherwise.

(6) Argument head-word - The head word of the relation if the node is an internal node or the lexical item (word) if it is a leaf.

(7) Argument head-word - The head word of the relation if the node is an internal node or the lexical item (word) if it is a leaf.

(8) Head-word POS tag - The POS tag of the head word.

(9) c-label pattern of argument - The left to right chain of c-labels of the argument and its siblings.

(10) d-label pattern - The left to right chain of d-labels of the argument and its siblings.

(11) c-label & d-label of argument combined - The c-label of the argument concatenated with its d-label.

The training set consists of predicate/argument pairs encoded in training instances. Each instance contains features of a predicate and its candidate argument. Candidate arguments are nodes (constituents) in the dependency tree. This pair-wise approach is analogous to earlier work by van den Bosch et al. (2004) and Tjong Kim Sang et al. (2005) in which instances were build from verb/phrase pairs from which the phrase parent is an ancestor of the verb. We adopted their approach to dependency trees: only siblings of the verb (predicate) are considered as candidate arguments.

In comparison to experiments in earlier work, we had relatively few training data available: our training corpus consisted of 2,395 sentences which comprise 3066 verbs, 5271 arguments and 3810 modifiers.[6] To overcome our data sparsity problem, we trained the classifier using the leave one out (LOO) method (`-t leave_one_out` option in TiMBL). With this option set, every data item in turn is selected once as a test item, and the classifier is trained on all remaining items. Except for the LOO option, we only used the default TiMBL settings during training, to prevent overfitting because of data sparsity.

7 Results & Evaluation

Table 2 shows the performance of the TiMBL classifier on our annotated dependency treebank. From these sentences, 12,113 instances were extracted. To measure the performance of the systems, the automatically assigned labels were compared to the labels assigned by a human annotator.

Table 2: Results of TiMBL classification

Label	Precision	Recall	$F_{\beta=1}$
Overall	70.27%	70.59%	70.43
Arg0	90.44%	86.82%	88.59
Arg1	87.80%	84.63%	86.18
Arg2	63.34%	59.10%	61.15
Arg3	21.21%	19.18%	20.14
Arg4	54.05%	54.05%	54.05
ArgM-ADV	54.98%	51.85%	53.37
ArgM-CAU	47.24%	43.26%	45.16
ArgM-DIR	36.36%	33.33%	34.78
ArgM-DIS	74.27%	70.71%	72.45
ArgM-EXT	29.89%	28.57%	29.21
ArgM-LOC	57.95%	54.53%	56.19
ArgM-MNR	52.07%	47.57%	49.72
ArgM-NEG	68.00%	65.38%	66.67
ArgM-PNC	68.61%	64.83%	66.67
ArgM-PRD	45.45%	40.63%	42.90
ArgM-REC	86.15%	84.85%	85.50
ArgM-TMP	55.95%	53.29%	54.58

It is difficult to compare our results with those obtained with other existing systems, since our system is the first one to be applied to Dutch sentences. Moreover, our data format, data size and evaluation methods (separate test/train/develop sets versus LOO) are different from earlier research. However, to put our results somewhat in perspective, we looked mainly at systems that participated in the CoNLL shared tasks on semantic role labeling.

The best performing system that participated in CoNLL 2005 reached an F_1 of 80. There were seven systems with an F_1 performance in the 75-78 range, seven more with performances in the 70-75 range and five with a performance between 65 and 70 (Carreras and Màrquez, 2005).

A system that did not participate in the CoNLL task, but still provides interesting material for comparison since it is also based on dependency structures, is the system by Hacioglu (2004). This system scored 85,6% precision, 83,6% recall and 84,6 F_1 on the CoNLL data set, which is even higher than the best results published so far on the PropBank data

[6]We refer to (Oostdijk and Boves, 2006) for general information about the domain of the D-Coi corpus and its design.

sets (Pradhan et al., 2005): 84% precision, 75% recall and 79 F_1. These results support our claim that dependency structures can be very useful in the SRL task.

As one would expect, the overall precision and recall scores of the classifier are higher than those of the XARA rule-based system. Yet, we expected a better performance of the classifier on the lower numbered arguments (ARG0 and ARG1). Our hypothesis is that performance on these arguments can be improved by by adding semantic features to our feature set.

Examples of such features are the subcategorization frame of the predicate and the semantic category (e.g. WordNet synset) of the candidate argument. We expect that such semantic features will improve the performance of the classifier for certain types of verbs and arguments, especially the lower numbered arguments ARG0 and ARG1 and temporal and spatial modifiers. For example, the Dutch preposition *over* can either head a phrase indicating a location or a time-span. The semantic category of the neighboring noun phrase might be helpful in such cases to choose the right PropBank label. Thanks to new lexical resources, such as Cornetto (Vossen, 2006), and clustering techniques based on dependency structures (van de Cruys, 2005), we might be able to add lexical semantic information about noun phrases in future research.

Performance of the classifier can also be improved by automatically optimizing the feature set. The optimal set of features for a classifier can be found by employing bi-directional hill climbing (van den Bosch et al., 2004). There is a wrapper script (Paramsearch) available that can be used with TiMBL and several other learning systems that implements this approach[7]. In addition, iterative deepening (ID) can be used as a heuristic way of finding the optimal algorithm parameters for TiMBL.

8 Conclusions & Future work

We have presented an approach to automatic semantic role labeling based on three steps: bootstrapping from a syntactically annotated Dutch corpus with a rule-based tagger developed for this purpose, manual correction and training a machine learning system on the manually corrected data.

The promising results in this area obtained for English on the basis of PropBank role labels was a decisive factor for our choice to adopt the PropBank annotation scheme which has been adapted for the annotation of the Dutch corpus. However, we would like to adopt the conceptual structure of FrameNet, even though not necessarily the granularity of its role assignment approach, to this end we are linking manually the predicates annotated with the PropBank semantic roles to the FrameNet ontology.

Only a small part of the D-Coi corpus has been annotated with semantic information, in order to yield information with respect to its feasibility. We believe that a more substantial annotation task will be carried out in the framework of a follow-up project aiming at the construction of a 500 million word corpus, in which one million words will be annotated with semantic information. Hopefully, in the follow-up project, it will be possible to carry out experiments and measure inter-annotator agreement since due to financial constraints only one annotator has annotated the current corpus.

Finally, it would be interesting to see how the classifier would perform on larger collections and new genres of data. The follow-up of the D-Coi project will provide new semantically annotated data to facilitate research in this area.

[7]URL: http://ilk.uvt.nl/software.html#paramsearch

References

G. Bouma and G. Kloosterman. 2002. Querying dependency treebanks in xml. In *Proceedings of the Third international conference on Language Resources and Evaluation (LREC)*. Gran Canaria.

G. Bouma, G. van Noord, and R. Malouf. 2000. Alpino: wide-coverage computational analysis of dutch.

X. Carreras and L. Màrquez. 2005. Introduction to the conll-2005 shared task: Semantic role labeling. In *Proceedings of the Eighth Conference on Computational Natural Language Learning (CoNLL-2005)*. Boston, MA, USA.

J. Clark and S. DeRose. 1999. Xml path language (xpath). *W3C Recommendation 16 November 1999*. URL: http://www.w3.org/TR/xpath.

D. Daelemans, D. Zavrel, K. van der Sloot, and A. van den Bosch. 2004. Timbl: Tilburg memory based learner, version 5.1, reference guide. ILK Technical Report Series 04-02, Tilburg University.

M. Dzikovska, M. Swift, and J. Allen. 2004. Building a computational lexicon and ontology with framenet. In *Proceedings of the workshop Building Lexical Resources with Semantically Annotated Corpora (LREC) 2004*. Lisbon.

D. Gildea and D. Jurafsky. 2002. Automatic labeling of semantic roles. *Comput. Linguist.*, 28(3):245–288.

K. Hacioglu. 2004. Semantic role labeling using dependency trees. In *COLING '04: Proceedings of the 20th international conference on Computational Linguistics*, page 1273. August 2004.

C. R. Johnson, C. J. Fillmore, M. R. L. Petruck, C. F. Baker, M. J. Ellsworth, J. Ruppenhofer, and E. J. Wood. 2002. *FrameNet:Theory and Practice.*

S. Pado K. Erk, A. Kowalski and M. Pinkal. 2003. Towards a resource for lexical semantics: A large german corpus with extensive semantic annotation. In *Proceedings of ACL 2003*. Sapporo.

P. Kingsbury, M. Palmer, and M. Marcus. 2002. Adding semantic annotation to the penn treebank. In *Proceedings of the Human Language Technology Conference (HLT'02)*.

P. Monachesi and J. Trapman. 2006. Merging framenet and propbank in a corpus of written dutch. In *Proceedings of (LREC) 2006*. Genoa.

M. Moortgat, I. Schuurman, and T. van der Wouden. 2000. CGN syntactische annotatie. *Internal report Corpus Gesproken Nederlands.*

N. Oostdijk and L. Boves. 2006. User requirements analysis for the design of a reference corpus of written dutch. In *Proceedings of (LREC) 2006*. Genoa.

N. Oostdijk. 2002. The design of the spoken dutch corpus. In P. Peters, P. Collins, and A. Smith, editors, *New Frontiers of Corpus Research*, pages 105–112. Amsterdam: Rodopi.

S. Pradhan, K., V. Krugler, W. Ward, J. H. Martin, and D. Jurafsky. 2005. Support vector learning for semantic argument classification. *Machine Learning Journal*, 1-3(60):11–39.

E. Tjong Kim Sang, S. Canisius, A. van den Bosch, and T. Bogers. 2005. Applying spelling error correction techniques for improving semantic role labeling. In *Proceedings of the Ninth Conference on Natural Language Learning (CoNLL-2005)*. Ann Arbor, MI, USA.

I. Schuurman and P. Monachesi. 2006. The contours of a semantic annotation scheme for dutch. In *Proceedings of Computational Linguistics in the Netherlands 2005*. University of Amsterdam. Amsterdam.

G. Stevens. 2006. Automatic semantic role labeling in a dutch corpus. Master's thesis, Universiteit Utrecht.

C. Subirats and H. Sato. 2004. Spanish framenet and framesql. In *4th International Conference on Language Resources and Evaluation. Workshop on Building Lexical Resources from Semantically Annotated Corpora*. Lisbon (Portugal), May 2004.

J. Trapman and P. Monachesi. 2006. Manual for the annotation of semantic roles in d-coi. Technical report, University of Utecht.

Tim van de Cruys. 2005. Semantic clustering in dutch. In *Proceedings of CLIN 2005*.

A. van den Bosch, S. Canisius, W. Daelemans, I. Hendrickx, and E. Tjong Kim Sang. 2004. Memory-based semantic role labeling: Optimizing features, algorithm, and output. In H.T. Ng and E. Riloff, editors, *Proceedings of the Eighth Conference on Computational Natural Language Learning (CoNLL-2004)*. Boston, MA, USA.

G. van Noord. 2006. At last parsing is now operational. In *Proceedings of TALN 06*. Leuven.

P. Vossen. 2006. Cornetto: Een lexicaal-semantische database voor taaltechnologie. *Dixit Special Issue*. Stevin.

A Search Tool for Parallel Treebanks

Martin Volk, Joakim Lundborg and Maël Mettler
Stockholm University
Department of Linguistics
106 91 Stockholm, Sweden
volk@ling.su.se

Abstract

This paper describes a tool for aligning and searching parallel treebanks. Such treebanks are a new type of parallel corpora that come with syntactic annotation on both languages plus sub-sentential alignment. Our tool allows the visualization of tree pairs and the comfortable annotation of word and phrase alignments. It also allows monolingual and bilingual searches including the specification of alignment constraints. We show that the TIGER-Search query language can easily be combined with such alignment constraints to obtain a powerful cross-lingual query language.

1 Introduction

Recent years have seen a number of initiatives in building parallel treebanks. Our group has participated in these efforts by building a tri-lingual parallel treebank called SMULTRON (Stockholm MULtilingual TReebank).[1] Our parallel treebank consists of syntactically annotated sentences in three languages, taken from translated (i.e. parallel) documents. In addition, the syntax trees of corresponding sentence pairs are aligned on a sub-sentential level. This means they are aligned on word level or phrase level (some phrases can be as large as clauses). Parallel treebanks can be used as training or evaluation corpora for word and phrase alignment, as input for example-based machine translation (EBMT), as training corpora for transfer rules, or for translation studies.

Similar projects include Croco (Hansen-Schirra et al., 2006) which is aimed at building a German-English parallel treebank for translation studies, LinES an English-Swedish parallel treebank (Ahrenberg, 2007), and the Czech-English parallel dependency treebank built in Prague (Cmejrek et al., 2005).

SMULTRON is an English-German-Swedish parallel treebank (Samuelsson and Volk, 2006; Samuelsson and Volk, 2007). It contains the first two chapters of Jostein Gaarder's novel "Sofie's World" with about 500 sentences. In addition it contains 500 sentences from economy texts (a quarterly report by a multinational company as well as part of a bank's annual report). We have (semi-automatically) annotated the German sentences with Part-of-Speech tags and phrase structure trees (incl. edges labeled with functional information) following the NEGRA/TIGER guidelines for German treebanking.

For English we have used the Penn Treebank guidelines which are similar in that they also prescribe phrase structure trees (with PoS tags, but only partially annotated with functional labels). However they differ from the German guidelines in many details. For example the German trees use crossing edges for discontinuous units while the English trees introduce symbols for empty tokens plus secondary edges for the representation of such phenomena.

For Swedish there were no appropriate guidelines available. Therefore we have adapted the German

[1]We gratefully acknowledge financial support for the SMULTRON project by Granholms stiftelse and Rausings stiftelse.

Proceedings of the Linguistic Annotation Workshop, pages 85–92,
Prague, June 2007.

guidelines to Swedish. The general annotation strategy for Swedish was the same as for German: PoS tags, phrase structure trees (incl. functional edge labels) and crossing branches for discontinuous units. But, of course, there are linguistic differences between German and Swedish that required special attention (e.g. Swedish prepositions that introduce sentences).

The treebanks for all three languages were annotated separately with the help of the treebank editor ANNOTATE. After finishing the monolingual treebanks, the trees were exported from the accompanying SQL database and converted into an XML format as input to our alignment tool, the Stockholm TreeAligner.

In this paper we will first describe this alignment tool and then focus on its new search facility. To our knowledge this is the first dedicated tool that combines visualization, alignment and searching of parallel treebanks (although there are others who have experimented with parallel corpus searches (Nygaard and Johannesen, 2004; Petersen, 2006)).

2 The Stockholm TreeAligner

When our monolingual treebanks were finished, the trees were exported from the editor system and converted into TIGER-XML. TIGER-XML is a line-based (i.e. not nested and thus database-friendly) representation for graph structures which supports crossing edges and secondary edges.[2] TIGER-XML has been defined as input format for TIGER-Search, a query tool for monolingual treebanks (see section 3). We use this format also as input format for our alignment tool, the Stockholm TreeAligner (Volk et al., 2006).

The TreeAligner program is a graphical user interface to specify (or correct) word and phrase alignments between pairs of syntax trees.[3] The TreeAligner is roughly similar to alignment tools such as I*Link (Ahrenberg et al., 2002) or Cairo (Smith and Jahr, 2000) but it is especially tailored to visualize and align full syntax trees (including trees with crossing edges).

[2]For information about TIGER-XML see www.ims.uni-stuttgart.de/projekte/TIGER

[3]The TreeAligner is freely available at www.ling.su.se/DaLi/downloads/treealigner/index.htm

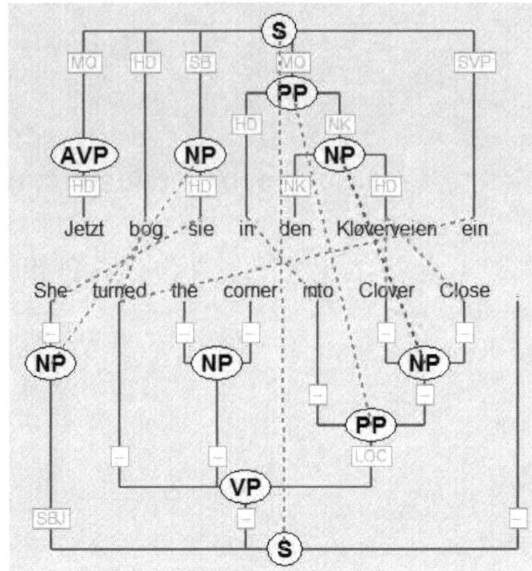

Figure 1: Tree pair German-English in the TreeAligner.

The TreeAligner operates on an alignment file in an XML format developed by us. This file describes the alignments between two TIGER-XML treebanks (specified in the alignment file) holding the trees from language one and language two respectively. For example the alignment between two nodes is represented as:

```
<align type="exact">
  <node id="s13_505" tb_id="DE"/>
  <node id="s14_506" tb_id="EN"/>
</align>
```

This says that node 505 in sentence 13 of the German treebank is aligned with node 506 in sentence 14 of the English treebank. The node identifiers refer to the ids in the TIGER-XML treebanks. The alignment is given the label “exact” if the corresponding token sequences are equivalent in meaning.

The alignment file might initially be empty when we want to start manual alignment from scratch, or it might contain automatically computed alignments for correction. The TreeAligner displays tree pairs with the trees in mirror orientation (one top-up and one top-down). See figure 1 for an example. The trees are displayed with node labels and edge labels. The PoS labels are omitted in the display since they are not relevant for the alignment task.[4]

[4]During the development of our treebanks we discovered

Each alignment is displayed as a dotted line between two nodes (or words) across two trees. Clicking on a node (or a word) in one tree and dragging the mouse pointer to a node (or a word) in the other tree inserts an alignment line. Currently the TreeAligner supports two types of alignment lines (displayed in different colors) which are used to indicate exact translation correspondence vs. approximate translation correspondence. However, our experiments indicate that eventually more alignment types will be needed to precisely represent different translation differences. The alignment type attribute can be used to describe many different levels or types of alignment. These distinctions could prove useful when exploiting the aligned treebanks for Machine Translation and other applications.

Often one tree needs to be aligned to two (or more) trees in the other language. The TreeAligner therefore provides the option to browse the trees independently. For instance, if we have aligned only a part of a tree T_i from language one to tree T_k of language two, we may scroll to tree T_{k+1} of language two in order to align the remaining parts of T_i. Special [Forward] and [Back] buttons are provided to browse through the multiple-aligned trees systematically.

The TreeAligner is designed as a stand-alone tool (i.e. it is not prepared for collaborative annotation). It stores every alignment in an XML file (in the format described above) as soon as the user moves to a new tree pair.

The TreeAligner was implemented in Python by Joakim Lundborg. Python has become popular in Language Technology in recent years. It is a high level programming language that allows different programming styles including a good support for object-oriented programming. It is an interpreted language that uses a dynamic type system. It is therefore mostly compared to its siblings Perl, Tcl and Ruby, even though the influence of other languages like Smalltalk and Haskell are probably stronger on a conceptual level.

One of Python's strengths is the ease with which a programmer can manipulate primitive data types like strings or numbers. Python's string objects are an excellent match to the needs of linguistic processing. In addition to the primitive data types, Python also features higher level data types: lists, tuples and dictionaries. The combination of these built-in data types, the vast standard library and the simple and straightforward syntax make Python the perfect tool for a wide range of scientific programming.

The TreeAligner served us well for creating the alignments, but it soon became evident that we needed suitable tools to explore and exploit the aligned data. The most apparent need was a search module for aligned trees. We decided to design our search module after TIGER-Search.

3 TIGER-Search

TIGER-Search is a powerful treebank query tool developed at the University of Stuttgart by Wolfgang Lezius (cf. (König and Lezius, 2002; Lezius, 2002). Its query language allows for feature-value descriptions of syntax graphs. It is similar in expressiveness to tgrep (Rohde, 2005) but it comes with graphical output and highlighting of the syntax trees plus nice frequency tables for objects identified in the query. TIGER-Search has been implemented in Java and is freely available for research purposes. Because of its clearly defined input format (TIGER-XML) and its powerful query language, it has become the corpus query system of choice for many linguists.

The TIGER-Search query language is based on feature-value descriptions of all linguistic objects (tokens and constituents), dominance, precedence and sibling relations in the tree, graph predicates (e.g. with respect to token arity and continuity), variables for referencing objects, regular expressions over values for varying the query precision, and queries over secondary edges (which constitute a secondary graph level).

A complex query might look like in the following example (with > denoting direct dominance, $>*$ denoting general dominance, the dot denoting immediate precedence, and the # symbol introducing variables). This query is meant to find instances of two ambiguously located PPs that are both attached to the first noun (as illustrated by the example tree in figure 2).

that the TreeAligner is also useful for displaying different versions of the same treebank (e.g. before and after corrections, or manually vs. automatically parsed). Therefore we plan to add a tree-diff module which will highlight the differences between a pair of trees over the same token sequence.

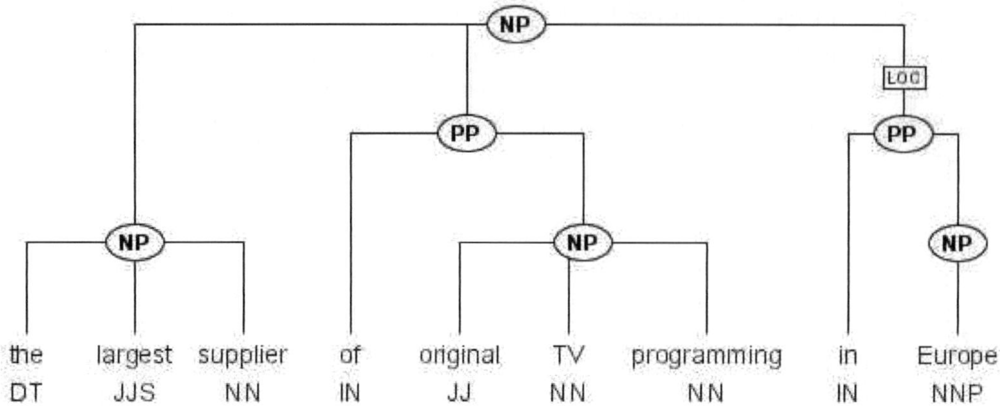

Figure 2: Noun phrase tree from the Penn Treebank

```
#np:[cat="NP"] >* #n1:[pos="NN"]&
#np  >  #pp1:[cat="PP"] &
#n1  .  #pp1 &
#pp1 >* #n2:[pos="NN"] &
#np  >  #pp2:[cat="PP"] &
#n2  .  #pp2
```

This query says: Search for an NP (call it #np) that dominates a noun #n1 (line 1) and two PPs (lines 2 and 5). #pp1 must follow immediately after the noun #n1 (line 3), and #pp2 must follow immediately after the noun within the #pp1 (lines 4 and 6).

TIGER-Search handles such queries efficiently based on a intricate indexing scheme. It finds all matching instances in a given treebank and allows to browse (and to export) the resulting trees. The matching objects in the resulting trees are highlighted.

TIGER-Search is limited in that it only allows manually entered queries (rather than processing a batch of queries from a file). Furthermore it is limited with regard to negation. The TIGER-Search query language includes a negation operator but this is of limited usefulness. The reason is that "For the sake of computational simplicity and tractability, the universal quantifier is (currently) not part of the TIGER language" (quoted from the TIGER-Search online help manual). This means that typical negated queries such as "Find all VPs which do **not** contain any NP" are not possible.

And clearly TIGER-Search is a tool for querying monolingual treebanks and thus needed to be extended for our purposes, i.e. querying parallel treebanks.

4 The TreeAligner Search Module

(Merz and Volk, 2005) had listed the requirements for a parallel treebank search tool. Based on these we have now re-implemented TIGER-Search for parallel treebanks and integrated it into the TreeAligner.

The idea is to allow the power of TIGER-Search queries on both treebanks plus additional alignment constraints. For example, a typical query could ask for a verb phrase VP dominating a prepositional phrase PP in treebank one. This query can be combined with the constraint that the VP in treebank one is aligned to a sentence S in treebank two which also dominates a PP. Such a query would be expressed in 3 lines as:

```
#t1:[cat="VP"] > [cat="PP"]
#t2:[cat="S"] > [cat="PP"]
#t1 * #t2
```

These three lines are entered into three separate input fields in the user interface (cf. the three input fields in the bottom left in figure 3). Lines 1 and 2 contain the queries over the monolingual treebanks 1 and 2. And line 3 contains the alignment constraint. Note that the treebank queries 1 and 2 closely follow the TIGER-Search syntax. In particular they allow the binding of variables (marked with #) to specific linguistic objects in the query. And these variables are used in the alignment constraint in line 3. The reuse of the variables is the cru-

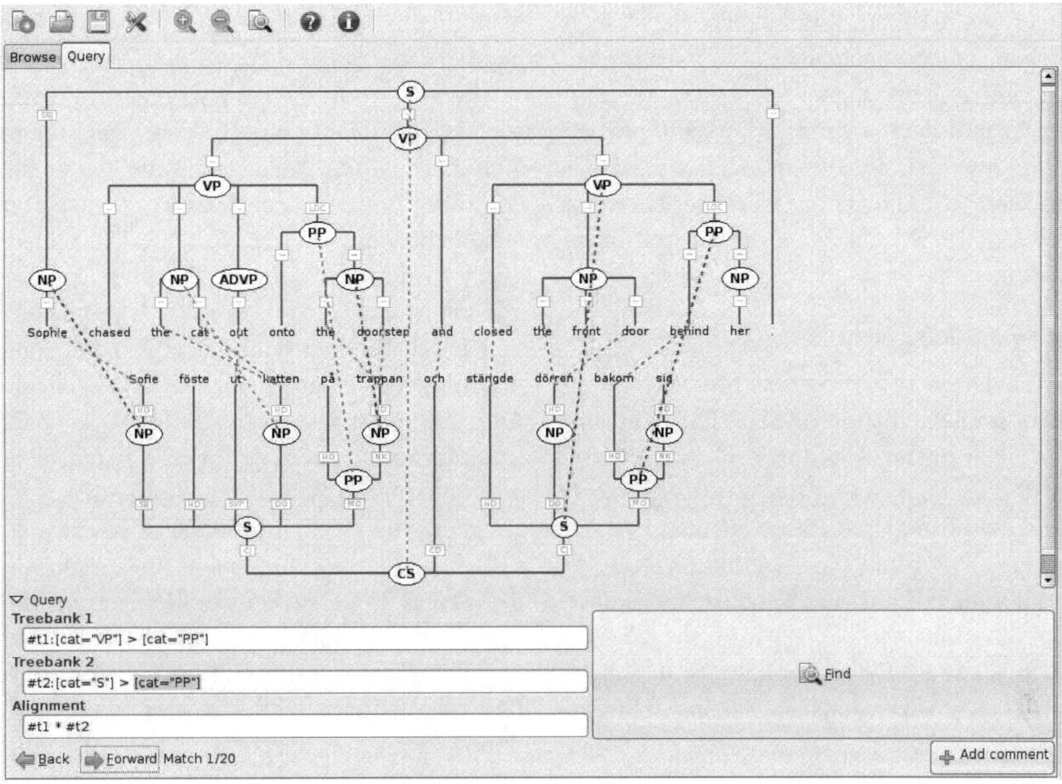

Figure 3: Screenshot of the TreeAligner with the Search Module.

cial idea which enabled a clear design of the Search Module by keeping the alignment constraints separate from the queries over the two treebanks.

So the above query will find the tree pair in figure 3 because it matches the alignment between the English VP *closed the front door behind her* and the elliptical Swedish sentence *stängde dörren bakom sig* (which lacks the subject, but is still annotated as S).

The Search Module has recently been added to the TreeAligner. It is intended to be used with any parallel treebank where the monolingual treebanks can be converted into TIGER-XML and where the alignment information can be converted to the SMULTRON alignment format. The separation of these parts makes it possible to query each treebank separately as well. The system is divided into a monolingual query facility and an alignment query facility that makes use of the former to perform its job. This design choice made it necessary to (re)implement the following in Python:

1. TIGER-Search
2. The alignment query facility
3. The integration into the TreeAligner

The choice of reimplementing TIGER-Search in Python influenced the feature set. Even though the implementation of TIGER-Search is well documented (in (Lezius, 2002) among others) and the source codes are available under an Open Source license, this is still a non-trivial task. In order to narrow down the amount of work in a first phase, it was decided to restrict the implementation to a subset of the TIGER-Search query language. The implementation of negation within the queries was therefore postponed (with the exception of negations used in regular expressions within a feature definition). As discussed in section 3, negations are limited even in TIGER-Search, and we plan to implement a comprehensive support for negation at a later stage. The code already has hooks for this extension.

The language for the alignment constraints is kept simple as well. The user can specify that two linguistic objects must be aligned (with exact alignment or approximate alignment). And such constraints can be combined with *AND* statements into more complex constraints. Currently, we cannot foresee exactly how a parallel treebank will be queried. We have therefore focused on a clear design of the Search Module rather than overloading it with features. This will facilitate the integration of more features as they are requested by users.

4.1 Implementation Details

The implementation of the Search Module started as a close re-implementation of the TIGER-Search system described in (Lezius, 2002). During the development it became apparent that some of Lezius' design choices did not translate well into Python. Moreover, the advancements concerning speed and memory in computer hardware in recent years have made it possible for us to deviate from the original design towards a more Python-oriented and simpler code with less considerations for resource limitations (see (Mettler, 2007)).

This code base can be divided into four types of functionality classes: helper, index, parser and processor. The **helper** classes are the smallest pieces of code and perform trivial tasks like sorting or set operations and are called from the other classes. The query system as such consists of the index, the parsers and processors. The **parsers** are used to transform a string such as the TIGER-XML files or the queries into objects. These parse objects are then used to create the index or are passed to a processor object to get the results of a query.

The **index** consists of four classes. The Corpus class governs the three others which are used to store the data for the graphs and the attribute value register that is defined in the TIGER-XML head. Each graph is contained within its own object. The attribute value register consists of one object that governs a range of attribute value lookup tables. There are three parser classes and one parser method. Each of these parser classes handles a different input. The first parses TIGER-XML, the second parses the node definitions within a TIGER-Search query (contained within the square brackets), and the third parser class uses them to parse complete TIGER-Search queries. As the syntax for the alignment constraints is simple, this was done within a method of the parallel query processor class. This is likely to change with the increasing feature set for parallel queries.

The last part of the system consists of two **processor** classes. The first is the class used for monolingual queries. On instantiation the class takes an index object and a query parser object as arguments. When the object's query method is called with a query string, the object lets the query parser produce a parse object from the string. The parse object is then processed to produce an object that contains the matching graph parts using the index. The processor for parallel queries works similarly. On instantiation a monolingual processor for each language is passed as arguments to the object. When the query method is called, the parallel processor objects gets the results from the monolingual processors first and then parses and processes the parallel query using the results from the monolingual processing step. The result of a query is a list with the two aligned sentence IDs.

4.2 Evaluation of the Search Module

The TreeAligner Search module was first tested by running a set of representative queries over a part of our English-German parallel treebank (500 tree pairs). This test set included:

- dominance relations (direct dominance, general dominance, labeled dominance, right and left corner dominance)
- precedence relations (immediate precedence, general precedence, sibling precedence, precedence distance)
- queries over secondary edges
- graph predicates (root, arity, tokenarity)

For the monolingual queries we checked whether the number of hits in our TreeAligner Search corresponded to the number of hits in TIGER-Search. This worked nicely. For bilingual queries we manually checked the correctness of the results.

We also tested the system for robustness and scalability. Since we currently do not have a large parallel treebank, we took the German NEGRA treebank with 10,000 trees and used it for both language one and language two in our TreeAligner. This means we used each tree aligned to a copy of itself as the basic data. This treebank contains around 81,000 nodes. We automatically generated an alignment file that contains each node aligned to its copy in the corresponding tree. This means we were using an alignment file with 81,000 alignments.

Unfortunately the time for loading this data set into the TreeAligner was prohibitively long (while loading a monolingual treebank with 10,000 trees into TIGER-Search takes less than a minute for indexing it once, plus few seconds for loading the index before starting the searches). Obviously, we need to improve the scalability of the TreeAligner.

When we redid the experiment with 1000 trees from the NEGRA treebank (with 35,756 alignments), it worked fine. Loading takes about one minute, and queries like the one given in the example above are processed in less than one minute. The system is currently not optimized for speed. It is a proof-of-concept system to demonstrate that the (monolingual) TIGER-Search query language can be elegantly extended with alignment constraints for parallel treebank searches.

Lately we have tested the use of serialized indexes. We have observed that they are much faster, but that the speed-up factor decreases with increasing file size. It seems that eventually we will have to switch to a custom binary format as was done in TIGER-Search, if we want to provide a smooth work experience with parallel treebanks of 10,000 and more trees.

5 Conclusions

We have built a TreeAligner for displaying and searching parallel aligned trees. The tool is written in Python and freely available. In particular it allows to align nodes and words across languages by drawing lines. We distinguish between exact and approximate alignment types. The search module which was recently added supports queries over both treebanks in combination with alignment constraints. The query language follows TIGER-Search (though negation is not included yet). The alignment constraints use the variables bound to linguistic objects in the monolingual queries.

In the future we will improve the TreeAligner in three directions: features, usability and evaluation. The feature part consists of providing full support for TIGER-Search queries (in particular the implementation of negation) and improving the parallel query facilities (with a variety of alignment constraints).

Moreover we are in the process of extending the TreeAligner to handling dependency trees. The TreeAligner currently imports only treebanks in TIGER-XML. This format is well suited for representing phrase structure trees but less for dependency trees. We will therefore extend the support to appropriate XML import formats.

Usability is the broadest group and aims at improvements like creating an installation routine for all operating systems, improving speed and making sure that UTF8 support works properly.

Finally, more systematic evaluations are needed. We plan to enlarge our standard set of queries to cover all possible combinations. This query set could then be used to test the speed and performance of our system (and for the comparison with other systems). We hope that the TreeAligner will gain a broad user community which will help to drive improvements in alignment and querying.

References

Lars Ahrenberg, Magnus Merkel, and Mikael Andersson. 2002. A system for incremental and interactive word linking. In *Proc. of LREC-2002*, pages 485–490, Las Palmas.

Lars Ahrenberg. 2007. LinES: An English-Swedish parallel treebank. In *Proc. of Nodalida*, Tartu.

Martin Cmejrek, Jan Curín, and Jirí Havelka. 2005. Prague Czech-English dependency treebank. Resource for structure-based MT. In *Proceedings of EAMT 10th Annual Conference*, Budapest.

Silvia Hansen-Schirra, Stella Neumann, and Mihaela Vela. 2006. Multi-dimensional annotation and alignment in an English-German translation corpus. In *Proceedings of the EACL Workshop on Multidimensional Markup in Natural Language Processing (NLPXML-2006)*, pages 35– 42, Trento.

Esther König and Wolfgang Lezius. 2002. The TIGER language - a description language for syntax graphs. Part 1: User's guidelines. Technical report.

Wolfgang Lezius. 2002. *Ein Suchwerkzeug für syntaktisch annotierte Textkorpora*. Ph.D. thesis, IMS, University of Stuttgart, December. Arbeitspapiere des

Instituts für Maschinelle Sprachverarbeitung (AIMS), volume 8, number 4.

Charlotte Merz and Martin Volk. 2005. Requirements for a parallel treebank search tool. In *Proceedings of GLDV-Conference*, Sprache, Sprechen und Computer / Computer Studies in Language and Speech, Bonn, March. Peter Lang Verlag.

Maël Mettler. 2007. Parallel treebank search - the implementation of the Stockholm TreeAligner search. C-uppsats, Stockholm University, March.

Lars Nygaard and Janne Bondi Johannesen. 2004. SearchTree - a user-friendly treebank search interface. In *Proc. of 3rd Workshop on Treebanks and Linguistic Theories*, pages 183–189, Tübingen, December.

Ulrik Petersen. 2006. Querying both parallel and treebank corpora: Evaluation of a corpus query system. In *Proc. of LREC*, Genua.

Douglas L. T. Rohde, 2005. *TGrep2 User Manual*. MIT. Available from http://tedlab.mit.edu/ ~dr/Tgrep2/.

Yvonne Samuelsson and Martin Volk. 2006. Phrase alignment in parallel treebanks. In Jan Hajic and Joakim Nivre, editors, *Proc. of the Fifth Workshop on Treebanks and Linguistic Theories*, pages 91–102, Prague, December.

Yvonne Samuelsson and Martin Volk. 2007. Alignment tools for parallel treebanks. In *Proceedings of GLDV Frühjahrstagung 2007*.

Noah A. Smith and Michael E. Jahr. 2000. Cairo: An alignment visualization tool. In *Proc. of LREC-2000*, Athens.

Martin Volk, Sofia Gustafson-Capková, Joakim Lundborg, Torsten Marek, Yvonne Samuelsson, and Frida Tidström. 2006. XML-based phrase alignment in parallel treebanks. In *Proc. of EACL Workshop on Multi-dimensional Markup in Natural Language Processing*, Trento, April.

Annotating Expressions of Appraisal in English

Jonathon Read, David Hope and John Carroll
Department of Informatics
University of Sussex
United Kingdom
{j.l.read,drh21,j.a.carroll}@sussex.ac.uk

Abstract

The Appraisal framework is a theory of the language of evaluation, developed within the tradition of systemic functional linguistics. The framework describes a taxonomy of the types of language used to convey evaluation and position oneself with respect to the evaluations of other people. Accurate automatic recognition of these types of language can inform an analysis of document sentiment. This paper describes the preparation of test data for algorithms for automatic Appraisal analysis. The difficulty of the task is assessed by way of an inter-annotator agreement study, based on measures analogous to those used in the MUC-7 evaluation.

1 Introduction

The Appraisal framework (Martin and White, 2005) describes a taxonomy of the language employed in communicating evaluation, explaining how users of English convey attitude (emotion, judgement of people and appreciation of objects), engagement (assessment of the evaluations of other people) and how writers may modify the strength of their attitude/engagement. Accurate automatic analysis of these aspects of language will augment existing research in the fields of sentiment (Pang et al., 2002) and subjectivity analysis (Wiebe et al., 2004), but assessing the usefulness of analysis algorithms leveraging the Appraisal framework will require test data.

At present there are no machine-readable Appraisal-annotated texts publicly available. Real-world instances of Appraisal in use are limited to example extracts that demonstrate the theory, coming from a wide variety of genres as disparate as news reporting (White, 2002; Martin, 2004) and poetry (Martin and White, 2005). These examples, while useful in demonstrating the various aspects of Appraisal, can only be employed in a qualitative analysis and would bring about inconsistencies if analysed collectively — one can expect the writing style to depend upon the genre, resulting in significantly different syntactic constructions and lexical choices.

We therefore need to examine Appraisal across documents in the same genre and investigate patterns within that particular register. This paper discusses the methodology of an Appraisal annotation study and an analysis of the inter-annotator agreement exhibited by two human judges. The output of this study has the additional benefit of bringing a set of machine-readable annotations of Appraisal into the public domain for further research.

This paper is structured as follows. The next section offers an overview of the Appraisal framework. Section 3 discusses the methodology adopted for the annotation study. Section 4 discusses the measures employed to assess inter-annotator agreement and reports the results of these measures. Section 5 offers an analysis of cases of systematic disagreement. Other computational work utilising the Appraisal framework is reviewed in Section 6. Section 7 summarises the paper and outlines future work.

2 The linguistic framework of Appraisal

The Appraisal framework (Martin and White, 2005) is a development of work in Systemic Functional

Proceedings of the Linguistic Annotation Workshop, pages 93–100,
Prague, June 2007. ©2007 Association for Computational Linguistics

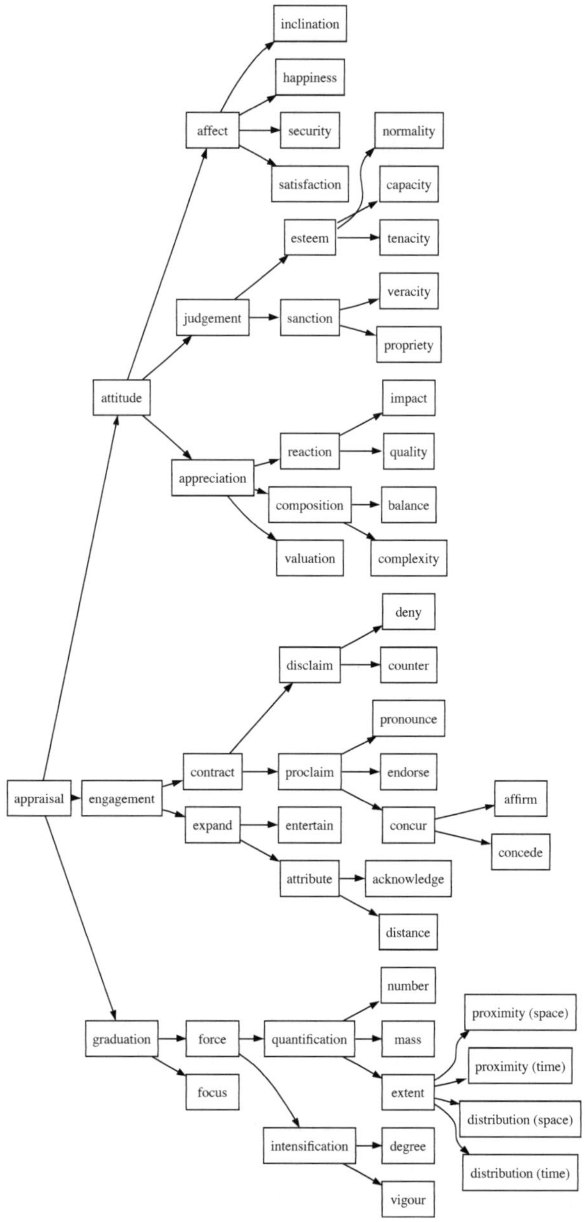

Figure 1: The Appraisal framework.

Linguistics (Halliday, 1994) and is concerned with interpersonal meaning in text—the negotiation of social relationships by communicating emotion, judgement and appreciation. The taxonomy described by the Appraisal framework is depicted in Figure 1.

Appraisal consists of three subsystems that operate in parallel: **attitude** looks at how one expresses private state (Quirk et al., 1985) (one's emotion and opinions); **engagement** considers the positioning of oneself with respect to the opinions of others and **graduation** investigates how the use of language functions to amplify or diminish the attitude and engagement conveyed by a text.

2.1 Attitude: emotion, ethics and aesthetics

The Attitude sub-system describes three areas of private state: emotion, ethics and aesthetics. An attitude is further qualified by its polarity (*positive* or *negative*). Affect identifies feelings—author's emotions as represented by their text. Judgement deals with authors' attitude towards the behaviour of people; how authors applaud or reproach the actions of others. Appreciation considers the evaluation of things—both man-made and natural phenomena.

2.2 Engagement: appraisals of appraisals

Through engagement, Martin and White (2005) deal with the linguistic constructions by which authors construe their point of view and the resources used to adopt stances towards the opinions of other people. The theory of engagement follows Stubbs (1996) in that it assumes that all utterances convey point of view and Bakhtin (1981) in supposing that all utterances occur in a miscellany of other utterances on the same motif, and that they carry both implicit and explicit responses to one another. In other words, all text is inherently dialogistic as it encodes authors' reactions to their experiences (including previous interaction with other writers). Engagement can be both retrospective (that is, an author will acknowledge and agree or disagree with the stances of others who have previously appraised a subject), and prospective (one may anticipate the responses of an intended audience and include counter-responses in the original text).

2.3 Graduation: strength of evaluations

Martin and White (2005) consider the resources by which writers alter the strength of their evaluation as a system of graduation. Graduation is a general property of both attitude and engagement. In attitude it enables authors to convey greater or lesser degrees of positivity or negativity, while graduation of engagements scales authors' conviction in their utterance.

Graduation is divided into two subsystems. Force alters appraisal propositions in terms of its intensity, quantity or temporality, or by means of spatial metaphor. Focus considers the resolution of semantic categories, for example:

They play *real* jazz.
They play jazz, *sort of.*

In real terms a musician either plays jazz or they do not, but these examples demonstrate how authors blur the lines of semantic sets and how binary relationships can be turned into scalar ones.

3 Annotation methodology

The corpus used in this study consists of unedited book reviews. Book reviews are good candidates for this study as, while they are likely to contain similar language by virtue of being from the same genre of writing, we can also expect examples of Appraisal's many classes (for example, the emotion attributed to the characters in reviews of novels, judgements of authors' competence and character, appreciation of the qualities of books and engagement with the propositions put forth by the authors under review).

The articles were taken from the web sites of four British newspapers (The Guardian, The Independent, The Telegraph and The Times) on two different dates—31 July 2006 and 11 September 2006. Each review is attributed to a unique author. The corpus is comprised of 38 documents, containing a total of 36,997 tokens in 1,245 sentences.

Two human annotators, d and j, participated in this study, assigning tags independently. The annotators were well-versed in the Appraisal framework, having studied the latest literature. The judges were asked to annotate appraisal-bearing terms with the appraisal type presumed to be intended by the author of the text. They were asked to highlight each example of appraisal and specify the type of attitude, engagement or graduation present. They also assigned a *polarity* (positive or negative) to attitudinal items and a *scaling* (up or down) to graduating items, employing a custom-developed software tool to annotate the documents.

Four alternative annotation strategies were considered. One approach is to allow only a single token per annotation. However, this is too simplistic for an Appraisal annotation study—a unit of Appraisal is frequently larger than a single token. Consider the following examples:

(1)
The design was *deceptively*–VERACITY *simple*–COMPLEXITY. (∗)

(2)
The design was *deceptively simple*–COMPLEXITY.

Example 1 demonstrates that a single-token approach is inappropriate as it ascribes a judgement of someone's honesty, whereas Example 2 indicates the correct analysis—the sentence is an appreciation of the simplicity of the "design". This example shows how it is necessary to annotate larger units of appraisal-bearing language.

Including more tokens, however, increases the complexity of the annotation task, and reduces the likelihood of agreement between the judges, as the annotated tokens of one judge may be a subset of, or overlap with, those of another. We therefore experimented with tagging entire sentences in order to constrain the annotators' range of choices. This resulted in its own problems as there is often more than one appraisal in a sentence, for example:

(3)
The design was *deceptively simple*–COMPLEXITY and belied his *ingenuity*–CAPACITY.

An alternative approach is to permit annotators to tag an arbitrary number of contiguous tokens. Arbitrary-length tagging is disadvantageous as the judges will frequently tag units of differing length, but this can be compensated for by relaxing the rules for agreement—for example, by allowing intersecting annotations to match successfully (Wiebe et al., 2005). Bruce and Wiebe (1999) employ another approach, creating units from every non-compound sentence and each conjunct of every compound sentence. This side-steps the problem of ambiguity in appraisal unit length, but will still fail to capture both appraisals demonstrated in the second conjunct of Example 4.

(4)
The design was *deceptively simple*–COMPLEXITY and belied his *remarkable*–NORMALITY *ingenuity*–CAPACITY.

Ultimately in this study, we permitted judges to annotate any number of tokens in order to allow for multiple Appraisal units of differing sizes within sentences. Annotation was carried out over two rounds, punctuated by an intermediary analysis of

	d	j		d	j		d	j
Inclination	1.26	3.50	Balance	2.64	1.84	Distance	0.69	0.59
Happiness	2.80	2.32	Complexity	2.52	2.74	Number	0.82	2.63
Security	4.31	2.22	Valuation	6.08	9.29	Mass	0.22	1.63
Satisfaction	1.67	2.32	Deny	3.05	3.67	Proximity (Space)	0.09	0.14
Normality	8.00	4.44	Counter	4.79	3.78	Proximity (Time)	0.03	0.55
Capacity	11.46	9.63	Pronounce	3.84	1.21	Distribution (Space)	0.41	1.39
Tenacity	3.72	4.44	Endorse	2.05	1.49	Distribution (Time)	0.82	2.56
Veracity	3.15	2.01	Affirm	0.54	1.14	Degree	4.38	5.72
Propriety	13.32	12.61	Concede	0.38	0.03	Vigour	0.60	0.45
Impact	6.11	4.23	Entertain	2.27	2.43	Focus	3.02	2.29
Quality	2.55	3.40	Acknowledge	2.42	3.33			

Table 1: The distribution of the Appraisal types selected by each annotator (%).

	d	j
Documents	115.74	77.21
Sentences	3.65	2.43
Words	0.12	0.08

Table 2: The density of annotations relative to the number of documents, sentences and words.

agreement and disagreement between the two annotators. The judges discussed examples of the most common types of disagreement in an attempt to acquire a common understanding for the second round, but annotations from the first round were left unaltered.

Following the methodology described above, d made 3,176 annotations whilst j made 2,886 annotations. The distribution of the Appraisal types ascribed is shown in Table 1, while Table 2 details the density of annotations in documents, sentences and words.

4 Measuring inter-annotator agreement

The study of inter-annotator agreement begins by considering the level of agreement exhibited by the annotators in deciding which tokens are representative of Appraisal, irrespective of the type. As discussed, this is problematic as judges are liable to choose different length token spans when marking up what is essentially the same appraisal, as demonstrated by Example 5.

(5)
[d] It is tempting to point to the bombs in London and elsewhere, to the *hideous mess*–QUALITY in Iraq, to recent victories of the Islamists, to the *violent and polarised rhetoric*–PROPRIETY and answer yes.

[j] It is tempting to point to the bombs in London and elsewhere, to the *hideous*–QUALITY *mess*–BALANCE in Iraq, to recent victories of Islamists, to the *violent*–PROPRIETY and *polarised*–PROPRIETY rhetoric and answer yes.

Wiebe et al. (2005), who faced this problem when annotating expressions of opinion under their own framework, accept that it is necessary to consider the validity of all judges' interpretations and therefore consider intersecting annotations (such as "hideous" and "hideous mess") to be matches. The same relaxation of constraints is employed in this study.

Tasks with a known number of annotative units can be analysed with measures of agreement such as Cohen's κ Coefficient (1960), but the judges' freedom in this task prohibits meaningful application of this measure. For example, consider how word sense annotators are obliged to choose from a limited fixed set of senses for each token, whereas judges annotating Appraisal are free to select one of thirty-two classes for any contiguous substring of any length within each document; there are $16\,(n^2 - n)$ possible choices in a document of n tokens (approximately 6.5×10^8 possibilities in this corpus).

A wide range of evaluation metrics have been employed by the Message Understanding Conferences (MUCs). The MUC-7 tasks included extraction of named entities, equivalence classes, attributes, facts and events (Chinchor, 1998). The participating systems were evaluated using a variety of related measures, defined in Table 3. These tasks are similar to Appraisal annotation in that the units are formed of an arbitrary number of contiguous tokens.

In this study the agreement exhibited by an annotator a is evaluated as a pair-wise comparison against the other annotator b. Annotator b provides

COR	Number correct	
INC	Number incorrect	
MIS	Number missing	
SPU	Number spurious	
POS	Number possible	= COR + INC + MIS
ACT	Number actual	= COR + INC + SPU
FSC	F-score	= (2 × REC × PRE) / (REC + PRE)
REC	Precision	= COR/POS
PRE	Recall	= COR/ACT
SUB	Substitution	= INC/ (COR + INC)
ERR	Error per response	= (INC + SPU + MIS) / (COR + INC + SPU + MIS)
UND	Under-generation	= MIS/POS
OVG	Over-generation	= SPU/ACT

Table 3: MUC-7 score definitions (Chinchor 1998).

	FSC	**REC**	**PRE**	**ERR**	**UND**	**OVG**
d	0.682	0.706	0.660	0.482	0.294	0.340
j	0.715	0.667	0.770	0.444	0.333	0.230
$\bar{x}$	0.698	0.686	0.711	0.462	0.312	0.274

Table 4: MUC-7 test scores, evaluating the agreement in text anchors selected by the annotators. $\bar{x}$ denotes the average value, calculated using the harmonic mean.

a presumed gold standard for the purposes of evaluating agreement. Note, however, that in this case it does not necessarily follow that REC (a w.r.t. b) = PRE (b w.r.t. a). Consider that a may tend to make one-word annotations whilst b prefers to annotate phrases; the set of a's annotations will contain multiple matches for some of the phrases annotated by b (refer to Example 5, for instance). The 'number correct' will differ for each annotator in the pair under evaluation.

Table 4 lists the values for the MUC-7 measures applied to the text spans selected by the annotators. Annotator d is inclined to identify text as Appraisal more frequently than annotator j. This results in higher recall for d, but with lower precision. Naturally, the opposite observation can be made about annotator j. Both annotators exhibit a high error rate at 48.2% and 44.4% for d and j respectively. The substitution rate is not listed as there are no classes to substitute when considering only text anchor agreement. The second round of annotation achieved slightly higher agreement (the mean F-score increased by 0.033).

	FSC	**REC**	**PRE**	**SUB**	**ERR**
0	0.698	0.686	0.711	0.000	0.462
1	0.635	0.624	0.647	0.090	0.511
2	0.528	0.518	0.538	0.244	0.594
3	0.448	0.441	0.457	0.357	0.655
4	0.396	0.388	0.403	0.433	0.696
5	0.395	0.388	0.403	0.433	0.696

Table 5: Harmonic means of the MUC-7 test scores evaluating the agreement in text anchors and Appraisal classes selected by the annotators, at each level of hierarchical abstraction.

Having considered the annotators' agreement with respect to text anchors, we go on to analyse the agreement exhibited by the annotators with respect to the types of Appraisal assigned to the text anchors. The Appraisal framework is a hierarchical system—a tree with leaves corresponding to the annotation types chosen by the judges. When investigating agreement in Appraisal type, the following measures include not just the leaf nodes but also their parent types, collapsing the nodes into increasingly abstract representations. For example *happiness* is a kind of *affect*, which is a kind of *attitude*, which is a kind of *appraisal*. These relationships are depicted in full in Figure 2. Note that in the following measurements of inter-annotator agreement leaf nodes are included in subsequent levels (for example, *focus* is a leaf node at level 2, but is also considered to be a member of levels 3, 4 and 5).

Table 5 shows the harmonic means of the MUC-7 measures of the annotators' agreement at each of the levels depicted in Figure 2. As one might expect, the agreement steadily drops as the classes become more concrete—classes become more specific and more numerous so the complexity of the task increases.

Table 5 also lists the average rate of substitutions as the annotation task's complexity increases, showing that the annotators were able to fairly easily distinguish between instances of the three subsystems of Appraisal (Attitude, Engagement and Graduation) as the substitution rate at level 1 is low (only 9%). As the number of possible classes increases annotators are more likely to confuse appraisal types, with disagreement occurring on approximately 44% of annotations at level 5. The second round of annotations resulted in slightly improved agreement at

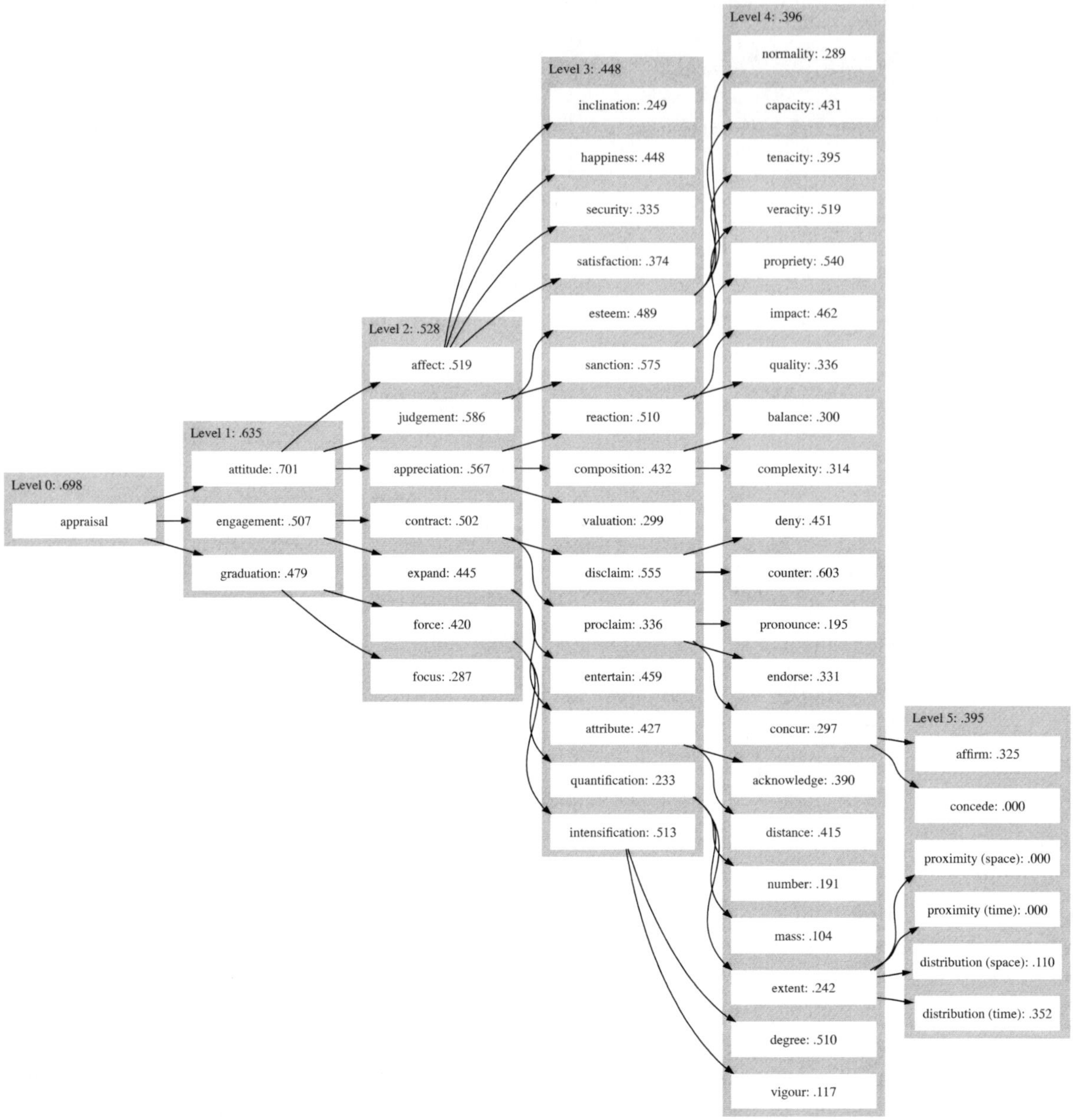

Figure 2: The Appraisal framework with hierarchical levels highlighted. Appraisal classes and levels are accompanied by the harmonic mean of the F-scores of the annotators for that class/level.

each level of abstraction (the mean F-score increased by 0.051 at the most abstract level).

Of course, some Appraisal classes are easier to identify than others. Figure 2 summarises the agreement for each node in the Appraisal hierarchy with the harmonic mean of the F-scores of the annotators for each class. Typically, the attitude annotations are easiest to identify, whereas the other subsystems of engagement and graduation tend to be more difficult.

The Proximity children of Extent exhibited no agreement whatsoever. This seems to have arisen from the differences in the judges' interpretations of proximity. In the case of Proximity (Space), for example, one judge annotated words that function to modify the spatial distance of other concepts (e.g. *near*), whereas the other selected words placing concepts at a specific location (e.g. *homegrown, local*). This confusion between modifying words and specific locations also accounts for the low agreement in the Distribution (Space) type.

The measures show that it is also difficult to achieve a consensus on what qualifies as engagements of the Pronounce type. Both annotators select expressions that assert the irrefutability of a proposition (e.g. *certainly* or *in fact* or *it has to be said*). Judge d, however, tends to perceive pronouncement as occurring wherever the author makes an assertion (e.g. *this is* or *there will be*). Judge j seems to require that the assertion carry a degree of emphasis to include a term in the Pronounce class.

The low agreement of the Mass graduations can also be explained in this way, as both d and j select strong expressions relating to size (e.g. *massive* or *scant*). Annotator j found additional but weaker terms like *largely* or *slightly*.

The Pronounce and Mass classes provide typical examples of the disagreement exhibited by the annotators. It is not that the judges have wildly different understandings of the system, but rather they disagree in the bounds of a class—one annotator may require a greater degree of strength of a term to warrant its inclusion in a class.

Contingency tables (not depicted due to space constraints) reveal some interesting tendencies for confusion between the two annotators. Approximately 33% of d's annotations of Proximity (Space) were ascribed as Capacity by j. The high percentage is due to the rarity of annotations of Proximity (Space), but the confusion comes from differing units of Appraisal, as shown in Example 6.

(6)
[d] But at key points in this story, one gets the feeling that the essential factors are operating *just outside*–PROXIMITY (SPACE) *James's field of vision*–CAPACITY.

[j] But at key points in this story, one gets the feeling that the essential factors are operating just *outside James's field of vision*–CAPACITY.

Another interesting case of frequent confusion is the pair of Satisfaction and Propriety. Though not closely related in the Attitude subsystem, j chooses Propriety for 21% of d's annotations of Satisfaction. The confusion is typified by Example 7, where it is apparent that there is disagreement in terms of *who* is being appraised.

(7)
[d] Like him, Vermeer – or so he chose to believe – was an artist *neglected*–SATISFACTION and *wronged*–SATISFACTION by critics and who had died an almost unknown.

[j] Like him, Vermeer – or so he chose to believe – was an artist *neglected and wronged*–PROPRIETY by critics and who had died an almost unknown.

Annotator d believes that the author is communicating the artist's dissatisfaction with the way he is treated by critics, whereas j believes that the critics are being reproached for their treatment of the artist. This highlights a problem with the coding scheme, which simplifies the task by assuming only one type of Appraisal is conveyed by each unit.

5 Related work

Taboada and Grieve (2004) initiated computational experimentation with the Appraisal framework, assigning adjectives into one of the three broad attitude classes. The authors apply SO-PMI-IR (Turney, 2002) to extract and determine the polarity of adjectives. They then use a variant of SO-PMI-IR to determine a 'potential' value for affect, judgement and appreciation, calculating the mutual information between the adjective and three pronoun-copular pairs: *I was* (affect); *he was* (judgement) and *it was* (appreciation). While the pairs seem compelling markers of the respective attitude types, they incorrectly assume that appraisals of affect are limited to the first person whilst judgements are made only of the third person. We can expect a high degree of overlap between the sets of documents retrieved by queries formed using these pairs (e.g. *I was a happy* $\langle X \rangle$; *he was a happy* $\langle X \rangle$; *It was a happy* $\langle X \rangle$).

Whitelaw et al. (2005) use the Appraisal framework to specify frames of sentiment. These "Appraisal Groups" are derived from aspects of Attitude and Graduation:

Attitude:	affect | judgement | appreciation
Orientation	positive | negative
Force:	low | neutral | high
Focus:	low | neutral | high
Polarity:	marked | unmarked

Their process begins with a semi-automatically constructed lexicon of these Appraisal groups, built using example terms from Martin and White (2005) as seeds into WordNet synsets. The frames supplement bag of words-based machine learning techniques for sentiment analysis and they achieve minor improvements over unigram features.

6 Summary

This paper has discussed the methodology of an exercise annotating book reviews according to the Appraisal framework, a functional linguistic theory of evaluation in English. The agreement exhibited by two human judges was measured by analogy with the evaluation employed for the MUC-7 shared tasks (Chinchor, 1998).

The agreement varied greatly depending on the level of abstraction in the Appraisal hierarchy (a mean F-score of 0.698 at the most abstract level through to 0.395 at the most concrete level). The agreement also depended on the type being annotated—there was more agreement evident for types of attitude compared to types of engagement or graduation.

The exercise is the first step in an ongoing study of approaches for the automatic analysis of expressions of Appraisal. The primary output of this work is a corpus of book reviews independently annotated with Appraisal types by two coders. Agreement was in general low, but if one assumes that the intersection of both sets of annotations contains reliable examples, this leaves 2,223 usable annotations.

Future work will employ these annotations to evaluate algorithms for the analysis of Appraisal, and investigate the usefulness of the Appraisal framework when in the computational analysis of document sentiment and subjectivity.

Acknowledgments

We would like to thank Bill Keller for advice when designing the annotation methodology. The work of the first author is supported by a UK EPSRC studentship.

References

M. M. Bakhtin. 1981. *The Dialogic Imagination*. University of Texas Press, Austin. Translated by C. Emerson & M. Holquist.

Rebecca Bruce and Janyce Wiebe. 1999. Recognizing subjectivity: a case study in manual tagging. *Natural Language Engineering*, 5(1):1–16.

N. Chinchor. 1998. MUC-7 test scores introduction. In *Proceedings of the Seventh Message Understanding Conference*.

Jacob Cohen. 1960. A coefficient of agreement for nominal scales. *Educational and Psychological Measures*, 20:37–46.

M. A. K. Halliday. 1994. *An Introduction to Functional Grammar*. Edward Arnold, London.

J. R. Martin and P. R. R. White. 2005. *Language of Evaluation: Appraisal in English*. Palgrave Macmillan.

J. R. Martin. 2004. Mourning: how we get aligned. *Discourse & Society*, 15(2-3):321–344.

Bo Pang, Lillian Lee, and Shivakumar Vaithyanathan. 2002. Thumbs up? Sentiment classification using machine learning techniques. In *Proceedings of the 2002 Conference on Empirical Methods in Natural Language Processing*, Philadelphia, PA, USA.

Randolph Quirk, Sidney Greenbaum, Geoffrey Leech, and Jan Svartvik. 1985. *A Comprehensive Grammar of the English Language*. Longman.

M. Stubbs. 1996. Towards a modal grammar of English: a matter of prolonged fieldwork. In *Text and Corpus Analysis*. Blackwell, Oxford.

Maite Taboada and Jack Grieve. 2004. Analyzing Appraisal automatically. In *Spring Symposium on Exploring Attitude and Affect in Text*. American Association for Artificial Intelligence, Stanford. AAAI Technical Report SS-04-07.

Peter D. Turney. 2002. Thumbs up or thumbs down? Semantic orientation applied to unsupervised classification of reviews. In *Proceedings of the 40th Annual Meeting of the Association for Computational Linguistics*, Philadelphia, PA, USA.

P. R. R. White. 2002. Appraisal — the language of evaluation and stance. In Jef Verschueren, Jan-Ola Östman, Jan Blommaert, and Chris Bulcaen, editors, *Handbook of Pragmatics*, pages 1–27. John Benjamins, Amsterdam.

Casey Whitelaw, Navendu Garg, and Shlomo Argamon. 2005. Using appraisal groups for sentiment analysis. In *Proceedings of the 14th ACM international conference on Information and knowledge management*.

Janyce Wiebe, Theresa Wilson, Rebecca Bruce, Matthew Bell, and Melanie Martin. 2004. Learning subjective language. *Computational linguistics*, 30(3):277–308.

Janyce Wiebe, Theresa Wilson, and Claire Cardie. 2005. Annotating expressions of opinions and emotions in language. *Language Resources and Evaluation*, 39(2-3):165–210.

Active Learning for Part-of-Speech Tagging: Accelerating Corpus Annotation

Eric Ringger*, Peter McClanahan*, Robbie Haertel*, George Busby*, Marc Carmen, James Carroll*, Kevin Seppi*, Deryle Lonsdale****

*Computer Science Department; **Linguistics Department
Brigham Young University
Provo, Utah, USA 84602

Abstract

In the construction of a part-of-speech annotated corpus, we are constrained by a fixed budget. A fully annotated corpus is required, but we can afford to label only a subset. We train a Maximum Entropy Markov Model tagger from a labeled subset and automatically tag the remainder. This paper addresses the question of where to focus our manual tagging efforts in order to deliver an annotation of highest quality. In this context, we find that active learning is always helpful. We focus on Query by Uncertainty (QBU) and Query by Committee (QBC) and report on experiments with several baselines and new variations of QBC and QBU, inspired by weaknesses particular to their use in this application. Experiments on English prose and poetry test these approaches and evaluate their robustness. The results allow us to make recommendations for both types of text and raise questions that will lead to further inquiry.

1 Introduction

We are operating (as many do) on a fixed budget and need annotated text in the context of a larger project. We need a fully annotated corpus but can afford to annotate only a subset. To address our budgetary constraint, we train a model from a manually annotated subset of the corpus and automatically annotate the remainder. At issue is where to focus manual annotation efforts in order to produce a complete annotation of highest possible quality. A follow-up question is whether these techniques work equally well on different types of text.

In particular, we require part-of-speech (POS) annotations. In this paper we employ a state-of-the-art tagger on both prose and poetry, and we examine multiple known and novel active learning (or sampling) techniques in order to determine which work best in this context. We show that the results obtained by a state-of-the-art tagger trained on a small portion of the data selected through active learning can approach the accuracy attained by human annotators and are on par with results from exhaustively trained automatic taggers.

In a study based on English language data presented here, we identify several active learning techniques and make several recommendations that we hope will be portable for application to other text types and to other languages. In section 2 we briefly review the state of the art approach to POS tagging. In section 3, we survey the approaches to active learning employed in this study, including variations on commonly known techniques. Section 4 introduces the experimental regime and presents results and their implications. Section 5 draws conclusions and identifies opportunities for follow-up research.

2 Part of Speech Tagging

Labeling natural language data with part-of-speech tags can be a complicated task, requiring much effort and expense, even for trained annotators. Several efforts, notably the Alembic workbench (Day et al., 1997) and similar tools, have provided interfaces to aid annotators in the process.

Automatic POS tagging of text using probabilistic models is mostly a solved problem but requires supervised learning from substantial amounts of training data. Previous work demonstrates the suitability of Hidden Markov Models for POS tagging (Kupiec, 1992; Brants, 2000). More recent work has achieved state-of-the-art results with Maxi-

Proceedings of the Linguistic Annotation Workshop, pages 101–108,
Prague, June 2007.

mum entropy conditional Markov models (MaxEnt CMMs, or MEMMs for short) (Ratnaparkhi, 1996; Toutanova & Manning, 2000; Toutanova et al., 2003). Part of the success of MEMMs can be attributed to the absence of independence assumptions among predictive features and the resulting ease of feature engineering. To the best of our knowledge, the present work is the first to present results using MEMMs in an active learning framework.

An MEMM is a probabilistic model for sequence labeling. It is a Conditional Markov Model (CMM as illustrated in Figure 1) in which a Maximum Entropy (MaxEnt) classifier is employed to estimate the probability distribution $p(t_i \mid \underline{w}, \underline{t}_{1..i-1}) \approx p_{ME}(t_i \mid w_i, \underline{f_i}, t_{i-1}, t_{i-2})$ over possible labels t_i for each element in the sequence—in our case, for each word w_i in a sentence $\underline{w}$. The MaxEnt model is trained from labeled data and has access to any predefined attributes (represented here by the collection $\underline{f_i}$) of the entire word sequence and to the labels of previous words ($\underline{t}_{1..i-1}$). Our implementation employs an order-two Markov assumption so the classifier has access only to the two previous tags t_{i-1}, t_{i-2}. We refer to the features $(w_i, \underline{f_i}, t_{i-1}, t_{i-2})$ from which the classifier predicts the distribution over tags as "the local trigram context".

A Viterbi decoder is a dynamic programming algorithm that applies the MaxEnt classifier to score multiple competing tag-sequence hypotheses efficiently and to produce the best tag sequence, according to the model. We approximate Viterbi very closely using a fast beam search. Essentially, the decoding process involves sequential classification, conditioned on the (uncertain) decisions of the previous local trigram context classifications. The chosen tag sequence $\hat{\underline{t}}$ is the tag sequence maximizing the following quantity:

$$\begin{aligned}\hat{\underline{t}} &= \arg\max_{\underline{t}} P(\underline{t} \mid \underline{w}) \\ &= \arg\max_{\underline{t}} \prod_{i=1..n} p_{ME}(t_i \mid w_i, \underline{f_i}, t_{i-1}, t_{i-2})\end{aligned}$$

The features used in this work are reasonably typical for modern MEMM feature-based POS tagging and consist of a combination of lexical, orthographic, contextual, and frequency-based information. In particular, for each word the following features are defined: the textual form of the word itself, the POS tags of the preceding two words, and the textual form of the following word. Following Toutanova and Manning (2000) approximately, more information is defined for words that are considered rare (which we define here as words that occur fewer than fifteen times). We consider the tagger to be near-state-of-the-art in terms of tagging accuracy.

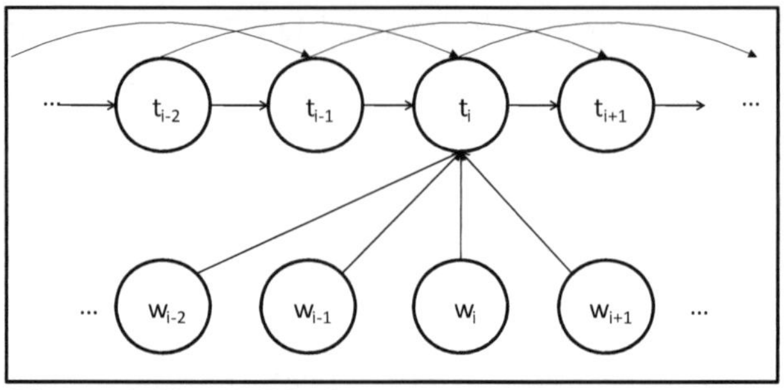

Figure 1. Simple Markov order 2 CMM, with focus on the i-th hidden label (or tag).

3 Active Learning

The objective of this research is to produce more high quality annotated data with less human annotator time and effort. Active learning is an approach to machine learning in which a model is trained with the selective help of an oracle. The oracle provides labels on a sufficient number of "tough" cases, as identified by the model. Easy cases are assumed to be understood by the model and to require no additional annotation by the oracle. Many variations have been proposed in the broader active learning and decision theory literature under many names, including "active sampling" and "optimal sampling."

In active learning for POS tagging, as in other applications, the oracle can be a human. For experimental purposes, a human oracle is simulated using pre-labeled data, where the labels are hidden until queried. To begin, the active learning process requires some small amount of training data to seed the model. The process proceeds by identifying the data in the given corpus that should be tagged first for maximal impact.

3.1 Active Learning in the Language Context

When considering the role of active learning, we were initially drawn to the work in active learning for classification. In a simple configuration, each instance (document, image, etc.) to be labeled can be considered to be independent. However, for active learning for the POS tagging problem we considered the nature of human input as an oracle for the task. As an approximation, people read sentences as propositional atoms, gathering contextual cues from the sentence in order to assemble the meaning of the whole. Consequently, we thought it unreasonable to choose the word as the granularity for active learning. Instead, we begin with the assumption that a human will usually require much of the sentence or at least local context from the sentence in order to label a single word with its POS label. While focusing on a single word, the human may as well label the entire sentence or at least correct the labels assigned by the tagger for the sentence. Consequently, the sentence is the granularity of annotation for this work. (Future work will question this assumption and investigate tagging a word or a subsequence of words at a time.) This distinguishes our work from active learning for classification since labels are not drawn from a fixed set of labels. Rather, every sentence of length n can be labeled with a tag sequence drawn from a set of size T^n, where T is the size of the per-word tag set. Granted, many of the options have very low probability.

To underscore our choice of annotating at the granularity of a sentence, we also note that a maximum entropy classifier for isolated word tagging that leverages attributes of neighboring words—but is blind to all tags—will underperform an MEMM that includes the tags of neighboring words (usually on the left) among its features. Previous experiments demonstrate the usefulness of tags in context on the standard Wall Street Journal data from the Penn Treebank (Marcus et al., 1999). A MaxEnt isolated word tagger achieves 93.7% on words observed in the training set and 82.6% on words unseen in the training set. Toutanova and Manning (2000) achieves 96.9% (on seen) and 86.9% (on unseen) with an MEMM. They surpassed their earlier work in 2003 with a "cyclic dependency network tagger", achieving 97.2%/89.05% (seen/unseen) (Toutanova et al., 2003). The generally agreed upon upper bound is around 98%, due to label inconsistencies in the Treebank. The main point is that effective use of contextual features is necessary to achieve state of the art performance in POS tagging.

In active learning, we employ several sets of data that we refer to by the following names:

- Initial Training: the small set of data used to train the original model before active learning starts
- Training: data that has already been labeled by the oracle as of step i in the learning cycle
- Unannotated: data not yet labeled by the oracle as of step i
- Test (specifically Development Test): labeled data used to measure the accuracy of the model at each stage of the active learning process. Labels on this set are held in reserve for comparison with the labels chosen by the model. It is the accuracy on this set that we report in our experimental results in Section 4.

Note that the Training set grows at the expense of the Unannotated set as active learning progresses.

Active Learning for POS Tagging consists of the following steps:

1. Train a model with Initial Training data
2. Apply model to Unannotated data
3. Compute potential informativeness of each sentence
4. Remove top n sentences with most potential informativeness from Unannotated data and give to oracle
5. Add n sentences annotated (or corrected) by the oracle to Training data
6. Retrain model with Training data
7. Return to step 2 until stopping condition is met.

There are several possible stopping conditions, including reaching a quality bar based on accuracy on the Test set, the rate of oracle error corrections in the given cycle, or even the cumulative number of oracle error corrections. In practice, the exhaustion of resources, such as time or money, may completely dominate all other desirable stopping conditions.

Several methods are available for determining which sentences will provide the most information. Expected Value of Sample Information (EVSI) (Raiffa & Schlaiffer, 1967) would be the optimal approach from a decision theoretic point of view, but it is computationally prohibitive and is not considered here. We also do not consider the related notion of query-by-model-improvement or other methods (Anderson & Moore, 2005; Roy & McCallum, 2001a, 2001b). While worth exploring, they do not fit in the context of this current work and should be considered in future work. We focus here on the more widely used Query by Committee (QBC) and Query by Uncertainty (QBU), including our new adaptations of these.

Our implementation of maximum entropy training employs a convex optimization procedure known as LBFGS. Although this procedure is relatively fast, training a model (or models in the case of QBC) from scratch on the training data during every round of the active learning loop would prolong our experiments unnecessarily. Instead we start each optimization search with a parameter set consisting of the model parameters from the previous iteration of active learning (we call this "Fast MaxEnt"). In practice, this converges quickly and produces equivalent results.

3.2 Query by Committee

Query by Committee (QBC) was introduced by Seung, Opper, and Sompolinsky (1992). Freund, Seung, Shamir, and Tishby (1997) provided a careful analysis of the approach. Engelson and Dagan (1996) experimented with QBC using HMMs for POS tagging and found that selective sampling of sentences can significantly reduce the number of samples required to achieve desirable tag accuracies. Unlike the present work, Engelson & Dagan were restricted by computational resources to selection from small windows of the Unannotated set, not from the entire Unannotated set. Related work includes learning ensembles of POS taggers, as in the work of Brill and Wu (1998), where an ensemble consisting of a unigram model, an N-gram model, a transformation-based model, and an MEMM for POS tagging achieves substantial results beyond the individual taggers. Their conclusion relevant to this paper is that different taggers commit complementary errors, a useful fact to exploit in active learning. QBC employs a committee of N models, in which each model votes on the correct tagging of a sentence. The potential informativeness of a sentence is measured by the total number of tag sequence disagreements (compared pair-wise) among the committee members. Possible variants of QBC involve the number of committee members, how the training data is split among the committee members, and whether the training data is sampled with or without replacement.

A potential problem with QBC in this application is that words occur with different frequencies in the corpus. Because of the potential for greater impact across the corpus, querying for the tag of a more frequent word may be more desirable than querying for the tag of a word that occurs less frequently, even if there is greater disagreement on the tags for the less frequent word. We attempted to compensate for this by weighting the number of disagreements by the corpus frequency of the word in the full data set (Training and Unannotated). Unfortunately, this resulted in worse performance; solving this problem is an interesting avenue for future work.

3.3 Query by Uncertainty

The idea behind active sampling based on uncertainty appears to originate with Thrun and Moeller (1992). QBU has received significant attention in general. Early experiments involving QBU were conducted by Lewis and Gale (1994) on text classification, where they demonstrated significant benefits of the approach. Lewis and Catlett (1994) examined its application for non-probabilistic learners in conjunction with other probabilistic learners under the name "uncertainty sampling." Brigham Anderson (2005) explored QBU using HMMs and concluded that it is sometimes advantageous. We are not aware of any published work on the application of QBU to POS tagging. In our implementation, QBU employs a single MEMM tagger. The MaxEnt model comprising the tagger can assess the probability distribution over tags for any word in its local trigram context, as illustrated in the example in Figure 2.

			NN	*0 .85*
			VB	*0.13*
			...	
RB	**DT**	**JJS**	*CD*	*2.0E-7*
Perhaps	**the**	**biggest**	**hurdle**	...

Figure 2. Distribution over tags for the word "hurdle" in italics. The local trigram context is in boldface.

In Query by Uncertainty (QBU), the informativeness of a sample is assumed to be the uncertainty in the predicted distribution over tags for that sample, that is the entropy of $p_{ME}(t_i \mid w_i, f_i, t_{i-1}, t_{i-2})$. To determine the potential informativeness of a word, we can measure the entropy in that distribution. Since we are selecting sentences, we must extend our measure of uncertainty beyond the word.

3.4 Adaptations of QBU

There are several problems with the use of QBU in this context:

- Some words are more important; i.e., they contain more information perhaps because they occur more frequently.

- MaxEnt estimates per-word distributions over tags, not per-sentence distributions over tag sequences.
- Entropy computations are relatively costly.

We address the first issue in a new version of QBU which we call "Weighted Query by Uncertainty" (WQBU). In WQBU, per-word uncertainty is weighted by the word's corpus frequency.

To address the issue of estimating per-sentence uncertainty from distributions over tag *sequences*, we have considered several different approaches. The per-word (conditional) entropy is defined as follows:

$$H(T_i \mid w_i, \underline{f_i}, t_{i-1}, t_{i-2}) \\ = -\sum_{t_i \in Tagset} p_{ME}(t_i \mid w_i, \underline{f_i}, t_{i-1}, t_{i-2}) \\ \cdot \log p_{ME}(t_i \mid w_i, \underline{f_i}, t_{i-1}, t_{i-2})$$

where T_i is the random variable for the tag t_i on word w_i, and the features of the context in which w_i occurs are denoted, as before, by the collection $\underline{f_i}$ and the prior tags t_{i-1}, t_{i-2}. It is straightforward to calculate this entropy for each word in a sentence from the Unannotated set, if we assume that previous tags t_{i-1}, t_{i-2} are from the Viterbi (best) tag sequence (for the entire sentence) according to the model.

For an entire sentence, we estimate the tag-sequence entropy by summing over all possible tag sequences. However, computing this estimate exactly on a 25-word sentence, where each word can be labeled with one of 35 tags, would require $35^{25} = 3.99 * 10^{38}$ steps. Instead, we approximate the per-sentence tag sequence distribution entropy by summing per-word entropy:

$$\hat{H}(\underline{T} \mid \underline{w}) \approx -\sum_{w_i \in \underline{w}} H(T_i \mid w_i, \underline{f_i}, t_{i-1}, t_{i-2})$$

This is the approach we refer to as QBU in the experimental results section. We have experimented with a second approach that estimates the per-sentence entropy of the tag-sequence distribution by Monte Carlo decoding. Unfortunately, current active learning results involving this MC POS tagging decoder are negative on small Training set sizes, so we do not present them here. Another alternative approximation worth pursuing is computing the per-sentence entropy using the n-best POS tag sequences. Very recent work by Mann and McCallum (2007) proposes an approach in which exact sequence entropy can be calculated efficiently. Further experimentation is required to compare our approximation to these alternatives.

An alternative approach that eliminates the overhead of entropy computations entirely is to estimate per-sentence uncertainty with $1 - P(\hat{t})$, where $\hat{t}$ is the Viterbi (best) tag sequence. We call this scheme QBUV. In essence, it selects a sample consisting of the sentences having the highest probability that the Viterbi sequence is wrong. To our knowledge, this is a novel approach to active learning.

4 Experimental Results

In this section, we examine the experimental setup, the prose and poetry data sets, and the results from using the various active learning algorithms on these corpora.

4.1 Setup

The experiments focus on the annotation scenario posed earlier, in which budgetary constraints afford only some number x of sentences to be annotated. The x-axis in each graph captures the number of sentences. For most of the experiments, the graphs present accuracies on the (Development) Test set. Later in this section, we present results for an alternate metric, namely number of words corrected by the oracle.

In order to ascertain the usefulness of the active learning approaches explored here, the results are presented against a baseline in which sentences are selected randomly from the Unannotated set. We consider this baseline to represent the use of a state-of-the-art tagger trained on the same amount of data as the active learner. Due to randomization, the random baseline is actually distinct from experiment to experiment without any surprising deviations. Also, each result curve in each graph represents the average of three distinct runs.

Worth noting is that most of the graphs include active learning curves that are run to completion; namely, the rightmost extent of all curves represents the exhaustion of the Unannotated data. At this extreme point, active learning and random sample selection all have the same Training set. In the scenarios we are targeting, this far right side is not of interest. Points representing smaller amounts of annotated data are our primary interest.

In the experiments that follow, we address several natural questions that arise in the course of applying active learning. We also compare the variants of QBU and QBC. For QBC, committee members divide the training set (at each stage of the active learning process) evenly. All committee members and final models are MEMMs. Likewise, all variants of QBU employ MEMMs.

4.2 Data Sets

The experiments involve two data sets in search of conclusions that generalize over two very different kinds of English text. The first data set consists of English prose from the POS-tagged one-million-word Wall Street Journal text in the Penn Treebank (PTB) version 3. We use a random sample of the corpus constituting 25% of the traditional training set (sections 2–21). Initial Training data consists of 1% of this set. We employ section 24 as the Development Test set. Average sentence length is approximately 25 words.

Our second experimental set consists of English poetry from the British National Corpus (BNC) (Godbert & Ramsay, 1991; Hughes, 1982; Raine, 1984). The text is also fully tagged with 91 parts of speech from a different tag set than the one used for the PTB. The BNC XML data was taken from the files B1C.xml, CBO.xml, and H8R.xml. This results in a set of 60,056 words and 8,917 sentences.

4.3 General Results

To begin, each step in the active learning process adds a batch of 100 sentences from the Unannotated set at a time. Figure 3 demonstrates (using QBU) that the size of a query batch is not significant in these experiments.

The primary question to address is whether active learning helps or not. Figure 4 demonstrates that QBU, QBUV, and QBC all outperform the random baseline in terms of total, per-word accuracy on the Test set, given the same amount of Training data. Figure 5 is a close-up version of Figure 4, placing emphasis on points up to 1000 annotated sentences. In these figures, QBU and QBUV vie for the best performing active learning algorithm. These results appear to give some useful advice captured in Table 1. The first column in the table contains the starting conditions. The remaining columns indicate that for between 800-1600 sentences of annotation, QBUV takes over from QBU as the best selection algorithm.

The next question to address is how much initial training data should be used; i.e., when should we start using active learning? The experiment in Figure 6 demonstrates (using QBU) that one should use as little data as possible for Initial Training Data. There is always a significant advantage to starting early. In the experiment documented in

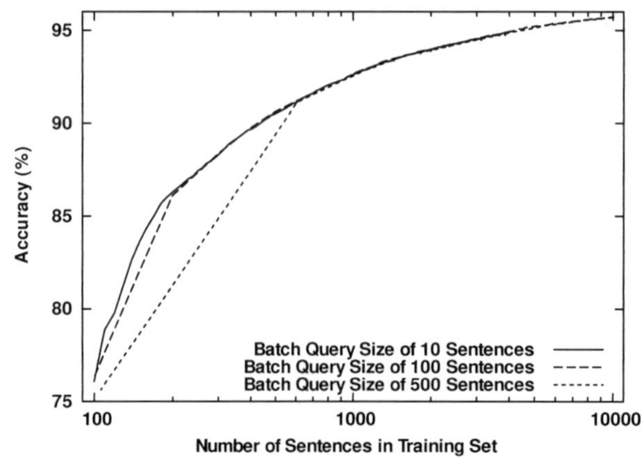

Figure 3. Varying the size of the query batch in active learning yields identical results after the first query batch.

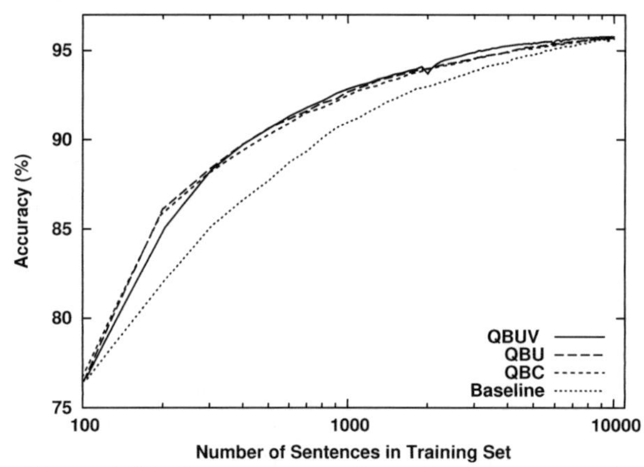

Figure 4. The best representatives of each type of active learner beat the baseline. QBU and QBUV trade off the top position over QBC and the Baseline.

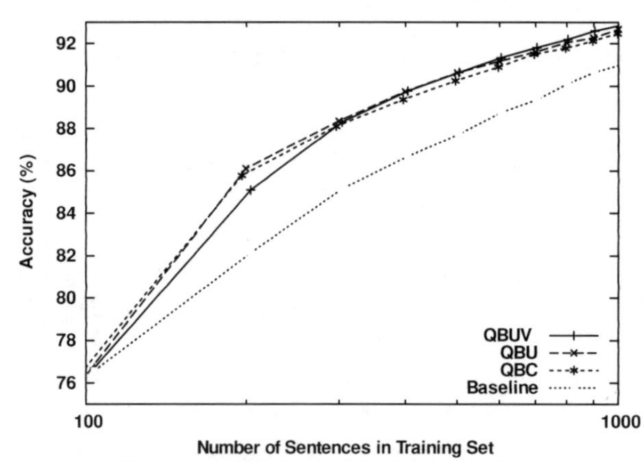

Figure 5. Close-up of the low end of the graph from Figure 4. QBUV and QBU are nearly tied for best performance.

this figure, a batch query size of one was employed in order to make the point as clearly as possible. Larger batch query sizes produce a graph with similar trends as do experiments involving larger Unannotated sets and other active learners.

	100	200	400	800	1600	3200	6400
QBU	76.26	**86.11**	**90.63**	**92.27**	93.67	94.65	95.42
QBUV	**76.65**	85.09	89.75	92.24	**93.72**	**94.96**	**95.60**
QBC	76.19	85.77	89.37	91.78	93.49	94.62	95.36
Base	76.57	82.13	86.68	90.12	92.49	94.02	95.19

Table 1. The best models (on PTB WSJ data) with various amounts of annotation (columns).

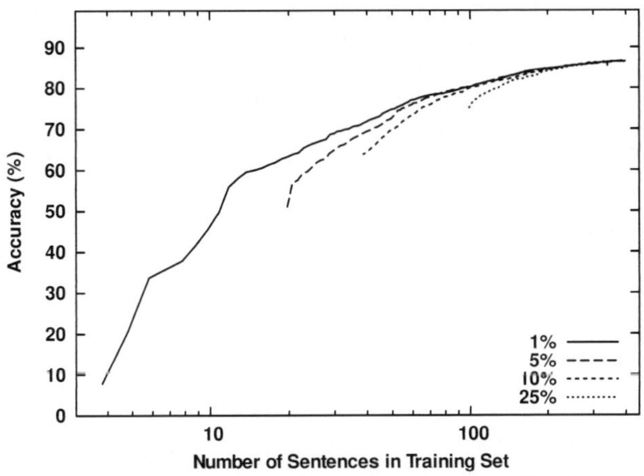

Figure 6. Start active learning as early as possible for a head start.

4.4 QBC Results

An important question to address for QBC is what number of committee members produces the best results? There was no significant difference in results from the QBC experiments when using between 3 and 7 committee members. For brevity we omit the graph.

4.5 QBU Results

For Query by Uncertainty, the experiment in Figure 7 demonstrates that QBU is superior to QBUV for low counts, but that QBUV slightly overtakes QBU beyond approximately 300 sentences. In fact, all QBU variants, including the weighted version, surpassed the baseline. WQBU has been omitted from the graph, as it was inferior to straightforward QBU.

4.6 Results on the BNC

Next we introduce results on poetry from the British National Corpus. Recall that the feature set employed by the MEMM tagger was optimized for performance on the Wall Street Journal. For the experiment presented in Figure 8, all data in the Training and Unannotated sets is from the BNC, but we employ the same feature set from the WSJ experiments. This result on the BNC data shows first of all that tagging poetry with this tagger leaves a final shortfall of approximately 8% from the WSJ results. Nonetheless and more importantly, the active learning trends observed on the WSJ still hold. QBC is better than the baseline, and QBU and QBUV trade off for first place. Furthermore, for low numbers of sentences, it is overwhelmingly to one's advantage to employ active learning for annotation.

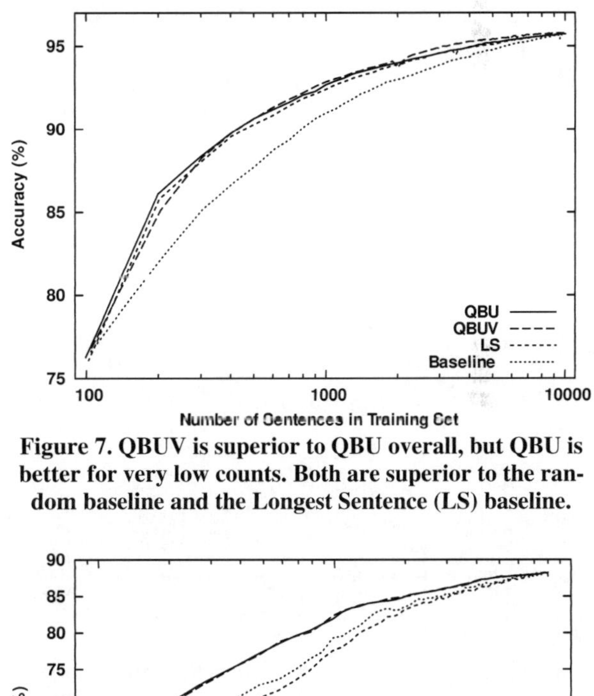

Figure 7. QBUV is superior to QBU overall, but QBU is better for very low counts. Both are superior to the random baseline and the Longest Sentence (LS) baseline.

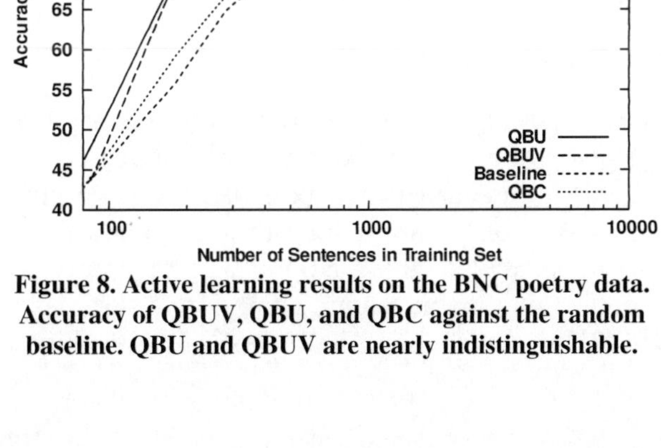

Figure 8. Active learning results on the BNC poetry data. Accuracy of QBUV, QBU, and QBC against the random baseline. QBU and QBUV are nearly indistinguishable.

4.7 Another Perspective

Next, briefly consider a different metric on the vertical axis. In Figure 9, the metric is the total number of words changed (corrected) by the oracle. This quantity reflects the cumulative number of differences between the tagger's hypothesis on a sentence (at the point in time when the oracle is queried) and the oracle's answer (over the training set). It corresponds roughly to the amount of time that would be required for a human annotator to correct the tags suggested by the model. This figure reveals that QBUV makes significantly more changes than QBU, QBC, or LS (the Longest Sentence baseline). Hence, the superiority of QBU over QBUV, as measured by this metric, appears to outweigh the small wins provided by QBUV when measured by accuracy alone. That said, the random baseline makes the fewest changes of all. If this metric (and not some combination with accuracy) were our only consideration, then active learning would appear not to serve our needs.

This metric is also a measure of how well a particular query algorithm selects sentences that especially require assistance from the oracle. In this sense, QBUV appears most effective.

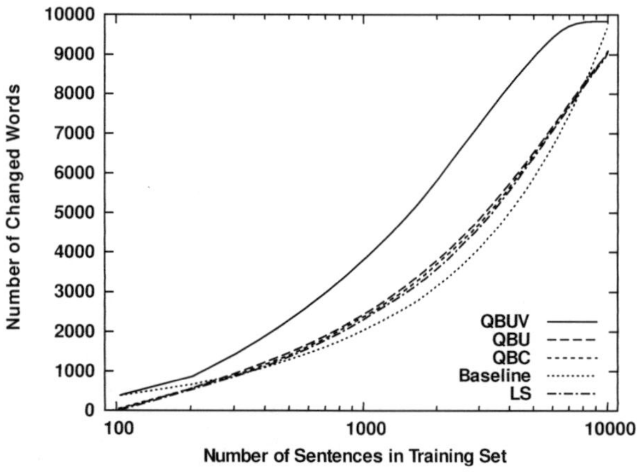

Figure 9. Cumulative number of corrections made by the oracle for several competitive active learning algorithms. QBU requires fewer corrections than QBUV.

5 Conclusions

Active learning is a viable way to accelerate the efficiency of a human annotator and is most effective when done as early as possible. We have presented state-of-the-art tagging results using a fraction of the labeled data. QBUV is a cheap approach to performing active learning, only to be surpassed by QBU when labeling small numbers of sentences.

We are in the midst of conducting a user study to assess the true costs of annotating a sentence at a time or a word at a time. We plan to incorporate these specific costs into a model of cost measured in time (or money) that will supplant the metrics reported here, namely accuracy and number of words corrected. As noted earlier, future work will also evaluate active learning at the granularity of a word or a subsequence of words, to be evaluated by the cost metric.

References

Anderson, B., and Moore, A. (2005). "Active Learning for HMM: Objective Functions and Algorithms." ICML, Germany.

Brants, T., (2000). "TnT -- a statistical part-of-speech tagger." ANLP, Seattle, WA.

Brill, E., and Wu, J. (1998). "Classifier combination for improved lexical disambiguation." Coling/ACL, Montreal, Quebec, Canada. Pp. 191-195.

Day, D., et al. (1997). "Mixed-Initiative Development of Language Processing Systems." ANLP, Washington, D.C.

Engelson, S. and Dagan, I. (1996). "Minimizing manual annotation cost in supervised training from corpora." ACL, Santa Cruz, California. Pp. 319-326.

Freund, Y., Seung, H., Shamir, E., and Tishby, N. (1997). "Selective sampling using the query by committee algorithm." Machine Learning, 28(2-3):133-168.

Godbert, G. and Ramsay, J. (1991). "For now." In the British National Corpus file B1C.xml. London: The Diamond Press (pp. 1-108).

Hughes, T. (1982). "Selected Poems." In the British National Corpus file H8R.xml. London: Faber & Faber Ltd. (pp. 35-235).

Kupiec, J. (1992). "Robust part-of-speech tagging using a hidden Markov model." Computer Speech and Language 6, pp. 225-242.

Lewis, D., and Catlett, J. (1994). "Heterogeneous uncertainty sampling for supervised learning." ICML.

Lewis, D., and Gale, W. (1995). "A sequential algorithm for training text classifiers: Corrigendum and additional data." SIGIR Forum, 29 (2), 13--19.

Mann, G., and McCallum, A. (2007). "Efficient Computation of Entropy Gradient for Semi-Supervised Conditional Random Fields". NAACL-HLT.

Marcus, M. et al. (1999). "Treebank-3." Linguistic Data Consortium, Philadelphia, PA.

Raiffa, H. and Schlaiffer, R. (1967). *Applied Statistical Decision Theory*. New York: Wiley Interscience.

Raine, C. (1984). "Rich." In the British National Corpus file CB0.xml. London: Faber & Faber Ltd. (pp. 13-101).

Ratnaparkhi, A. (1996). "A Maximum Entropy Model for Part-Of-Speech Tagging." EMNLP.

Roy, N., and McCallum, A. (2001a). "Toward optimal active learning through sampling estimation of error reduction." ICML.

Roy, N. and McCallum, A. (2001b). "Toward Optimal Active Learning through Monte Carlo Estimation of Error Reduction." ICML, Williamstown.

Seung, H., Opper, M., and Sompolinsky, H. (1992). "Query by committee". COLT. Pp. 287-294.

Thrun S., and Moeller, K. (1992). "Active exploration in dynamic environments." NIPS.

Toutanova, K., Klein, D., Manning, C., and Singer, Y. (2003). "Feature-Rich Part-of-Speech Tagging with a Cyclic Dependency Network." HLT-NAACL. Pp. 252-259.

Toutanova, K. and Manning, C. (2000). "Enriching the Knowledge Sources Used in a Maximum Entropy Part-of-Speech Tagger." EMNLP, Hong Kong. Pp. 63-70.

Combining Independent Syntactic and Semantic Annotation Schemes

Marc Verhagen, Amber Stubbs and James Pustejovsky
Computer Science Department
Brandeis University, Waltham, USA
{marc,astubbs,jamesp}@cs.brandeis.edu

Abstract

We present MAIS, a UIMA-based environment for combining information from various annotated resources. Each resource contains one mode of linguistic annotation and remains independent from the other resources. Interactions between annotations are defined based on use cases.

1 Introduction

MAIS is designed to allow easy access to a set of linguistic annotations. It embodies a methodology to define interactions between separate annotation schemes where each interaction is based on a use case. With MAIS, we adopt the following requirements for the interoperability of syntactic and semantic annotations:

1. Each annotation scheme has its own philosophy and is independent from the other annotations. Simple and generally available interfaces provide access to the content of each annotation scheme.

2. Interactions between annotations are not defined a priori, but based on use cases.

3. Simple tree-based and one-directional merging of annotations is useful for visualization of overlap between schemes.

The annotation schemes currently embedded in MAIS are the Proposition Bank (Palmer et al., 2005), NomBank (Meyers et al., 2004) and TimeBank (Pustejovsky et al., 2003). Other linguistics annotation schemes like the opinion annotation (Wiebe et al., 2005), named entity annotation, and discourse annotation (Miltsakaki et al., 2004) will be added in the future.

In the next section, we elaborate on the first two requirements mentioned above and present the MAIS methodology to achieve interoperability of annotations. In section 3, we present the XBank Browser, a unified browser that allows researchers to inspect overlap between annotation schemes.

2 Interoperability of Annotations

Our goal is not to define a static merger of all annotation schemes. Rather, we avoid defining a potentially complex interlingua and instead focus on how information from different sources can be combined pragmatically. A high-level schematic representation of the system architecture is given in figure 1.

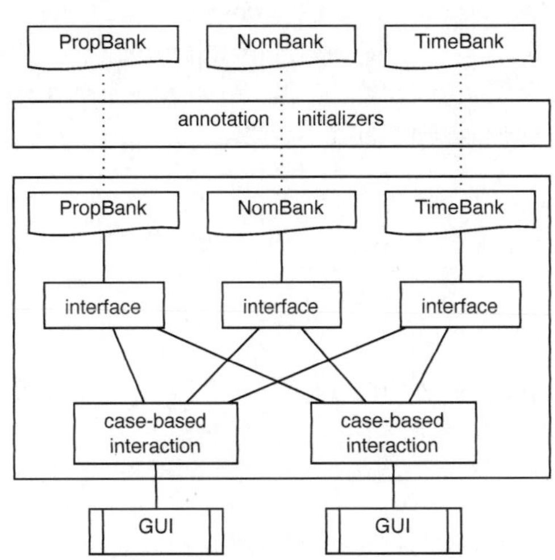

Figure 1: Architecture of MAIS

Proceedings of the Linguistic Annotation Workshop, pages 109–112,
Prague, June 2007.

The simple and extensible interoperability of MAIS can be put in place using three components: a unified environment that stores the annotations and implements some common functionality, a set of annotation interfaces, and a set of case-based interactions.

2.1 Unified Environment

All annotations are embedded as stand-off annotations in a unified environment in which each annotation has its own namespace. This unified environment takes care of some basic functionality. For example, given a tag from one annotation scheme, there is a method that returns tags from other annotation schemes that have the same text extent or tags that have an overlap in text extent. The unified environment chosen for MAIS is UIMA, the open platform for unstructured information analysis created by IBM.[1]

UIMA implements a common data representation named CAS (Common Analysis Structure) that provides read and write access to the documents being analyzed. Existing annotations can be imported into a CAS using CAS Initializers. UIMA also provides a framework for Analysis Engines: modules that can read from and write to a CAS and that can be combined into a complex work flow.

2.2 Annotation Interfaces

In the unified environment, the individual annotations are independent from each other and they are considered immutable. Each annotation defines an interface through which salient details of the annotations can be retrieved. For example, annotation schemes that encodes predicate-argument structure, that is, PropBank and NomBank, define methods like

```
args-of-relation(pred)
arg-of-relation(pred, arg)
relation-of-argument(arg)
```

Similarly, the interface for TimeBank includes methods like

```
rel-between(event_i, event_j)
events-before(event)
event-anchorings(event)
```

[1] `http://www.research.ibm.com/UIMA/`

The arguments to these methods are not strings but text positions, where each text position contains an offset and a document identifier. Return values are also text positions. All interfaces are required to include a method that returns the tuples that match a given string:

```
get-locations(string, type)
```

This method returns a set of text positions. Each text position points to a location where the input string occurs as being of the given type. For TimeBank, the type could be `event` or `time`, for PropBank and NomBank, more appropriate values are `rel` or `arg0`.

2.3 Case-based Interactions

Most of the integration work occurs in the interaction components. Specific interactions can be built using the unified environment and the specified interfaces of each annotation scheme.

Take for example, the use case of an entity chronicle (Pustejovsky and Verhagen, 2007). An entity chronicle follows an entity through time, displaying what events an entity was engaged in, how these events are anchored to time expressions, and how the events are ordered relative to each other. Such an application depends on three kinds of information: identification of named entities, predicate-argument structure, and temporal relations. Each of these derive from a separate annotation scheme. A use case can be built using the interfaces for each annotation:

- the named entity annotation returns the text extents of the named entity, using the general method `get-locations(string, type)`
- the predicate-argument annotation (accessed through the PropBank and NomBank interfaces) returns the predicates that go with a named-entity argument, repeatedly using the method `relation-of-argument(arg)`
- finally, the temporal annotation returns the temporal relations between all those predicates, calling `rel-between(event_i, event_j)` on all pairs of predicates

Note that named entity annotation is not integrated into the current system. As a stopgap measure we use a pre-compiled list of named entities and feed elements of this list into the PropBank and NomBank interfaces, asking for those text positions where the entity is expressed as an argument. This shows the utility of a general method like `get-locations(string, type)`.

Each case-based interaction is implemented using one or more UIMA analysis engines. It should be noted that the analysis engines used for the entity chronicler do not add data to the common data representation. This is not a principled choice: if adding new data to the CAS is useful then it can be part of the case-based interaction, but these added data are not integrated into existing annotations, rather, they are added as a separate secondary resource.[2]

The point of this approach is that applications can be built pragmatically, using only those resources that are needed. It does not depend on fully merged syntactic and semantic representations. The entity chronicle, for example, does not require discourse annotation, opinion annotation or any other resource except for the three discussed before. An a priori requirement to have a unified representation introduces complexities that go beyond what's needed for individual applications.

This is not to say that a unified representation is not useful on its own, there is obvious theoretical interest in thoroughly exploring how annotations relate to each other. But we feel that the unified representation is not needed for most, if not all, practical applications.

3 The XBank Browser

The unified browser, named the XBank Browser, is intended as a convenience for researchers. It shows the overlap between different annotations. Annotations from different schemes are merged into one XML representation and a set of cascading style sheets is used to display the information.

[2]In fact, for the entity chronicle it would be useful to have extra data available. The current implementation uses what's provided by the basic resources plus a few heuristics to superficially merge data from separate documents. But a more informative chronicle along the lines of (Pustejovsky and Verhagen, 2007) would require more temporal links than available in TimeBank. These can be pre-compiled and added using a dedicated analysis engine.

The XBank Browser does not adhere to the MAIS philosophy that all resources are independent. Instead, it designates one syntactic annotation to provide the basic shape of the XML tree and requires tags from other annotations to find landing spots in the basic tree.

The Penn Treebank annotation (Marcus et al., 1993) was chosen to be the first among equals: it is the starting point for the merger and data from other annotations are attached at tree nodes. Currently, only one heuristic is used to merge in data from other sources: go up the tree to find a Treebank constituent that contains the entire extent of the tag that is merged in, then select the head of this constituent. A more sophisticated approach would consist of two steps:

- first try to find an exact match of the imported tag with a Treebank constituent,
- if that fails, find the constituent that contains the entire tag that is merged in, and select this constituent

In the latter case, there can be an option to select the head rather than the whole constituent. In any case, the attached node will be marked if its original extent does not line up with the extent at the tree node.

It should be noted that this merging is one-directional since no attempt is made to change the shape of the tree defined by the Treebank annotation.

The unified browser currently displays markups from the Proposition Bank, NomBank, TimeBank and the Discourse Treebank. Tags from individual schemes can be hidden as desired. The main problem with the XBank Browser is that there is only a limited amount of visual clues that can be used to distinguish individual components from each other and cognitive overload restricts how many annotation schemes can be viewed at the same time. Nevertheless, the browser does show how a limited number of annotation schemes relate to each other.

All functionality of the browser can be accessed at `http://timeml.org/ula/`. An idea of what it looks like can be gleaned from the screenshot displayed in figure 2. In this figure, boxes represent relations from PropBank or NomBank and shaded

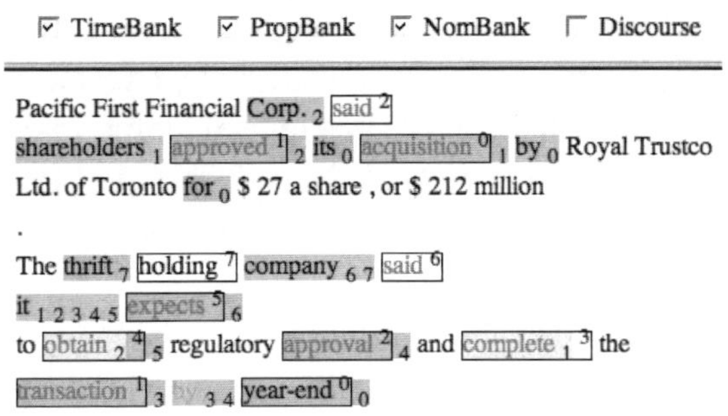

Figure 2: A glimpse of the XBank Browser

backgrounds represent arguments. Superscripts are indexes that identify relations, subscripts identify what relation an argument belongs to. Red fonts indicate events from TimeBank. Note that the real browser is barely done justice by this picture because the browser's use of color is not visible.

4 Conclusion

We described MAIS, an environment that implements interoperability between syntactic and semantic annotation schemes. The kind of interoperability proposed herein does not require an elaborate representational structure that allows the interaction. Rather, it relies on independent annotation schemes with interfaces to the outside world that interact given a specific use case. The more annotations there are, the more interactions can be defined. The complexity of the methodology is not bound by the number of annotation schemes integrated but by the complexity of the use cases.

5 Acknowledgments

The work reported in this paper was performed as part of the project "Towards a Comprehensive Linguistic Annotation of Language", and supported under award CNS-0551615 of the National Science Foundation.

References

Mitchell Marcus, Beatrice Santorini, and Mary Ann Marcinkiewicz. 1993. Building a Large Annotated Corpus of English: The Penn Treeb. *Computational Linguistics*, 19(2):313–330.

A. Meyers, R. Reeves, C. Macleod, R. Szekely, V. Zielinska, B. Young, and R. Grishman. 2004. The nombank project: An interim report. In A. Meyers, editor, *HLT-NAACL 2004 Workshop: Frontiers in Corpus Annotation*, pages 24–31, Boston, Massachusetts, USA, May 2 - May 7. Association for Computational Linguistics.

Eleni Miltsakaki, Rashmi Prasad, Aravind Joshi, and Bonnie Webber. 2004. The penn discourse treebank. In *Proceedings of the Language Resources and Evaluation Conference*, Lisbon, Portugal.

Martha Palmer, Paul Kingsbury, and Daniel Gildea. 2005. The Proposition Bank: An Annotated Corpus of Semantic Roles. *Computational Linguistics*, 31(1):71–106.

James Pustejovsky and Marc Verhagen. 2007. Constructing event-based entity chronicles. In *Proceedings of the IWCS-7*, Tilburg, The Netherlands.

James Pustejovsky, Patrick Hanks, Roser Saurí, Andrew See, Robert Gaizauskas, Andrea Setzer, Dragomir Radev, Beth Sundheim, David Day, Lisa Ferro, and Marcia Lazo. 2003. The timebank corpus. In *Proceedings of Corpus Linguistics*, pages 647–656.

Janyce Wiebe, Theresa Wilson, and Claire Cardie. 2005. Annotating expressions of opinions and emotions in language. *Language Resources and Evaluation*, 39(2-3):165–210.

XARA: An XML- and rule-based semantic role labeler

Gerwert Stevens
University of Utrecht, the Netherlands
gerwert.stevens@let.uu.nl

Abstract

XARA is a rule-based PropBank labeler for Alpino XML files, written in Java. I used XARA in my research on semantic role labeling in a Dutch corpus to bootstrap a dependency treebank with semantic roles. Rules in XARA are based on XPath expressions, which makes it a versatile tool that is applicable to other treebanks as well.

In addition to automatic role annotation, XARA is able to extract training instances (sets of features) from an XML based treebank. Such an instance base can be used to train machine learning algorithms for automatic semantic role labeling (SRL). In my semantic role labeling research, I used the Tilburg Memory Learner (TiMBL) for this purpose.

1 Introduction

Ever since the pioneering article of Gildea and Jurafsky (2002), there has been an increasing interest in automatic semantic role labeling (SRL). In general, classification algorithms (a supervised machine learning strategy) are used for this purpose. Manual annotated corpora provide a gold standard for such classifiers.

Starting manual annotation from scratch is very time consuming and therefore expensive. A possible solution is to start from a (partially) automatically annotated corpus. In fact, this reduces the manual *annotation* task to a manual *correction* task. Initial automatic annotation of a corpus is often referred to as *bootstrapping* or *unsupervised SRL*.

In recent years relatively little effort has gone into the development of unsupervised SRL systems. This is partly because semantically annotated English corpora, such as PropBank (Kingsbury et al., 2002) and FrameNet (Johnson et al., 2002), currently contain enough data to develop and test SRL systems based on machine learning. Therefore, bootstrapping large collections of English texts has no priority anymore. For languages other than English however, annotated corpora are rare and still very much needed. Therefore, the development of bootstrapping techniques is very relevant.

One of the languages for which the creation of semantically annotated corpora has lagged dramatically behind, is Dutch. Within the project *Dutch Language Corpus Initiative* (D-Coi)[1], the first steps have been taken towards the development of a large semantically annotated Dutch corpus. The D-Coi project is a preparatory project which will deliver a blueprint and the tools needed for the construction of a 500-million-word reference corpus of contemporary written Dutch. The corpus will be annotated with several layers of annotation, amongst others with semantic roles.

In the context of this project, I developed XARA: (**X**ML-based **A**utomatic **R**ole-labeler for **A**lpino-trees). In my research, XARA was used for two purposes:

- Bootstrap a dependency treebank with semantic roles

[1] http://lands.let.ru.nl/projects/d-coi/

Proceedings of the Linguistic Annotation Workshop, pages 113–116,
Prague, June 2007.

- Extract an instance base for the training of a semantic role classifier.

2 Rule-based role labeling

2.1 The Alpino XML-format

The input for the semantic role tagger is a set of sentences annotated by the Dutch dependency parser Alpino (Bouma et al., 2000) [2]. Alpino is based on a hand-crafted Head-driven Phrase Structure Grammar (HPSG).

The annotation scheme of Alpino dependency trees is based on the Spoken Dutch Corpus (CGN) (Oostdijk, 2002) annotation format. In Alpino trees the same labels are used as in their CGN counterparts and nodes are structured in the same way. The XML-format used to store dependency trees however differs. In the CGN, sentences are stored in the TIGER-XML format (Lezius, 2002) [3], Alpino uses its own XML format to store parsed sentences (Bouma and Kloosterman, 2002). In our treebank, every sentence was encoded in a separate XML file. An example of an Alpino dependency tree annotated with semantic roles is shown in figure 1. Below, the corresponding XML output is shown:

```
<node rel="top">
 <node cat="top" rel="top">
  <node cat="smain" rel="--">
  <node cat="np" rel="su">
   <node pos="det" rel="det" word="de"/>
   <node pos="noun" rel="hd" word="jongen"/>
  </node>
  <node pos="verb" rel="hd" word="aait"/>
  <node cat="np" rel="obj1">
   <node pos="det" rel="det" word="de"/>
   <node pos="adj" rel="mod" word="zwarte"/>
   <node pos="noun" rel="hd" word="hond"/>
  </node>
 </node>
</node>
```

The structure of Alpino XML documents directly corresponds to the structure of the dependency tree: dependency nodes are represented by NODE elements, attributes of the node elements are the c-label, d-label, pos-tag, etc. The format is designed to support a range of linguistic queries on the dependency trees in XPath directly (Bouma and Kloosterman, 2002). XPath (Clark and DeRose, 1999) is a powerful query language for the XML format and it is the cornerstone of XARA's rule-based approach.

[2] A demonstration of the Alpino parser can be found on the following website: http://ziu.let.rug.nl/vannoord_bin/alpino

[3] see also http://www.ims.uni-stuttgart.de/projekte/TIGER/TIGERSearch/index.shtml

Figure 1: Example CGN dependency graph ('The boy pets the black dog')

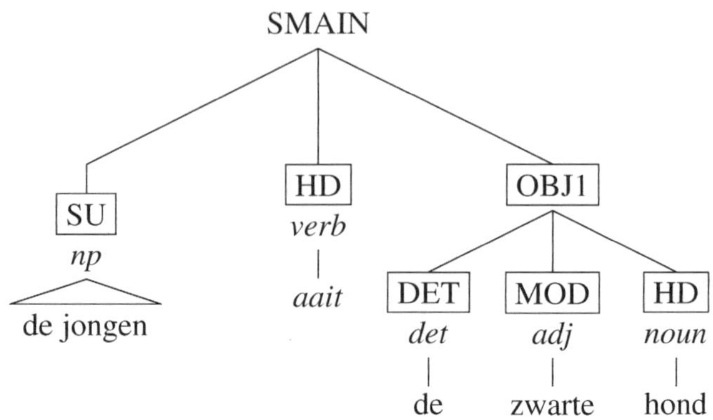

I would like to stress that although our SRL research focused on Alpino structures, XARA can be used with any XML-based treebank, thanks to the fact that XPath and XML are widely accepted standards. This property satisfies one of the major design criteria of the system: reusability.

2.2 The annotation process

The input for the tagger is set of directories containing Alpino XML files, called a *treebank*. Each sentence is annotated separately by applying a set of rules. Rules are applied to local dependency domains (subtrees of the complete dependency tree). The local dependency domain to which a rule is applied, is called the rule's *context*. A context is simply defined by an XPath expression which selects a group of nodes.

Suppose for example that we want to apply a certain rule to nodes that are part of a passive participle, i.e the context of our rule are passive participles. Passive participles in Alpino trees are local dependency domains with a root node with c-label PPART. An example is shown in figure 2.

The dark colored nodes are the ones we are interested in. To select these nodes, the following XPath expression can be used:

Figure 2: Example PropBank annotation on a Dependency tree ('She is never seen')

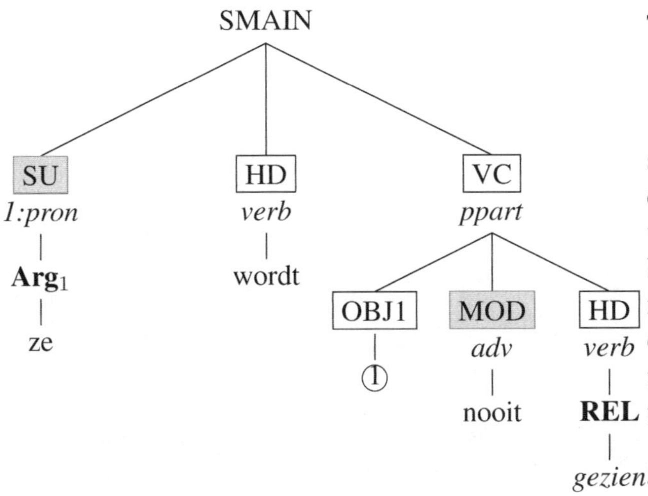


```
//node[@cat='ppart']
[preceding-sibling::
node[@rel='hd' and (@root='word')]]
```

which says that we are looking for nodes with the c-label PPART and the auxiliary verb indicating passive tense (*word*) as preceding sibling.

Once a context is defined, rules can be applied to nodes in this context. Rules consist of an XPath expression which specifies a relative path from the context's root node to the target node and an output label. Upon application of the rule, the target node will be labeled with output label.

The output label can have three kinds of values:

- A positive number n, to label a node with ARGn.
- The value -1, to label the node with the first available numbered argument.
- A string value, to label the node with an arbitrary label, for example an ARGM.

Notice that because the label can be specified as a string value, the set of possible labels is not restricted. In my work, I used PropBank labels, but other labels - such as generic thematic roles - can be used just as well.

Formally, a rule in XARA can be defined as a $(path, label)$ pair. Suppose for example that we want to select direct object nodes in the previously defined context and assign them the label ARG1. This can be formulated as:

```
(./node[@rel='obj1'],1)
```

The first element of this pair is an XPath expression that selects direct object daughters, the second element is a number that specifies which label we want to assign to these target nodes. In this case the label is a positive integer 1, which means the target node will receive the label ARG1. Upon application of a rule, an attribute ("pb") is added to the target node element in the XML file. This attribute contains the PropBank label.

3 Feature extraction

Besides bootstrapping an unannotated corpus, training a SRL classifier was another important part of my automatic SRL strategy. The learning tool I used for this purpose was TiMBL (Tilburg Memory Based Learner) (Daelemans et al., 2004).

In order to be able to train a TiMBL classifier, a file with training data is needed. Training data is represented as a text file containing instances. Each line in the text file represents a single instance. An instance consists of a set of features separated by commas and a target class. XARA is able to create such an instance base from a set of XML files automatically.

3.1 The automatic feature extraction process

The target instance base consists of predicate/argument pairs encoded in training instances. Each instance contains features of a predicate and its candidate argument. Candidate arguments are nodes (constituents) in the dependency tree. This pair-wise approach is analogous to earlier work by van den Bosch et al. (2004) and Tjong Kim Sang et al. (2005) in which instances were built from verb/phrase pairs from which the phrase parent is an ancestor of the verb.

Once it is clear how instances will be encoded, an instance base can be extracted from the annotated corpus. For example, the following instances can be extracted from the tree in figure 2:

```
zie,passive,mod,adv,#
zie,passive,su,pron,ARG1
```

These two example instances consist of 4 features and a target class each. In this example, the predicate lemma (stem) and voice, and the candidate argument c-label, d-label are used. For null values the hash symbol (#) is specified. The first instance represents the predicate/argument pair $(zie, nooit)$ ('see,never'), the second instance represents the pair (zie, ze) ('see, she').

The extraction of instances from the annotated corpus can be done fully automatically by XARA from the command line. The resulting feature base can be directly used in training a TiMBL classifier.

4 Performance

In order to evaluate the labeling of XARA, the output of XARA's semantic role tagger was compared with the manual corrected annotation of 2,395 sentences. The results are shown in table 1.

Table 1: Overall performance

Precision	Recall	$F_{\beta=1}$
65,11%	45,83%	53,80

Since current rules in XARA cover only a subset of PropBank labels, recall is notably lower than precision. However, current overall performance of XARA is encouraging. Our expectation is that, especially if the current rule set is improved and/or extended, XARA can be a very useful tool in current and future SRL research.

References

G. Bouma and G. Kloosterman. 2002. Querying dependency treebanks in xml. In *Proceedings of the Third international conference on Language Resources and Evaluation (LREC)*. Gran Canaria.

G. Bouma, G. van Noord, and R. Malouf. 2000. Alpino: wide-coverage computational analysis of dutch.

J. Clark and S. DeRose. 1999. Xml path language (xpath). *W3C Recommendation 16 November 1999*. URL: http://www.w3.org/TR/xpath.

D. Daelemans, D. Zavrel, K. van der Sloot, and A. van den Bosch. 2004. Timbl: Tilburg memory based learner, version 5.1, reference guide. ILK Technical Report Series 04-02, Tilburg University.

D. Gildea and D. Jurafsky. 2002. Automatic labeling of semantic roles. *Comput. Linguist.*, 28(3):245–288.

C. R. Johnson, C. J. Fillmore, M. R. L. Petruck, C. F. Baker, M. J. Ellsworth, J. Ruppenhofer, and E. J. Wood. 2002. *FrameNet:Theory and Practice*.

P. Kingsbury, M. Palmer, and M. Marcus. 2002. Adding semantic annotation to the penn treebank. In *Proceedings of the Human Language Technology Conference (HLT'02)*.

W Lezius. 2002. *Ein Suchwerkzeug für syntaktisch annotierte Textkorpora*. Ph.D. thesis, University of Stuttgart.

N. Oostdijk. 2002. The design of the spoken dutch corpus. In P. Peters, P. Collins, and A. Smith, editors, *New Frontiers of Corpus Research*, pages 105–112. Amsterdam: Rodopi.

E. Tjong Kim Sang, S. Canisius, A. van den Bosch, and T. Bogers. 2005. Applying spelling error correction techniques for improving semantic role labeling. In *Proceedings of the Ninth Conference on Natural Language Learning (CoNLL-2005)*. Ann Arbor, MI, USA.

A. van den Bosch, S. Canisius, W. Daelemans, I. Hendrickx, and E. Tjong Kim Sang. 2004. Memory-based semantic role labeling: Optimizing features, algorithm, and output. In H.T. Ng and E. Riloff, editors, *Proceedings of the Eighth Conference on Computational Natural Language Learning (CoNLL-2004)*. Boston, MA, USA.

ITU Treebank Annotation Tool

Gülşen Eryiğit
Department of Computer Engineering
Istanbul Technical University
Istanbul, 34469, Turkey
gulsen.cebiroglu@itu.edu.tr

Abstract

In this paper, we present a treebank annotation tool developed for processing Turkish sentences. The tool consists of three different annotation stages; morphological analysis, morphological disambiguation and syntax analysis. Each of these stages are integrated with existing analyzers in order to guide human annotators. Our semi-automatic treebank annotation tool is currently used both for creating new data sets and correcting the existing Turkish treebank.

1 Introduction

Annotated corpora is essential for most of the natural language processing tasks. Developing new annotated corpora becomes crucial especially for lesser studied languages where we encounter many difficulties for finding such data. Turkish is one of the languages which still suffer from scarcity of annotated resources. The most reliable data set for Turkish is the Metu-Sabancı Turkish Treebank (Oflazer et al., 2003) consisting of 5635 sentences annotated with dependency structures. Unfortunately, the data size of this treebank remained unchanged during recent years. There exist also some other small data sets manually pos-tagged by different research groups.

In this study, we introduce our treebank annotation tool developed in order to improve the size of the existing data sets for Turkish (particularly the treebank). Our main motivation for developing a new tool is the inability of the existing tools (e.g. Atalay et al. (2003) and DepAnn (Kakkonen, 2006) which seems to be the most suitable tools for our task) in either reflecting the peculiar morphological and dependency structure of Turkish or providing suitable automatic analyses for guidance. We also aim to speed up the annotation process by using graphical user-friendly interfaces and transforming the annotation process from a manual (starting from scratch) procedure into a controlling and correcting procedure. In the rest of this paper, we first introduce the framework of the tool and then the details of its different annotation stages. We then close with conclusions and future work.

2 Framework

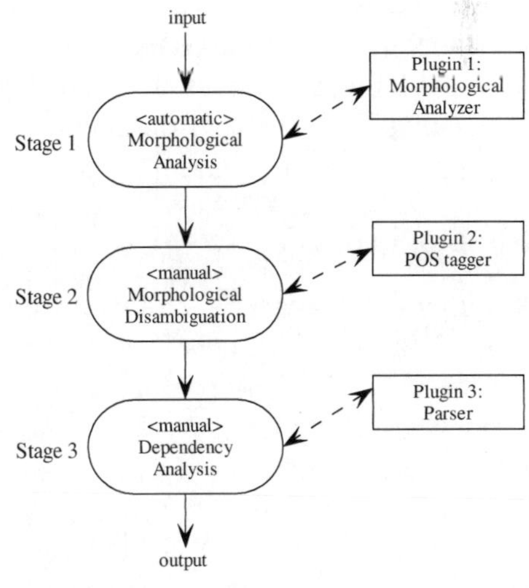

Figure 1: Data Flow

ITU treebank annotation tool takes raw sentences as input and produces results in both the Turkish treebank original XML format (Atalay et al., 2003) and Conll treebank data format (Buchholz and

Proceedings of the Linguistic Annotation Workshop, pages 117–120,
Prague, June 2007.

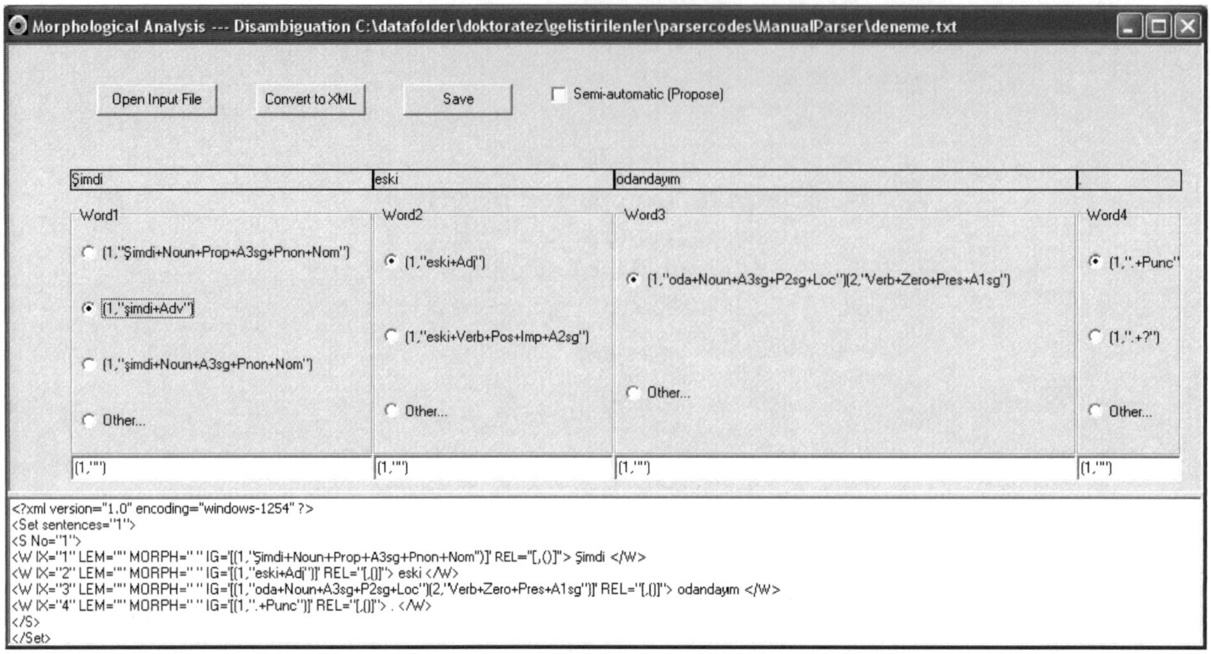

Figure 2: Morphological Analysis and Disambiguation Screen

Marsi, 2006) which is now recognized by many of the state of the art dependency parsers.

The tool consists of three levels of annotation and can be used to produce results for each of them; these are morphological analysis, morphological disambiguation and syntax analysis stages. Each of these stages uses plugins in order to guide the human annotators (referred as *annotator*s in the remaining part). Figure 1 gives the data flow between the annotation stages and the plugins which will be explained in detail in the following sections.

3 Morphological Analysis

The most important characteristic of Turkish which distinguishes it from most of the well-studied languages is its very rich morphological structure. Turkish which is an agglutinative language has a very productive derivational and inflectional morphology. This rich structure of the language has been represented in the literature (Oflazer et al., 2003; Hakkani-Tür et al., 2002; Eryiğit and Oflazer, 2006) by splitting the words into inflectional groups (IGs) which are separated from each other by derivational boundaries. Each IG is then annotated with its own part-of-speech and inflectional features.

We are using the morphological analyzer of Oflazer (1994) which provides all the possible morphological analyses together with the IG structure. The output provided by the morphological analyzer for each word in the example sentence "*Şimdi eski odandayım.*" (I'm now in your old room.) can be seen from Figure 2 (the listed items under each word with radio buttons in front). We can see from the figure that the derived word "*odandayım*" (I'm in your room) is composed of two IGs:

$$\underbrace{\text{(1,"oda+Noun+A3sg+P2sg+Loc")}}_{IG_1}\underbrace{\text{(2,"Verb+Zero+Pres+A1sg")}}_{IG_2}$$

The first IG is the noun "*oda*" (room) which takes the meaning of "in your room" after taking the 3rd singular number-person agreement (+A3sg) , 2nd person possessive agreement (+P2sg) and locative case (+Loc) inflectional features. The second IG is the derived verb "being in your room" in present tense (+Pres), with 1st singular number-person agreement (+A1sg) inflectional features[1].

The morphological analysis stage is totally automatic except that the user can enter other analyses to the text boxes under each word if the correct one is not within the above listed items or the analyzer couldn't suggest any analysis. This latter case generally occurs for numerical values (e.g., numbers,

[1] +Zero means no additional suffix is used for the derivation.

dates) and unknown words. For numerical values, we use a preprocessor to produce the analysis, but for unknown words, the annotators are asked to enter the appropriate analysis.

4 Morphological Disambiguation

The second stage is the morphological disambiguation where the annotator is asked to choose one of the possible analyses for each word. The annotator may consult to an automatic analyzer by clicking the checkbox at the top of the screen in Figure 2. In this case we activate the part-of-speech tagger of Yüret and Türe (2006) which uses some rules automatically derived from a training corpus. The results of this tagger is reflected to the screen by selecting automatically the appropriate radio button for each word. After finishing the disambiguation, the annotator saves the results in XML format (shown at the bottom panel of Figure 2) and proceeds trough the syntax analysis.

5 Syntax Analysis

The syntactic annotation scheme used in the Turkish treebank is the dependency grammar representation. The aim of the dependency analysis is to find the binary relationships between dependent and head units. The dependency structure of Turkish has been mentioned in many studies (Oflazer et al., 2003; Oflazer, 2003; Eryiğit et al., 2006) and it is argued that for Turkish, it is not just enough to determine the relationships between words and one should also determine the relationships between inflectional groups. Figure 3 gives an example of this structure[2]. In this screen, the annotator first selects a dependent unit by selecting the check box under it and then a head unit and the appropriate dependency relation from the combo box appearing under the constructed dependency. In this figure, we see that the adjective "*eski*" (old) is connected to the first IG of the word "*odandayım*" since it is the word "*oda*" (room) which is modified by the adjective, not the derived verb form "*odandayım*" (I'm in your room). On the other hand, the adverb "*şimdi*" (now) is connected to the second IG of this word and modifies the verb "being in the room". The graphical interface is designed so that the annotator can easily determine the correct head word and its correct IG.

[2]The arrows in the figure indicates the dependencies emanating from the dependent unit towards the head unit.

In each step of the syntactic annotation, the partially built dependency tree is shown to the annotators in order to reduce the number of mistakes caused by the inattentiveness of the annotators (such as the errors encountered in the original Turkish treebank; cycled dependencies, erroneous crossing dependencies, unconnected items, dependencies to nonexistent items). Extra cautions are taken with similar reasons in order to force the annotators to only make valid annotations:

- Only the check boxes under final IGs of the words become active when the annotator is about to select a dependent since the dependencies can only emanate from the last IGs of the dependents.
- The dependents may only be connected to the IGs of other words, thus the check boxes of the IGs within the dependent word become passive when selecting a head unit.

Similar to the morphological disambiguation stage, the annotator may want to consult to an automatic analyzer. We use the data-driven dependency parser of Nivre et al. (2006) as an external parsing guide which is shown to give the highest accuracy for Turkish and for many other languages. The out put of the parser (pre-trained on the Turkish treebank) is reflected to the screen by automatically constructing the dependency tree. The annotator may then change the dependencies which he/she finds in correct.

6 Conclusions and Future Work

ITU treebank annotation tool is a semi-automatic annotation tool tailored for the particular morphological structure of Turkish where we need to annotate units smaller than words. It has three annotation levels and uses pluggable analyzers in order to automate these levels. These are a rule-based morphological analyzer, and machine learning based part-of-speech tagger and dependency parser. The tool which aims to provide a user-friendly platform for the human annotators, also tries to minimize the number of errors due to the complexity of the annotation process of Turkish. The tool is designed and used only for Turkish in its current state, however it can be used for other languages with similar morphological structure (particularly other Turkic lan-

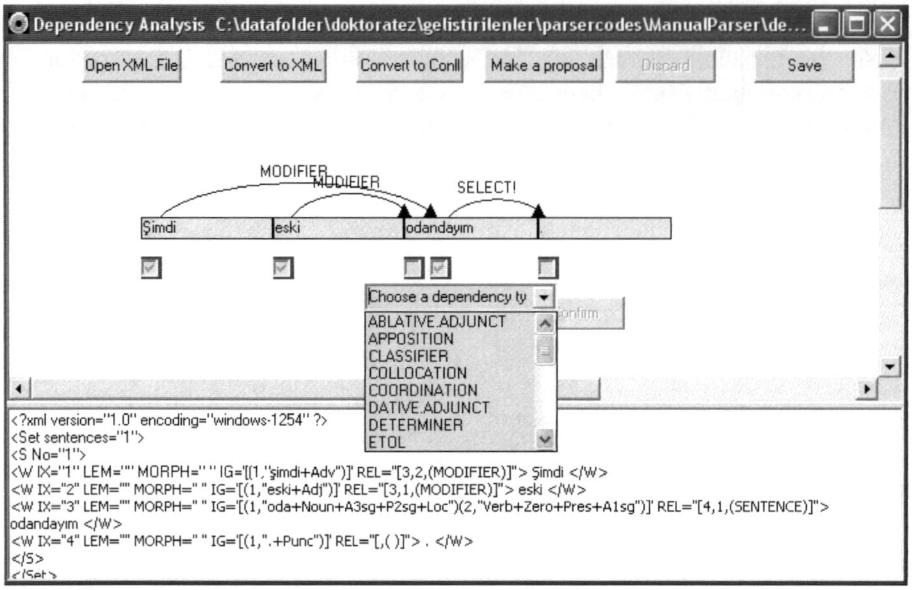

Figure 3: Dependency Analysis Screen

guages) by replacing the external analyzers. By using this tool, we observed significant acceleration both in correcting the existing treebank and developing new data sets. However education of new human annotators still remains as a difficult point and requires a lot of time. Hence in the future, we aim to develop online education tools which teach the annotators and tests their performance. We also aim to carry the platform to the web and supply an environment which can be reached from different places by volunteer researchers and collect the data in a single place.

Acknowledgment

The author wants to thank Kemal Oflazer for his valuable comments, Engin Taşkın and Cihat Eryiğit for their help during the development of the tool.

References

Nart B. Atalay, Kemal Oflazer, and Bilge Say. 2003. The annotation process in the Turkish treebank. In *Proc. of the 4th International Workshop on Linguistically Interpreteted Corpora*, Budapest.

Sabine Buchholz and Erwin Marsi. 2006. Conll-X shared task on multilingual dependency parsing. In *Proc. of the 10th CoNLL*, pages 149–164, New York, NY.

Gülşen Eryiğit and Kemal Oflazer. 2006. Statistical dependency parsing of Turkish. In *Proc. of the EACL*, pages 89–96, Trento.

Gülşen Eryiğit, Joakim Nivre, and Kemal Oflazer. 2006. The incremental use of morphological information and lexicalization in data-driven dependency parsing. In *Proc. of the ICCPOL*, pages 498–507, Singapore.

Dilek Hakkani-Tür, Kemal Oflazer, and Gökhan Tür. 2002. Statistical morphological disambiguation for agglutinative languages. *Journal of Computers and Humanities*, 36(4):381–410.

Tuomo Kakkonen. 2006. Depann - an annotation tool for dependency treebanks. In *Proc. of the 11th ESSLLI Student Session*, pages 214–225, Malaga.

Joakim Nivre, Johan Hall, Jens Nilsson, Gülşen Eryiğit, and Stetoslav Marinov. 2006. Labeled pseudo-projective dependency parsing with support vector machines. In *Proc. of the CoNLL-X*, pages 221–225, New York, NY.

Kemal Oflazer, Bilge Say, Dilek Z. Hakkani-Tür, and Gökhan Tür. 2003. Building a Turkish treebank. In A. Abeillé, editor, *Treebanks: Building and Using Parsed Corpora*, pages 261–277. Kluwer, Dordrecht/Boston/London.

Kemal Oflazer. 1994. Two-level description of Turkish morphology. *Literary and Linguistic Computing*, 9(2):137–148.

Kemal Oflazer. 2003. Dependency parsing with an extended finite-state approach. *Computational Linguistics*, 29(4):515–544.

Deniz Yüret and Ferhan Türe. 2006. Learning morphological disambiguation rules for Turkish. In *Proc. of the HLT-NAACL*, pages 328–334, New York, NY.

Two Tools for Creating and Visualizing Sub-sentential Alignments of Parallel Text

Ulrich Germann
University of Toronto
germann@cs.toronto.edu

Abstract

We present two web-based, interactive tools for creating and visualizing sub-sentential alignments of parallel text. *Yawat* is a tool to support distributed, manual word- and phrase-alignment of parallel text through an intuitive, web-based interface. *Kwipc* is an interface for displaying words or bilingual word pairs in parallel, word-aligned context.

A key element of the tools presented here is the interactive visualization: alignment information is shown only for one pair of aligned words or phrases at a time. This allows users to explore the alignment space interactively without being overwhelmed by the amount of information available.

1 Introduction

Sub-sentential alignments of parallel text play an important role in statistical machine translation (SMT). They establish which parts of a sentence correspond to which parts of the sentence's translation, and thus form the basis of a compositional approach to translation that models the translation of a sentence as a sequence of individual translation decisions for basic units of meaning. The simplest assumption is that typographic words, i.e., strings of letters delimited by punctuation and white space, constitute the basic units of translation. In reality, of course, things are more complicated. One word in one language may have to be translated into several in the other or not at all, or several words may form a conceptual unit that cannot be translated word for word. Because of its central role in building machine translation systems and because of the complexity of the task, sub-sentential alignment of parallel corpora continues to be an active area of research (e.g., Moore *et al.*, 2006; Fraser and Marcu, 2006), and this implies a continuing demand for manually created or human-verified gold standard alignments for development and evaluation purposes.

We present here two tools that are designed to facilitate the process and allow human inspection of automatically aligned parallel corpora for the study of translation. The first is a web-based interface for manual sub-sentential alignment of parallel sentences. The second is an extension of the traditional keywords-in-context tools to the bilingual case. A distinctive feature of both tools is that they are based on an interactive process. Rather than showing all alignment information at once, they hide most information most of the time and visualize alignment information only selectively and only on demand.

2 Visualization schemes for sub-sentential text alignment information

In this section, we briefly review existing visualization schemes for word-level alignments.

2.1 Drawing lines

Word alignment visualization by drawing lines is shown in Figure 1. This visualization technique has several limitations.

- The parallel text cannot be wrapped easily. Each sentence has to be represented as a straight line or column of text. If the word

Proceedings of the Linguistic Annotation Workshop, pages 121–124,
Prague, June 2007.

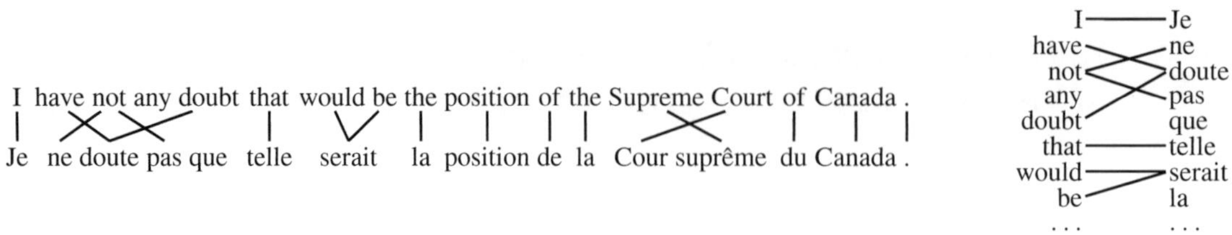

Figure 1: Visualization of word alignments by drawing lines.

alignment is known, it may be possible to presegment the parallel text into smaller blocks of text such that all word alignment links are contained within these blocks of text. For manual word alignment from scratch, this is impossible, for lack of prior word alignment information. In consequence, the sentence pair often will not fit on the computer screen entirely, so that users have to scroll back and forth to view and create alignment links.

- Especially when the two aligned sentences show differences in word order, many of the lines representing word alignments will cross one another, leading to a cluttered and hard-to-follow display.

- There is no good way to represent the alignment on the phrase level, especially when the phrases contain gaps. If the phrases involved are contiguous, we can use brackets or boxes to group words into phrases, but this does not work for phrases that contain gaps. Another way to visualize phrase alignments is to link each word in each of the two phrases with each word in the respective other phrase. This acerbates the aforementioned problem of visual clutter.

2.2 Alignment matrices

Alignment matrices such as the one shown in Figure 2 map the words of one sentence onto the rows and the words of the other sentence onto the columns of a two-dimensional table. Each cell (r, c) in the table represents a potential alignment between the word in the r-th position of the first sentence and the word in the c-th position in the second sentence. If the two words are in fact aligned, the respective

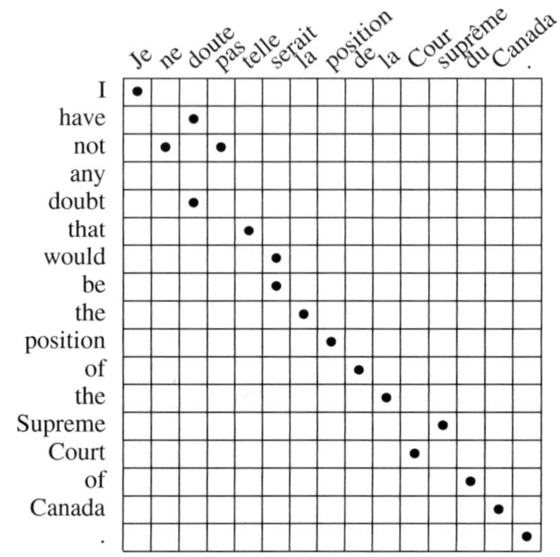

Figure 2: Visualization of word alignments with an alignment matrix.

cell contains a dot, otherwise it is empty. This technique allows the visualization of phrase-level alignments even of discontinuous phrases (by filling the cells representing the cross-product of the two sets of words involved). Fitting the matrix for pairs of long sentences onto the screen is still a problem, however.

2.3 Coloring

A third way of visualizing word alignments is the use of colors. This technique has two draw-backs. First, it may be difficult to find enough colors that are easily distinguished to mark up all alignments in pairs of long sentences, and second, actually tracking alignments is tedious and requires a lot of concentration.

2.4 Interactive visualization

Our solution to the visualization problem is to take an interactive approach. We use the coloring approach, but use only one or two colors to mark up

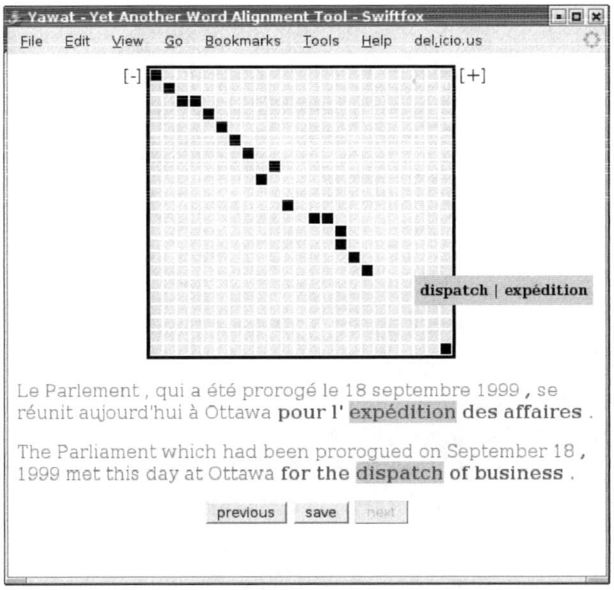

Figure 3: Manual word alignment with *Yawat*. The image shows the state of the screen with the mouse hovering over the alignment matrix cell corresponding to *dispatch* ↔ *expédition*. A click onto the cell links the two words.

alignment pairs, and we mark up alignment pairs only one at a time. By positioning the mouse pointer over a word of interest, the user indicates which alignment he or she would like to see. All other alignments are hidden.

3 The tools

3.1 Yawat

Yawat (***Y**et **A**nother **W**ord **A**lignment **T**ool*) is a tool for manual alignment of parallel sentences. It consists of a cgi-script responsible for retrieving and storing sentence pairs and their alignments from a database on the server side and marking them up in HTML, and client-side functionality that handles the interactive aspects of word-alignment and display and reports changes back to the server-side script.

The user interface combines alignment matrix visualization with interactive colorization. Figure 3 shows the typical *Yawat* interface. The alignment matrix on top gives a birds-eye view of the alignment relations in the sentence. If the mouse is positioned over one of the cells, a tool-tip window pops up showing the row and column labels of the respective cell. If the cell is 'active' (i.e., represents part of an alignment relation), the corresponding alignment pair is highlighted in the text section below. Rows and columns of the alignment matrix are deliberately not labeled so that the alignment matrix can be kept small. Its size is adjustable via the [–] and [+] buttons to its left and right.

The text section below the matrix shows the actual sentence pair. Moving the mouse over an aligned word highlights the respective alignment pair in the text as well as the corresponding cells in the matrix.

The tool was designed to minimize the number of mouse clicks and mouse travel necessary to align words. Clicking on an empty cell in the matrix aligns the respective words. The effect of clicking on an active cell depends on whether the cell represents an exclusive link between two single words, or is part of a larger alignment group. In the former case, the link is simply removed, in the latter, the respective alignment group is opened for editing. Once an alignment group is open for editing, a left-click with the mouse adds or removes words. Selecting a word that is currently part of another alignment group automatically removes it from that group. An alignment group is closed by a right-click on one of its members. A right click on a non-member adds it to the group and then closes the group for editing. This allows us to perform single word alignments with two simple mouse clicks: left-click on the first word and right click on the second, without the need to move the mouse on a visual 'link words' button in the interface.

Unaligned text in the sentence pair is represented in red, aligned text in gray. This allows the annotator to immediately spot unaligned sections without having to refer to the alignment matrix or to scan the text with the mouse to find unaligned words.

We have not performed a formal user study, but we have found the tool very efficient in our own experience.

3.2 Kwipc

Kwipc (***K**ey **W**ords **I**n **P**arallel **C**ontext*) uses the same interactive visualization technique to display word alignments for multiple sentence pairs. It currently uses a very simple search interface that allows the user to specify regular expressions for one or both of the sentences in the sentence pair. The server-side cgi-script searches the corpus lin-

Table 1: Word alignment visualization and editing tools

name	visualization	editing
Cairo[a]	lines	no
Alpaco[b]	lines	yes
Lingua-AlignmentSet[c]	matrix	no
UMIACS WA Interface[d]	lines	yes
HandAlign[e]	lines	yes
Ilink[f]	static colors	yes
UPlug[g]	matrix	yes
ICA[h]	matrix	yes
ReWrite Decoder	interactive, colors	no
Yawat	matrix, interactive, colors	yes
Kwipc	interactive, colors	no

[a] http://www.clsp.jhu.edu/ws99/projects/mt/toolkit/

[b] http://www.d.umn.edu/~tpederse/parallel.html

[c] http://gps-tsc.upc.es/veu/personal/lambert/\newlinesoftware/AlignmentSet.html

[d] http://www.umiacs.umd.edu/~nmadnani/\newlinealignment/forclip.htm

[e] http://www.cs.utah.edu/~hal/HandAlign/

[f] http://www.ida.liu.se/~nlplab/ILink/

[g] http://stp.ling.uu.se/cgi-bin/joerg/Uplug

[h] Tiedemann (2006)

early and returns a list of marked-up sentence pairs that contain matching expressions (which are highlighted in red) and provides the same interactive alignment visualization as *Yawat*. For lack of space, we cannot provide a screen shot here.

4 Related work

There are numerous tools available for the visualization and creation of word alignments, most of which are listed on Rada Mihalcea's web site on word alignment at http://www.cs.unt.edu/~rada/wa/. A comparison of these tools is shown in Table 1. Most tools use line drawing or alignment matrices for visualization. Only *Ilink* (Ahrenberg *et al.*, 2002) relies on colors to visualize alignments, but it implements a static colorization scheme. The interactive visualization scheme was first used in the HTML output of the *ISI ReWrite Decoder*[1], but the formatting used there relies on an obsolete Document Object Model and is not functional any more. The use of different colors to distinguish aligned and unaligned sections of text can also be found in *HandAlign*.

5 Conclusion

We have presented two web-based tools that use an interactive visualization method to display word- and phrase-alignment information for parallel sentence pairs, thus reducing visual clutter in the display and providing users with focussed access to the alignment information they are actually interested in. The editing tool *Yawat* was designed to minimize unnecessary scrolling, mouse clicks and mouse travel to provide the annotator with an efficient tool to perform manual word- and phrase-alignment of parallel sentences. Delivery of the application through the web browser allows collaborative alignment efforts with a central repository of alignments and without the need to install the software locally.

6 Availability

The tools are available at http://www.cs.toronto.edu/compling/Software.

References

Ahrenberg, Lars, Mikael Andersson, and Magnus Merkel. 2002. "A system for incremental and interactive word linking." *Proc. LREC 2002*, 485–490. Las Palmas, Spain.

Fraser, Alexander and Daniel Marcu. 2006. "Semi-supervised training for statistical word alignment." *Proc. COLING-ACL 2006*, 769–776. Sydney, Australia.

Moore, Robert C., Wen-tau Yih, and Andreas Bode. 2006. "Improved discriminative bilingual word alignment." *Proc. COLING-ACL 2006*, 513–520. Sydney, Australia.

Tiedemann, Jörg. 2006. "ISA & ICA — Two web interfaces for interactive alignment of bitexts." *Proc. LREC 2006*. Genoa, Italy.

[1] http://www.isi.edu/publications/licensed-sw/rewrite-decoder/index.html

Building Chinese Sense Annotated Corpus with the Help of Software Tools

Yunfang Wu
School of Electronic Engineering and Computer Science, Peking University, Beijing 100871
wuyf@pku.edu.cn

Peng Jin
School of Electronic Engineering and Computer Science, Peking University, Beijing 100871
jandp@pku.edu.cn

Tao Guo
School of Electronic Engineering and Computer Science, Peking University, Beijing 100871
gtwcq@pku.edu.cn

Shiwen Yu
School of Electronic Engineering and Computer Science, Peking University, Beijing 100871
yusw@pku.edu.cn

Abstract

This paper presents the building procedure of a Chinese sense annotated corpus. A set of software tools is designed to help human annotator to accelerate the annotation speed and keep the consistency. The software tools include 1) a tagger for word segmentation and POS tagging, 2) an annotating interface responsible for the sense describing in the lexicon and sense annotating in the corpus, 3) a checker for consistency keeping, 4) a transformer responsible for the transforming from text file to XML format, and 5) a counter for sense frequency distribution calculating.

1 Introduction

There is a strong need for a large-scale Chinese corpus annotated with word senses both for word sense disambiguation (WSD) and linguistic research. Although much research has been carried out, there is still a long way to go for WSD techniques to meet the requirements of practical NLP programs such as machine translation and information retrieval. It was argued that no fundamental progress in WSD could be made until large-scale lexical resources were built (Veronis, 2003). In English a word sense annotated corpus SEMCOR (Semantic Concordances) (Landes et al., 1999) has been built, which was later trained and tested by many WSD systems and stimulated large amounts of WSD work. In Japanese the Hinoki Sensebank is constructed (Tanaka et al., 2006). In the field of Chinese corpus construction, plenty of attention has been paid to POS tagging and syntactic structures bracketing, for instance the Penn Chinese Treebank (Xue et al., 2002) and Sinica Corpus (Huang et al., 1992), but very limited work has been done with semantic knowledge annotation. Huang et al. (2004) introduced the Sinica sense-based lexical knowledge base, but as is well known, Chinese pervasive in Taiwan is not the same as mandarin Chinese. SENSEVAL-3 provides a Chinese word sense annotated corpus, which contains 20 words and 15 sentences per meaning for most words, but obviously the data is too limited to achieve wide coverage, high accuracy WSD systems.

This paper is devoted to building a large-scale Chinese corpus annotated with word senses. A small part of the Chinese sense annotated corpus has been adopted as one of the SemEval-2007 tasks namely "Multilingual Chinese-English Lexical Sample Task" This paper concentrates on the description of the manually annotating schemes

Proceedings of the Linguistic Annotation Workshop, pages 125–131,
Prague, June 2007.

with the help of software tools. The software tools will help human annotators mainly in the two aspects: 1) Reduce the labor time and accelerate the speed; 2) Keep the inter-annotator agreement. The overall procedure along with the software tools is illustrated in figure 1.

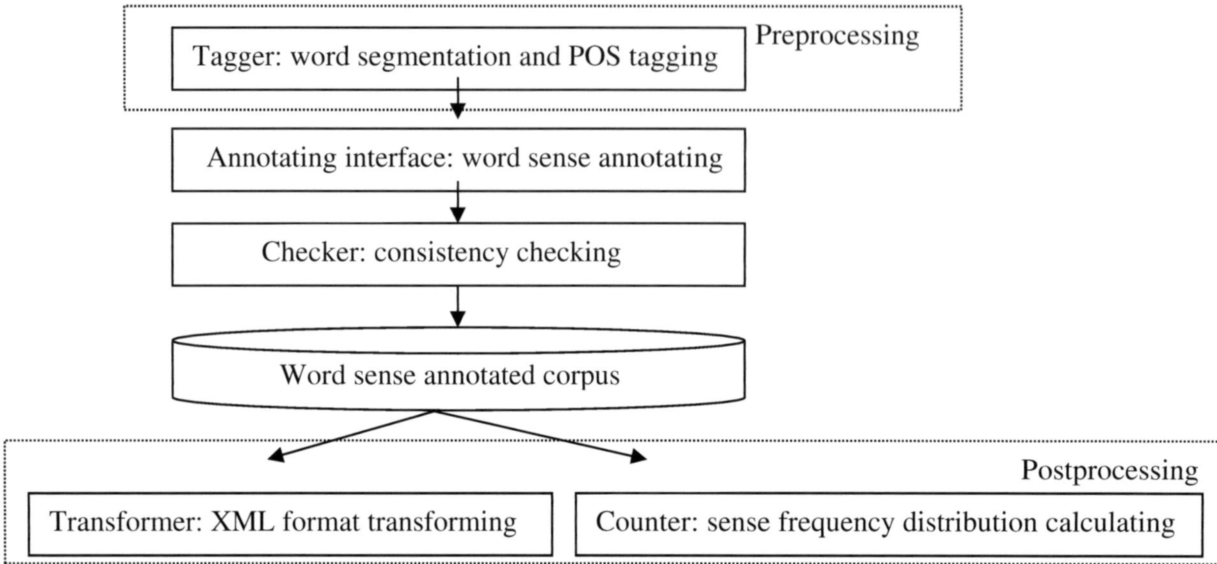

Fig.1.The overall procedure along with the software tools

This paper is so organized as follows. In section 2 the preprocessing stage (word segmentation and POS tagging) is discussed. Then in section 3 the annotating scheme and the annotating interface are demonstrated in detail. The strategy to keep consistency is addressed in section 4. And then in section 5 and 6 the two postprocessing stages are respectively presented. Finally in section 7 conclusions are drawn and future works are presented.

2 Word segmentation and POS tagging

The input data for word sense annotating is firstly word segmented and POS tagged using Peking University's POS tagger (Yu et al., 2003). The POS tagging precision is up to 97.5%, which lays a sound foundation for researches on sense annotating. This is actually to make use of the full-fledged syntactic processing techniques to deal with the semantic annotation problems. Different senses of one ambiguous word sometimes behave so differently that they bear different POS tags. Take "把握/hold" in sentence (1) as an example. The noun of "把握/hold" means "confidence", but the verb means "grasp".

(1) a 有(have) 把握/n(confidence)

b 把握/v(grasp) 住(ZHU) 机会(chance)

Due to the unique characteristic of Chinese language that lacks word inflection, the ambiguous words with different POSs are very common. According to the research of Li (1999), after POS tagging the ratio of ambiguous word occurrences in the text of People's Daily is reduced from 42% to 26%. Therefore the emphasis of manually sense annotating in this paper falls on the ambiguous words with the same part of speech. This will in turn save 16% of the annotation effort compared with the sense annotating before the preprocessing of POS tagging.

3 Word sense annotating

The resulting lexical knowledge base in this project will contain three major components: 1) a corpus annotated with Chinese word senses namely Chinese Senses Pool (CSP); 2) a lexicon containing sense distinction and description namely Chinese Semantic Dictionary (CSD); 3) the linking between the CSD and the Chinese Concept Dictionary (CCD) (Liu et al., 2002). The corpus CSP, the lexicon CSD and CCD constitute a highly relational and tightly integrated system: 1) In CSD the sense distinctions are described relying on the corpus; 2) In CSP the word occurrences are assigned sense tags according to the sense entry specified in CSD; 3) The linking between the sense entry in CSD and CCD synsets are established. The dynamic model is shown in figure 2. A software tool is developed in Java to be used as the word sense annotating interface (figure 3), which embodies the spirit of the dynamic model properly.

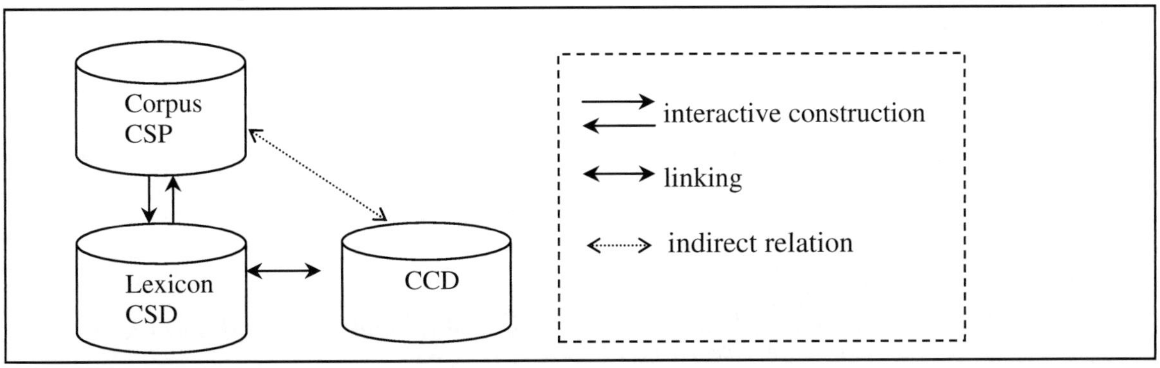

Fig 2. The dynamic model between the CSP, CSD and CCD

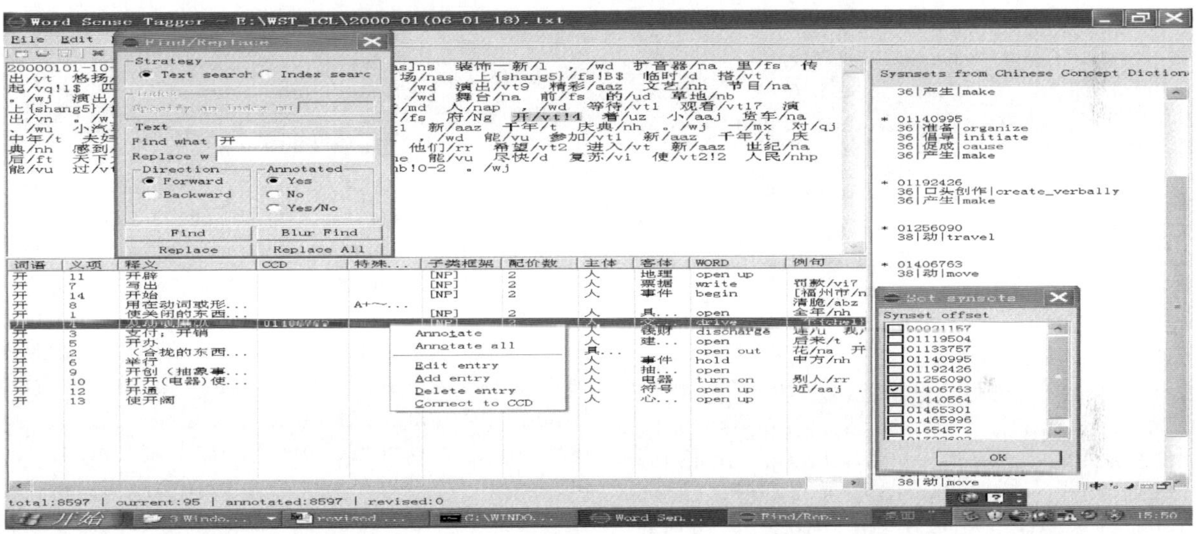

Fig3. The word sense annotating interface

3.1 Sense describing in the lexicon and sense annotating in the corpus

In this project the lexicon CSD containing sense descriptions and the corpus CSP annotated with senses are built interactively, simultaneously and dynamically. On one hand, the sense distinctions in the lexicon are made relying heavily on the corpus usage. On the other hand, using the sense information specified in the lexicon the human annotators assign semantic tags to all the instances of the word in a corpus.

In the word sense annotating interface, the sentences from CSP containing the target ambiguous words are displayed in the upper section, and the word senses with feature-based description from CSD are displayed in the bottom section.

Through reading the context in the corpus, the human annotator decides to add or delete or edit a sense entry in the lexicon. The default value of the range of the context is within a sentence, and the surrounding characters in the left and right of the target word can be specified by the annotator. Annotators can do four kinds of operations in CSD: 1) Add a sense entry and then fill in all the features; 2) Delete a sense entry along with all its feature description; 3) Edit a sense entry and change any of the features; 4) Select a sample sentence form the CSP and add it to the lexicon in the corresponding sense entry.

According to the sense specification in CSD the human annotator assigns semantic tags to the word occurrences in CSP. The operation is quite easy. When the annotator double clicks the appropriate sense entry in CSD the sense tag is automatically added to the target word.

The notable feature in this word sense annotating interface is that it provides flexible searching schemes. 1) Search sequentially (forward or backward) all the instances of an ambiguous words regardless of the annotating state; 2) Search sequentially (forward or backward) the already annotated instances; 3) Search sequentially (forward or backward) the yet un-annotated instances and 4) Search the instances of a specific ambiguous word (the window named Find/Replace in figure3, and again is shown in figure 4 for clearness).

The tool of Find/Replace is widely used in this project and has proven to be effective in annotating word senses. It allows the annotator to search for a specific word to finish tagging all its occurrences in the same period of time rather than move sequentially through the text. The consistency is more easily kept when the annotator manages many different instances of the same word than handle a few occurrences of many different words in a specific time frame, because the former method enables the annotator to establish an integrative knowledge system about a specific word and its sense distinction. Also the tool of Find/Replace provides flexible searching schemes for a specific ambiguous word. For instance, search in the corpus with different directions (forward/backward) and search with different annotating states (annotated/un-annotated/both). Using the tool the annotator can also replace some specific word occurrences in the corpus (often with special POS tags) with a sense tag, thus can finish annotating the corpus quickly and with a batch method. For instance the POS tag of "vq" (means verb complement) often uniquely corresponds to a specific verb sense such as "开/vq→开/vq!8".

There is the status bar in the bottom line of the word sense annotating interface, and there clearly show the annotating status: the total word occurrences, the serial number of the current processing instance and the number of the already annotated instances.

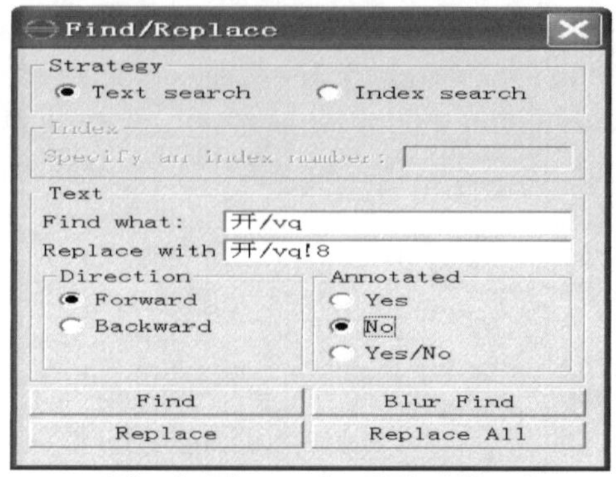

Fig.4 The tool of Find/Replace

3.2 Linking between CSD and CCD

The feature-based description of word meanings in CSD describes mainly the syntagmatic information, such as the subcategory frames of verbs, the semantic categories of the head noun of adjectives, but cannot include the paradigmatic relations. WordNet is a popular open resource and has been widely experimented in WSD researches. Chinese Concept Dictionary (CCD) is a WordNet-like Chinese lexicon (Liu et al., 2002), which carries the main relations defined in WordNet and can be seen as a bilingual concept lexicon with the parallel Chinese-English concepts to be simultaneously included. So the linking between the sense entries in CSD and the synsets in CCD is tried to establish in this project. After the linking has been established, the paradigmatic relations (such as hypernym / hyponym, meronym / holonym) expressed in CCD can map automatically to the sense entry in CSD. What's more, the many existing WSD approaches based on WordNet can be trained and tested on the Chinese sense tagged corpus.

In the right section of the word sense annotating interface there displays the synset information from CCD. When coping with a specific ambiguous word (such as "开/open") in CSD, the linking between CSD and CCD is automatically established with the word itself ("开/open") as the primary key. And then all the synsets of the word ("开/open") in CCD, along with the hypernyms of each sense (expressed by the first word in a synset), are displayed in the right section. A synset selection window (namely Set synsets) containing the offset numbers of the synsets then appears in the right section. The annotator clicks on the appropriate box(es) before the corresponding offset number and then the offset number is automatically added to the feature "CCD" in the currently selected sense entry in CSD.

The linking is now done manually. Unfortunately some of the ambiguous words existing in CSD are not included in CCD. This also provides a good way to improve the coverage and quality of CCD.

4 Consistency Checking

Consistency is always an important concern for hand-annotated corpus, and is even critical for the sense tagged corpus due to the subtle meanings to handle. A software tool namely Sense Consistency Checker is developed in the checking procedure. The checker extracts all the instances of a specific ambiguous word into a checking file with the format of the sense concordances (as shown in figure 5). The checking file enables the checker to have a closer examination of how the senses are used and distributed, and to form a general view of how the sense distinctions are made. The inter-annotator in-agreement thus can be reached quickly and correctly. As illustrated in figure 5, it is obviously an error to assign the same semantic tag to "开/drive 倒车/car" and "会议/meeting 开/held". Simply as it is the checker greatly accelerates the checking speed and improve the consistency.

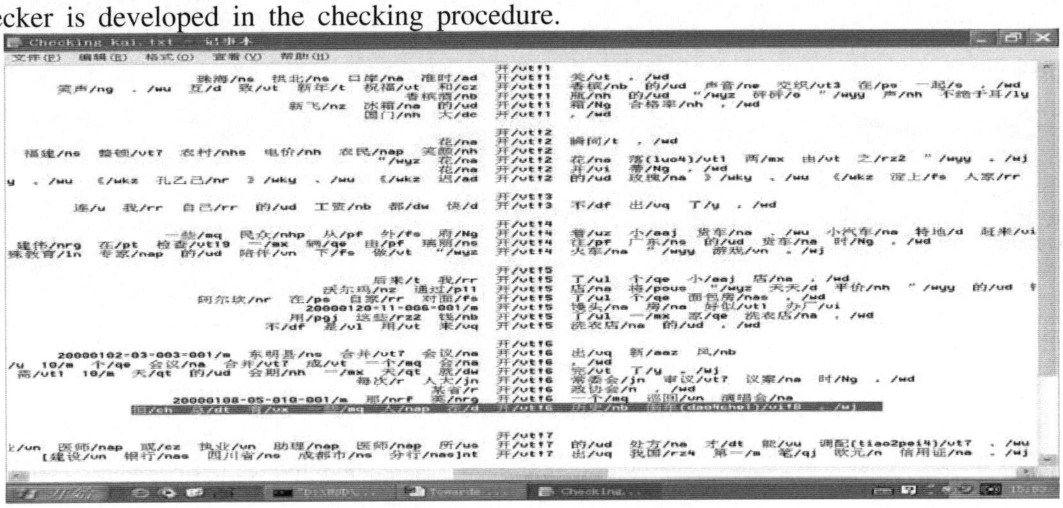

Fig. 5. Some example sentences in the checking file of "开/open"

Together five researchers took part in the annotation, of which three are majored in linguistics and two are majored in computational linguistics. In this project the annotators are also checkers, who check other annotators' work. A text generally is first tagged by one annotator and then verified by two checkers.

After the preprocessing of word segmentation and Pos tagging, the word sense annotating and the consistency checking, the Chinese word sense annotated corpus is constructed. And then other software tools are needed to do further processing in the sense annotated corpus.

5 XML format transforming

The original format of the Chinese sense annotated corpus is in text file as shown in figure 6. In the text file the sign following "/" denotes the POS tag, and the number following "!" indicates the sense ID. The text file complies with the other language resources at the Institute of Computational Linguistics, Peking University, which provides a quite easy way to make full use of the existing resources and techniques at ICL/PKU when constructing the sense annotated corpus.

At the same time in order to exchange and share information easily with other language resources in the world, a software tool namely Text-to-XML Transformer is developed to change the text to XML format (as shown in figure 7). In the XML file, the item "pos" denotes the POS tag of the word, and the item "senseid" denotes sense ID of the ambiguous word.

Thus there are two kinds of format for the Chinese sense annotated corpus, each of which has its advantages and can be adopted to meet different requirements in different situations.

严格/a 的/u 管理/vn 使/vt!2 整个/b 企业/n 像/p 一/m 架/q!1 各/r2 部位/n 零件/n 咬合/vi 得/u 十分/d 紧密/a 的/u 机器/n ，/w 生产/vn 成本/n 逐年/d 下降/vt 。/w 去年/t 电解铝/n 每/r 吨/q 制造/vn 成本/n 已/d 降/vt!3 到 /v 9000/m 多/m 元/q 。/w

Fig. 6. The sense annotated corpus in text file


```
<head date="20000201" page="01" articleno="003" passageno="019">
<passage>
严格的管理使整个企业像一架各部位零件咬合得十分紧密的机器，生产成本逐年下降。去年电解铝每吨制造成本已降到 9000 多元
</passage>
<postagging>
<word id="0" pos="a" senseid="">
<token>严格</token>
</word>
<word id="1" pos="u" senseid="">
<token>的</token>
</word>
<word id="2" pos="vn" senseid="">
<token>管理</token>
</word>
<word id="3" pos="vt" senseid="2">
<token>使</token>
</word>
…… ……
```


Fig. 7. The sense annotated corpus in XML format

6 Sense frequency calculating

Word sense frequency distribution in the real texts is a vital kind of information both for the algorithms of word sense disambiguation and for the research on lexical semantics. In the postprocessing stage a software tool namely Sense Frequency Counter is developed to make statistics on the sense frequency distribution. Quite valuable information can be acquired through the counter based on the sense annotated corpus: 1) The amount of all the instances of an ambiguous word; 2) The number of the already annotated instances; 3) The occurrence of each sense of an ambiguous word and 4) The sense frequency. Table 1 illustrates the sense frequency distribution of ambiguous verb "开/open" in 10 day's People's Daily.

7 Conclusions

This paper describes the overall building procedure of a Chinese sense annotated corpus. The corpus is firstly word segmented and POS tagging using Peking University's tagger in the preprocessing stage. Then the lexicon Chinese Semantic Dictionary (CSD) containing sense descriptions and the corpus Chinese Senses Pool (CSP) annotated with senses are built interactively, simultaneously and dynamically using the word sense annotating interface. At the same time the linking between the sense entries in CSD and the synsets in Chinese Concept Dictionary (CCD) are manually established. And then the Sense Consistency Checker is used to keep the inter-annotator agreement. Finally two software tools are developed to do further processing based on the sense annotated corpus. A software tool namely Text-to-XML Transformer is developed to change the text to XML format, and the Sense Frequency Counter is developed to make statistics on the sense frequency distribution. The annotation schemes and all the software tools have been experimented in building the SemEval-2007 task 5 "Multilingual Chinese-English Lexical Sample Task", and have proven to be effective.

Table 1 the sense frequency distribution of ambiguous verb "开/open"

Ambiguous verbs	Sense ID	Occurrences	Frequency(%)
开	8	30	32.26
开	4	13	13.98
开	6	12	12.90
开	7	8	8.60
开	0	6	6.45
开	1	6	6.45
开	9	4	4.30
开	12	4	4.30
开	11	3	3.23
开	2	3	3.23
开	10	3	3.23
开	14	1	1.08
开	15	0	0.00
开	3	0	0.00
开	5	0	0.00
开	13	0	0.00

Acknowledgments. This research is supported by Humanity and Social Science Research Project of China State Education Ministry (No. 06JC740001) and National Basic Research Program of China (No. 2004CB318102).

References

Huang, Ch. R and Chen, K. J. 1992. A Chinese Corpus for Linguistics Research. In Proceedings of COLING-1992.

Huang, Ch. R., Chen, Ch. L., Weng C. X. and Chen. K. J. 2004. The Sinica Sense Management System: Design and Implementation. In Recent advancement in Chinese lexical semantics.

Landes, S., Leacock, C. and Tengi, R. 1999. Building Semantic Concordances. In Christiane Fellbaum (Ed.) WordNet: an Electronic Lexical Database. MIT Press, Cambridge.

Li, J. 1999. The research on Chinese word sense disambiguation. Doctoral dissertation in computer science department of Tsinghua University.

Liu, Y., Yu, S. W. and Yu, J.S. 2002. Building a Bilingual WordNet-like Lexicon: the New Approach and Algorithms. In Proceedings of COLING 2002.

Tanaka, T., Bond F. and Fujita, S. 2006. The Hinoki Sensebank----A large-scale word sense tagged corpus of Japanese. In Proceedings of the Workshop on Frontiers in Linguistically Annotated Corpora 2006.

Veronis, J. 2003. Sense Tagging: Does It Make Sense? In Wilson et al. (Eds). Corpus Linguistics by the Rule: a Festschrift for Geoffrey Leech.

Xue, N., Chiou, F. D. and Palmer, M. 2002. Building a Large-Scale Annotated Chinese Corpus. In Proceedings of COLING 2002.

Yu, S. W., Duan, H. M., Zhu, X. F., Swen, B. and Chang, B. B. 2003. Specification for Corpus Processing at Peking University: Word Segmentation, POS tagging and Phonetic Notation. Journal of Chinese Language and Computing.

Annotating a Japanese Text Corpus with Predicate-Argument and Coreference Relations

Ryu Iida, Mamoru Komachi, Kentaro Inui and Yuji Matsumoto
Graduate School of Information Science,
Nara Institute of Science and Technology
8916-5 Takayama, Ikoma, Nara, 630-0192, Japan
{ryu-i,mamoru-k,inui,matsu}@is.naist.jp

Abstract

In this paper, we discuss how to annotate coreference and predicate-argument relations in Japanese written text. There have been research activities for building Japanese text corpora annotated with coreference and predicate-argument relations as are done in the Kyoto Text Corpus version 4.0 (Kawahara et al., 2002) and the GDA-Tagged Corpus (Hasida, 2005). However, there is still much room for refining their specifications. For this reason, we discuss issues in annotating these two types of relations, and propose a new specification for each. In accordance with the specification, we built a large-scaled annotated corpus, and examined its reliability. As a result of our current work, we have released an annotated corpus named the *NAIST Text Corpus*[1], which is used as the evaluation data set in the coreference and zero-anaphora resolution tasks in Iida et al. (2005) and Iida et al. (2006).

1 Introduction

Coreference resolution and predicate-argument structure analysis has recently been a growing field of research due to the demands from NLP application such as information extraction and machine translation. With the research focus placed on these tasks, the specification of annotating corpora and the data sets used in supervised techniques (Soon et al., 2001; Ng and Cardie, 2002, etc.) have also grown in sophistication.

For English, several annotation schemes have already been proposed for both coreference relation and argument structure, and annotated corpora have been developed accordingly (Hirschman, 1997; Poesio et al., 2004; Doddington et al., 2004). For instance, in the Coreference task on Message Understanding Conference (MUC) and the Entity Detection and Tracking (EDT) task in the Automatic Content Extraction (ACE) program, which is the successor of MUC, the details of specification of annotating coreference relation have been discussed for several years. On the other hand, the specification of predicate-argument structure analysis has mainly been discussed in the context of the CoNLL shared task[2] on the basis of the PropBank (Palmer et al., 2005).

In parallel with these efforts, there have also been research activities for building Japanese text corpora annotated with coreference and predicate-argument relations such as the Kyoto Text Corpus version 4.0 (Kawahara et al., 2002) and the GDA[3]-Tagged Corpus (Hasida, 2005). However, as we discuss in this paper, there is still much room for arguing and refining the specification of such sorts of semantic annotation. In fact, for neither of the above two corpora, the adequacy and reliability of the annotation scheme has been deeply examined.

In this paper, we discuss how to annotate coreference and predicate-argument relations in Japanese

[1]The NAIST Text Corpus is downloadable from http://cl.naist.jp/nldata/corpus/, and it has already been downloaded by 102 unique users.

[2]http://www.lsi.upc.edu/~srlconll/

[3]The Global Document Annotation

Proceedings of the Linguistic Annotation Workshop, pages 132–139,
Prague, June 2007. ©2007 Association for Computational Linguistics

text. In Section 2 to Section 4, we examine the annotation issues of coreference, predicate-argument relations, and event-nouns and their argument relations respectively, and define adequate specification of each annotation task. Then, we report the results of actual annotation taking the Kyoto Corpus 3.0 as a starting point. Section 6 discusses the open issues of each annotation task and we conclude in Section 7.

2 Annotating coreference relations

2.1 Approaches to coreference annotation

Coreference annotation in English has been evolving mainly in the context of information extraction. For instance, in the 6th and 7th Message Understanding Conferences (MUC), coreference resolution is treated as a subtask of information extraction[4]. The annotated corpora built in the MUC contain coreference relations between NPs, which are used as a gold standard data set for machine learning-based approaches to coreference resolution by researchers such as Soon et al. (2001) and Ng and Cardie (2002). However, van Deemter and Kibble (1999) claim that the specification of the MUC coreference task guides us to annotate expressions that are not normally considered coreferential, such as appositive relations (e.g. *Julius Caesar*$_i$, *a well-known emperor*$_i$, ...).

In the task of Entity Detection and Tracking (EDT) in the Automatic Content Extraction (ACE) program (Doddington et al., 2004), the successor of MUC, the coreference relations are redefined in terms of two concepts, *mentions* and *entities*, in order to avoid inappropriate co-indexing. In the specification of EDT, mentions are defined as the expressions appearing in the texts, and entities mean the collective set of specific entities referred to by the mentions in the texts. Entities are limited to named entities such as PERSON and ORGANIZATION for adequacy and reliability of annotation. Therefore, the ACE data set has the drawback that not all coreference relations in the text are exhaustively annotated. It is insufficient to resolve only the annotated coreference relations in order to properly analyze a text.

[4] http://www-nlpir.nist.gov/related_projects/muc/proceedings/co_task.html

2.2 Coreference annotated corpora of Japanese

In parallel with these efforts, Japanese corpora have been developed that are annotated with coreference relations, such as the Kyoto Text Corpus version 4.0 (Kawahara et al., 2002) and GDA-Tagged Corpus (Hasida, 2005). Before reviewing these works, we explain the relationship between anaphora and coreference in Japanese, referring to the following examples. In example (1), the pronoun *sore*$_i$ *(it)* points back to *iPod*$_i$, and these two mentions refer to the same entity in the world and thus are considered both anaphoric and coreferential.

(1) *Tom-wa* *iPod*$_i$*-o* *ka-tta* .
Tom-TOP iPod$_i$-ACC buy-PAST PUNC
Tom bought an iPod.
kare-wa *sore*$_i$*-de* *ongaku-o* *ki-ita* .
he-TOP it$_i$-INS music-ACC listen to-PAST PUNC
He listened to music on it.

On the other hand, in example (2), we still see an anaphoric relation between *iPod*$_i$ *(iPod*$_i$*)* and *sore*$_j$ *(it*$_j$*)* and *sore*$_j$ points back to iPod$_i$. However, these two mentions are not coreferential since they refer to different entities in the world.

(2) *Tom-wa* *iPod*$_i$*-o* *ka-tta* .
Tom-TOP iPod$_i$-ACC buy-PAST PUNC
Tom bought an iPod.
Mary-mo *sore*$_j$*-o* *ka-tta* .
Mary-TOP one$_j$-ACC buy-PAST PUNC
Mary also bought one.

As in the above examples, an anaphoric relation can be either coreferential or not. The former case is called an *identity-of-reference anaphora* (*IRA*) and the latter an *identity-of-sense anaphora* (*ISA*) (see Mitkov (2002)). In English the difference between IRA and ISA is clearly expressed by the anaphoric relations formed with 'it' and 'one' respectively. This makes it possible to treat these classes separately. However, in Japanese, no such clear lexical distinction can be drawn. In both the Kyoto Corpus and GDA-Tagged Corpus, there is no discussion in regards to distinction between ISA and IRA, thus it is unclear what types of coreference relations the annotators annotated. To make matters worse, their approaches do not consider whether or not a mention refers to a specific entity like in the EDT task.

2.3 Annotating IRA relations in Japanese

As described in the previous section, conventional specifications in Japanese are not based on a precise definition of coreference relations, resulting in inappropriate annotation. On the other hand, in our specification, we consider two or more mentions as coreferential in case they satisfy the following two conditions:

- The mentions refer to not a generic entity but to a specific entity.
- The relation between the mentions is considered as an IRA relation.

3 Annotating predicate-argument relations

3.1 Labels of predicate-argument relations

One debatable issue in the annotation of predicate-argument relations is what level of abstraction we should label those relations at.

The GDA-Tagged Corpus, for example, adopts a fixed set of somewhat "traditional" semantic roles such as Agent, Theme, and Goal that are defined across verbs. The PropBank (Palmer et al., 2005), on the other hand, defines a set of semantic roles (labeled ARG0, ARG1, and AM-ADV, etc.) for each verb and annotates each sentence in the corpus with those labels as in (3).

(3) [ARGM−TMP *A year earlier*], [ARG0 *the refiner*] [rel *earned*] [ARG1 *$66 million, or $1.19 a share*].

In the FrameNet (Fillmore and Baker, 2000), a specific set of semantic roles is defined for each set of semantically-related verbs called a FrameNet frame. However, there is still only limited consensus on how many kinds of semantic roles should be identified and which linguistic theory we should adopt to define them at least for the Japanese language.

An alternative way of labeling predicate-argument relations is to use syntactic cases as labels. In Japanese, arguments of a verb are marked by a postposition, which functions as a case marker. In sentence (4), for example, the verb *tabe* has two arguments, each of which is marked by a postposition, *ga* or *o*.

(4) *Tom-ga* *ringo-o* *tabe-ru*
Tom-NOM apple-ACC eat-PRES
(Tom eats an apple.)

Labeling predicate-argument relations in terms of syntactic cases has a few more advantages over semantic roles as far as Japanese is concerned:

- Manual annotation of syntactic cases is likely to be more cost-efficient than semantic roles because they are often explicitly marked by case markers. This fact also allows us to avoid the difficulties in defining a label set.
- In Japanese, the mapping from syntactic cases to semantic roles tends to be reasonably straightforward if a semantically rich lexicon of verbs like the VerbNet (Kipper et al., 2000) is available.
- Furthermore, we have not yet found many NLP applications for which the utility of semantic roles is actually demonstrated. One may think of using semantic roles in textual inference as exemplified by, for example, Tatu and Moldovan (2006). However, similar sort of inference may well be realized with syntactic cases as demonstrated in the information extraction and question answering literature.

Taking these respects into account, we choose to label predicate-argument relations in terms of syntactic cases, which follows the annotation scheme adopted in the Kyoto Corpus.

3.2 Syntactic case alternation

Once the level of syntactic cases is chosen for our annotation, another issue immediately arises, alteration of syntactic cases by syntactic transformations such as passivization and causativization. For example, sentence (5) is an example of causativization, where *Mary* causes *Tom*'s eating action.

(5) *Mary-ga* *Tom-ni* *ringo-o* *tabe-saseru*
Mary-NOM Tom-DAT apple-ACC eat-CAUSATIVIZED
(Mary helps Tom eat an apple.)

One way of annotating these arguments is something like (6), where the relations between the causativized predicate *tabe-saseru (to make someone eat)* and its arguments are indicated in terms of surface syntactic cases.

(6) [REL=*tabe-saseru* (eat-CAUSATIVE), GA=*Mary*, NI=*Tom*, O=*ringo* (apple)]

In fact, the Kyoto Corpus adopts this way of labeling.

An alternative way of treating such case alternations is to identify *logical* (or deep) case relations, i.e. the relations between the *base form* of each predicate and its arguments. (7) illustrates how the arguments in sentence (5) are annotated with logical case relations: *Tom* is labeled as the *ga*-case (Nominative) filler of the verb *tabe (to eat)* and *Mary* is labeled as the *Extra-Nominative* (EX-GA) which we newly invent to indicate the Causer of a syntactically causativized clause.

(7) [REL=*tabe-(ru)* (eat), GA=*Tom*, O=*ringo* (apple), EX-GA=*Mary*]

In the NAIST Text Corpus, we choose to this latter way of annotation motivated by such considerations as follows:

- Knowing that, for example, *Tom* is the filler of the *ga*-case (Nominative) of the verb *tabe (to eat)* in (5) is more useful than knowing that *Tom* is the *ni*-case (Dative) of the causativized verb *tabe-saseru (to make someone eat)* for such applications as information extraction.
- The mapping from syntactic cases to semantic roles should be described in terms of logical case relations associated with bare verbs.

3.3 Zero-anaphora

In the PropBank the search space for a given predicate's arguments is limited to the sentence that predicate appears in, because, syntactically, English obligatory arguments are overtly expressed except pro-form (e.g. *John hopes* [PRO *to leave.*]).

In contrast, Japanese is characterized by extensive use of nominal ellipses, called zero-pronouns, which behave like pronouns in English texts. Thus, if an argument is omitted, and an expression corresponding to that argument does not appear in the same sentence, annotators should search for its antecedent outside of the sentence. Furthermore, if an argument is not explicitly mentioned in the text, they need to annotate that relation as "exophoric." In the second sentence of example (8), for instance, the *ga* (Nominative) argument of the predicate *kaeru (go back)* is omitted and refers to *Tom* in the first sentence. The *kara* (Ablative) argument of that predicate is also omitted, however the corresponding argument does not explicitly appear in the text. In such cases, omitted arguments should be considered as "*exophoric*."

(8) Tom_i*-wa* *kyo* *gakko-ni* *it-ta* .
Tom_i-TOP today school-LOC go-PAST PUNC
Tom went to school today.
(ϕ_i*-ga*) ($\phi_{exophoric}$*-kara*) *kae-tte* *suguni*
ϕ_i-NOM $\phi_{exophoric}$-ABL go back immediately
(ϕ_i*-ga*) *kouen-ni* *dekake-ta* .
ϕ_i-NOM park-LOC go out-PAST PUNC
He went to the park as soon as he came back from school.

Table 1: Comparison of annotating predicate-argument relations

corpus	label	search space
PropBank	semantic role	intra
GDA Corpus	semantic role	inter, exo
Kyoto Corpus	surface case (voice alternation involved)	intra, inter, exo
NAIST Corpus (our corpus)	logical (deep) case (relation with bare verb)	intra, inter, exo

intra: intra-sentential relations, inter: inter-sentential relations, exo: exophoric relations

To the best of our knowledge, the GDA-Tagged Corpus does not contain intra-sentential zero-anaphoric relations as predicate-argument relations, so it has a serious drawback when used as training data in machine learning approaches.

Unlike coreference between two explicit nouns where only an IRA is possible, the relation between a zero-pronoun and its antecedent can be either IRA or ISA. For example, in example (8), ϕ_i is annotated as having an IRA relation with its antecedent Tom_i. In contrast, example (9) exhibits an ISA relation between $iPod_i$ and ϕ_i.

(9) *Tom-wa* $iPod_i$*-o* ka_a*-tta* .
Tom-TOP $iPod_i$-ACC buy_a-PAST PUNC
Tom bought an iPod.
Mary-mo (ϕ_i*-o*) ka_b*-tta* .
Mary-TOP ϕ_i-ACC buy_b-PAST PUNC
Mary also bought one.
[REL=*ka-(u)* (buy), GA=*Mary*, O=$iPod_i$]

The above examples indicate that predicate-argument annotation in Japanese can potentially be annotated as either an IRA or ISA relation. Note that in Japanese these two relations cannot be explicitly separated by syntactic clues. Thus, in our corpus we annotate them without explicit distinction. It is arguable that separate treatment of IRA and ISA in predicate-argument annotation could be preferable. We consider this issue as a task of future work.

A comparison of the specification is summarized in Table 1.

4 Annotating event-noun-argument relations

Meyers et al. (2004) propose to annotate semantic relations between nouns referring to an event in the context, which we call event-nouns in this paper. They release the NomBank corpus, in which PropBank-style semantic relations are annotated for event-nouns. In (10), for example, the noun "*growth*" refers to an event and "*dividends*" and "*next year*" are annotated as ARG1 (roughly corresponding to the theme role) and ARGM-TMP (temporal adjunct).

(10) *12% growth in dividends next year* [REL=*growth*, ARG1=*in dividends*, ARGM-TMP=*next year*]

Following the PropBank-style annotation, the NomBank also restricts the search space for the arguments of a given event-noun to the sentence in which the event-noun appears. In Japanese, on the other hand, since predicate-argument relations are often zero-anaphoric, this restriction should be relaxed.

4.1 Labels of event-noun-relations

Regarding the choice between semantic roles and syntactic cases, we take the same approach as that for predicate-argument relations, which is also adopted in the Kyoto Corpus. For example, in (11), *akaji*$_i$ *(deficit)* is identified as the *ga* argument of the event-noun *eikyo (influence)*.

(11) *kono* *boueki* *akaji*$_i$*-wa* *waga* *kuni-no*
this trade deficit-TOP our country-OF
kyosoryoku$_j$*-ni* *eikyo-o* *oyobosu*
competitiveness-DAT influence-ACC affect
[REL=*eikyo* (influence), GA=*akaji*$_i$ (deficit), O=*kyosoryoku*$_j$ *(competitiveness)*]
The trade deficit affects our competitiveness.

Note that unlike verbal predicates, event-nouns can never be a subject of voice alternation. An event-noun-argument relation is, therefore, necessarily annotated in terms of the relation between the bare verb corresponding to the event-noun and its argument. This is another reason why we consider it reasonable to annotate the logical case relations between bare verbs and their arguments for predicate-argument relations.

4.2 Event-hood

Another issue to be addressed is on the determination of the "event-hood" of noun phrases, i.e. the task of determining whether a given noun refers to an event or not. In Japanese, since neither singular-plural nor definite-indefinite distinction is explicitly marked, event-hood determination tends to be highly context-dependent. In sentence (12), for example, the first occurrence of *denwa (phone-call)*, subscripted with *i*, should be interpreted as *Tom*'s calling event, whereas the second occurrence of the same noun *denwa* should be interpreted as a physical telephone (cellphone).

(12) *kare*$_a$*-karano* *denwa*$_i$*-niyoruto* *watashi*$_b$*-wa*
he$_a$-ABL phone-call$_i$ according to I$_b$-NOM
kare-no *ie-ni* *denwa*$_j$*-o* *wasure-tarasii*
his-OF home-LOC phone$_j$-ACC leave-PAST
According to his phone call, I might have left my cell phone at his home.

To control the quality of event-hood determination, we constrain the range of potential event-nouns from two different points of view, neither of which is explicitly discussed in designing the specifications of the Kyoto Corpus.

First, we impose a POS-based constraint. In our corpus annotation, we consider only verbal nouns (*sahen*-verbs; e.g. *denwa (phone)*) and deverbal nouns (the nominalized forms of verbs; e.g. *furumai (behavior)*) as potential event-nouns. This means that event-nouns that are not associated with a verb, such as *jiko (accident)*, are out of scope of our annotation.

Second, the determination of the event-hood of a noun tends to be obscure when the noun constitutes a compound. In (13), for example, the verbal noun *kensetsu (construction)* constituting a compound *douro-kensetsu (road construction)* can be interpreted as a constructing event. We annotate it as an event and *douro (road)* as the *o* argument.

(13) *(ϕ-ga)* *douro-kensetsu-o* *tsuzukeru*
ϕ-NOM road construction-ACC continue
Someone continues road construction.

In (14), on the other hand, since the compound *furansu kakumei (French Revolution)* is a named-entity and is not semantically decomposable, it is not reasonable to consider any sort of predicate-argument-like relations between its constituents *furansu (France)* and *kakumei (revolution)*.

(14) *furansu-kakumei-ga* *okoru*
French Revolution-NOM take place
The French Revolution took place.

We therefore do not consider constituents of such semantically non-decomposable compounds as a target of annotation.

5 Statistics of the new corpus

Two annotators annotated predicate-argument and coreference relations according to the specifications, using all the documents in Kyoto Text Corpus version 3.0 (containing 38,384 sentences in 2,929 texts) as a target corpus. We have so far annotated predicate-argument relations with only three major cases: *ga* (Nominative), *o* (Accusative) and *ni* (Dative). We decided not to annotate other case relations like *kara*-case (Ablative) because the annotation of those cases was considered even further unreliable at the point where we did not have enough experiences in this annotation task. Annotating other cases is one of our future directions.

The numbers of the annotated predicate-argument relations are shown in Table 2. These relations are categorized into five cases: (a) a predicate and its argument appear in the same phrase, (b) the argument syntactically depends on its predicate or vice versa, (c) the predicate and its argument have an intra-sentential zero-anaphora relation, (d) the predicate and its argument have an inter-sentential zero-anaphora relation and (e) the argument does not explicitly appear in the text (i.e. exophoric). Table 2 shows that in annotation for predicates over 80% of both *o*- and *ni*-arguments were found in dependency relations, while around 60% of *ga*-arguments were in zero-anaphoric relations. In comparison, in the case of event-nouns, *o*- and *ni*-arguments are likely to appear in the same phrase of given event-nouns, and about 80% of *ga*-arguments have zero-anaphoric relations with event-nouns. With respect to the corpus size, we created a large-scaled annotated corpus with predicate-argument and coreference relations. The data size of our corpus along with other corpora is shown in Table 3.

Next, to evaluate the agreement between the two human annotators, 287 randomly selected articles were annotated by both of them. The results are evaluated by calculating recall and precision in which one annotation result is regarded as correct and the other's as the output of system. Note that only the predicates annotated by both annotators are used in calculating recall and precision. For evaluation of coreference relations, we calculated recall and precision based on the MUC score (Vilain et al., 1995). The results are shown in Table 4, where we can see that most annotating work was done with high quality except for the *ni*-argument of event-nouns. The most common source of error was caused by verb alternation, and we will discuss this issue in detail in Section 6. Such investigation of the reliability of annotation has not been reported for either the Kyoto Corpus or the GDA-Tagged Corpus. However, our results also show that each annotating task still leaves room for improvement. We summarize open issues and discuss the future directions in the next section.

Table 3: Data size of each corpus

corpus	size
PropBank I	7,891 sentences
NomBank 0.8	24,311 sentences
ACE (2005 English)	269 articles
GDA Corpus	2,177 articles
Kyoto Corpus	555 articles (5,127 sentences)
NAIST Corpus (ours)	2,929 articles (38,384 sentences)

Table 4: Agreement of annotating each relation

	recall	precision
predicate	0.947 (6512/6880)	0.941 (6512/6920)
ga (NOM)	0.861 (5638/6549)	0.856 (5638/6567)
o (ACC)	0.943 (2447/2595)	0.919 (2447/2664)
ni (DAT)	0.892 (1060/1189)	0.817 (1060/1298)
event-noun	0.905 (1281/1415)	0.810 (1281/1582)
ga (NOM)	0.798 (1038/1300)	0.804 (1038/1291)
o (ACC)	0.893 (469/525)	0.765 (469/613)
ni (DAT)	0.717 (66/92)	0.606 (66/109)
coreference	0.893 (1802/2019)	0.831 (1802/2168)

6 Discussion

6.1 Identification of predicates and event-nouns

Identification of predicates is sometimes unreliable due to the ambiguity between a literal usage and a compound functional usage. For instance, the expression "*to-shi-te*", which includes the verb *shi* (to do), is ambiguous: either the verb *shi* functions as a content word, i.e. an event-denoting word, or it constitutes a multi-word expression together with *to* and *te*. In the latter case, it does not make sense to interpret the verb *shi* to denote an event. However, this judgment is highly context-dependent and we have not been able to devise a reliable criterion for it.

Tsuchiya et al. (2006) have built a functional expression-tagged corpus for automatically classifying these usages. They reported that the agreement ratio of functional expressions is higher than ours. We believe their findings to also become helpful information for annotating predicates in our corpus.

With regards to event-nouns, a similar problem

Table 2: Statistics: annotating predicate-arguments relations

		ga (Nominative)		*o* (Accusative)		*ni* (Dative)	
predicates	(a) in same phrase	177	(0.002)	60	(0.001)	591	(0.027)
106,628	(b) dependency relations	44,402	(0.419)	35,882	(0.835)	18,912	(0.879)
	(c) zero-anaphoric (intra-sentential)	32,270	(0.305)	5,625	(0.131)	1,417	(0.066)
	(d) zero-anaphoric (inter-sentential)	13,181	(0.124)	1,307	(0.030)	542	(0.025)
	(e) exophoric	15,885	(0.150)	96	(0.002)	45	(0.002)
	total	105,915	(1.000)	42,970	(1.000)	21,507	(1.000)
event-nouns	(a) in same phrase	2,195	(0.077)	5,574	(0.506)	846	(0.436)
28,569	(b) dependency relations	4,332	(0.152)	2,890	(0.263)	298	(0.154)
	(c) zero-anaphoric (intra-sentential)	9,222	(0.324)	1,645	(0.149)	586	(0.302)
	(d) zero-anaphoric (inter-sentential)	5,190	(0.183)	854	(0.078)	201	(0.104)
	(e) exophoric	7,525	(0.264)	42	(0.004)	10	(0.005)
	total	28,464	(1.000)	11,005	(1.000)	1,941	(1.000)

also arises. If, for example, a compound noun contains a verbal noun, we have to judge whether the verbal noun can be interpreted as an event-noun or not. Currently, we ask annotators to check if the meaning of a given compound noun can be compositionally decomposed into those of its constituents. However, the judgement of compositionality tends to be highly subjective, causing the degradation of the agreement ratio of event-nouns as shown in Table 4. We are planning to investigate this problem more closely and refine the current compositionality criterion. One option is to build lexical resources of multi-word expressions and compounds.

6.2 Identification of arguments

As we mentioned in 3.1, we use (deep) cases instead of semantic roles as labels of predicate-argument relations. While it has several advantages as discussed in 3.1, this choice has also a drawback that should be removed. The problem arises from lexical verb alternation. It can sometimes be hard for annotators to determine a case frame of a given predicate when verb alternation takes place. For example, sentence (15) can be analyzed simply as in (16a). However, since the verb *shibaru* (bind) has also another alternative case frame as in (16b), the labeling of the case of the argument *kisoku* (rule), i.e. either GA (NOM) or DE (INST) may be undecidable if the argument is omitted.

(15) *kisoku-ga* *hitobito-o* *shibaru*
rule-NOM people-ACC bind
The rule binds people.

(16) a. [REL = *shibaru* (bind), GA = *kisoku* (rule), O = *hitobito* (people)]

b. [REL = *shibaru* (bind), GA = ϕ (exophoric), O = *hitobito* (people), DE (Instrumental) = *kisoku* (rule)]

Similar problems occur for event-nouns as well. For example, the event-noun *hassei (realization)* has both transitive and intransitive readings, which may produce awkward ambiguities.

To avoid this problem, we have two options; one is to predefine the preference in case frames as a convention for annotation and the other is to deal with such alternations based on generic resources of lexical semantics such as Lexical Conceptual Structure (LCS) (Jackendoff, 1990). Creating a Japanese LCS dictionary is another on-going project, so we can collaborate with them in developing the valuable resources.

6.3 Event-hood determination

Event-nouns of some semantic types such as *keiyaku (contract)*, *kisei (regulation)* and *toushi (investment)* are interpreted as either an event or an entity resulting from an event depending on are context. However, it is sometimes difficult to judge whether such an event-noun should be interpreted as an event or a resultant entity even by considering the whole context, which degrades the stability of annotation. This phenomena is also discussed in the NomBank, and we will share their insights and refine our annotation manual in the next step.

6.4 Identification of coreference relation

Even though coreference relation is defined as IRA relations, the lack of agreement on the granularity of noun classes makes the agreement ratio worse. In other words, it is crucial to decide how to annotate abstract nouns in order to improve the annotation.

Annotators judge coreference relations as whether or not abstract nouns refer to the same entity in the world. However, the equivalence of the referents of abstract nouns cannot be reconciled based on real-world existence since by definition abstract nouns have no physical entities in the real world.

As far as predicate-argument relation is concerned, there might be a need for treating generic entities in addition to specific entities as coreferential in some application. For example, one may want to relate *kids* to *children* in sentence (17).

(17) We all want *children* to be fit and healthy. However, the current invasion of fast food is creating overweight and unhealthy *kids*.

The coreference relation between generic nouns are missed in the current specification since we annotate only IRA relations between specific nouns. Even though there are various discussions in the area of semantics, the issue of how to deal with generic nouns as either coreferential or not in real texts is still left open.

7 Conclusion

In this paper, we reported on the current specification of our annotated corpus for coreference resolution and predicate-argument analysis. Taking the previous work of corpus annotation into account, we decided to annotate predicate-argument relations by ISA and IRA relations, and coreference relations according to IRA relations. With the Kyoto Text Corpus version 3.0 as a starting point, we built a large annotated corpus. We also discussed the revelations made from annotating our corpus, and discussed future directions for refining our specifications of the NAIST Text Corpus.

Acknowledgement

This work is partially supported by the Grant-in-Aid for Scientific Research in Priority Areas JAPANESE CORPUS (http://tokuteicorpus.jp).

References

G. Doddington, A. Mitchell, M. Przybocki, L. Ramshaw, S. Strassel, and R. Weischedel. 2004. Automatic content extraction (ace) program - task definitions and performance measures. In *Proceedings of the 4rd International Conference on Language Resources and Evaluation (LREC-2004)*, pages 837–840.

Charles J. Fillmore and Collin F. Baker. 2000. Framenet: Frame semantics meets the corpus. In *Proceedings of the 74th Annual Meeting of the Linguistic Society of America.*

K. Hasida. 2005. Global document annotation (gda) annotation manual. http://i-content.org/tagman.html.

L. Hirschman. 1997. *MUC-7 coreference task definition*. version 3.0.

R. Iida, K. Inui, and Y. Matsumoto. 2005. Anaphora resolution by antecedent identification followed by anaphoricity determination. *ACM Transactions on Asian Language Information Processing (TALIP)*, 4:417–434.

R. Iida, K. Inui, and Y. Matsumoto. 2006. Exploiting syntactic patterns as clues in zero-anaphora resolution. In *Proceddings of the 21st International Conference on Computational Linguistics and 44th Annual Meeting of the Association for Computational Linguistics (COLING-ACL)*, pages 625–632.

R. Jackendoff. 1990. *Semantic Structures*. Current Studies in Linguistics 18. The MIT Press.

D. Kawahara, T. Kurohashi, and K. Hasida. 2002. Construction of a japanese relevance-tagged corpus (in japanese). In *Proceedings of the 8th Annual Meeting of the Association for Natural Language Processing*, pages 495–498.

K. Kipper, H. T. Dang, and M. Palmer. 2000. Class-based construction of a verb lexicon. In *Proceedings of the 17th National Conference on Artificial Intelligence and 12th Conference on on Innovative Applications of Artificial Intelligence*, pages 691–696.

A. Meyers, R. Reeves, C. Macleod, R. Szekely, V. Zielinska, B. Young, and R. Grishman. 2004. The nombank project: An interimreport. In *Proceedings of the HLT-NAACL Workshop on Frontiers in Corpus Annotation.*

Ruslan Mitkov. 2002. *Anaphora Resolution*. Studies in Language and Linguistics. Pearson Education.

V, Ng and C. Cardie. 2002. Improving machine learning approaches to coreference resolution. In *Proceedings of the 40th ACL*, pages 104–111.

M. Palmer, D. Gildea, and P. Kingsbury. 2005. The proposition bank: An annotated corpus of semantic roles. *Computational Linguistics*, 31(1):71–106.

M. Poesio, R. Mehta, A. Maroudas, and J. Hitzeman. 2004. Learning to resolve bridging references. In *Proceddings of the 42nd Annual Meeting of the Association for Computational Linguistics (ACL)*, pages 144–151.

W. M. Soon, H. T. Ng, and D. C. Y. Lim. 2001. A machine learning approach to coreference resolution of noun phrases. *Computational Linguistics*, 27(4):521–544.

M. Tatu and D. Moldovan. 2006. A logic-based semantic approach to recognizing textual entailment. In *Proceddings of the 21st International Conference on Computational Linguistics and 44th Annual Meeting of the Association for Computational Linguistics (COLING-ACL)*, pages 819–826.

M. Tsuchiya, T. Utsuro, S. Matsuyoshi, S. Sato, and S. Nakagawa. 2006. Development and analysis of an example database of japanese compound functional expressions. *IPSJ Journal*, 47(6):1728–1741.

K. van Deemter and R. Kibble. 1999. What is coreference, and what should coreference annotation be? In *Proceedings of the ACL '99 Workshop on Coreference and its applications*, pages 90–96.

M. Vilain, J. Burger, J. Aberdeen, D. Connolly, and L. Hirschman. 1995. A model-theoretic coreference scoring scheme. In *Proceedings of the 6th Message Understanding Conference (MUC-6)*, pages 45–52.

Web-based Annotation of Anaphoric Relations and Lexical Chains

Maik Stührenberg and **Daniela Goecke** and **Nils Diewald** and **Alexander Mehler**
Bielefeld University
Germany
{maik.stuehrenberg|daniela.goecke|nils.diewald|alexander.mehler}@uni-bielefeld.de

Irene Cramer
Dortmund University
Germany
irene.cramer@uni-dortmund.de

Abstract

Annotating large text corpora is a time-consuming effort. Although single-user annotation tools are available, web-based annotation applications allow for distributed annotation and file access from different locations. In this paper we present the web-based annotation application *Serengeti* for annotating anaphoric relations which will be extended for the annotation of lexical chains.

1 Introduction

The relevance of corpus work for different tasks in the fields of linguistics is widely accepted. This holds especially for the area of (semi-)automatic text and discourse analysis which demands reference corpora in which instances of various levels of discourse structure have been annotated. Such annotation tasks are typically carried out by a combination of automatic and manual techniques. Manual annotation of large text corpora is a time consuming effort. Therefore, annotation tools are an indispensable means to overcome the limits of manual annotations. In spite of their limited level of automatization, such tools nevertheless help to semi-automatically support the annotation process and to secure consistency of manual annotations. This paper describes such an annotation tool which focuses on a certain type of discourse structures. More specifically, we deal with anaphoric relations and lexical cohesion. Our starting point is the observation that these two resources of textual cohesion (Halliday and Hasan, 1976) homogeneously induce *chain-like* discourse structures: one the one hand we have reference chains started by some antecedence and continued by some anaphora linked to the same antecedence. On the other hand, lexical cohesion generates so called *lexical chains* of semantically related tokens. Based on this observation we describe the annotation tool *Serengeti* which reflects this structural homogeneity on the level of its structural representation model as well as by its procedural annotation model. *Serengeti* includes an annotation scheme which is extended in order to support the annotation of reference chains and lexical chains. The paper is organized as follows: Section 2.1 describes the application scenario of anaphoric relations and the scheme we use to annotate them. Section 2.2 deals with the second application scenario: lexical chains. As our starting point was the former scenario, its extension to the latter one will be motivated by a separate case study of lexical chaining. Section 3 refers to related work, while Section 4 describes our annotation tool in detail. Finally, the application of *Serengeti* to annotating lexical chains is described in Section 5.

2 Annotating Large Text Corpora

The main focus of the joint work presented in this paper[1] is text technological information modelling and analysis of various types of discourse. Within our research group we deal with the integration of

[1]The work presented in this paper is a joint effort of the projects A2, A4 and B1 of the Research Group *Text-technological modelling of information* funded by the German Research Foundation. See http://www.text-technology.de for further details.

Proceedings of the Linguistic Annotation Workshop, pages 140–147,
Prague, June 2007. ©2007 Association for Computational Linguistics

heterogeneous linguistic resources. This applies especially to the *Sekimo* project (A2) which focusses on the application domain of anaphora resolution. We use the term 'heterogeneity' to refer to resources that differ either in terms of form (text, audio, video) or in terms of function (e. g. lexicons, annotated texts). Connection between these resources can be established with the means of XML, cf. Simons (2004). Integrating resources via an abstract interface is necessary due to different reasons: The resources used have often been developed independently from each other and a cascaded application of one resource to the output of another resource is not always possible. Furthermore, the output of different resources often cannot be encoded in a single structure without driving into incompatibilites (i. e. XML overlap). Therefore an architecture was developed which allows for the combination of the output structures of several linguistic resources into a single XML annotated document and which is described in detail in Witt et al. (2005) and Stührenberg et al. (2006) .

2.1 Anaphoric Relations

Motivation and Background Resolving anaphoric relations needs a variety of different information (e. g. POS, distance information, grammatical function, semantic knowledge, see, for example, Mitkov (2002) for an overview). Several resources are applied to a corpus of 47 texts and the output structures are combined into a single XML document using the architecture mentioned above. In order not only to integrate but also evaluate resources for a given linguistic task formally in terms of precision and recall, it should be possible to either switch on or switch off a given resource. In the application domain of anaphora resolution evaluation is done as follows. Each *discourse entity* or *referent* (cf. Karttunen (1976)) is annotated as an XML element which holds a variety of attribute information. Each XML element is reinterpreted as a feature vector; pairs of discourse entities between which an anaphoric relation holds form a single feature vector with additional information relevant for anaphora resolution (e. g. distance information, identity of grammatical form, semantic relatedness of underlying lemmata and the like). In order to evaluate different resource settings, decision trees with varying sets of feature vectors are used for the process of anaphora resolution. Xiaofeng et al. (2004) or Strube and Müller (2003) have shown the feasibility of decision trees for the domain of anaphora resolution; we have chosen this approach as it makes it possible to easily switch the information set for training and evaluation as opposed to e. g. rewriting rule sets. Both, training and evaluation as well as empirically based analysis of anaphora need an annotated reference corpus (Poesio et al., 2002). Scheme and annotation process are described in the following section.

The Annotation Scheme for Anaphoric Relations Several annotation schemes for annotating anaphoric relations have been developed in the last years, e. g. the UCREL anaphora annotation scheme (Fligelstone, 1992; Garside et al., 1997), the SGML-based MUC annotation scheme (Hirschmann, 1997), and the MATE/GNOME Scheme (Poesio, 2004), amongst others. In order to annotate discourse relations – either anaphoric relations or lexical chains (cf. Section 2.2) – two types of information have to be specified. First, the *markables*, i. e. the elements that can be part of a relation, have to be specified (cf. Müller and Strube (2003)). Second, the *relation(s)* between markables and their respective types and subtypes have to be defined. The markables form a basis for the annotation process and therefore have to be annotated in advance. Normally, for a domain under investigation, elements are denoted as being markables either via a specific element or via the use of a universal attribute. In our system, discourse entities are detected automatically on the basis of POS and parsing information. The annotation scheme for annotating anaphoric relations is an extension of the scheme presented by Holler et al. (2004) that has been developed for annotations in the context of text-to-hypertext conversion in the project B1 *HyTex*. We adopt the distinction between coreference and cospecification but we extend the annotation scheme for an explicit distinction between cospecification (direct anaphora) and bridging (associative or indirect anaphora). Thus, we add the primary relation type *bridgingLink* (denoting bridging) to the already existing one (*cospecLink*). Each primary relation type includes different secondary relation

Listing 1: The annotation format for anaphoric relations. Shortened and manually revised output

```
1  <chs:chs>
2   <chs:text>
3    <cnx:de deID="de8" deType="namedEntity" headRef="w36">
4     <cnx:token ref="w36">Maik</cnx:token></cnx:de>
5    <cnx:token ref="w37">hat</cnx:token> <cnx:token ref="w38">kein</cnx:token>
6    <cnx:token ref="w39">eigenes</cnx:token> <cnx:token ref="w40">Fahrrad</cnx:token>,
7    <cnx:token ref="w42">und</cnx:token>
8    <cnx:de deID="de10" deType="namedEntity" headRef="w43">
9     <cnx:token ref="w43">Marie</cnx:token></cnx:de>
10   <cnx:token ref="w45">fährt</cnx:token> <cnx:token ref="w46">nicht</cnx:token>
11   <cnx:token ref="w47">in</cnx:token>
12   <cnx:de deID="de11" deType="nom" headRef="w49">
13    <cnx:token ref="w48">den</cnx:token>
14    <cnx:token ref="w49">Urlaub</cnx:token></cnx:de>.
15   <cnx:de deID="de12" deType="nom" headRef="w53">
16    <cnx:token ref="w52">Zwei</cnx:token>
17    <cnx:token ref="w53">Kinder</cnx:token></cnx:de>,
18   <cnx:de deID="de13" deType="nom" headRef="w56">
19    <cnx:token ref="w55">eine</cnx:token>
20    <cnx:token ref="w56">Gemeinsamkeit</cnx:token></cnx:de>:
21  </chs:text>
22  <cnx:token_ref id="w36" head="w37" pos="N" syn="@NH" depV="subj" morph="MSC␣SG␣NOM" />
23  <chs:semRel>
24   <chs:bridgingLink relType="hasMember" antecedentIDRefs="de8␣de10" phorIDRef="de12"/>
25  </chs:semRel>
26 </chs:chs>
```

types that specify the subtype of the relation, e. g. *ident* or *hypernym* as secondary types of cospecLink or *meronym* or *setMember* as secondary types of bridgingLink. An example annotation of an indirect anaphoric relation (element `bridgingLink`, line 30) between the discourse entities `de12` (lines 18 to 21) and `de8` (lines 3 to 5) and `de10` (lines 9 to 11) can be seen in Listing 1.

2.2 Lexical Chaining

Motivation and Background Based on the concept of lexical cohesion (Halliday and Hasan, 1976), computational linguists (inter alia Morris and Hirst (1991)) developed a method to compute a partial text representation: *lexical chains*. These span over passages or even the complete text linking lexical items. The exemplary annotation in Figure 1 illustrates that lexical chaining is achieved by the selection of vocabulary and significantly accounts for the cohesive structure of a text passage. Items in a lexical chain are connected via semantic relations. Accordingly, lexical chains are computed on the basis of a lexical semantic resource such as WordNet (Fellbaum, 1998). Figure 1 also depicts several unsystematic relations, which should in principle be considered. Unfortunately, common lexical resources do not incorporate them sufficiently. Most systems consist of the fundamental modules shown in Table 1.

> Jan sat down to rest at the foot of a huge beech-tree. Now he was so tired that he soon fell asleep; and a leaf fell on him, and then another, and then another, and before long he was covered all over with leaves, yellow, golden and brown.
>
> **Chain 1:** sat down, rest, tired, fell asleep
> **Chain 2:** beech-tree, leaf, leaves
>
> Unsystematic relations not yet considered in lexical chaining: foot / huge – beech-tree; yellow / golden / brown – leaves

Figure 1: Chaining Example (adapted from Halliday et al. (1976))

However, in order to formally evaluate the performance of a given chainer in terms of precision and recall, a (preferably standardized and freely available) test set would be required. To our knowledge such a resource does not exist – neither for English

Module	Subtasks
chaining candidate selection	preprocessing of corpora: determine chaining window, sentence boundaries, tokens, POS-tagging chunks etc.
calculation of chains / meta-chains	look-up: lexical semantic resource (e.g. WordNet), scoring of relations, sense disambiguation
output creation	rate chain strength (e.g. select strong chains), build application specific representation

Table 1: Overview of Chainer Modules

nor for German. We therefore plan to develop an evaluation corpus (gold standard), which on the one hand includes the annotation of lexical chains and on the other hand reveals the rich interaction between various principles to achieve a cohesive text structure. In order to systematically construct sound guidelines for the annotation of this gold standard, we conducted a case study.

Case Study Six subjects were asked to annotate lexical chains in three short texts and in doing so record all challenges and uncertainties they experienced. The subjects were asked to read three texts – a `wikipedia` entry (137 words), a newspaper article (233 words), and an interview (306 words). They were then given a list of all nouns occurring in the articles (almost all chainers exclusively consider nouns as chaining candidates), which they had to rate with respect to their 'importance' in understanding the text. On this basis they were asked to determine the semantic relations of every possible chaining candidate pair, thus chain the nouns and annotate the three texts. Just like previously reported case studies (Beigman Klebanov, 2005; Morris and Hirst, 2004; Morris and Hirst, 2005) aiming at the annotation of lexical chains, we found that the inter-annotator agreement was in general relatively low. Only the annotation of very prominent items in the three texts, which accounted for approximately one fifth of the chaining candidates, resulted in a satisfying agreement (that is: the majority of the subjects produced an identical or very similar annotation). However, all subjects complained about the task. They found it rather difficult to construct linearized or quasi-linearized structures, in short, chains. Instead, most of the subjects built clusters and drew very complex graphs to illustrate the cohesive relations they found. They also pointed out that only a small fraction of the candidate list contributed to their text understanding. This clearly supports our observation that most of the subjects *first* skimmed through the text to find the most prominent items, established chains for this selection and *then* worked the text over to distribute the remaining items to these chains. We therefore assume that lexical chains do not directly reflect reading and understanding processes. Nevertheless, they do in some way contribute to them. Many subjects additionally noted that a reasonable candidate list should also include multi-word units (e.g. technical terms) or even phrases. Furthermore, as already reported in previous work (Morris and Hirst, 2004), the semantic relations usually considered seem not to suffice. Accordingly, some subjects proposed new relations to characterize the links connecting candidate pairs. Given our own findings and the results reported in previous work, it is obviously demanding to find a clear-cut border between the concepts of lexical chaining, semantic fields, and co-reference/anaphora resolution. Definitely, the annotation of co-reference/anaphora and lexical chains is inherently analogous. In both cases an annotation layer consisting of labelled edges between pairs of annotation candidates is constructed. However, we assume that the lexical chaining layer might contain more edges between annotation candidates. As a consequence, its structure presumably is more complex and its connectivity higher. We thus plan to conduct an extended follow-up study in order to explore these differences between the annotation of lexical chains and co-reference/anaphora. We also intend to take advantage of – amongst other aspects – the inter-annotator comparison functionality provided by *Serengeti* (see Section 4 for a detailed description) in order to implement a formally correct inter-annotator agreement test.

3 Available Tools for Annotating Linguistic Corpora

Both the anaphora resolution and the lexical chaining scenario have shown the importance of an easy-to-use annotation tool. Although a wide range of annotation tools is available, one has to separate tools for annotating multimodal corpora from tools for annotating unimodal (i. e. text) corpora. Dipper et al. (2004) evaluated some of the most commonly used tools of both categories (TASX Annotator, EXMARaLDA, MMAX, PALinkA and Systematic Coder). Besides, other tools such as ELAN[2] or Anvil[3] are available as well, as are tool kits such as the Annotation Graph Toolkit (AGTK)[4] or the NITE XML Toolkit.[5] While multimodal annotation demands a framework supporting the time-aligned handling of video and audio streams and, therefore, much effort has been spent on the design and development of tools, unimodal annotation has often been fulfilled by using ordinary XML editors which can be error-prone. Nevertheless, specialized annotation frameworks are available as well, e. g. MMAX can be used for multi-level annotation projects (cf. Müller and Strube (2001; 2003)). However, as annotation projects grow in size and complexity (often multiple annotation layers are generated), collaborative annotation and the use of annotation tools is vital.

- Ma et al. (2002), for example, describe collaborative annotation in the context of the AGTK. But since most of the aforementioned applications have to be installed locally on a PC, working on a corpus and managing annotations externally can be difficult.

- Another problem worth to be mentioned is data management. Having several annotators working on one text, unification and comparison of the markup produced is quite difficult.

- Furthermore, annotation tools help to increase both the quality and quantity of the annotation process.

Recent web technologies allow the design of web-based applications that resemble locally installed desktop programs on the one hand and provide central data management on the other hand. Therefore distributed annotation is possible regardless of location, provided that an internet connection is available. In this paper we propose the web-based annotation application *Serengeti*.

4 A new Approach: Serengeti

As the *Sekimo* project is part of a research group with interrelated application domains, annotation layers from different projects have been evaluated for their interrelationship (e. g. Bayerl et al. (2003; 2006)). This led directly to the open design of *Serengeti* – an annotation tool with the fundamental idea in mind: making possible the annotation of a single layer (or resource) and the use of the best annotation possible and the best available resources. *Serengeti* allows for several experts to annotate a single text at the same time as well as to compare the different annotations (inter-annotator-agreement) and merge them afterwards. Access to the documents is available from everywhere (an internet connection and a browser is required).

4.1 Technical Overview

Serengeti is a web application developed for Mozilla Firefox,[6] thus its architecture is separated into a client and a server side, following the principles and tools of AJAX (Asynchronous JavaScript and XML, cf. Garrett (2005)). While groups, documents and annotations are managed centrally on the server side, all user interactions are rendered locally on the client side.[7]

4.2 Graphical User Interface

The Graphical User Interface (GUI) of *Serengeti* is subdivided into several areas (cf. Figure 2). The main area renders the text to be annotated, roughly laid out in terms of paragraphs, lists, tables and non-text sections according to the input XML data. Additionally, predefined markables are underlined and followed by boxes containing the markables' unique identifiers. These boxes serve as clickable buttons to choose markables during the annotation. At this

[2] `http://www.lat-mpi.eu/tools/elan/`
[3] `http://www.dfki.de/~kipp/anvil/`
[4] `http://agtk.sourceforge.net/`
[5] `http://www.ltg.ed.ac.uk/NITE/`

[6] *Serengeti* is targeted at platform independence, so we've chosen Firefox, which is freely available for several operating systems. Future versions will support other browsers as well.

[7] Each *Serengeti* installation supports more than one workgroup. Server sided data management allows the use of versioning systems like *CVS* or, in our case, *Subversion*.

time, adding markables, i. e. changing the input data, is not allowed.[8] This ensures that all annotators use the same base layer. A section at the bottom of the interface represents the annotation panel with a list of all annotated relations on the left and all editing tools on the right side. An application bar at the top of the GUI provides functions for choosing and managing groups, documents and annotations.

4.3 Annotation Process

After logging in and choosing a document to annotate, new relations between markables can be created. The markables that take part in the relation are chosen by left-clicking the boxes attached to the underlined markables in the text and, if necessary, unchecked by clicking them once again. To encode the type of a relation between chosen markables, an input form at the bottom right of the page provides various options for specifying the relation according to the annotation scheme. The OKAY command adds created relations to the list, which can subsequently be edited or deleted. In regard to their state, relation bars in the list can be highlighted differently to simplify the post-editing (i. e. new relations, old/saved relations, commented relations or incomplete relations).[9] The user can save his work to the server at any time. After the annotation process is completed, the COMMIT command (located in the document menu) declares the annotation as finished.

4.4 Comparing Annotations and Reaching a Consensus

In order to achieve the best annotation results it is necessary to provide an opportunity for the evaluation of single annotations or comparing of multiple annotations on one single document (either by different annotators or identical annotators at different points in time). This allows for verification of the quality of the annotation scheme and for valid training data for automated natural language processing tools. For this purpose, a special user access, the *Consensus User (CU)*, has been developed as part of *Serengeti*'s concept. Loading a document as a CU, it is possible to choose a single annotation done by any other annotator (either work in progress or committed) as the basis for the final annotation. This is done with the same tools as those for the annotation process. If satisfied, the CU can declare the annotation as ultimately closed via the COMMIT command.

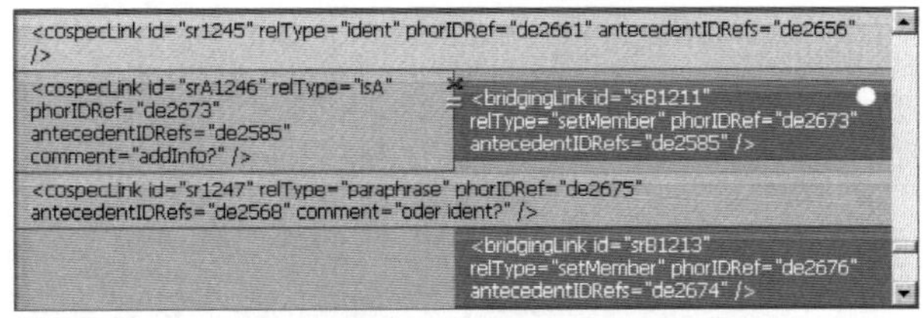

Figure 3: *Serengeti*'s comparison window in the lower left part of the GUI.

Furthermore, the CU can compare two annotations with each other. The relations annotated by both users are then displayed in the relation list and juxtaposed in case they differ in at least one aspect (e. g. different relation types as in Figure 3).[10] On this basis the CU can decide which relation to accept and which one to reject. Again, all editing options are at the user's disposal.
While editing single or multiple user annotations, the CU can save the current state of his work at any time. Afterwards these annotations will appear in the ANNOTATIONS MENU as well and can be selected for further evaluation and comparison.[11]

5 Extending Serengeti

Although one might doubt that *Serengeti* is directly applicable to annotating lexical chains, this can nevertheless be done straightforwardly using the annotation described in Section 2.1. Our starting point is as follows: As markables we refer to entities of the parser output (i. e. tokens) where a user can mark a token as the initial vertex of a chain. In order to reflect the findings of our case study on lexical chaining we distinguish two cases: Either the annotator decides that a newly entered token enlarges

[8]The definition of XML elements as markables and the layout and relation type specification is driven via an external configuration script, adjustable for each group.

[9]It is possible to hide relations according to their state as well.

[10]At this point the assignment of relations is important. Anaphoric relations, for example, are assigned to each other if their anaphoric element is the same. If there is more than one relation with identical anaphoric elements, the relations are sorted by their relation types and their antecedent(s).

[11]Comparisons require conflictless annotations, i. e. saved comparisons have to be free from juxtaposed relations.

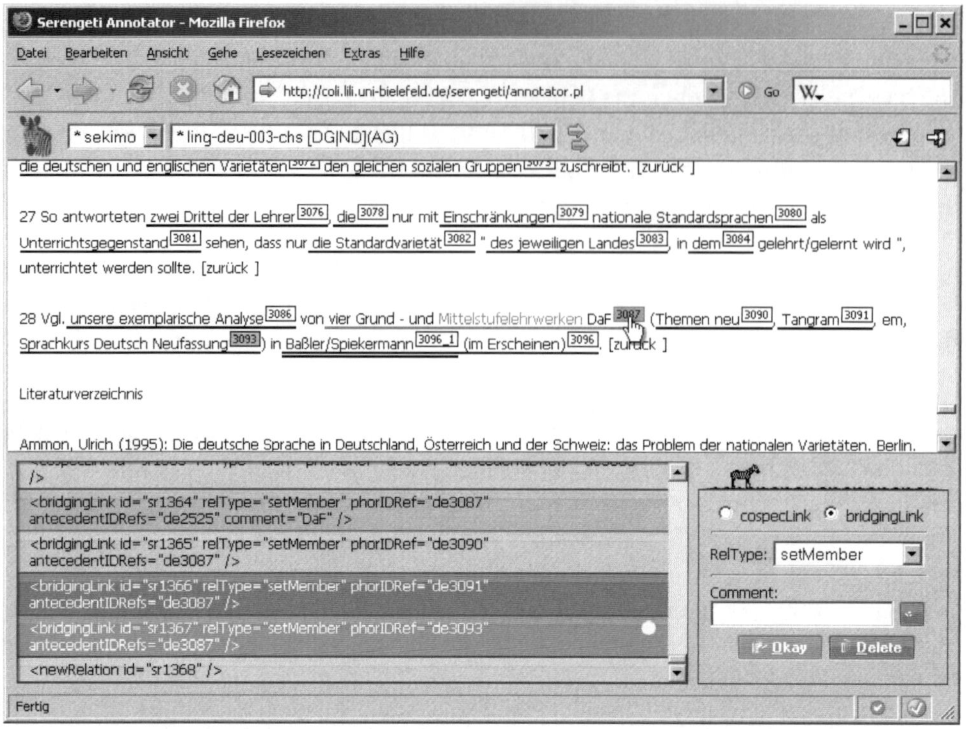

Figure 2: *Serengeti*'s User Interface. Screenshots of *Serengeti* Version 0.7.1

an already marked-up chain by explicitly relating it to one of its links or he implicitly assigns the token to that chain as a whole which is visually represented as part of *Serengeti*'s interface. In the first case we just face another use case of our annotation scheme, that is, a link between two tokens or spans of a text where this link may be typed according to some linguistic relation that holds between the spans, e. g. hyponymy. In the second case of an implicit chain assignment we proceed as follows: We link the newly processed token to the last vertex of the lexical chain to which the token is attached and type this relation non-specifically as *association*. As a result, we reduce this use case to the one already mapped by our general annotation scheme. In order to make this a workable solution, we will integrate a representation of lexical chains by means of *tag clouds* where each chain is represented by a subset of those lexical units which because of their frequency are most important in representing that chain. Following this line of extending *Serengeti*, we manage to use it as an annotation tool which handles anaphoric relations *as well as* lexical chains.

6 Discussion and Outlook

Serengeti can be used to create corpus data for training and evaluation purposes. An installation of *Serengeti* is available online.[12] Currently, the tool is being generalized to allow the annotation of lexical chains and several other annotation tasks. More specifically, we plan to incorporate any kind of chain-like structuring of text segments and to make the chains an object of annotation so that they can be interrelated. This will allow to incorporate constituency relations into the annotation process. Beyond that we will incorporate metadata handling to document all steps of the annotation process.

References

P. S. Bayerl, H. Lüngen, D. Goecke, A. Witt, and D. Naber. 2003. Methods for the Semantic Analysis of Document Markup. In C. Roisin, E. Muson, and C. Vanoirbeek, editors, *Proceedings of the 2003 ACM symposium on Document engineering (DocEng)*, pages 161–170, Grenoble. ACM Press.

[12] `http://coli.lili.uni-bielefeld.de/serengeti/`

B. Beigman Klebanov. 2005. Using readers to identify lexical cohesive structures in texts. In *Proceedings of ACL Student Research Workshop*.

S. Dipper, M. Götze, and M. Stede. 2004. Simple Annotation Tools for Complex Annotation Tasks: an Evaluation. In *Proceedings of the LREC Workshop on XML-based Richly Annotated Corpora*, pages 54–62, Lisbon, Portugal.

C. Fellbaum, editor. 1998. *WordNet. An Electronic Lexical Database*. The MIT Press.

S. Fligelstone. 1992. Developing a Scheme for Annotating Text to Show Anaphoric Relations. In G. Leitner, editor, *New Directions in English Language Corpora: Methodology, Results, Software Developments*, pages 153–170. Mouton de Gruyter, Berlin.

J. J. Garrett, 2005. *AJAX: A New Approach to Web Applications*. Adaptive Path LLC, February, 18. Online: `http://www.adaptivepath.com/publications/essays/archives/000385.php`.

R. Garside, S. Fligelstone, and S. Botley. 1997. Discourse Annotation: Anaphoric Relations in Corpora. In R. Garside, G. Leech, and A. McEnery, editors, *Corpus Annotation: Linguistic Information from Computer Text Corpora*, pages 66–84. Addison-Wesley Longman, London.

D. Goecke and A. Witt. 2006. Exploiting Logical Document Structure for Anaphora Resolution. In *Proceedings of the 5th International Conference.*, Genoa, Italy.

Michael A. K. Halliday and Ruqaiya Hasan. 1976. *Cohesion in English*. Longman, London.

L. Hirschmann. 1997. MUC-7 Coreference Task Definition (version 3.0). In L. Hirschman and N. Chinchor, editors, *Proceedings of Message Understanding Conference (MUC-7)*.

A. Holler, J.-F. Maas, and A. Storrer. 2004. Exploiting Coreference Annotations for Text-to-Hypertext Conversion. In *Proceeding of LREC*, volume II, pages 651–654, Lisbon, Portugal.

L. Karttunen. 1976. Discourse Referents. *Syntax and Semantics: Notes from the Linguistic Underground*, 7:363–385.

X. Ma, L. Haejoong, S. Bird, and K. Maeda. 2002. Models and Tools for Collaborative Annotation. In *Proceedings of the Third International Conference on Language Resources and Evaluation*, Paris. European Language Resources Association.

R. Mitkov. 2002. *Anaphora Resolution*. Longman, London.

J. Morris and G. Hirst. 1991. Lexical cohesion computed by thesaural relations as an indicator of the structure of text. *Computational linguistics*, 17(1):21–48, March.

J. Morris and G. Hirst. 2004. Non-classical lexical semantic relations. In *Proceedings of HLT-NAACL Workshop on Computational Lexical Semantics*.

J. Morris and G. Hirst. 2005. The subjectivity of lexical cohesion in text. In J. C. Chanahan, C. Qu, and J. Wiebe, editors, *Computing attitude and affect in text*. Springer.

C. Müller and M.l Strube. 2001. Annotating Anaphoric and Bridging Relations with MMAX. In *Proceedings of the 2nd SIGdial Workshop on Discourse and Dialogue*, pages 90–95, Aalborg, Denmark.

C. Müller and M. Strube. 2003. Multi-Level Annotation in MMAX. In *Proceedings of the 4th SIGdial Workshop on Discourse and Dialogue*, pages 198–207, Sapporo, Japan.

M. Poesio, T. Ishikawa, S. Schulte im Walde, and R. Viera. 2002. Acquiring lexical knowledge for anaphora resolution. In *Proc. of the 3rd Conference on Language Resources and Evaluation (LREC)*.

M. Poesio. 2004. The MATE/GNOME Scheme for Anaphoric Annotation, Revisited. In *Proceedings of SIGDIAL*, Boston, April.

G. Simons, W. Lewis, S. Farrar, T. Langendoen, B. Fitzsimons, and H. Gonzalez. 2004. The semantics of markup. In *Proceedings of the ACL 2004 Workshop on RDF/RDFS and OWL in Language Technology (NLPXML-2004)*, Barcelona.

M. Strube and C. Müller. 2003. A Machine Learning Approach to Pronoun Resolution in Spoken Dialogue. In *Proceedings of the 41st Annual Meeting on Association for Computational Linguistics*, volume 1, pages 168–175. ACL 03.

M. Stührenberg, A. Witt, D. Goecke, D. Metzing, and O. Schonefeld. 2006. Multidimensional Markup and Heterogeneous Linguistic Resources. In D. Ahn, E. T. K. Sang, and G. Wilcock, editors, *Proceedings of the 5th Workshop on NLP and XML (NLPXML-2006): Multi-Dimensional Markup in Natural Language Processing*, pages 85–88.

A. Witt, D. Goecke, F. Sasaki, and H. Lüngen. 2005. Unification of XML Documents with Concurrent Markup. *Literary and Lingustic Computing*, 20(1):103–116.

Y. Xiaofeng, J. Su, G. Zhou, and C. L. Tan. 2004. Improving Pronoun Resolution by Incorporating Coreferential Information of Candidates. In *Proceedings of ACL*.

Standoff Coordination for Multi-Tool Annotation in a Dialogue Corpus

Kepa Joseba Rodríguez♣, Stefanie Dipper♠, Michael Götze♠, Massimo Poesio△, Giuseppe Riccardi◇, Christian Raymond◇, Joanna Wisniewska‡

♣Piedmont Consortium for Information Systems (CSI-Piemonte)
KepaJoseba.Rodriguez@csi.it
♠Department of Linguistics. University of Potsdam.
{dipper|goetze}@ling.uni-potsdam.de
△Center for Mind/Brain Sciences. University of Trento.
massimo.poesio@unitn.it
◇Department of Information and Communication Technology. University of Trento.
{christian.raymond|riccardi}@dit.unitn.it
‡Institute of Computer Science. Polish Academy of Science.
jwisniewska@poczta.uw.edu.pl

Abstract

The LUNA corpus is a multi-lingual, multi-domain spoken dialogue corpus currently under development that will be used to develop a robust natural spoken language understanding toolkit for multilingual dialogue services. The LUNA corpus will be annotated at multiple levels to include annotations of syntactic, semantic, and discourse information; specialized annotation tools will be used for the annotation at each of these levels. In order to synchronize these multiple layers of annotation, the PAULA standoff exchange format will be used. In this paper, we present the corpus and its PAULA-based architecture.[1]

1 Introduction

XML standoff markup (Thompson and McKelvie, 1997; Dybkjær et al., 1998) is emerging as the cleanest way to organize multi-level annotations of corpora. In many of the current annotation efforts based on standoff a single multi-purpose tool such as the NITE XML Toolkit (Carletta et al., 2003) or WordFreak (Morton and LaCivita, 2003) is used to annotate as well as maintain all annotation levels (cf. the SAMMIE annotation effort (Kruijff-Korbayová et al., 2006b)).

However, it is often the case that specialized tools are developed to facilitate the annotation of particular levels: examples include tools for segmentation and transcription of the speech signal like PRAAT (Boersma and Weenink, 2005) and TRANSCRIBER (Barras et al., 1998), the SALSA tools for FrameNet-style annotation (Burchardt et al., 2006), and MMAX (Müller and Strube, 2003) for coreference annotation. Even in these cases, however, it may still be useful, or even necessary, to be able to visualize more than one level at once, or to 'knit' together[2] multiple levels to create a file that can be used to train a model for a particular type of annotation. The Linguistic Annotation Framework by (Ide et al., 2003) was proposed as a unifying markup format to be used to synchronize heterogeneous markup formats for such purposes.

In this paper, we discuss how the PAULA representation format, a standoff format inspired by the Linguistic Annotation Framework, is being used to synchronize multiple levels of annotation in the LUNA corpus, a corpus of spoken dialogues in multiple languages and multiple domains that is being created to support the development of robust spoken language understanding models for multilingual dialogue services. The corpus is richly annotated with linguistic information that is considered relevant for research on dialogue, including chunks, named entities, argument structure, coreference, and dialogue acts. We chose to adopt specialized tools for each level: e.g.,

[1] The members of the LUNA project consortium are: Piedmont Consortium for Information Systems (IT), University of Trento (IT), Loquendo SpA (IT), RWTH-Aachen (DE), University of Avignon (FR), France Telecom R&D Division S.A. (FR), Polish-Japanese Institute of Information Technology (PL) and the Institute for Computer Science of the Polish Academy of Sciences (PL), http://www.ist-luna.eu.
This research was performed in the LUNA project funded by the EC, DG Infso, Unit E1 and in the Collaborative Research Center 632 "Information Structure", funded by the German Science Foundation, http://www.sfb632.uni-potsdam.de.

[2] In the sense of the knit tool of the LT-XML suite.

Proceedings of the Linguistic Annotation Workshop, pages 148–155,
Prague, June 2007.

transcription using TRANSCRIBER, coreference using MMAX, attributes using SEMANTIZER, etc. To synchronize the annotation and allow cross-layer operations, the annotations are mapped to a common representation format, PAULA.

The structure of the paper is as follows. In Section 2, we present the LUNA project and the LUNA corpus with its main annotation levels. In Section 3, we introduce the PAULA exchange format, focusing on the representation of time alignment and dialogue phenomena. Finally we show how PAULA is used in the LUNA corpus and discuss alternative formats.

2 The LUNA project

The aim of the LUNA project is to advance the state of the art in understanding conversational speech in Spoken Dialogue Systems (Gupta et al., 2005), (Bimbot et al., 2006).

Three aspects of Spoken Language Understanding (SLU) are of particular concern in LUNA: generation of semantic concept tags, semantic composition into conceptual structures and context sensitive validation using information provided by the dialogue manager. In order to train and evaluate SLU models, we will create an annotated corpus of spoken dialogues in multiple domains and multiple languages: French, Italian, and Polish.

2.1 The LUNA corpus

The LUNA corpus is currently being collected, with a target to collect 8100 human-machine dialogues and 1000 human-human dialogues in Polish, Italian and French. The dialogues are collected in the following application domains: stock exchange, hotel reservation and tourism inquiries, customer support service/help-desk and public transportation.

2.2 Multilevel annotation

Semantic interpretation involves a number of subtasks, ranging from identifying the meaning of individual words to understanding which objects are being referred to up to recovering the relation between different semantic objects in the utterance and discourse level to, finally, understanding the communicative force of an utterance.

In some annotation efforts–e.g., in the annotation of the French MEDIA Corpus (Bonneau-Maynard and Rosset, 2003)– information about the meaning of semantic chunks, contextual information about coreference, and information about dialogue acts are all kept in a single file. This approach however suffers from a number of problems, including the fact that errors introduced during the annotation at one level may make other levels of annotation unusable as well, and that it is not possible for two annotators to work on different types of annotation for the same file at the same time. Most current annotation efforts, therefore, tend to adopt the 'multilevel' approach pioneered during the development of the MAPTASK corpus and then developed as part of work on the EU-funded MATE project (McKelvie et al., 2001), in which each aspect of interpretation is annotated in a separate **level**, independently maintained. This approach is being followed, for instance, in the ONTONOTES project (Hovy et al., 2006) and the SAMMIE project (Kruijff-Korbayova et al., 2006a).

For the annotation of the LUNA corpus, we decided to follow the multilevel approach as well. That allows us to achieve more granularity in the annotation of each of the levels and to investigate more easily dependencies between features that belong to different levels. Furthermore, we can use different specialized off-the-shelf annotation tools, splitting up the annotation task and thus facilitating consistent annotation.

2.3 Annotation levels

The LUNA corpus will contain different types of information. The first levels are necessary to prepare the corpus for subsequent semantic annotation, and include segmentation of the corpus in dialogue turns, transcription of the speech signal, and syntactic preprocessing with POS-tagging and shallow parsing.

The next level consists of the annotation of domain information using attribute-value pairs. This annotation will be performed on all dialogues in the corpus.

The other levels of the annotation scheme are not mandatory, but at least a part of the dialogues will be annotated in order to investigate contextual aspects of the semantic interpretation. These levels include the predicate structure, the relations between referring expressions, and the annotation of dialogue acts.

2.3.1 Segmentation and transcription of the speech signal

Before transcription and annotation can begin, it is necessary to segment the speech signal into dialogue turns and annotate them with speaker identity and mark where speaker overlap occurs. The goal of this segmentation is to be able to perform a transcription and annotation of the dialogue turns with or without dialogue context. While dialogue context is preferable for semantic annotation, it slows down the annotation process.

The tool we will use for the segmentation and transcription of the speech signal is the open source tool TRANSCRIBER[3] (Barras et al., 1998).

The next step is the transcription of the speech signal, using conventions for the orthographic transcription and for the annotation of non-linguistic acoustic events.

2.3.2 Part Of Speech Tagging and Chunking

The transcribed material will be annotated with POS-tags, morphosyntactic information like agreement features, and segmented based on syntactic constituency.

For the POS-tags and morphosyntactic features, we will follow the recommendations made in EAGLES (EAGLES, 1996), which allows us to have a unified representation format for the corpus, independently of the tools used for each language.

2.3.3 Domain Attribute Annotation

At this level, semantic segments will be annotated following an approach used for the annotation for the French MEDIA dialogue corpus (Bonneau-Maynard and Rosset, 2003).

We specify the domain knowledge in domain ontologies. These are used to build domain-specific dictionaries. Each dictionary contains:

- Concepts corresponding to classes of the ontology and attributes of the annotation.
- Values corresponding to the individuals of the domain.
- Constraints on the admissible values for each concept.

The concept dictionaries are used to annotate semantic segments with attribute-value pairs. The semantic segments are produced by concatenation of the chunks produced by the shallow parser. A semantic segment is a unit that corresponds unambiguously to a concept of the dictionary.

(1) buongiorno lei [può iscriversi]$_{concept1}$ [agli esami]$_{concept2}$ [oppure]$_{concept3}$ [ottenere delle informazioni]$_{concept4}$ come la posso aiutare[4]

```
<concept1 action:inscription>
<concept2 objectDB:examen>
<concept3 conjunctor:alternative>
<concept4 action:obtain_info>
```

2.3.4 Predicate structure

The annotation of predicate structure facilitates the interpretation of the relation between entities and events occurring in the dialogue.

There are different approaches to annotate predicate structure. Some of them are based upon syntactic structure, with PropBank (Kingsbury and Palmer, 2003) being one of the most relevant, building the annotation upon the syntactic representation of the TreeBank corpus (Marcus et al., 1993). An alternative to syntax-driven approaches is the annotation using semantic roles as in FrameNet (Baker et al., 1998).

For the annotation of predicate structure in the LUNA corpus, we decided to use a FrameNet-like approach, rather than a syntax-based approach:

1. Annotation of dialogue interaction has to deal with disfluencies, non-complete sentences, ungrammaticality, etc., which complicates the use of deep syntactic representations.

2. If we start from a syntactic representation, we have to follow a long way to achieve the semantic interpretation. Syntactic constituents must be mapped to θ-roles, and then to semantic roles. FrameNet offers the possibility of annotating using directly semantic criteria.

[3] http://trans.sourceforge.net

[4] Good morning, you can register for the exam or obtain information. How can I help you?

For each domain, we define a set of frames. These frames are defined based on the domain ontology, with the named entities providing the frame elements. For all the frames we introduce the negation as a default frame element.

For the annotation, first of all we annotate the entities with a frame and a frame element.

Then if the target is overtly realized we make a pointer from the frame elements to the target. The next step is putting the frame elements and the target (if overtly realized) in a set.

(2) buongiorno [lei]$_{fe1}$ [può iscriversi]$_{fe2}$ [agli esami]$_{fe3}$ oppure [ottenere delle informazioni]$_{fe4}$ come la posso aiutare

set1 = {id1, id2, id3}
frame: inscription
frame-elements:{student, examen, date}
set2 = {id4}
frame = info-request
frame-elements:{student, addressee, topic}

```
<fe1 frame="inscription"
FE="student" member="set1"
pointer="fe2">
<fe2 frame="inscription"
FE="target" member="set1">
<fe3 frame="inscription"
FE="examen" member="set1"
pointer="fe2">
<fe4 frame="information"
FE="target" member="set2">
```

2.3.5 Coreference / Anaphoric relations

To annotate anaphoric relations we will use an annotation scheme close to the one used in the ARRAU project (Artstein and Poesio, 2006). This scheme has been extensively tested with dialogue corpora and includes instructions for annotating a variety of anaphoric relations, including bridging relations. A further reason is the robustness of the scheme that doesn't require one single interpretation in the annotation.

The first step is the annotation of the information status of the markables with the tags `given` and `new`. If the markables are annotated with `given`, the annotator will select the most recent occurrence of the object and add a pointer to it. If the markable is annotated with `new`, we distinguish between markables that are related to a previously mentioned object (associative reference) or don't have such a relation.

If there are alternative interpretations, which of a list of candidates can be the antecedent, the annotator can annotate the markable as `ambiguous` and add a pointer to each of the possible antecedents.

(3) **Wizard:** buongiorno [lei]$_{cr1}$ [può iscriversi]$_{cr2}$ [agli esami]$_{cr3}$ oppure ottenere [delle informazioni]$_{cr4}$ come la posso aiutare

```
<cr1 inf_status="new" related="no">
<cr2 inf_status="new" related="no">
<cr3 inf_status="new" related="no">
<cr4 inf_status="new" related="no">
```

Caller: [iscrizione]$_{cr5}$ [esami]$_{cr6}$[5]

```
<cr5 inf_status="given"
single_phrase_antecedent="cr2"
ambiguity="unambiguous">
<cr6 inf_status="given"
single_phrase_antecedent="cr3"
ambiguity="unambiguous">
```

2.3.6 Dialogue acts

In order to associate the intentions of the speaker with the propositional content of the utterances, the segmentation of the dialogue turns in utterances is based on the annotation of predicate structure. Each set of frame elements will correspond to an utterance.

Each utterance will be annotated using a multidimensional annotation scheme partially based on the DAMSL scheme (Allen and Core, 1997) and on the proposals of ICSI-MRDA (Dhillon et al., 2004).

We have selected nine dialogue acts from the DAMSL scheme as initial tagset, that can be extended for the different application domains. Each utterance will be annotated with as many tags as applicable.

(4) **Wizard:** [buongiorno]$_{utt1}$ [lei può iscriversi agli esami]$_{utt2}$ oppure [ottenere delle

[5]Register for the exam.

informzaioni]$_{utt3}$ [come la posso aiutare]$_{utt4}$

```
<utt1 d-act="opening/closing">
<utt2 d-act="statement"
link-frame="set1">
<utt3 d-act="statement"
link-frame="set2">
<utt4 d-act="info-request">
```

Caller: [iscrizione esami]$_{utt5}$

```
<utt5 d-act="answer;statement"
link-frame="set3">
```

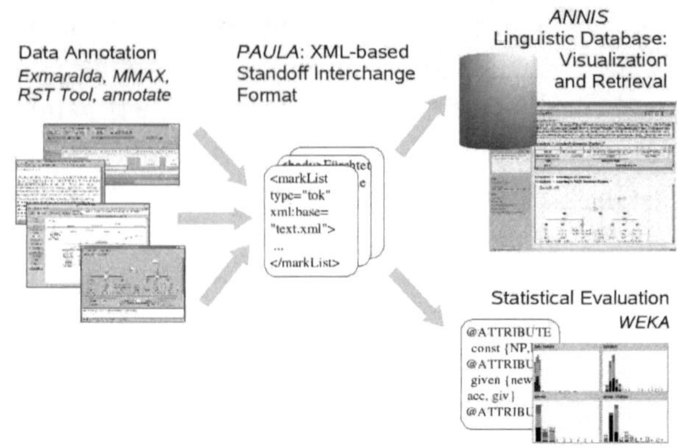

Figure 1: PAULA annotation scenario

3 PAULA - a Linguistic Standoff Exchange Format

PAULA stands for *Potsdamer Austauschformat für linguistische Annotation* ("Potsdam Interchange Format for Linguistic Annotation") and has been developed for the representation of data annotated at multiple layers. The application scenario is sketched in Fig 1: researchers use multiple, specialized off-the-shelf annotation tools, such as EXMARALDA or MMAX, to enrich data with linguistic information. The tools store the data in tool-specific formats and, hence, it is not straightforward to combine information from different sources and, e.g., to search for correlations across multiple annotation layers.

This is where PAULA comes in: PAULA maps the tool-specific formats to a common format and serves as an interchange format between these tools.[6] Moreover, the annotations from the different sources are merged into one single representation. PAULA makes this data available for further applications, such as searching the data by means of the tool ANNIS[7], or to feed statistical applications like WEKA[8].

PAULA is an XML-based standoff format for linguistic annotations, inspired by the "dump format" of the Linguistic Annotation Framework (Ide et al., 2003).[9] With PAULA, not only is the primary data separated from its annotations, but individual annotation layers (such as parts of speech and dialogue acts) are separated from each other as well. The standoff approach allows us to mark overlapping segments in a straightforward way: by distributing annotations over different files (XML as such does not easily account for overlapping segments, since its object model is a hierarchical, tree-like structure). Moreover, new annotation layers can be added easily.

PAULA assumes that a representation of the primary data is stored in a file that optionally specifies a header with meta information, followed by a tag `<body>`, which contains a representation of the primary data. In Fig. 2, the first box displays the transcription, with all contributions from the first speaker coming first, and the contributions from the other speaker(s) following (put in italics in the Figure).

The basic type of "annotation" are *markables*, encoded by the XML element `<mark>`. Markables specify "anchors", i.e., locations or ranges that can be annotated by linguistic information. The locations and ranges are positions or spans in the source text or timeline, which are referenced by means of XLinks and XPointer expressions. For instance, the "Token" markables in Fig. 2 define spans that cor-

[6]Currently, we provide PAULA import filters for the following tools and formats: Exmaralda, MMAX, RST Tool/URML, annotate/TIGER XML. Export from PAULA to the tool formats is at present supported for the original source format only. We plan to support the export of selected annotations to other tools. This is, however, not a trivial task since it may involve loss of information.

[7]ANNIS: `http://www.sfb632.uni-potsdam.de/annis`

[8]WEKA: `http://www.cs.waikato.ac.nz/ml/weka`

[9]The term 'standoff' describes the situation where primary data (e.g., the transcription) and annotations of this data are stored in separate files (Thompson and McKelvie, 1997).

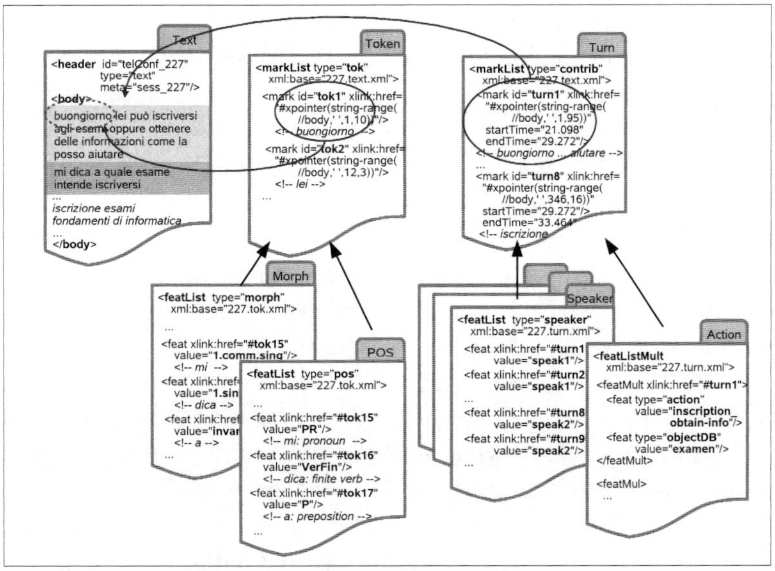

Figure 2: PAULA sample annotation

respond to words. The first markable, with the ID `tok1`, specifies the span that starts at character position 1 and is of length 10: *buongiorno*. Similarly, the speakers' individual turns are specified by the "Turn" markables. Here, the first markable (ID `turn1`) specifies the entire dialogue turn of the first speaker (which corresponds to the part marked in light grey within the text file). Additionally, the markable encodes the time range that is occupied by that turn: it starts at time point 21.098, and ends at time point 29.272.

Markables represent a special kind of annotation: they mark linguistic units. The actual annotation, though, specifies properties of these units, such as part of speech or dialogue acts. For the encoding of these properties, PAULA provides `<feat>` elements, which point to `<mark>` elements by referencing their IDs. Token markables are annotated by "Morph" and "POS" features. The name of the annotated feature is specified by the attribute `type` of the `<featList>` element; the value of the feature is given by the attribute `value` of the `<feat>` elements. For instance, the token with ID `tok15` is annotated with `morph="1.comm.sing"` and `pos="PR"`. Similarly, the Turn markables are specified for the speakers uttering the turns ("Speaker" features), and details of the dialogue acts ("Action") are given. The file with the dialogue act annotations specify multiple features within one tag `<feat>`, rather than distributing the features over several files, as we do in the case of morphology and POS annotations. This way, we explicitely encode the fact that the individual annotations (`action="inscription_obtain-info"` and `objectDB="examen"`) jointly form one complex annotation.

PAULA markables can also refer to points or areas within pictures or videos (by referring to coordinates) or point to other markables (Fig. 2 does not illustrate these options). Moreover, for the encoding of hierarchical structures like graphs, PAULA provides `<struct>` (structure) elements (see Fig. 3 below for an example).

The PAULA standoff format is a generic format that does not necessarily prescribe in detail how to represent annotations. Often there is more than one way to represent the data in PAULA standoff format. In the next section, we present the way we intend to represent dialogue data, which involve possibly overlapping contributions by several speakers, and often include time-alignment information.

4 Representing LUNA Dialogue Annotations in PAULA

In this section, we illustrate the use of PAULA for the LUNA corpus with a more elaborated example, focusing on the representation of frame annotation. In Fig. 3, the top elements represent the dialogue turns and the semantic units underlying the frame annotations, which are defined on the base of the dialogue turns. "FrameUnit" markables define the scope or extension of the frames, and roughly correspond to a sentence or turn. "FrameP" markables specify the frame participants, i.e., all elements that receive a semantic role within some frame.

The annotations at the bottom contain information about individual frames. The frames are encoded as `<struct>` elements, constituting complex objects that group semantic units to form frames instances. In Fig. 3, the frame with ID `frame_1` consists of the frame unit, the lexical unit and the frame participants. The "FrameAnno" box encodes the name of the frame: "inscription". The frames can be defined by external "Framesets", such as FrameNet (Baker et al., 1998), which in our example is stored in an external XML-resource called `frameSet.xml`.

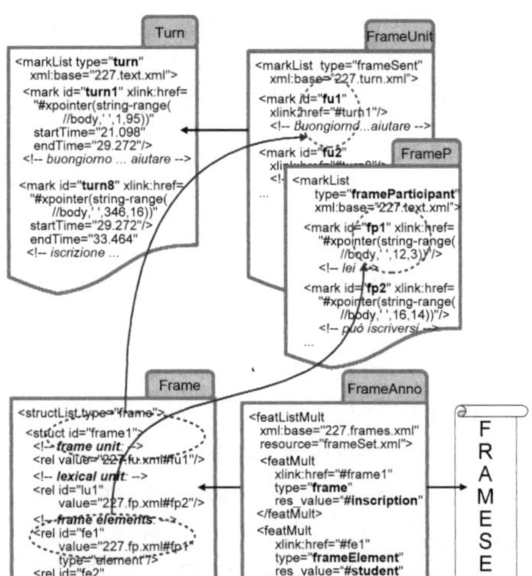

Figure 3: Frame annotation in PAULA

5 Alternative Formats

For richly annotated dialogue corpora, alternative representation formats have been proposed. Two of the most prominent ones are the NITE-XML[10] and the ELAN[11] format. Similar to PAULA, NITE-XML focuses on richly annotated corpus data. It comes with a rich data model and employs a rich meta specification, which determines—based upon the individual corpus characteristics— the concrete linearization of the respective XML representation. Furthermore, it is accompanied by a JAVA API and a query tool, forming a valuable toolkit for corpus engineers who can adapt available resources to their specific needs. The ELAN format is used by a family of tools developed primarily for language documentation, of which the most advanced one is ELAN, a robust, ready-to-use tool for multi-level annotation of video. Its underlying data model is the *Abstract Corpus Model (ACM)* (Brugman and Russel, 2004).

PAULA aims at an application scenario different from both of these formats. First, it builds upon the usage of specialized off-the-shelf annotation tools for the variety of annotation tasks. Both the NITE-XML and ELAN approaches require additional effort and skills from the user, to add the required functionality, which PAULA aims to avoid. Second, PAULA takes care of *merging* the annotations from different sources, which is not in focus of ELAN or NITE.

6 Discussion and Future Directions

We presented the LUNA dialogue corpus and its representation format, the standoff exchange format PAULA.

In contrast to other formats, PAULA focuses on an application scenario in which different annotations come in their own specific format and are to be merged into one corpus representation. This includes, for instance, the use of specialized off-the-shelf annotation tools for specific annotation tasks, as well as distributed and incremental annotation. The creation of the LUNA dialogue corpus is a prototypical example for this scenario.

However, the usefulness of a format also depends on its interoperability and the available tools. With its import filters, PAULA already serves the needs of linguists of different linguistic communities, while more export functionality is still to be integrated. With the export to WEKA, a first step in this direction is done. Furthermore, ANNIS –a web-based tool for visualizing and searching complex multi-level

[10]NITE: `http://http://www.ltg.ed.ac.uk/NITE`

[11]ELAN: `http://www.lat-mpi.eu/tools/elan`

annotations– is available and will be developed further.

In our next steps, we will focus on a deliberate extension of the PAULA format for further and more complex dialogue annotations, which will enable the use of PAULA as an exchange format also in this domain.

References

J. Allen and M. Core. 1997. Draft of DAMSL: Dialog Act Markup in Several Layers.

R. Artstein and M. Poesio, 2006. *ARRAU Annotation Manual (TRAINS dialogues).* Univerity of Essex, U.K.

C. F. Baker, C. J. Fillmore, and J. B. Lowe. 1998. The Berkeley FrameNet project. In *Proceedings of COLING-ACL*. Association for Computational Linguistics.

C. Barras, W. Geoffrois, Z. Wu, and M. Libermann. 1998. Transcriber: a free tool for segmenting, labeling and transcribing speech. In *Proceedings of the First International Conference on Language Ressources and Evaluation (LREC)*.

F. Bimbot, M. Faundez-Zanuy, and R. deMori, editors. 2006. *Special Issue on Spoken Language Understanding*, volume 48 of *Speech Communication*. Elsevier.

P. Boersma and D. Weenink. 2005. Praat: doing phonetics by computer (Version 4.3.14). `http://www.praat.org`.

H. Bonneau-Maynard and S. Rosset. 2003. A semantic representation for spoken dialogues. In *Proceedings of Eurospeech*, Geneva.

H. Brugman and A. Russel. 2004. Annotating multimedia/multi-modal resources with ELAN. In *Proceedings of the Fourth International Conference on Language Resources and Evaluation*, pages 2065–2068, Paris: ELRA.

A. Burchardt, K. Erk, A. Frank, A. Kowalski, and S. Pado. 2006. SALTO – A Versatile Multi-Level Annotation Tool. In *Proceedings of LREC 2006*.

J. Carletta, S. Evert, U. Heid, J. Kilgour, J. Robertson, and H. Voormann. 2003. The NITE XML Toolkit: flexible annotation for multi-modal language data. *Behavior Research Methods, Instruments, and Computers – special issue on Measuring Behavior,*, 35(3).

R. Dhillon, S. Bhagat, H. Carvez, and E. Shriberg. 2004. Meeting Recorder Project: Dialog Act Labeling Guide. Technical report, TR-04-002 ICSI.

L. Dybkjær, N.O. Bernsen, H. Dybkjær, D. McKelvie, and A. Mengel. 1998. The MATE markup framework. MATE Deliverable D1.2.

EAGLES. 1996. Recommendations for the Morphosyntactic Annotation of Corpora. EAGLES Document EAG-TCWG-MAC/R.

N. Gupta, G. Tur adn D. Hakkani-Tur, S. Bangalore, G. Riccardi, and M. Rahim. 2005. The AT&T Spoken Language Understanding System. *IEEE Transactions on Speech and Audio*, PP(99).

E. Hovy, M. Marcus, M. Palmer, L. Ramshaw, and R. Weischedel. 2006. Ontonotes: the 90% solution. In *Proc. HLT-NAACL*.

N. Ide, L. Romary, and E. de la Clergerie. 2003. International standard for a linguistic annotation framework. In *Proceedings of HLT-NAACL'03 Workshop on The Software Engineeri ng and Architecture of Language Technology*.

P. Kingsbury and M. Palmer. 2003. PropBank: the Next Level of TreeBank. In *Proceedings of the Second Workshop on Treebanks and Linguistic Theories (TLT)*.

I. Kruijff-Korbayova, C. Gerstenberger, V. Rieser, and J. Schehl. 2006a. The SAMMIE multimodal dialogue corpus meets the NITE XML toolkit. In *Proc. LREC*, Genoa.

I. Kruijff-Korbayová, V. Rieser, J. Schehl, and T. Becker. 2006b. The Sammie Multimodal Dialogue Corpus Meets the Nite XML Toolkit. In *Proceedings of the Fifth Workshop on multi-dimensional Markup in Natural Language Processing, EACL2006*. EACL.

M. Marcus, B. Santorini, and M.A. Marcinkiewicz. 1993. Building a large annotated corpus of English. *Coputational Linguistics*, (19).

D. McKelvie, A. Isard, A. Mengel, M. B. Moeller, M. Grosse, and M. Klein. 2001. The MATE workbench - an annotation tool for XML corpora. *Speech Communication*, 33(1-2):97–112.

T. Morton and J. LaCivita. 2003. WordFreak: an open tool for linguistic annotation. In *Proceedings of the 2003 Conference of the North American Chapter of the Association for Computational Linguistics on Human Language Technology: Demonstrations*.

Ch. Müller and M. Strube. 2003. Multi-Level Annotation in MMAX. In *Proceedings of the 4th SIGdial Workshop on Discourse and Dialogue*.

H. Thompson and D. McKelvie. 1997. Hyperlink semantics for standoff markup of read-only documents. In *Proceedings of SGML Europe'97*. `http://www.ltg.ed.ac.uk/~ht/sgmleu97.html`.

PoCoS – Potsdam Coreference Scheme[1]

Olga Krasavina
Moscow State University
krasavina@gmx.net

Christian Chiarcos
University of Potsdam
chiarcos@ling.uni-potsdam.de

Abstract[1]

This document outlines minimal design principles underlying annotation of coreference relations in PoCoS, a scheme for cross-linguistic anaphoric annotation. We identify language-independent principles for markable identification which are essential for comparability of annotations produced for different languages. We further suggest a clear and motivated structure of annotation stages, the separation of a coarse-grained core and a family of more elaborate extended schemes, and strategies for the systematic treatment of ambiguity. Explicit mark-up of ambiguities is a novel feature. We implemented three instantiations of PoCoS for German, English and Russian applied to corpora of newspaper texts.

1 Introduction

Anaphoric annotation is notoriously problematic because of ambiguity and subjectivity issues. One has to deal with them at two stages: 1) by designing annotation guidelines; 2) by performing annotation. As for 1), it is a well-known problem that different schemes propose different annotation decisions. As for 2), different annotators may have different judgments on coreference-related issues. The current paper focuses on the general principles and strategies of annotating coreference – the theoretical core that should logically precede any annotation decisions or schemes, but has not been formulated explicitly by now.

The number of existing schemes released just in the last few years is overwhelming and is out of the scope here. The MUC is still generally accepted as the most standard-like annotation scheme (Hirschman, 1997). Given its simplicity is its most important advantage, it has been criticized for its limited coverage and its contra-intuitive understanding of coreference. One of the most well-known later approaches is MATE/GNOME (Poesio, 2004). As the author fairly notices, "there can be no such thing as a general-purpose anaphoric annotation instructions", due to the complexity of phenomena associated with the term of anaphora. So, its essential idea is combining a "general-purpose markup scheme" (MATE) with application-specific scheme instantiations (GNOME). In PoCoS, we adapted and elaborated this idea, by suggesting the Core and Extended Schemes.

The PoCoS, the Potsdam Coreference Scheme, both adapts selected features of existing schemes and implements a set of innovative features. We distinguish between the Core and Extended Scheme: the Core Scheme is general and reusable, while the Extended Scheme supports a wider range of specific extensions, see fig. 1. Here, we are talking about English and German instantiations of the PoCoS Core Scheme.

2 Coreference annotation

Coreference is a relation between textual elements, "referring expressions", which denote the same entity. Semantically, these expressions are prototypical objects or "(discourse) referents" (Karttunen, 1976). Given a pair of two coreferring expressions, the preceding expression is termed antecedent, the subsequent one is termed anaphor.

Subject to annotation are "markables" defined as a cover-term for potential anaphors and their antecedents. Coreference annotation consists of assignment of relations pointing from an anaphor to an antecedent markable. Whether two markables are co-referent, i.e. referring to the same discourse referent, can be determined by a *substitution test*. If

[1] The research by Olga Krasavina was supported by Russian Foundation for the Humanities, grant 05-04-04240a.

Proceedings of the Linguistic Annotation Workshop, pages 156–163,
Prague, June 2007.

the substitution of anaphor and antecedent yield the same interpretation of the text, these are deemed coreferential.

Syntactically, a markable is typically a phrase with a nominal or a pronominal head. According to the referential properties a syntactic construction typically has, we distinguish between *primary markables*, i.e. potential anaphors, and *secondary markables*, expressions which can not serve as anaphors, but only as antecedents.

3 Annotation principles

3.1 A principled approach

In order to develop an annotation scheme which is maximally consistent, we initially identified a set of axiomatic requirements:

- CONSTITUENCY
  - a primary or secondary markable must be an independent syntactic constituent
- COMPLETENESS
  - neither sub-tokens nor non-phrasal nominals are subject to annotation, only syntactic words (tokens) and phrases are
- CONSISTENCY
  - corresponding features have to be analyzed in a corresponding way

CONSTITUENCY and COMPLETENESS are necessary pre-conditions for an alignment between syntactic and anaphoric annotation, CONSISTENCY implies that annotation principles must be formulated in a way that allows for inter-subjective and cross-linguistically valid annotation decisions. While CONSTITUENCY and COMPLETENESS define constraints for markable identification, consistency also affects selection preferences among potential antecedents, and it motivates the explicit representation of anaphoric ambiguity in PoCoS.

In addition to these requirements, we add the preference for MAXIMAL ANALYSIS. It suggests longer anaphoric chains are preferred to the shorter ones by annotation. This defines preferences for coding decisions by ambiguity (see 4.1).

In the remainder of this section, annotation principles employed in the PoCoS scheme are shortly presented and discussed as to their relationship to these four requirements.

3.2 Markable identification

Cross-linguistically consistent markable identification strategies are a necessary pre-condition for a comparative evaluation of anaphor annotation and anaphor resolution across different languages. It has been controversial, however, how to set markable boundaries. So, for example, Ge et al. (1998) and, MUC (Hirschman, 1997) propose a minimal string constraint motivated by evaluation considerations. This procedure leads to systematic violations of the CONSTITUENCY and COMPLETENESS principles, though, cf. the potential markables `Denver` and `bankruptcy` in ex. (1)

> `(1) The [Denver]?-based concern, which emerged from bancruptcy ... its new, post-[bancruptcy]? law structure ..."` (WSJ, 1328)

We explicitly propose a maximum size principle as an alternative to the minimum string constraint (see Principle 1 below). So, a markable consists of the head, usually a noun or a pronoun, and of all modifiers, attributes, relative clauses, appositions, and dislocated elements attached to the head.

Principle 1 Maximum size

> One markable includes all modifications of its head.

Prepositions can be regarded as modifications of a noun as well, and following this line of argumentation, the seemingly clear-cut differentiation between NPs and PPs becomes questionable, cf. the unclear status of Japanese postpositions that can also be interpreted as morphological case markers (Givón 2001:115f).

Further, in most European languages, functional elements such as prepositions and determiners tend to be fused. In combination with the COMPLETENESS constraint, a possible NP-preference for the selection of markables will result in the selection of either PPs or non-phrasal markables if preposition-determiner fusion occurs.

In order to achieve a more consistent analysis, in which the syntactic status of a markable does not depend on surface phenomena such as the (optional) fusion of prepositions and determiner, function words are integrated into a markable if they modify it. As a consequence, CONSISTENCY considerations call for the choice of PPs rather than NPs as markables where possible.

Principle 2 Syntactic characterization
If a referring expression is modified by function words, e.g. a determiner or an adposition, these are to be integrated into the markable.

Like Principle 1, Principle 2 originates from CONSISTENCY and COMPLETENESS requirements applied both within one language and considering cross-linguistic validity, as the function of inflectional marking in one language and the function of prepositions in another language are exchangeable.

If a markable includes another markable, both are specified as markables in annotation. Such treatment provides consistency across languages, (cf. the fragment of parallel text in ex. 2), and has an additional advantage of representing the syntactic structure of a markable.

(2) [Dieses Recht]$_{right}$ kann nicht in Anspruch genommen werden [im Falle einer Strafverfolgung auf Grund von Handlungen, die [gegen die Ziele [der Vereinten Nationen]$_{UN}$]$_{purp}$ verstoßen]$_{prosec}$.

[This right]$_{right}$ may not be invoked [in the case of prosecutions arising from acts contrary [to the purposes [of the United Nations]$_{UN}$]$_{purp}$]$_{prosec}$.

[Это право]$_{right}$ не может быть использовано [в случае преследования, основанного на совершении деяния, противоречащего [целям [Организации Объединенных Наций]$_{UN}$]$_{purp}$]$_{prosec}$. (www.unhchr.ch/udhr, shortened)

3.3 Antecedent selection

For interconnecting co-referring expressions three basic strategies can be employed: (i) leave this decision to an annotator, (ii) connect all mentions to the first one, or (iii) connect each following mention to the immediately preceding one. In line with previous research and in order to enhance consistency, we opted for (iii), as Principle 3 states:

Principle 3 Chain principle
Mark the most recent mention of a referent as antecedent, so that all mentions of the same referent make up an ordered chain.

Possessive pronouns can often be used at the beginning of a sentence, in case they are resolved in the same sentence as in (3) and (4). The chain principle suggests selecting a pronoun as the chain-initial element which is contra-intuitive in this case: a pronoun introduces no lexical material which serves for subsequent re-identification of a referent. In order to respect the inter-subjective intuition to identify the controller of the possessive as a markable, we posit an exception to the chain principle for the case of pronominal cataphora. According to the CONSISTENCY requirement (see 3.1), *any* bound pronoun, no matter if its is chain-initial or not, has to be treated this way.

Principle 4 Cataphora at sentence level

If a pronoun which is typically used as a bound pronoun is bound by an intrasentential controller, annotate a pointing relation to the controller rather than to a candidate antecedent in previous discourse.

In the Core Scheme for German, English and Russian, Principle 4 applies to possessive pronouns only.

(3) Through [his]$_a$ lawyers, [Mr. Antar]$_a$ has denied allegations in the SEC suit...(WSJ, 3)

(4) [Die einstige Fußball-Weltmacht]$_d$ zittert [vor einem Winzling]$_s$. Mit [seinem]$_s$ Tor zum 1:0 [für die Ukraine]$_u$ stürzte [der 1,62 Meter große Gennadi Subow]$_s$ [die deutsche Nationalelf]$_d$ vorübergehend in ein Trauma... (PCC, 10374)
"[The former football World Power]$_d$ is shivering [in the face of a mite]$_s$. By [his]$_s$ goal that set the score to 1:0 [for Ukraine]$_u$ pitched [Gennadi Subow]$_s$, 1.62 Meter tall, [the German National Eleven]$_d$ in a shock for a while..."

3.4 Identifying pointing relations

A special case for annotation is pronominal or nominal reference by plural or NPs or *both* to *multiple* concrete antecedents mentioned at different points in a text. Thus, they cannot be regarded as single constituent. Since a referent of a plural NP is not the same as the sum of its parts, we deal with multiple antecedents by introducing a separate annotation layer called *groups*. Group referents are linked to their anaphors by regular anaphoric relations, see (5).

(5) `[Montedison]`$_m$ `now owns about 72% of [Erbamont's]`$_e$ `shares outstanding. [The companies]`$_{m+e}$ `said ... a sale of all of [Erbamont's]`$_e$ `assets ... [to Montedison]`$_m$ `... [The companies]`$_{m+e}$ `said ...` (WSJ, 660)

Special treatment of groups is important as they introduce an exception to the Chain Principle. Formally, the same group of people can be referred to at different points of time. However, following the preference for MAXIMAL ANALYSIS (see 3.1), longer anaphoric chains are preferred, and thus, once a pre-established group reference exists, it is marked as an antecedent instead of establishing a new group referent. Accordingly, in ex. (5), the preferred antecedent of the second `companies` is the previously established group reference `The companies`. More generally, this is formulated in Principle 5.

Principle 5 Maximize anaphoric chains

The annotation of anaphoric references is preferred over the annotation of alternative analyses.

This principle is motivated by CONSISTENCY and coverage considerations.

4 Dealing with vagueness

4.1 Ambiguity resolution strategies

The problem of identifying an appropriate pointing relation is especially acute in connection with anaphoric ambiguity. As opposed to general annotation strategies, however, the ambiguity strategies apply only in case of doubt, i.e. if the annotator perceives different readings as equally possible. Consider ex. (6) as a continuation of ex. (4):

(6) `Je kleiner [die Kicker]`$_{u?/d?}$ `daherkommmen, desto größer wird [der Gegner]`$_{d?/u?}$ `geredet.` (PCC, 10374)
„The smaller [the kickers]$_{u?/d?}$ are, the greater [the rivals]$_{d?/u?}$ are rumoured to be."

Antecedent of `die Kicker` "kickers" depends on the understanding of the "size" metaphor, it can be either the Ukrainian team (presented as having short players), or the German team (which has not been favored in the first match), or a generic description (which would mean that the sentence is not directly linked with the discourse). Here, also Principle 5 can be applied, since we are facing alternative readings, and accordingly, the generic reading in the example is excluded. This application of Principle 5 is reformulated in Principle 6.

Principle 6 Primacy of anaphora

In case of uncertainty between different readings prefer anaphoric interpretation to antecedentless one.

However, in the example under consideration, we still have the choice between two possible antecedents. The substitution test (see Sec. 2) fails to determine a unique antecedent, as both possible substitutions are plausible, depending on whether "size" refers to physical size or anticipated defeat. From the preference for MAXIMAL ANALYSIS, however, a more rigid version of Principle 5 can be motivated, cf. Principle 7.

Principle 7 Avoid ambiguous antecedents

In case of two possible antecedents, primary markable is preferred to secondary ones or to group referents.
In case of two primary markables are possible antecedents, choose the one which leads to the longer anaphoric chain.

In ex. (6), this results in a preference for the German team as the antecedent of `die Kicker`.

Finally, in order to narrow down the scope of ambiguity, another exception to the chain principle is necessary. Markables with ambiguous reference should be avoided as antecedents, but rather the last unambiguously coreferential expression.

Principle 8 Primary markables as preferred antecedents

Prefer antecedents which are unambiguous in their reference to antecedents which are ambiguous.

4.2 Annotation of ambiguities

In order to investigate the effect of ambiguity and to document its influence on inter-annotator-agreement, ambiguities are to be explicitly marked. For this purpose, we classified ambiguities as follows.

Ambiguous antecedent ambiguity of antecedent of a markable, cf. (6).

Ambiguous relation ambiguity wrt relation between a markable and the context:

`(7) Weil [die Polizei]`$_p$ `das weiß, richten sich [die Beamten]`$_?$ `… auf viele Anzeigen ... ein. (PCC, 19442)`

"As [the police]$_p$ knows this, [the officials]$_?$ are expecting … a lot of statements…"

The relation between *"the police"* and *"the policemen"* is either bridging (part-whole) or coreference.

Ambiguous idiomatic ambiguity wrt whether a markable could be either understood as coreferential or as a part of an idiom. In (8), *der Spatz in der Hand*, a definite NP in German, can be generic, part of an idiom, or referring:

`(8) Lieber [der Spatz in der Hand] als [die Taube auf dem Dach] (PCC, 12666)`

„A bird in the hand is worth two in the bush" (Context: a mayor finds an investor for his town willing to make only minimal investments).

5 PoCoS annotation scheme

PoCoS disposes of three annotation levels: markables, relations and attributes (5.1, 5.2. and 5.3). In what follows, we concentrate on the Core Scheme because of relevance and space considerations.

5.1 Markables

Primary markables are all potential anaphors, i.e. referential forms which can be used to indicate subsequent mentions of a previously introduced referent in the discourse, such as definite NPs, pronouns, and proper names. *Secondary markables* are expressions that normally indicates non-reference (e.g. indefinites; in the Extended Scheme also clauses). Secondary markables are subject to annotation only if they serve as antecedents of a primary markable.

The basic distinctive feature between primary and secondary markables is if they can refer to previously mentioned nominals or not. Using the above-mentioned grammatical criteria, most probable referring expressions (i.e. primary markables) can be extracted automatically from syntactic annotation, which is an important advantage.

Further, using this differentiation a more precise definition of the coreference annotation task can be given. Coreference annotation is *complete*, if all primary markables are classified as having an antecedent or not.

5.2 Coreference Relations

We distinguish between two types of coreference: nominal and non-nominal. The Core Scheme only deals with *nominal* coreference, which we define as reference of NPs to explicitly mentioned NPs establishing a relation of identity (cf. Mitkov's (2002) "identity-of-reference direct nominal anaphora"). If a relation other than identity holds between a primary markable and an element from the preceding context, e.g. the bridging relation, the relation remains underspecified and can be assigned later, as part of Extended Scheme.

Differently from MUC, we do not consider predicative nominals as coreferential with the subject in the sense of textual coreference defined above (for similar view, see van Deemter and Kibble, 1999), as the relationship with the hypothetical antecedent is expressed by syntactic means.

5.3 Annotation principles

In sec. 3 and 4, we outlined a small set of heuristics serving to guide annotators to more consistent annotation decisions. These principles are, however, not equal in their restrictive force, but rather they build the following preference hierarchy (cf. Carlson et al., 2003):

obligatory principles > exception principles > default principles > ambiguity principles

Principles 1 and 2 are *obligatory* and do not allow exceptions; 4, 5 and 8 are *exceptions* to the *default*, i.e. the Chain Principle (3). 6 and 7 are applied only if interpretation-dependent *ambiguities* occur, thus being no exceptions to default principles.

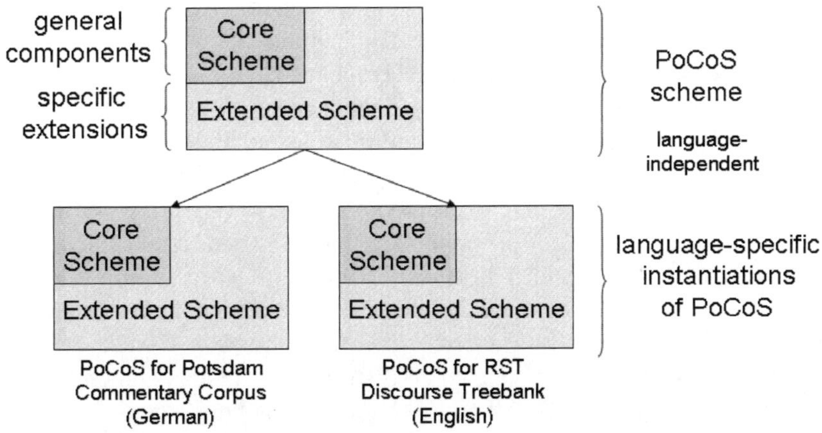

Figure 1. PoCoS: Core Scheme, Extended Scheme and language-specific instantiations

5.4 Attributes

Markables and relations are enriched by a set of additional features. These features encode attributes of pointing relations (e.g. anaphora type) or specify parameters of anaphoricity (e.g. referentiality, ambiguity). Further, certain grammatical features of markables are integrated which are of general interest when analyzing patterns of anaphora in corpora and can be extracted from other preexisting annotations. This way we gain a common minimal representation of grammatical features which can be extracted from different annotation schemes. This allows us to abstract from language-, tool- or annotation-specific expressions of, say, grammatical roles. As a consequence, the scheme is self-contained to a higher degree, and thus, the cross-linguistic validity of the assembled data is enhanced.

5.5. Annotation procedure

The scheme suggests structuring annotation into several annotation cycles performed manually or semi-automatically:

I. Core Scheme Annotation

1. Identify primary markables
2. Connect markables with coreference links
    a. assign to every primary markable a unique antecedent
    b. if antecedent is not a primary markable, annotate it is as secondary markable if necessary
3. Set attribute values

II. Extended Scheme: steps 1 to 3 accordingly

These stages correspond to the 3 annotation levels within the Core and Extended Schemes respectively, because annotating at all levels at the same time has proved to be very labor-intensive and more time-consuming than one level at a time.

6 Application and evaluation

The original annotation guidelines were drafted in 2004 by the authors for the annotation of the Potsdam Commentary Corpus of German newspaper commentaries (PCC) (Stede, 2004) and the RST Discourse Treebank of Wall Street Journal articles (WSJ) (Carlson et al., 2003).

After a series of annotation experiments, the PoCoS Core Scheme was applied to the PCC by two instructed annotators, students of linguistics, whose portions had an overlap of 19 texts (11%). Based upon these texts, inter-annotator agreement was calculated using different agreement scores along the methodology of Popescu-Belis et al. (2004). So, with respect to German, we achieved moderate to substantial agreement (full chains, κ=0.61 with union of markables; κ=0.77 with intersection of markables).

Part of the WSJ corpus has been performed in co-operation with A.A. Kibrik, Moscow State University. Fourteen instructed annotators, also students of linguistics, worked on the RST Discourse Treebank with pair-wise overlapping portions. Regarding 8 texts from 6 annotators, we also found substantial agreement (κ=0.71 with union; κ=0.96 with intersection).

These results are reasonable in the light of κ values reported for an annotation experiment by Artstein and Poesio (2005, p.22) on English which yielded κ=0.48. However, κ is affected by parameters of the text as a whole, and thus should be interpreted with certain reservations. The texts of the PCC are generally short, but very demanding in their interpretation.

A detailed study of outliers revealed several sources of errors in both corpora. Besides „soft errors“ such as inclusion of punctuation and conjunctions within markables, occasionally missed integration of function words into markables, or obviously missed anaphors, we found several „hard“ errors on syntax (e.g. different assumptions about PP attachment), semantics (e.g. vagueness, exact relationship between abstract concepts in a given context), and pragmatics (e.g. differentiation between metonymy and bridging). Above, we suggested the annotation of ambiguity as an attempt to capture typical semantic and pragmatic sources of disagreement (cf. sec. 4.2 for examples).

In order to evaluate the impact of such „hard errors“ in the German data, two instructed annotators corrected 13 texts from the overlapping part of the portions independently. As a concequence, the original κ values increased by about 7%: original κ = 0.69 (union)/0.82 (intersection), and corrected κ =0.76 (union)/0.89 (intersection). These results, however, still suffer from the special problems with the demanding – though, very interesting – type of texts assembled in the PCC as well.

Note that in spite of these short remarks, this paper has focused on the *presentation* of the scheme principles rather than on its evaluation. Currently, the PCC is annotated with information structure and a more thorough evaluation addressing both information status and co-reference is in preparation. A corpus of Russian is currently under construction, which PoCoS is being applied to (cf. Krasavina et al. 2007).

7 Discussion

The majority of earlier coreference annotation experiences were dealing with English, including the standard-like MUC-scheme (Hirschman, 1997). MATE was an attempt to extend annotation to other languages than English (Poesio, 2004). For German, several annotation schemes appeared and were applied to annotation of corpora recently: for newspaper texts, such as the TüBa-D/Z (Naumann, 2006) and for hypertexts, Holler et al. (2004). As for Slavic languages, the Prague Dependency Treebank has been recently enriched by coreference annotation, see Kučová and Hajičová (2004) . For Russian, though, we are aware of no similar experiences so far. The current approach is an advance on the existing work as it attempts at providing language-independent and systematic annotation principles, including a language-neutral repertoire of relations and a language-neutral apparatus for identification of markables. This makes the resulting annotation scheme extendable and applicable across languages.

The Core Scheme is comparable to MUC by Hirschman, 1997; DRAMA by Passonneau, 1996; MATE by Poesio, 2004. Its specific instantiations formalized in a family of Extended Scheme(s) are comparable to Rocha, 1997, GNOME by Poesio, 2004. By distinguishing between fundamental ("obligatory"), project-specific ("recommended") and language-specific ("optional") levels of annotation (cf. Leech and Wilson, 1996), a compromise between a general character and a greater level of detail is achieved.

A central innovation is the dichotomy of primary and secondary markables. As both are defined on the basis of their syntactic properties, we recommend identifying primary markables automatically, but annotate secondary markables manually and only if needed. The separation between both leads to a reduction of the number of possible attribute values subject to annotation, and thus to reduction of complexity. The definition of primary and secondary markables makes use of language-specifics such as existence of a definite determiner, etc. These specifications, although formulated here specifically for German and English, are subject to language-specific alternative instantiations of the PoCoS Scheme. Note that in Russian, the differentiation between primary and secondary markables is made on the basis of different linguistic cues, as definiteness is not explicitly marked. Therefore, in Russian, secondary markables are only certain quantified expressions. Nevertheless, the function of primary and secondary markables remains the same. Further, existence of a pre-determined set of potential anaphors allows to verify if all primary markables are assigned a relation or have been explicitly marked as non-referring.

Another important novel aspect is the systematic treatment of ambiguity in the annotation of large corpora. This aspect has never been included in coreference annotation before (except for one experiment described by Poesio and Artstein, 2005) and thus defines the task of coreference annotation in a more precise way. Moreover, we specified a set of heuristic rules to guide an annotator to a specific decision in case of ambiguity or vagueness. These rules are ranked according to their priority. Similarly, Versley (2006) has recently argued that a "light-weight theory" of anaphoric ambiguity is due, in order to ensure consistent coding decisions.

Finally, splitting annotation procedure into stages allows explicit structuring of the process, in existing approaches presented no more than implicitly (cf. Naumann, 2006, see p. 12).

8 Conclusion

This paper has presented the general coreference annotation framework and the PoCoS Scheme for coreference annotation. As an innovative feature for coreference annotation, it implements ambiguity resolution strategies and proposes annotation of ambiguities. Also, by introducing language-neutral criteria for identification of markables, it both reduces the notorious complexity of anaphoric annotation on the systematic basis and enables applicability of similar principles across languages. Thus, it has a better portability and cross-language comparability as compared to the previous work. One possible field of application of the scheme can be seen in its utilisation for the anaphoric annotation of parallel corpora, an idea which is currently explored by the authors.

References

Artstein, R. and M. Poesio. 2005. Kappa[3]=Alpha (or Beta). Technical Report CSM-437, Univ. of Essex.

Carlson, L., D. Marcu and M. E. Okurowski. 2003. Building a Discourse-Tagged Corpus in the Framework of Rhetorical Structure Theory. Current directions in discourse and dialogue, Kluwer.

Deemter van, K. and R Kibble. 1999. What is coreference, and what should coreference annotation be? Proc. of the ACL Workshop on Coreference.

Ge, M, J. Hale, and E. Charniak. 1998. A statistical approach to anaphora resolution. Proc. of the Sixth Workshop on very Large Corpora.

Holler, A., J.F.Maas and A.Storrer. 2004. Exploiting Coreference Annotations for Text-to-Hypertext Conversion. Proc. of LREC 2004, Lissabon, Portugal.

Hirschman, L. 1997. MUC-7 coreference task definition. Version 3.0.

Karttunen, L. 1976. Discourse referents. Syntax and Semantics. J. McCawley, New York Academic Press.

Krasavina, O., Ch. Chiarcos and D. Zalmanov. 2007. Aspects of topicality in the use of demonstrative expressions in German, English and Russian. Proc. of DAARC-2007, Lagos, Portugal, 29-30 March.

Kučová, L. and E. Hajičová (2004). Prague Dependency Treebank: Enrichment of the Underlying Syntactic Annotation by Coreferential Mark-Up. The Prague Bulletin of Mathematical Linguistics 81.

Leech, G. and J. Svartvik. 2003. A communicative grammar of English. London [u.a.].

Leech, G. and A. Wilson. 1996. EAGLES Recommendations for the Morphosyntactic Annotation of Corpora. www.ilc.cnr.it/EAGLES/annotate/annotate.html

Mitkov, R. 2002. Anaphora resolution. London [u.a.].

Naumann, K. 2006. Manual for the Annotation of in-document Referential Relations. http://www.sfs.uni-tuebingen.de/de_tuebadz.shtml (July 2006).

Passonneau, R. 1996. Instructions for applying Discourse Reference Annotation for Multiple Applications (DRAMA). Unpublished document.

Poesio, M. 2004 The MATE/GNOME Proposals for Anaphoric Annotation, Revisited. Proc. of SIGDIAL.

Poesio, M. and R. Artstein, 2005. Annotating (Anaphoric) Ambiguity. Proc. of Corpus Linguistics-05.

Popescu-Belis, A., L. Rigouste, S. Salmon-Alt, and L-Romary. 2004, Online Evaluation of Coreference Resolution. Proc. of LREC 2004.

Rocha de, M. 1997. Supporting anaphor resolution with a corpus-based probabilistic model. Proc. of the ACL'97 workshop on Operational factors in practical, robust anaphora resolution. Madrid, Spain.

Stede, M. 2004. The Potsdam Commentary Corpus. Proc. of ACL-04 Workshop on Discourse Annotation, Barcelona, July.

Versley, Y. 2006. Disagreement Dissected: Vagueness as a Source of Ambiguity in Nominal (Co-) Reference. Proceedings of the ESSLLI 2006 Workshop on Ambiguity in Anaphora.

Multiple-step treebank conversion: from dependency to Penn format

Cristina Bosco
Dipartimento di Informatica, Università di Torino
Corso Svizzera 185
10149 Torino - Italia
bosco@di.unito.it

Abstract

Whilst the degree to which a treebank subscribes to a specific linguistic theory limits the usefulness of the resource, the availability of more formats for the same resource plays a crucial role both in NLP and linguistics. Conversion tools and multi-format treebanks are useful for investigating portability of NLP systems and validity of annotation. Unfortunately, conversion is a quite complex task since it involves grammatical rules and linguistic knowledge to be incorporated into the converter program.
The paper focusses on a methodology for treebank conversion which consists in splitting the process in steps corresponding to the kinds of information that have to be converted, i.e. morphological, structural or relational syntactic. The advantage is the generation of a set of parallel treebanks featuring progressively differentiated formats. An application to the case of an Italian dependency-based treebank in a Penn like format is described.

1 Introduction

The usefulness of a treebank can be potentially limited by the degree to which it subscribes to a specific linguistic theory, and when a new annotation is devised which employs a different linguistic framework than a standard, the problem of how to relate the syntactic schemes to one another arises. The increasing availability of multi-format treebanks (e.g. (Bick, 2006)) and the automatic conversion from some formats to others, e.g. (Collins et al, 1999; Bahgat Shehata and Zanzotto, 2006), are attempts to overcome this problem.
The automatic conversion of a treebank plays an important role in NLP and linguistics. First, it increases the exportability of the treebank, making usable tools developed for other resources. Second, it underlies a full check on correctness and consistency of the treebank annotation. Moreover, it is an explicit comparison among formats and linguistic frameworks. Therefore, a conversion is crucial for overcoming the limits imposed by data in formats that realize different grammatical theories to very important activities such as parsing evaluation and comparative testing of the adequateness of a representation for particular linguistic phenomena, languages and/or tasks. For instance, the availability of parallel annotations, and among them one in Penn format, can be of some aid in investigating the irreproducibility of the state-of-the-art results on treebanks or languages other than Penn and English, as empirically demonstrated by, e.g., (Collins et al, 1999) on Czech, (Dubey and Keller, 2003) on German, (Corazza et al, 2004) on Italian.
The paper, first, presents a methodology for the conversion, then an application of the methodology to the conversion of a dependency-based treebank into a Penn-like format, and finally some remarks on the implementation.

2 On the conversion methodology

The conversion of a treebank, annotated with some format A, into format B consists in a simple filtering

Proceedings of the Linguistic Annotation Workshop, pages 164–167,
Prague, June 2007.

and string manipulation only when A and B both follow the same linguistic framework. Elsewhere the conversion and development of parallel annotations is a challenging task, which involves grammatical rules and linguistic knowledge to be incorporated into the converter programs (see e.g.(Musillo and Sima'an, 2002) (Bick, 2006)). Nevertheless, parallel annotations which employ different linguistic frameworks may serve as a suitable infrastructure for comparisons among them. In fact, the definition of a conversion process is in itself a comparison between A and B, since it involves explicit assumptions about how A and B relate, and a virtually complete and correct mapping which translates every analysis in A into the corresponding analysis in B (Musillo and Sima'an, 2002).

We propose a methodology that consists in organizing the conversion in steps to be performed in cascade. Each step outputs a new annotation format, which differentiates from the previous one only with respect to a single kind of knowledge, e.g. morphological, structural or functional syntactic. The main advantage is in making available a set of parallel annotations for further use too.

In the next part, we describe the application of this methodology to the conversion of the Turin University Treebank (henceforth TUT), which exploits a dependency-based functionally rich annotation, into a Penn-like format.

3 Converting TUT

TUT is a project for an Italian treebank that features a dependency-based annotation following the dependency grammar major tenets (Hudson, 1984). The annotation is centred on a notion of morpho-syntactic-semantic grammatical relation which aims at represent the syntax-semantics interface by means of the Augmented Relational Structure (Bosco, 2004). TUT currently includes 2.000 sentences (see at http://www.di.unito.it/~tutreeb/) where 200 different dependency relations are annotated. The figure 1 a) shows an example of TUT tree.

Other Italian resources[1] implement, like TUT, particular representation formats and subscribe to specific linguistic frameworks, thus strongly limiting activities such as the application of state-of-the-art parsers and parsing evaluation for this language. The conversion of TUT in a Penn-like format is a crucial step towards the exportability of the resource, but also a first attempt at overcoming these limits by choosing as a further output a format of widespread use in training, testing and evaluating. Moreover, since the process is fully deterministic, even if currently applied on a small corpus, the conversion is in itself a preliminary validation of the resource and a demonstration that TUT annotation is expressive at least as Penn.

In the next sections, we show the translation of dependency into constituency trees and the management of differences in PoS tagging, structural syntactic, and syntactic-semantic relations faced during the conversion. For detailed information about the conversion of specific linguistic phenomena see at http://www.di.unito.it/~tutreeb/noteparallele.zip.

3.1 First step: morphology

Since Italian is inflectionally richer than English, TUT PoS tagset is richer than that of Penn (see at http://www.di.unito.it/~tutreeb/syntcat-22-7-02.doc), but we reduced it including only information that Penn makes explicit too, as usual in similar cases, see e.g. (Collins et al, 1999) and http://www.coli.uni-sb.de/sfb378/negra-corpus/. The major differences with respect to Penn concern tags of Verbs, which include fine-grained temporal information and are organized in three classes (Modal, Auxiliary, Main), rather than two like in Penn (Modal and non-Modal). Moreover, a fine-grained variety of Adjectives and Pronouns enables the recovery of information such as e.g. the owner of an object (possessive Adjective).

The output of this first step includes compact tags where features are expressed by short strings, like in (Collins et al, 1999). The following are examples of TUT PoS native vs reduced tags: for a common Noun 'nome' is (NOME NOUN COMMON M SING) reduced in (NOU~CS); for the main infinite Verb 'entrare' is (ENTRARE VERB MAIN INFINITE PRES INTRANS) reduced in (VMA~IN).

3.2 Second step: structural syntax

The main issue in this step is the conversion of dependency trees into Penn-like trees, i.e.

[1]Two other larger Italian treebanks exist: Venice Italian Treebank (VIT) (Delmonte, forthcoming) and Italian Syntactic Semantic Treebank (ISST) (Barsotti et al, 2001)

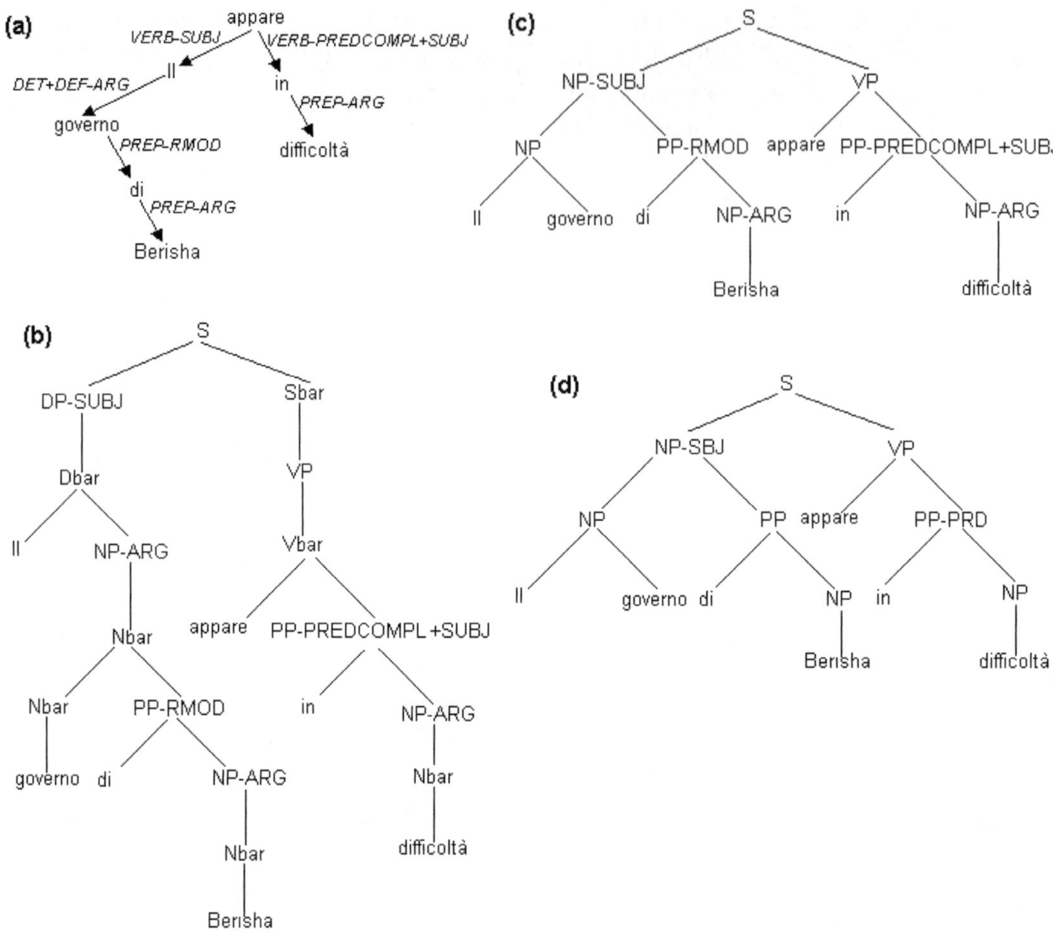

Figure 1: TUT (a), Constituency-TUT (b), Augmented-Penn (c) and Penn-like (d) representations of sentence ALB-4 "Il governo di Berisha appare in difficoltà" (The government of Berisha appears in trouble)

constituency structures implementing a minimal projection strategy. It is approached in two substeps: by first converting the TUT trees into a standard linguistically motivated Xbar form (i.e. Constituency-TUT), and then into Penn format (i.e. Augmented-Penn), but both including the functional syntactic information as TUT, i.e. the grammatical relations (annotated on constituents).

Constituency-TUT is a TUT-oriented constituency-based annotation that introduces in TUT trees the types of the multiple words syntactic units (e.g. VP and S). Each terminal category X corresponds to a word of a TUT tree, and projects into non-terminal nodes, namely the intermediate (Xbar) and maximal (XP) projections of X. The distinction between complements and adjuncts is here structurally marked.

Augmented-Penn instead features a format structurally isomorphic to Penn, but more functionally annotated. It applies to the Constituency-TUT structures the minimal projection strategy[2], and manages the smoothing of structures conceptually different in TUT and Penn, i.e. those of Determiners, auxiliary Verbs and relative clauses. In figure 1 you can see the same sentence in TUT, Constituency-TUT, Augmented-Penn and Penn format.

The conversion from dependency to constituency is not affected by the typical problem of non-projective structures, since TUT represents them through projective structures exploiting null elements. In dependency TUT, empty nodes also mark dropped subjects, and Constituency-TUT exploits

[2]Each terminal category projects only when the constituent includes more than one word

null elements for marking subjects which occur in non standard position with respect to the Verb (i.e. extraposed).

3.3 Third step: syntactic-semantic relations

While Penn features a description of relations based only on a single component, TUT features an explicit, systematic annotation of three components in each relation. Moreover, Penn includes a lower number of values for each component than TUT[3] and in various cases the Penn tags do not enable fine-grained distinctions as TUT.

We applied the original Penn tags that can be meaningful for Italian looking for correspondences between TUT and Penn relations (e.g. using the relation LOC for all TUT LOC+ relations)[4]. Nevertheless, the multi-step methodology makes available also a Penn-like format almost functionally rich as TUT, i.e. Augmented-Penn[5].

4 The converter

The five modules of the converter are: M_{reduc} for the reduction of PoS tags; M_{ctu} which converts in the Constituency-TUT format; M_{augp}, which converts Constituency-TUT in Augmented-Penn; M_{pen}, which takes Augmented-Penn and outputs Penn; M_{par} that generates the parenthetical notation of the output.

M_{ctu} manages the conversion from dependency to constituency by implementing the algorithm in (Xia, 2001). It recovers the types of phrases that (the grammatical category of) each node of the dependency tree projects by using the linguistic knowledge stored in dedicated tables.

The converter follows a lowest attachment strategy, i.e. the projection of a dependent attaches to a projection of its head as lowly as possible, but, in contrast with (Xia, 2001), it pursues a maximal rather than minimal projection heuristics, i.e. a category always projects into intermediate and maximal projections.

5 Conclusions

The methodology for treebank conversion here presented splits the process in steps, which correspond to the kinds of annotated linguistic knowledge that have to be converted. Since each step outputs a new annotation format, the advantage is the generation of set of parallel treebanks.

The application of the methodology in the conversion from a small Italian dependency-based treebank to a Penn like format is described.

[3] While Penn annotates 2 morpho-syntactic, 11 syntactic and 7 semantic relations, TUT features 40 morpho-syntactic, 55 functional-syntactic and 88 semantic items for building relations.

[4] The conversion from NEGRA to Penn maintains instead the NEGRA relations, see at http://www.coli.uni-sb.de/sfb378/negra-corpus/.

[5] The relations linking terminal nodes encompassed in a single constituent in Augmented-Penn are deleted during the conversion in this latter format.

References

A. Bahgat Shehata and F.M. Zanzotto. 2006. A dependency-based algorithm for grammar conversion. *Proc. of LREC '06*

F. Barsotti and R. Basili et al. 2001. *The Italian Syntactic-Semantic Treebank: Architecture, Annotation, Tools and Evaluation.* Kluwer, Dordrecht.

E. Bick. 2006. Turning a dependency-based treebank into a PSG-style constituent treebank. *Proc. of LREC 06.*

C. Bosco. 2004. *A grammatical relation system for treebank annotation.* PhD thesis, University of Torino.

M. Collins, J. Hajic, L. Ramshaw, and C. Tillmann. 1999. A statistical parser of Czech. *Proc. of ACL'99.*

A. Corazza, A. Lavelli, G. Satta, and R. Zanoli. 2004 Analyzing an Italian treebank with state-of-the-art statistical parser. In *Proc. of TLT-2004.*

R. Delmonte. forthcoming. *Strutture sintattiche dall'analisi computazionale di corpora di italiano* Franco Angeli, Milano, Italy.

A. Dubey and F. Keller. 2003. Probabilistic parsing for German using sister-head dependencies. *Proc. of ACL'03.*

R. Hudson. 1984. *Word Grammar.* Basil Blackwell, Oxford and New York.

G. Musillo and K. Sima'an. 2002. Towards comparing parsers from different linguistic frameworks. An information theoretic approach. *Proc. of Workshop Beyond PARSEVAL.*

F. Xia. 2001. *Automatic grammar generation from two different perspectives.* PhD thesis, University of Pennsylvania.

Experiments with an Annotation Scheme for a Knowledge-rich Noun Phrase Interpretation System

Roxana Girju
University of Illinois at Urbana-Champaign
girju@uiuc.edu

Abstract

This paper presents observations on our experience with an annotation scheme that was used in the training of a state-of-the-art noun phrase semantic interpretation system. The system relies on cross-linguistic evidence from a set of five Romance languages: Spanish, Italian, French, Portuguese, and Romanian. Given a training set of English noun phrases in context along with their translations in the five Romance languages, our algorithm automatically learns a classification function that is later on applied to unseen test instances for semantic interpretation. As training and test data we used two text collections of different genre: Europarl and CLUVI. The training data was annotated with contextual features based on two state-of-the-art classification tag sets.

1 Introduction

Linguistically annotated corpora are valuable resources for both theoretical and computational linguistics. They have played an important role in any aspect of natural language processing research, from supervised learning to evaluation, and have been used in many applications such as Syntactic and Semantic Parsing, Information Extraction, and Question Answering.

A long-term research topic in linguistics, computational linguistics[1], and artificial intelligence has been the semantic interpretation of noun phrases (NPs). The basic problem is simple to define: given a noun phrase constructed out of a pair of concepts expressed by words or phrases, $c_1 - c_2$, one representing the head and the other the modifier, determine the semantic relationship between the two concepts. For example, a compound *family estate* should be interpreted as the estate OWNED BY the family; an NP such as *dress of silk* should be interpreted as denoting a dress MADE FROM silk. The problem, while simple to state is hard to solve. The reason is that the meaning of these constructions is most of the time ambiguous or implicit.

Currently, the best-performing English NP interpretation methods in computational linguistics focus mostly on two consecutive noun instances (noun compounds) and are either (weakly) supervised, knowledge-intensive (Rosario and Hearst, 2001), (Rosario et al., 2002), (Moldovan et al., 2004), (Pantel and Pennacchiotti, 2006), (Pennacchiotti and Pantel, 2006), (Kim and Baldwin, 2006), (Snow et al., 2006), (Girju et al., 2005; Girju et al., 2006), or use statistical models on large collections of unlabeled data (Berland and Charniak, 1999), (Lapata and Keller, 2004), (Nakov and Hearst, 2005), (Turney, 2006). Unlike unsupervised models, supervised knowledge-rich approaches rely heavily on large sets of annotated training data. For example, we previously showed (Girju et al., 2006) that, for

[1]In the past few years at many workshops, tutorials, and competitions this research topic has received considerable interest from the computational linguistics community: Workshop on Multiword Expressions at COLING/ACL 2006, 2004, 2003; Computational Lexical Semantics Workshop at ACL 2004; Tutorial on Knowledge Discovery from Text at ACL 2003; Shared task on Semantic Role Labeling at CONLL 2005, 2004 and at SENSEVAL 2005.

Proceedings of the Linguistic Annotation Workshop, pages 168–175,
Prague, June 2007.

the task of automatic detection of part-whole relations, our system's learning curve reached a plateau at 74% F-measure when trained on approximatively 10,000 positive and negative examples.

Interpreting NPs correctly requires various types of information from world knowledge to complex context features. Since the training data needs to be as accurate as possible, many of such features are manually identified and annotated. Thus, the annotation process is an important task that requires not only considerable amount of time, but also experience with various annotation schemas and tools, and a good understanding of the research topic. Moreover, the extension of the noun phrase interpretation task to other natural languages brings forward new annotation issues.

This paper presents observations on our experience with an annotation scheme that was used in the training of a state-of-the-art noun phrase semantic interpretation system (Girju, 2007). The system relies on cross-linguistic evidence from a set of five Romance languages: Spanish, Italian, French, Portuguese, and Romanian. Given a training set of English noun phrases in context along with their translations in the five Romance languages, our algorithm automatically learns a classification function that is later on applied to unseen test instances for semantic interpretation. As training and test data we used two text collections of different genre: Europarl[2] and CLUVI[3]. The training data was annotated with contextual features based on two state-of-the-art classification tag sets: Lauer's set of 8 prepositions (Lauer, 1995) and our list of 22 semantic relations. The system achieved an accuracy of 77.9% (Europarl) and 74.31% (CLUVI).

The paper is organized as follows. Section 2 presents a summary of linguistic considerations of noun phrases. In Section 3 we describe the list of semantic interpretation categories used along with observations regarding their distribution on the two different cross-lingual corpora. Section 4 presents the data used along with observations on corpus annotation and inter-annotator agreement. Finally, Section 5 offers some discussion and conclusions.

2 Linguistic considerations of noun phrases

The automatic discovery of semantic relations must start with a thorough understanding of the linguistic aspects of the underlying relations. These considerations are not only employed as features in the supervised noun phrase interpretation model, but they are also used in the annotation process.

Noun phrases can be compositional when their meaning is derived from the meaning of the constituent nouns (e.g., *door knob* – PART-WHOLE, *kiss in the morning* – TEMPORAL), or idiosyncratic, when the meaning is a matter of convention (e.g., *soap opera*, *sea lion*). NPs can also express metaphorical names (eg, *ladyfinger*), proper names (e.g., *John Doe*), and binomial (dvandva) compounds in which neither noun is the head (e.g., *player-coach*).

NPs can also be classified into *synthetic* (verbal) and *root* (non-verbal) constructions. It is widely held (Levi, 1978), (Selkirk, 1982) that the modifier noun of a synthetic noun compound, for example, may be associated with a theta-role of the verbal head. For instance, in *truck driver*, the noun *truck* satisfies the THEME relation associated with the direct object in the corresponding argument structure of the verb *to drive*.

Studied cross-linguistically, noun phrases can express variations from one language to another. For example, English compounds of the form N_1 N_2 (e.g., *wood stove*) usually translate in Romance languages as N_2 P N_1 (e.g., *four á bois* (French) – *stove at/to wood*). Romance languages have very few N N compounds and they are of limited semantic categories, such as TYPE (e.g., *legge quadro* (Italian) – *framework law*). Moreover, while English N N compounds are right-headed (e.g., *framework*/modifier *law*/head), Romance compounds are left-headed (e.g., *legge*/head *quadro*/modifier).

For this research we focus only on English–Romance compositional noun phrases of the type N N and N P N and disregard metaphorical and

[2] http://www.isi.edu/koehn/europarl/
This corpus contains over 20 million words in eleven official languages of the European Union covering the proceedings of the European Parliament from 1996 to 2001.

[3] CLUVI - Linguistic Corpus of the University of Vigo Parallel Corpus 2.1 - http://sli.uvigo.es/CLUVI/. CLUVI is an open text repository of parallel corpora of contemporary oral and written texts in some of the Romance languages, such as Galician, French, Spanish, Portuguese, Basque parallel text collections.

proper names. In the following section we present two different state-of-the-art classification sets used in NP interpretation.

3 Lists of semantic classification relations

Although researchers (Downing, 1977), (Jespersen, 1954) argued that noun compounds, and NPs in general, encode an infinite set of semantic relations, many agree (Finin, 1980), (Levi, 1978) there is a limited number of relations that occur with high frequency in these constructions. However, the number and the level of abstraction of these frequently used semantic categories are not agreed upon. They can vary from a few prepositions (Lauer, 1995) to hundreds and even thousands more specific semantic relations (Finin, 1980). The more abstract the categories, the more noun phrases are covered, but also the more room for variation as to which category a phrase should be assigned. Lauer (Lauer, 1995), for example, considers a set of eight prepositions as semantic classification categories that can link the head and the modifier nouns in a noun compound: *of, for, with, in, on, at, about*, and *from*. However, according to this classification, the noun compound *love story*, for instance, can be classified both as *story* **of** *love* and *story* **about** *love*. The main problem with these abstract categories is that much of the meaning of individual compounds is lost, and sometimes there is no way to decide whether a form is derived from one category or another. On the other hand, lists of very specific semantic relations are difficult to build as they usually contain a very large number of predicates, such as the list of all possible verbs that can link the noun constituents. Finin (Finin, 1980), for example, uses semantic categories such as "**dissolved in**" to build interpretations of compounds such as "*salt water*" and "*sugar water*".

In this research we experiment with two sets of semantic classification categories defined at different abstraction levels. The first is a core set of 22 semantic relations (22 SRs), set which was identified by us from the linguistics literature and from various experiments after many iterations over a period of time (Moldovan and Girju, 2003)[4]. We proved empirically that this set is encoded by noun – noun pairs in noun phrases and is a subset of our larger list of 35 semantic relations. This list, presented in Table 1 along with examples and semantic argument frames, is general enough to cover a large majority of text semantics while keeping the semantic relations to a manageable number. A semantic argument frame is defined for each semantic relation and indicates the position of each semantic argument in the underlying relation. For example, "Arg_1 is part of (whole) Arg_2" identifies the part (Arg_1) and the whole (Arg_2) entities of this relation. This representation is important since it allows to distinguish between different arrangements of the arguments for given relation instances. For example, most of the time, in N N compounds Arg_1 precedes Arg_2, while in N P N constructions the position is reversed (Arg_2 P Arg_1). However, this is not always the case as shown by N N instances such as "*ham*/Arg1 *sandwich*/Arg2" and "*door*/Arg2 *knob*/Arg1". These argument frames were introduced to provide consistent guide to the annotators to easily test the goodness-of-fit of the relations.

The second set is Lauer's list of 8 prepositions and can be applied only to noun–noun compounds. We selected these two state-of-the-art sets as they are of different size and contain semantic classification categories at different levels of abstraction. Lauer's list is more abstract and, thus capable of encoding a large number of noun compound instances found in a corpus, while our list contains finer grained semantic categories. Details about the coverage of these semantic lists on the two different corpora (Europarl and CLUVI), how well they solve the interpretation problem of noun phrases, and the mapping from one list to another are provided in a companion paper (Girju, 2007).

4 The data

For a better understanding of the semantic relations encoded by N N and N P N instances, we analyzed the semantic behavior of these constructions on a large cross-linguistic corpora of examples. Our intention is to answer questions such as:

(1) *What syntactic constructions are used to translate the English instances to the target Ro-*

[4]There are also other lists of semantic relations used by the research community (e.g., (Barker and Szpakowicz, 1998)), but they overlap considerably with our list of 22-SR.

No.	Semantic Relations	Default argument frame	Examples
1	POSSESSION	Arg_1 POSSESSES Arg_2	*family#2/Arg_1 estate#2/Arg_2*
2	KINSHIP	Arg_1 IS IN KINSHIP REL. WITH Arg_2	*the boy#1/Arg_1's sister#1/Arg_2*
3	PROPERTY	Arg_2 IS PROPERTY OF Arg_1	*lubricant#1/Arg_1 viscosity#1/Arg_2*
4	AGENT	Arg_1 IS AGENT OF Arg_2	*investigation#2/Arg_2 of the crew#2/Arg_1*
5	TEMPORAL	Arg_2 IS TEMPORAL LOCATION OF Arg_1	*morning#1/Arg_2 news#3/Arg_1*
6	DEPICTION-DEPICTED	Arg_1 DEPICTS Arg_2	*a picture#1 Arg_1 of the nice#1/Arg_2*
7	PART-WHOLE	Arg_2 IS PART OF (whole) Arg_1	*faces#1/Arg_2 of children#1/Arg_1*
8	HYPERNYMY (IS-A)	Arg_2 IS A Arg_1	*daisy#1/Arg_2 flower#1/Arg_1*
9	CAUSE	Arg_1 CAUSES Arg_2	*scream#1/Arg_2 of pain#1/Arg_1*
10	MAKE/PRODUCE	Arg_1 PRODUCES Arg_2	*chocolate#2/Arg_2 factory#1/Arg_1*
11	INSTRUMENT	Arg_2 IS INSTRUMENT OF Arg_1	*laser#1/Arg_2 treatment#1/Arg_1*
12	LOCATION	Arg_2 IS LOCATED IN Arg_1	*castle#1/Arg_2 in the desert#1/Arg_1*
13	PURPOSE	Arg_2 IS PURPOSE OF Arg_1	*cough#1/Arg_2 syrup#1/Arg_1*
14	SOURCE	Arg_2 IS SOURCE OF Arg_1	*grapefruit#2/Arg_2 oil#3/Arg_1*
15	TOPIC	Arg_2 IS TOPIC OF Arg_1	*weather#1/Arg_2 report#2/Arg_2*
16	MANNER	Arg_2 IS MANNER OF Arg_1	*performance#3/Arg_1 with passion#1/Arg_2*
17	MEANS	Arg_2 IS MEANS OF Arg_1	*bus#1/Arg_2 service#1/Arg_1*
18	EXPERIENCER	Arg_1 IS EXPERIENCER OF Arg_2	*the girl#1/Arg_1's fear#1/Arg_2*
19	MEASURE	Arg_2 IS MEASURE OF Arg_1	*cup#2/Arg_2 of sugar#1/Arg_1*
20	RESEMBLANCE/TYPE	Arg_2 RESEMBLES OR IS A TYPE OF Arg_1	*framework#1/Arg_1 law#2/Arg_2*
21	THEME	Arg_2 IS THEME OF Arg_1	*acquisition#1/Arg_1 of stock#1/Arg_2*
22	BENEFICIARY	Arg_1 IS BENEFICIARY OF Arg_2	*reward#1/Arg_2 for the finder#1/Arg_1*
		OTHERS	*altar#1 boys#1*

Table 1: The set of 22 semantic relations along with examples interpreted in context and the semantic argument frame.

mance languages and vice-versa? (cross-linguistic syntactic mapping),

(2) *What semantic relations do these constructions encode?* (cross-linguistic semantic mapping),

(3) *What is the corpus distribution of the semantic relations per each syntactic construction?*, and finally

(4) *What is the role of English and Romance prepositions in the NP interpretation?*

Thus, we collected the data from two text collections with different distributions and of different genre, Europarl and CLUVI.

The Europarl text collection

Europarl is a parallel corpora of over 20 million words in eleven official languages of the European Union covering the proceedings of the European Parliament from 1996 to 2001. The corpus was assembled by combining four of the bilingual sentence-aligned corpora made public as part of the freely available Europarl corpus. Specifically, the Spanish-English, Italian-English, French-English and Portuguese-English corpora were automatically aligned based on exact matches of English translations. Then, only those English sentences which appeared verbatim in all four language pairs were considered. The resulting English corpus contained 10,000 sentences which were syntactically parsed (Charniak, 2000). From these we extracted the first 3,000 NP instances (N N: 48.82% and N P N: 51.18%).

The CLUVI text collection

CLUVI (Linguistic Corpus of the University of Vigo) is an open text repository of parallel corpora of contemporary oral and written languages, resource that besides Galician also contains literary text collections in other Romance languages. We focused only on the English-Portuguese and English-Spanish literary parallel texts from the works of John Steinbeck, H. G. Wells, J. Salinger, among others. Using the CLUVI search interface we created a sentence-aligned parallel corpus of 2,800 English-Spanish and English-Portuguese sentences. The English versions were automatically parsed after which each N N and N P N instance thus identified was manually mapped to the corresponding translations. The resulting corpus contains 2,200 English instances with a distribution of 26.77% N N and 73.23% N P N.

4.1 Corpus annotation

For each corpus, each NP instance was presented separately to two experienced annotators[5] in a web interface in context along with the English sentence and its translations. Since the corpora do not cover some of the languages (Romanian in Europarl and CLUVI, and Italian and French in CLUVI), three other native speakers of these languages and fluent in English provided the translations which were added to the list.

WordNet senses

The two computational semantics annotators had to tag each English constituent noun with its corresponding WordNet sense[6]. If the word was not found in WordNet the instance was not considered.

Tagging each noun constituent with the corresponding WordNet sense in context is important not only as a feature employed in the training models, but also as guidance for the annotators to select the right semantic relation. For instance, in the following sentences, *daisy flower* expresses a PART-WHOLE relation in (1) and a IS-A relation in (2) depending on the sense of the noun *flower* (cf. WordNet 2.1: *flower#2* is a "reproductive organ of angiosperm plants especially one having showy or colorful parts", while *flower#1* is "a plant cultivated for its blooms or blossoms").

(1) "Usually, more than one *daisy#1 flower#2* grows on top of a single stem."

(2) "Try them with orange or yellow flowers of red-hot poker, solidago or other late *daisy#1 flowers#1*, such as rudbeckias and heliopsis."

In cases where noun senses were not enough for relation selection, the annotators had to rely on a larger context provided by the sentence and its translations as shown below.

Semantic argument frame

The annotators were also asked to identify the translation phrases, tag each instance with the corresponding semantic relation, and identify the semantic arguments Arg_1 and Arg_2 in the semantic argument frame of the corresponding relation.

Thus, since the order of the semantic arguments in an NP is not fixed (Girju et al., 2005), the annotators were presented with the semantic argument frame for each of the 22 semantic relations and were asked to tag the NP instances accordingly. For example, in PART-WHOLE instances such as *chair*/Arg2 *arm*/Arg1 the part *arm* follows the whole *chair*, while in *button*/Arg1 *shirt*/Arg2 the order is reversed.

Translation instances

In the annotation process the annotators were asked to identify and use, if necessary, the five corresponding translations as additional information in selecting the semantic relation. Since only N N and N P N noun phrase constructions were considered, the annotators had to discard those instances encoded by different syntactic constructions in the Romance languages.

For instance, the context provided by the Europarl English sentence in (3) below does not give enough information for the disambiguation of the English noun phrase "*judgment of the presidency*" which can mean either AGENT or THEME. The annotators had to rely on the Romance translations in order to identify the correct meaning in context (in this case THEME): *valoración sobre la Presidencia* (Es.), *avis sur la présidence* (Fr.), *giudizio sulla Presidenza* (It.), *veredicto sobre a Presidência* (Port.), *evaluarea Presendiţiei* (Ro.)[7].

(3)

En.: "If you do , *our final judgment of the Spanish presidency* will be even more positive than it has been so far."

Es.: "Si se hace, nuestra valoración sobre la Presidencia española del Consejo será aún mucho más positiva de lo que es hasta ahora."

Fr.: "Si cela arrive, notre avis sur la présidence espagnole du Conseil sera encore beaucoup plus positif que ce n'est déjà le cas."

It.: "Se ci riuscirà il nostro giudizio sulla Presidenza spagnola sarà ancora più positivo di quanto non sia stato finora."

[5] The annotators have extensive expertise in computational semantics and are fluent in at least two of the Romance languages considered for this task.

[6] For the purpose of this research we used WordNet 2.1.

[7] En. means English, Es. – Spanish, Fr. – French, It. – Italian, Port. – Portuguese, and Ro. – Romanian.

Port.: "Se isso acontecer, o nosso veredicto sobre a Presidência espanhola será ainda muito mais positivo do que o actual."

Ro.: "Dacă are loc, evaluarea Preşedinţiei spaniole va fi încă mai pozitivă decât până acum."

Semantic relations

Whenever the annotators found an example encoding a semantic relation or a preposition paraphrase other than those provided or they didn't know what interpretation to give, they had to tag it as OTHER-SR and OTHER-PP, respectively . For example, in the CLUVI sentences (4) and (5) below, the noun phrases *melody of the pearl* and *cry of death* (the cry announcing death) were tagged as OTHER-SR since here the context of the sentences does not indicate the association between the two nouns. Moreover, noun compound instances such as *the corner box* and *knowledge searches* were tagged as OTHER-PP (*box* **in** *the corner*, *searches* **after** *knowledge*).

(3) LPE-284: "And because the need was great and the desire was great, the little secret *melody of the pearl* that might be was stronger this morning." (En.)

(4) LPE-1582: "And then Kino's brain cleared from its red concentration and he knew the sound - the keening, moaning, rising hysterical cry from the little cave in the side of the stone mountain, *the cry of death*." (En.)

Moreover, most of the time one instance was tagged with one semantic relation, and respectively preposition paraphrase, but there were also situations in which an example could belong to more than one classification category in the same context. For example, *Texas city* is tagged as PART-WHOLE/PLACE-AREA, but also as a LOCATION relation using the 22-SR classification category, and respectively as *of, from, in* based on the 8-PP category (e.g., *city of Texas*, *city from Texas*, and *city in Texas*). Other instances, however, can encode a total of three semantic relations in a particular context. One such instance is *cup#2 of hot_chocolate#1* in example (6) below, which was tagged in CLUVI as MEASURE/OTHER(CONTENT-CONTAINER)/LOC. Sense #2 of *cup* in WordNet refers to "the quantity the cup will hold" (cf. WordNet 2.1), thus mostly indicating a MEASURE relation.

(5) 557-AGU: "Wouldn't you like a cup of hot chocolate before you go?" (En.)

However, since most hot beverages (such as tea, coffee, and chocolate) are served in cups, it stands to reason that the instance can be easily paraphrased as a cup holding hold chocolate. Although our current NP interpretation system (Girju, 2007) does not differentiate between LOCATION and CONTENT-CONTAINER (as other researchers (Tyler and Evans, 2003)[8], we consider CONTENT-CONTAINER as a special type of LOCATION), we capture them in our annotation scheme.

Other examples of multiple annotations are MEASURE/PART-WHOLE (e.g., *an abundance of buildings, a bunch of guys*), Overall, 0.5% Europarl and 6.9% CLUVI instances were tagged with more than one semantic relation, and almost all noun compound instances were tagged with more than one preposition.

Thus, the annotated instances used in the corpus analysis and system training phases have the following format: <NP_{En} ;NP_{Es}; NP_{It}; NP_{Fr}; NP_{Port}; NP_{Ro}; target>. The word *target* is one of the 23 (22 + OTHER) semantic relations or one of the eight prepositions considered. For example, <*judgment#2/Arg_1 of presidency#2/Arg_2; valoración sobre la Presidencia; avis sur la présidence; giudizio sulla Presidenza; veredicto sobre a Presidência; evaluarea Preşedinţiei*; THEME>.

4.2 Inter-annotator agreement

The annotators' agreement was measured using Kappa statistics, one of the most frequently used measure of inter-annotator agreement for classification tasks: $K = \frac{Pr(A)-Pr(E)}{1-Pr(E)}$, where $Pr(A)$ is the proportion of times the annotators agree and $Pr(E)$ is the probability of agreement by chance. The K coefficient is 1 if there is a total agreement among the annotators, and 0 if there is no agreement other than that expected to occur by chance.

[8](Tyler and Evans, 2003) cite child language acquisition studies which show there is a strong cognitive relationship between LOCATION and CONTENT-CONTAINER.

The Kappa values obtained on each corpus are shown in Table 2. We also computed the number of pairs that were tagged with OTHER by both annotators for each semantic relation and preposition paraphrase, over the number of examples classified in that category by at least one of the judges. For the noun compound instances that encoded more than one classification category, the agreement was done on one of the relations only.

The agreement obtained for the Europarl corpus is higher than the one for CLUVI on both classification sets. This is partially explained by the distribution of semantic relations in both corpora. Overall, the K coefficient shows a fair to good level of agreement for the corpus data on the set of 22-SRs, taking into consideration the task difficulty. The level of agreement for the prepositional paraphrases was much higher. All these can be explained by the instructions the annotators received prior to the annotation and by their expertise in lexical semantics.

Corpus	Classification tag sets	Kappa Agreement N N	Kappa Agreement N P N	OTHER
Europarl	**8-PP**	0.80	N/A	91%
	22-SR	0.61	0.67	78%
CLUVI	**8-PP**	0.77	N/A	86%
	22-SR	0.56	0.58	69%

Table 2: The inter-annotator agreement on the NP annotation on the two corpora. For the noun compound instances that encoded more than one semantic classification category, the agreement was done on one of the relations only. "N/A" means not applicable.

13.05% of Europarl[9] and 1.9% of CLUVI instances that could not be tagged with Lauer's prepositions were included in OTHER-PP category. About 99% of the Europarl N N instances encode TYPE relations (e.g., *framework law*), while in CLUVI most of them were TYPE (e.g., *nightmare sensation*), followed by OTHER-SR (e.g., *altar boys*), and IS-A (e.g., *Winchester carbine*).

From the initial corpus we considered those English instances that had all the translations encoded by N N and N P N. Out of these, we selected only 1,023 Europarl and 1,008 CLUVI instances encoded by N N and N P N in all languages considered and resulted after agreement[10]. We split the corpora using a 8:2 training - test ratio and used it to train and test our system. Details about the experiments and the results obtained are presented in (Girju, 2007).

5 Discussion and conclusions

In this paper we presented some observations on our experience with an annotation scheme that was used in the training of a state-of-the-art noun phrase semantic interpretation system. These observations are defined in the framework of a larger project. This project is to investigate various linguistic issues and develop specific language models for the interpretation of noun phrase constructions in Germanic, Romance, and other classes of languages.

Our approach to NP interpretation, and thus annotation procedure, is novel in several ways. We define the problem in a cross-linguistic framework and provide empirical observations on various annotation issues based on a set of two different corpora using two state-of-the-art classification tag sets: Lauer's prepositions and our list of 22 relations.

The linguistic implications are also important to mention here. The annotation investigations done in this research provide new insights into the research topic at hand, the semantic interpretation of noun phrases, in particular and the identification of semantic relations between nominals (irrespective of the syntactic constructions that link the two nouns), in general. One such linguistic aspect is the importance of context for this task. Sometimes, the local context of the noun phrase is not enough to disambiguate the underlying instances. For this, the annotators need to relay on world and domain specific knowledge and the entire context of the sentence, or consider a larger context window (from a simple paragraph including the sentence, to the discourse of the text) as shown below in (6), (7), and (8). In (6) and (7), for example, neither the context of the sentence, nor the context of their paragraph provide the meaning of the NPs. Many of the CLUVI instances tagged as OTHER-SR (such as *the music of the pearl* in (6)), are naming phrases – they were defined only once in the text collection and later on mentioned to refer to the initial concept.

In (8), on the other hand, the meaning of the NP *the destruction of the Palestinian Authority* is THEME and not AGENT as might be considered by default.

[9] Only 5.70% of the TYPE instances in the Europarl corpus were unique.

[10] The annotated corpora resulted in this research are available at http://apfel.ai.uiuc.edu.

(6) LPE-390: "And *the music of the pearl* rose like a chorus of trumpets in his ears." (CLUVI)

(7) "Mr President, *the violent destruction of the State of Israel*." (Europarl)

(8) "The spread of the settlements, the seizing of land, the curfews, the Palestinians imprisoned in their own villages, the summary executions, the ambulances prevented from reaching their destinations, the women giving birth at check points, *the destruction of the Palestinian Authority*: these are not mistakes or accidents." (Europarl)

6 Acknowledgments

We would like to thank all the people who helped with the corpus creation and annotation, and those with whom we had nice discussions about various semantic relations. Without them this research wouldn't have been possible: Archna Bhatia, Gustavo Cavallin, Brian Drexler, Matt Garley, Tania Ionin, Matt Niemi, Dustin Parr, and Chris Struven. And last, but not least we like to thank the reviewers for their useful comments.

References

K. Barker and S. Szpakowicz. 1998. Semi-automatic recognition of noun modifier relationships. In *the Proceedings of the Association for Computational Linguistics / Conference on Computational Linguistics*.

M. Berland and E. Charniak. 1999. Finding Parts in Very Large Corpora. In *the Proceedings of the Association for Computational Linguistics (ACL)*, University of Maryland.

E. Charniak. 2000. A Maximum-entropy-inspired Parser. In *the Proceedings of the North American Chapter of the Association for Computational Linguistics (NAACL)*, Seattle, Washington.

P. Downing. 1977. On the Creation and Use of English Compound Nouns. *Language*, 53(4):810–842.

T. W. Finin. 1980. *The Semantic Interpretation of Compound Nominals*. Ph.D. thesis, University of Illinois at Urbana-Champaign.

R. Girju, D. Moldovan, M. Tatu, and D. Antohe. 2005. On the semantics of noun compounds. *Computer Speech and Language*, 19(4):479–496.

R. Girju, A. Badulescu, and D. Moldovan. 2006. Automatic discovery of part-whole relations. *Computational Linguistics*, 32(1).

R. Girju. 2007. Improving the interpretation of noun phrases with cross-linguistic information. In *the Proceedings of the Association for Computational Linguistics (ACL)*, Prague.

O. Jespersen. 1954. *A Modern English Grammar on Historical Principles*. London.

S. N. Kim and T. Baldwin. 2006. In *the Proceedings of the Association for Computational Linguistics*, Sydney, Australia.

M. Lapata and F. Keller. 2004. The Web as a baseline: Evaluating the performance of unsupervised Web-based models for a range of NLP tasks. In *the Proceedings of the Human Language Technology Conference / North American Chapter of the Association of Computational Linguistics (HLT-NAACL)*.

M. Lauer. 1995. Corpus statistics meet the noun compound: Some empirical results. In *the Proceedings of Association for Computational Linguistics (ACL)*, Cambridge, Mass.

J. Levi. 1978. *The Syntax and Semantics of Complex Nominals*. Academic Press, New York.

D. Moldovan and R. Girju. 2003. Knowledge discovery from text. In *the Tutorial Proceedings of the Association for Computational Linguistics (ACL)*, Sapporo, Japan.

D. Moldovan, A. Badulescu, M. Tatu, D. Antohe, and R. Girju. 2004. Models for the semantic classification of noun phrases. In *the Proceedings of the HLT/NAACL Workshop on Computational Lexical Semantics*, Boston, MA.

P. Nakov and M. Hearst. 2005. Search engine statistics beyond the n-gram: Application to noun compo und bracketing. In *the Proceedings of the Computational Natural Language Learning Conference*.

P. Pantel and M. Pennacchiotti. 2006. Espresso: Leveraging generic patterns for automatically harvesting semantic relations. In *the Proceedings of the International Conference for Computational Linguistics (COLING/ACL)*, Sydney, Australia.

M. Pennacchiotti and P. Pantel. 2006. Ontologizing semantic relations. In *the Proceedings of Conference on Computational Linguistics / Association for Computational Linguistics (COLING/ACL-06)*, Sydney, Australia. Association for Computational Linguistics.

B. Rosario and M. Hearst. 2001. Classifying the semantic relations in noun compounds. In *the Proceedings of the 2001 EMNLP Conference*.

B. Rosario, M. Hearst, and C. Fillmore. 2002. The descent of hierarchy, and selection in relational semantics. In *the Proceedings of the Association for Computational Linguistics*.

E. Selkirk. 1982. Syntax of words. In *Linguistic Inquiry Monograph*. MIT Press.

R. Snow, D. Jurafsky, and A. Ng. 2006. Semantic taxonomy induction from heterogenous evidence. In *the Proceedings of the Conference on Computational Linguistics / Association for Computational Linguistics (COLING-ACL)*, Sydney, Australia.

P. Turney. 2006. Expressing implicit semantic relations without supervision. In *the Proceedings of the Conference on Computational Linguistics / Association for Computational Linguistics (COLING/ACL)*, Sydney, Australia.

A. Tyler and V. Evans. 2003. *Spatial Experience, Lexical Structure and Motivation: The Case of In.* In G. Radden and K. Panther. Studies in Linguistic Motivation. Berlin and New York: Mouton de Gruyter.

IGT-XML: an XML format for interlinearized glossed texts

Alexis Palmer, Katrin Erk
Department of Linguistics
University of Texas at Austin
{alexispalmer,katrin.erk}@mail.utexas.edu

Abstract

We propose a new XML format for representing interlinearized glossed text (IGT), particularly in the context of the documentation and description of endangered languages. The proposed representation, which we call IGT-XML, builds on previous models but provides a more loosely coupled and flexible representation of different annotation layers. Designed to accommodate both selective manual reannotation of individual layers and semi-automatic extension of annotation, IGT-XML is a first step toward partial automation of the production of IGT.

1 Introduction

Much previous work on linguistic annotation has necessarily focused on resource-rich languages, as it is these languages for which we have large corpora in need of linguistic annotation. In contrast, development of annotation schemata and methodologies to be used with language data from endangered languages has been left largely to individual documentary and/or descriptive linguists working with particular languages.

This paper addresses linguistic annotation in the context of the documentation and description of endangered languages. One interesting feature of language documentation projects is that, while the languages studied differ widely, there is a quasi-standard for presenting the material, in the form of **interlinearized glossed text (IGT)**. IGT typically comprises at least four levels: (1) the original text, (2) a separation of the original text into individual morphemes, (3) a detailed morpheme-by-morpheme gloss, and (4) a free translation of each sentence. Another characteristic of language documentation projects is the tentative nature of many analyses, given that linguistic analysis is often occurring in tandem with the annotation process, sometimes for the first time in the recorded history of the language. Furthermore, language documentation projects require long-term accessibility of the collected language data as well as easy accessibility to community members as well as to linguists.

In this paper we propose a new XML format for representing IGT, which we call **IGT-XML**. We build on the model of Hughes et al (2003) (the **BHB model** from now on), who first proposed using the IGT structure directly as a basis for an XML format. While their format shows closely integrated annotation layers using XML embedding, our model has a more loosely coupled and flexible representation of different annotation layers, to accommodate (a) selective manual reannotation of individual layers, and (b) the (semi-)automatic extension of annotation, without the format posing an a priori restriction on the annotation levels that can be added. The IGT-XML representation is thus a first step toward partial automation of the production of IGT, which in turn is part of a larger project using techniques from machine learning and natural language processing to significantly reduce the time and money required to produce annotated texts.

Besides the BHB model, we build on the Open Languages Archiving Community (OLAC)[1] metadata standard. OLAC is developing best practice guidelines for archiving language resources digitally, including a list of metadata entries to record

[1] `http://www.language-archives.org`

Proceedings of the Linguistic Annotation Workshop, pages 176–183,
Prague, June 2007.

with language data.

Plan of the paper. After discussing interlinearized glosses in Section 2, we show the BHB model and corresponding XML format in Section 3. Section 4 presents the IGT-XML format that we propose. Section 5 demonstrates the applicability of IGT-XML to data from different languages and different documentation projects, and Section 6 concludes.

2 Interlinearized glossed text

IGT is a way of encoding linguistic data commonly used to present linguistic examples. The example below is a segment of IGT taken from Kuhn and Mateo-Toledo (2004). The language is Q'anjob'al, a Mayan language of Guatemala.

(1) `Maxab' ek'elteq ix unin yet sq'inib'alil tu.`

(2) `max-ab' ek'-el-teq ix unin y-et`
COM-EV pass-DIR-DIR CL child E3S-when
`s-q'inib'-al-il tu`
E3S-early-ABS-ABS DEM

'The child came out early that morning (they say)' [2]

The format of the IGT in this example is typical of the presentation of individual examples in the linguistics literature. The raw, unannotated text (1) is associated with three layers of annotation, shown in (2). The first annotation layer shows the same text with each word segmented into its constituent morphemes. The next layer, the gloss layer, is a combination of English translations of the Q'anjob'al lemmas and tags representing the linguistic information encoded by affixes on the lemmas. The third layer is an English translation.

IGT formats vary more widely in language documentation, where IGT is typically the product of linguistic analysis of texts transcribed from audio or audiovisual recordings. A broad survey of formats for interlinear texts (Bow et al., 2003) found variation in the number of rows, the type of analysis found in each row, as well as the level of granularity of analysis in each row.[3]

Tools using IGT Shoebox/Toolbox[4] (*Shoebox* in following text) is a system that is widely used in documentary linguistics for storing and managing language data. It provides facilities for lexicon management as well as text interlinearization.

Figure 1 shows one sentence of Q'anjob'al IGT in the Shoebox output format.[5] Shoebox exports texts as plain text files. The different annotation layers are marked by labels at the beginning of the line. For example, in Figure 1 the label `\tx` marks the original text and the line starting with `\dm` contains its morphological segmentation.

One important test case for any XML format for IGT is whether it can represent existing IGT data. As Shoebox is a widely used tool, we take the Shoebox data format as a representative case study. Specifically, in Section 5 we show how texts from two different languages, interlinearized using Shoebox and represented in the Shoebox output format, can be encoded in IGT-XML.

In this paper we focus on the question of representation rather than format transformation. Each system managing IGT data will have different output formats, requiring different techniques for transforming the data to XML. The aim of this paper is simply to describe and demonstrate the IGT-XML format; a detailed automatic transformation method mapping other formats to IGT-XML is beyond the scope of this paper and will be addressed separately.

3 Previous work

This section discusses previous work on representation formats and specifically XML formats for interlinear text.

The BHB model: four levels of interlinear text. Building on Bow et al.'s (2003) analysis of different IGT formats used in the literature, Hughes et al. (2003) propose a four-level hierarchical model for representing interlinear text. The four levels encode elements common to most instances of IGT: *text*, *phrase*, *word*, and *morpheme*. One *text* may consist of several individual *phrases*. A *phrase* consists of one or more *words*, each of which consists

[2] KEY: ABS=abstract, COM=completive, CL=classifier, DEM=demonstrative, E=ergative, EV=evidential, S=singular, 3=third person

[3] Hughes et al (2003) also discuss variation in presentational factors, which we choose not to encode in our XML format.

[4] `http://www.sil.org/computing/catalog/show_software.asp?id=79`

[5] Data from B'alam Mateo-Toledo, p.c.

```
\ref txt080_p2.002
\tx Exx  a    yet              junxa        tyempohal,  ayin ti'  xiwil+
\dm exxx a    y-    et         jun      - xa tyempo -al, ayin ti   xiwil+
\ge INTJ ENF  E3-   de/cuando ART/uno - ya tiempo -ABS yo   DEM  muchos
\cp intj part pref- sr         num      - adv s      -suf pro  part adv

\tes Eee en otro tiempo yo vi
```

Figure 1: Shoebox output: Q'anjob'al

```
<resource>
<interlinear_text>
 <item type="title">Example</item>
 <phrases>
   <phrase>
    <item type="gls">The child came out
    early that morning (they say)</item>
    <words>
      <word>
        <item type="txt">ek'elteq</item>
        <morphemes>
          <morph>
            <item type="txt">ek'</item>
            <item type="gls">pass</item>
          </morph>
          <morph>
            <item type="txt">el</item>
            <item type="gls">DIR</item>
          </morph>
          <morph>
            <item type="txt">teq</item>
            <item type="gls">DIR</item>
          </morph>
        </morphemes>
      </word>
    </words>
   </phrase>
 </phrases>
</interlinear_text>
</resource>
```

Figure 2: BHB IGT representation format: Q'anjob'al

of one or more *morphemes*. To make this more concrete, the example in (1) shows a single phrase (or a one-phrase text). The three annotation layers in (2) are situated at different levels in the hierarchy: The first and second annotation layers are both situated at the morpheme level, showing a separation of the original phrase into its constituent morphemes and a morpheme-by-morpheme gloss, respectively. The third annotation layer, the translation, is again situated at the phrase level, like the original text in (1).

The BHB model was originally developed in the context of the EMELD project,[6] which has focused on advancing the state of technologies, data representation formats, and methodologies for digital language documentation.

The BHB XML format. Figure 2 shows an example of the BHB XML format, which articulates the four nested levels of structure of the BHB model. It directly expresses the hierarchy of annotation levels in a nested XML structure, in which, for example, `<morph>` elements representing morphemes are embedded in `<word>` elements representing the corresponding words. The model maintains the link between the source text morpheme and the morpheme-level gloss annotation by embedding both as `<item>` elements within the `<morph>` and distinguishing the two by an attribute called `type`.

While this representation provides the needed link between morphemes and their glosses, it is rather inflexible because it is not modular: To add an additional annotation layer at the word level, one would need to access and change the representation of each word of each phrase. In this way, the BHB XML format is not ideally suited for an extensible annotation that would need to add additional layers of linguistic information in a flexible way.

[6] http://linguistlist.org/emeld

4 IGT-XML

In this section we propose a new XML representation for IGT, IGT-XML. Like the BHB XML format, it is based on the BHB four-level model, but it modularizes annotation levels. Linking between annotation levels is achieved via unique IDs.

The IGT-XML format.

Figure 3 illustrates the new IGT-XML format, showing a representation of the Q'anjob'al example of Figure 1, mostly restricted to a single word, *tyempohal*, for simplicity.

The IGT-XML format contains (at least) three main components:

- a *plaintext* component comprising phrases as well as the individual words making up each phrase, encased in the `<phrases>` XML element,
- a *morpheme* component giving a morphological analysis of the source text, encased in the `<morphemes>` XML element, and
- a *gloss* component including glosses at both the phrase and the word level.

Further annotation layers can be added by extending the format with additional components beyond these three, which describe the core four levels of interlinear text.

Within the `<phrases>` block, each individual phrase is encased in a `<phrase>` element, which includes the plain text within the `<plaintext>` element as well as each individual word of the plain text in a `<word>` element. Each `<phrase>` and each `<word>` has a globally unique ID, assigned in an `id` attribute. We choose to give explicit IDs to words, rather than rely on character offsets, to avoid possible problems with character encodings and mis-represented special characters.

The morphemes in the `<morphemes>` block are again organized by `<phrase>`. Each `<phrase>` in the `<morphemes>` block refers to the corresponding phrase in the `<phrases>` block by that phrase's unique ID.

Each individual morpheme, represented by a `<morph>` element, refers to the unique ID corresponding to the word of which it is a part. The linear order of morphemes belonging to the same word is reflected in the order in which `<morph>` elements appear, as well as in the running `id` of the morphemes. Morphemes have `id` attributes of their own such that further annotation levels can refer to the morphological segmentation of the source text, as is the case for the morpheme-by-morpheme gloss in the example in (2).

Whole-sentence glosses are collected in the `<translations>` block, while word-by-word glosses reside in the `<gloss>` block. Again, glosses are organized by `<phrase>`, linked to the original phrases by `idref` attributes. The glosses in `<gloss>` refer to individual morphemes, hence their `idref` attributes point to `id` attributes of the `<morphemes>` block.

Metadata information in the file header

As suggested in Figure 3, IGT-XML is easily extended with metadata for each text. We adopt the OLAC metadata set which uses the fifteen elements defined in the Dublin Core metadata standard (Bird and Simons, 2003a; Bird and Simons, 2001). These elements provide a framework for specifying key information such as annotators, format, and language of the text. In addition, the OLAC standard incorporates a number of qualifiers specific to the language-resource community, such as discourse types (story, conversation, etc.) and linguistic data types (lexicon, language description, primary text, etc.), and a process for adopting further extensions.

In addition to the metadata block at the head of the document, it would be possible to intersperse additional metadata blocks throughout the document, if for example we wanted to indicate change of speaker from one phrase to another in recorded conversation.

Discussion

Feature overview. The IGT-XML format we have presented groups annotation into blocks in a modular fashion. Each block represents an annotation layer. The format uses globally unique IDs (via `id` and `idref` attributes) rather than XML embedding for linking annotation layers. In particular, `<morph>` and `<word>` annotation is kept separate, such that additional layers of annotation at the word and morpheme levels can be added modularly without interfering with each other.

In its minimal form, the format has three blocks,

```
<text id="T1" lg="kjb" source_id="txt080_p2" title="Pixanej">
<metadata idref="T1">
  <!-- incorporate OLAC metadata standard -->
</metadata>
<body>
<phrases>
  <phrase id="T1.P2" source_id="txt080_p2.002">
    <plaintext>Exx a yet junxa tyempohal, ayin ti’ xiwil+</plaintext>
    <word id="T1.P2.W5" text="tyempohal"/>
  </phrase>
</phrases>
<morphemes source_layer="\dm">
  <phrase idref="T1.P2">
    <morph idref="T1.P2.W5" id="T1.P2.W5.M1" text="tyempo"/>
    <morph idref="T1.P2.W5" id="T1.P2.W5.M2" text="al">
      <type l="suf"/>
    </morph>
  </phrase>
</morphemes>
<gloss source_layer="\ge">
  <phrase idref="T1.P2">
    <gls idref="T1.P2.W5.M1" text="tiempo"/>
    <gls idref="T1.P2.W5.M2" text="ABS"/>
  </phrase>
</gloss>
<translations>
  <phrase idref="T1.P2">
    <trans id="T1.P2.Tr1" lg="en">Eee en otro tiempo yo vi</trans>
  </phrase>
</translations>
</body>
</text>
```

Figure 3: IGT-XML representation format: Q’anjob’al

for phrases, morphemes, and glosses, but it is extensible by further blocks, for example for POS-tags. It is also possible to have different types of annotation at the same linguistic level, for example manually created as well as automatically assigned POS-tags.

Mildly standoff annotation. The IGT-XML format keeps the plain text separate from all levels of annotation. However, it is not standoff in the strict sense of having all annotation levels refer to the plain text only and never to one another. The reason for this is that there is no clear "basic" level to which all other annotation could refer.

One obvious candidate is the plain text, but the morpheme-by-morpheme gloss refers not to words, but to the morpheme segmentation of the source text, as can be seen in example (2). This makes the morpheme-segmented source text another candidate for the basic level, but it is not guaranteed that this level of annotation will always be available. At the start of the annotation process the documentary linguist likely has a transcription and a translation, but he or she may or may not have determined the morphotactics of the language or even how to identify word boundaries.

So, in order (a) not to commit the annotator to one single order of annotation, or the presence of any particular annotation level besides the plain text, and (b) to allow annotation to refer to each of the levels identified in the BHB model – text, phrase, word, and morpheme –, we allow annotation levels to refer to each other via unique IDs.

Requirements for IGT formats. Given the nature of language documentation projects and IGT data, an IGT representation format should (1) support long term archiving of language data (Bird and Simons, 2003b), which requires platform-independent encoding, and it should (2) support a range of formats. IGT data from different sources may show differences in format and in what is annotated (Bow et al., 2003), and may be produced using different software systems. (3) It should be possible to add or exchange layers of annotation in a modular fashion. This is important because linguistic analysis in language documentation, which typically targets languages that are not well-studied, is often tentative and subject to change. This will also become increasingly important with the use of automation to aid and speed up language documentation: Automation techniques will typically target individual annotation layers, and it is desirable to be able to exchange automatic analysis tools freely.

Point (1), platform independence, is achieved by almost any XML format, since XML formats are plain text-based and mostly human-readable. Point (2), the coverage of IGT formats in all variants, can be achieved by adoption of the BHB model. Flexibility and modularity (point (3)) are the main motivations in the introduction of IGT-XML.

Beyond word-level annotation. For now the annotation focus in language documentation projects is mostly on the word level, especially on morphology and POS-tags. For annotation at the syntactic level, it is an open question what the features of a universally applicable annotation format should be. At the moment, TIGER XML (Mengel and Lezius, 2000), with its capability to represent discontinuous constituents, and constituent as well as dependency information, seems like a good candidate. Syntactic information could be represented in a separate top-level XML element, linking tree terminals to `<word>` elements by their ID attributes.

5 Data

An important goal of this research is to develop an XML format which will be viable for use in the broadest possible range of language documentation contexts. To that end, the format needs to stretch and morph with the needs and desires of the individual user. This section discusses some issues arising from actual use of the format. The points are illustrated with pieces of the XML representation rather than complete XML documents.

IGT-XML has been used to encode portions of texts from the Mayan language Q'anjob'al and the Mixe-Zoquean language Soteapanec (more commonly known as Sierra Popoluca). Q'anjob'al is spoken primarily in the northwestern regions of Guatemala, and Soteapanec is spoken in the southern part of the state of Veracruz, Mexico. Both texts come from ongoing documentation efforts, and both were first interlinearized using Shoebox.

5.1 Q'anjob'al

Figure 1 shows a Q'anjob'al sentence in the Shoebox export format. The annotation comprises original text (`\tx` level), morphological analysis (`\dm`), morpheme gloss (`\ge`), and parts of speech (`\cp`). The Q'anjob'al texts we received preserve links between Shoebox annotation layers only through typographical alignment. The IGT-XML representation makes these links explicit through global IDs using `id` and `idref` attributes. It also splits off punctuation, treating punctuation marks as separate words:

```
<word id="T1.P2.W5" text="tyempohal"/>
<word id="T1.P2.W6" text=","/>
<word id="T1.P2.W7" text="ayin"/>
```

In the part of speech annotation level (line `\cp`), the annotator has additionally marked prefixes and suffixes, using the labels `pref-` and `-suf`, respectively. In the IGT-XML, we have incorporated this information in the `<morphemes>` level as *type* information on a morpheme. Figure 3 shows an example of this, extended below:

```
<morph idref="T1.P2.W5" id="T1.P2.W5.M1"
       text="tyempo"/>
<morph idref="T1.P2.W5" id="T1.P2.W5.M2"
       text="al">
  <type l="suf"/>
</morph>
<morph idref="T1.P2.W6" id="T1.P2.W6.M1"
       text=",">
  <type l="punct"/>
</morph>
```

By encoding morpheme type as a `<type>` element embedded in the `<morph>`, we can allow a single morpheme to bear more than one type label. For example, an annotator may want to mark a single morpheme as being an inflectional morpheme which appears in a suffixal position. This would be indicated by associating multiple `<type>` elements with a single `<morph>` element, differentiating the `<type>` elements through use of the label (`l`) attribute, as shown in the constructed example below.

```
<morph idref="T3.P1.W3" id="T3.P1.W3.M2"
       text="al">
  <type l="suf"/>
  <type l="infl"/>
</morph>
```

Furthermore, as the type label is specified in an attribute value, each documentation project can specify its own list of possible labels.

```
\ref Jovenes 002
\t Weenyi  woony=jaych@@x+tyam
\mb weenyi  woonyi=jay.ty@@xi+tam
\gs algunos  varon+HPL

\t yo7om@7yyajpa+m
\mb 0+yoomo.7@7y-yaj-pa+m
\gs 3ABS+casar  con  mujer-3PL-INC+ALR

\f Algunos nin*os se casan.
```

Figure 4: Shoebox output: Soteapanec

5.2 Soteapanec

Figure 4 shows the Shoebox output for a Soteapanec phrase.[7] In the notation chosen in this project, the characters '7' and '@' refer to phonemes (glottal stop and mid high unrounded vowel, respectively), while '-', '+', '>', '=' and '.' all mark morpheme boundaries. Clitic boundaries are marked by '+', inflectional boundaries by '-', derivational boundaries by '>' or '.', and compounds are indicated with '='. The four different morpheme boundaries translate to morpheme types in the IGT-XML, which are encoded as in the Q'anjob'al case:

```
<morph idref="T1.P2.W1" id="T1.P2.W1.M1"
       text="weenyi"/>
<morph idref="T1.P2.W2" id="T1.P2.W2.M1"
       text="woonyi=jay">
  <type l="compound"/>
</morph>
<morph idref="T1.P2.W2" id="T1.P2.W2.M2"
       text="ty@@xi"/>
<morph idref="T1.P2.W2" id="T1.P2.W2.M3"
       text="tam">
  <type l="suf"/>
</morph>
```

The encoding of the compound represents one of many choices to be made by users of IGT-XML. We have chosen to present the compound *woonyi=jay* as a single morpheme, in line with the linguist's choice to notate the compounds this way in the text. An alternative would be to break the compound into two separate morphemes, each marked as a compound via the `l` attribute of the `<type>` element.

A similar choice exists with respect to the representation of other derivational morphology, both at the level of morphological segmentation and at the level of the plaintext. In this case, the plaintext of the Soteapanec includes boundary markers. IGT-XML

[7]Data from (Franco and de Jong Boudreault, 2005).

can accommodate this type of text as well as it can a truly plain text.

In this Shoebox output, there is no typographical alignment between annotation levels. So the manual transformation to IGT-XML had to rely on counting morphemes. However there are frequent mismatches between the number of morphemes in the morphological level (`\mb`) and the gloss level (`\gs`). The second group of lines in Figure 4 shows an example: There are six morphemes on the `\mb` level, but seven on the `\gs` level. We envision that automatic transformation to IGT-XML will flag such cases as mismatched, thus functioning as error detection for the annotation. Even in the manual transformation process, we have marked mismatches at the gloss level to facilitate adjudication by the annotator.

```
<morph idref="T1.P2.W2.M4"><gls text="HPL"
   flag="mismatch" flagsrc="amp"
   flagdate="031507"/>
</morph>
```

We also include the source and date of the flag, attributes which could easily be obtained automatically.

This section provides only a sample of the issues encountered using IGT-XML. One of our next steps is to work on automatic transformations from Shoebox data formats to IGT-XML, a stage at which many of these challenges will necessarily be addressed.

6 Conclusion

In this paper we have introduced a new XML format for representing language documentation data, IGT-XML. At the heart of the model is a representation of interlinearized glossed text (IGT). Building on the BHB model (Hughes et al., 2003), IGT-XML represents original text, its translation, a morphological analysis of the original text, and a morpheme-by-morpheme gloss. Different annotation layers are represented separately in a modular fashion, allowing for flexible annotation of individual layers as well as the extension by further annotation layers. Layers are linked explicitly via globally unique IDs, using `id` and `idref` attributes.

One main aim in the design of the IGT-XML format is to facilitate the (semi-)automatic annotation of language documentation data. In fact, our next step will be to explore the use of computational tools for speeding up and extending the annotation of less-studied languages. This connection of documentary and computational linguistics has the potential to be very useful to documentary linguists. It also represents an interesting opportunity for the use of semi-supervised machine learning techniques like active learning on a novel application.

Acknowledgments

We would like to thank Lynda de Jong Boudreault and B'alam Mateo-Toledo for sharing with us data collected in their documentation efforts.

References

Steven Bird and Gary Simons. 2001. The OLAC metadata set and controlled vocabularies. In *Proceedings of ACL Workshop on Sharing Tools and Resources for Research and Education*, pages 7–18, Toulouse.

Steven Bird and Gary Simons. 2003a. Extending Dublin Core Metadata to support the description and discovery of language resources. *Computing and the Humanities*, 37:375–388.

Steven Bird and Gary Simons. 2003b. Seven dimensions of portability for language documentation and description. *Language*, 79(3):557–582.

Catherine Bow, Baden Hughes, and Steven Bird. 2003. Towards a general model of interlinear text. In *Proceedings of EMELD Workshop 2003: Digitizing and Annotating Texts and Field Recordings*, LSA Institute: Lansing MI, USA.

Julia Albino Franco and Lynda de Jong Boudreault. 2005. Jovenes. Unpublished annotated text. University of Texas at Austin.

Baden Hughes, Steven Bird, and Catherine Bow. 2003. Encoding and presenting interlinear text using XML technologies. In Alistair Knott and Dominique Estival, editors, *Proceedings of the Australasian Language Technology Workshop*, pages 105–113.

Jonas Kuhn and B'alam Mateo-Toledo. 2004. Applying computational linguistic techniques in a documentary project for Q'anjob'al (Mayan, Guatemala). In *Proceedings of LREC 2004*, Lisbon, Portugal.

Andreas Mengel and Wolfgang Lezius. 2000. An XML-based encoding format for syntactically annotated corpora. In *Proceedings of LREC 2000*, Athens, Greece.

The Shared Corpora Working Group Report

Adam Meyers
New York University
New York, NY
meyers at cs.nyu.edu

Nancy Ide
Vassar College
Poughkeepsie, NY
ide at cs.vassar.edu

Ludovic Denoyer
University of Paris
Paris, France
ludovic.denoyer at lip6.fr

Yusuke Shinyama
New York University
New York, NY
yusuke at cs.nyu.edu

Abstract

We seek to identify a limited amount of representative corpora, suitable for annotation by the computational linguistics annotation community. Our hope is that a wide variety of annotation will be undertaken on the same corpora, which would facilitate: (1) the comparison of annotation schemes; (2) the merging of information represented by various annotation schemes; (3) the emergence of NLP systems that use information in multiple annotation schemes; and (4) the adoption of various types of best practice in corpus annotation. Such best practices would include: (a) clearer demarcation of phenomena being annotated; (b) the use of particular test corpora to determine whether a particular annotation task can feasibly achieve good agreement scores; (c) The use of underlying models for representing annotation content that facilitate merging, comparison, and analysis; and (d) To the extent possible, the use of common annotation categories or a mapping among categories for the same phenomenon used by different annotation groups.

This study will focus on the problem of identifying such corpora as well as the suitability of two candidate corpora: the Open portion of the American National Corpus (Ide and Macleod, 2001; Ide and Suderman, 2004) and the "Controversial" portions of the WikipediaXML corpus (Denoyer and Gallinari, 2006).

1 Introduction

This working group seeks to identify a limited amount of representative corpora, suitable for annotation by the computational linguistics annotation community. Our hope is that a wide variety of annotation will be undertaken on the same corpora, which would facilitate:

1. The comparison of annotation schemes
2. The merging of information represented by various annotation schemes
3. The emergence of NLP systems that use information in multiple annotation schemes; and
4. The adoption of various types of best practice in corpus annotation, including:
   (a) Clearer demarcation of the phenomena being annotated. Thus if predicate argument structure annotation adequately handles relative pronouns, a new project that is annotating coreference is less likely to include relative pronouns in their annotation; and
   (b) The use of particular test corpora to determine whether a particular annotation task can feasibly achieve good agreement scores.
   (c) The use of underlying models for representing annotation content that facilitate merging, comparison, and analysis.

Proceedings of the Linguistic Annotation Workshop, pages 184–190,
Prague, June 2007.

(d) To the extent possible, the use of common annotation categories or a mapping among categories for the same phenomenon used by different annotation groups.

In selecting shared corpora, we believe that the following issues must be taken into consideration:

1. The diversity of genres, lexical items and linguistic phenomena – this will ensure that the corpora will be useful to many different types of annotation efforts. Furthermore, systems using these corpora and annotation as data will be capable of handling larger and more varied corpora.

2. The availability of the same or similar corpora in a wide variety of languages;

3. The availability of corpora in a standard format that can be easily processed – there should be mechanisms in place to maintain the availability of corpora in this format in the future;

4. The ease in which the corpora can be obtained by anyone who wants to process or annotate them – corpora with free licenses or that are in the public domain are preferred

5. The degree with which the corpora is representative of text to be processed – this criterion can be met if the corpora is diverse (1 above) and/or if more corpora of the same kind is available for processing.

We have selected the following corpora for consideration:[1]

1. The OANC: the Open sections of the ANC corpus. These are the sections of the American National Corpus subject to the opened license, allowing them to be freely distributed. The full Open ANC (Version 2.0) contains about 14.5 megawords of American English and covers a variety of genres as indicated by the full pathnames taken from the ANC distribution (where a final 1 or 2 indicates which DVD the directory originates from):

   - spoken/telephone/switchboard
   - written_1/fiction/eggan
   - written_1/journal/slate
   - written_1/letters/icic
   - written_2/non-fiction/OUP
   - written_2/technical/biomed
   - written_2/travel_guides/berlitz1
   - written_2/travel_guides/berlitz2
   - written_1/journal/verbatim
   - spoken/face-to-face/charlotte
   - written_2/technical/911report
   - written_2/technical/plos
   - written_2/technical/government

2. The Controversial-Wikipedia-Corpus, a section of the Wikipedia XML corpus. WikipediaXML is a corpus derived from Wikipedia, converting Wikipedia into an XML corpus suitable for NLP processing. This corpus was selected from:

   - Those articles cited as controversial according to the November 28, 2006 version of the following Wikipedia page: http://en.wikipedia.org/wiki/Wikipedia:List_of_controversial_issues
   - The talk pages corresponding to these articles where Wikipedia users and the community debate aspects of articles. These debates may be about content or editorial considerations.
   - Articles in Japanese that are linked to the English pages (and the associated talk pages) are also part of our corpus.

2 American National Corpus

The American National Corpus (ANC) project (Ide and Macleod, 2001; Ide and Suderman, 2004) has released over 20 million words of spoken and written American English, available from the Linguistic Data Consortium. The ANC 2nd release consists of fiction, non-fiction, newspapers, technical reports, magazine and journal articles, a substantial amount of spoken data, data from blogs and other unedited web sources, travel guides, technical manuals, and other genres. All texts are annotated for sentence boundaries; token boundaries,

[1] These corpora can be downloaded from: http://nlp.cs.nyu.edu/wiki/corpuswg/SharedCorpora

lemma, and part of speech produced by two different taggers ; and noun and verb chunks. A subcorpus of 10 million words reflecting the genre distribution of the full ANC is currently being hand-validated for word and sentence boundaries, POS, and noun and verb chunks. For a complete description of the ANC 2nd release and its contents, see http://AmericanNationalCorpus.org.

Approximately 65 percent of the ANC data is distributed under an open license, which allows use and re-distribution of the data without restriction. The remainder of the corpus is distributed under a restricted license that disallows re-distribution or use of the data for commercial purposes for five years after its release date, unless the user is a member of the ANC Consortium. After five years, the data in the restricted portions of the corpus are covered by the open license.

ANC annotations are distributed as stand-off documents representing a set of graphs over the primary data, thus allowing for layering of annotations and inclusion of multiple annotations of the same type. Because most existing tools for corpus access and manipulation do not handle stand-off annotations, we have developed an easy-to-use tool and user interface to merge the user's choice of stand-off annotations with the primary data to form a single document in any of several XML and non-XML formats, which is distributed with the corpus. The ANC architecture and format is described fully in (Ide and Suderman, 2006).

2.1 The ULA Subcorpus

The Unified Linguistic Annotation (ULA) project has selected a 40,000 word subcorpus of the Open ANC for annotation with several different annotation schemes including: the Penn Treebank, PropBank, NomBank, the Penn Discourse Treebank, TimeML and Opinion Annotation.[2] This initial subcorpus can be broken down as follows:

- Spoken Language
  - charlotte: 5K words
  - switchboard: 5K words
- letters: 10K words
- Slate (Journal): 5K words
- Travel_guides: 5K words
- 911report: 5K words
- OUP books (Kaufman): 5K words

[2]Other corpora being annotated by the ULA project include sections of the Brown corpus and LDC parallel corpora.

As the ULA project progresses, the participants intend to expand the corpora annotated to include a larger subsection of the OANC. They believe that the diversity of this corpus make it a reasonable testbed for tuning annotation schemes for diverse modalities. The Travel_guides and some of the slate articles have already been annotated by the FrameNet project. Thus the inclusion of these documents furthered the goal of producing a multiply annotated corpus by one additional project.

It is the recommendation of this working group that: (1) other groups annotate these same subcorpora; and (2) other groups choose additional corpora from the OANC to annotate and publicly announce which subsections they choose. We would be happy to put all such subsections on our website for download. The basic idea is to build up a consensus of what should be mutually annotated, in part, based on what groups choose to annotate and to try to get annotation projects to gravitate toward multiply annotated, freely available corpora.

3 The WikipediaXML Corpus

3.1 Why Wikipedia?

The Wikipedia corpus consists of articles in a wide range of topics written in different genres and mainly (a) *main* pages are encyclopedia style articles; and (b) *talk* pages are discussions about main pages they are linked to. The topics of these discussions range from editing contents to disagreements about content. Although Wikipedia texts are mostly limited to these two genres, we believe that it is well suited as training data for natural language processing because:

1. they are lexically diverse (e.g., providing a lot of lexical information for statistical systems);
2. the textual information is well structured
3. Wikipedia is a large and growing corpus

4. the articles are multilingual (cf. section 3.4)
5. and the corpus has various other properties that many researchers feel would be interesting to exploit.

To date research in Computational Linguistics using Wikipedia includes: Automatic derivation of taxonomy information (Strube and Ponzetto, 2006; Suchanek et al., 2007; Zesch and Gurevych, 2007; Ponzetto, 2007); automatic recognition of pairs of similar sentences in two languages (Adafre and de Rijke, 2006); corpus mining (Rüdiger Gleim and Alexander Mehler and Matthias Dehmer, 2007), Named Entity Recognition (Toral and noz, 2007; Bunescu and Pasça, 2007) and relation extraction (Nguyen et al., 2007). In addition several shared tasks have been set up using Wikipedia as the target corpus including question answering (cf. (D. Ahn and V. Jijkoun and G. Mishne and K. Müller and M. de Rijke and S. Schlobach, 2004) and http://ilps.science.uva.nl/WiQA/); and information retrieval (Fuhr et al., 2006). Some other interesting properties of Wikipedia that have yet to be explored to our knowledge include: (1) Most main articles have talk pages which discuss them – perhaps this relation can be exploited by systems which try to detect discussions about topics, e.g., searches for discussions about current events topics; (2) There are various meta tags, many of which are not included in the WikipediaXML (see below), but nevertheless are retrievable from the original HTML files. Some of these may be useful for various applications. For example, the levels of disputability of the content of the main articles is annotated (cf. http://en.wikipedia.org/wiki/Wikipedia: Template_messages/Disputes).

3.2 Why WikipediaXML?

WikipediaXML (Denoyer and Gallinari, 2006) is an XML version of Wikipedia data, originally designed for Information Retrieval tasks such as INEX (Fuhr et al., 2006) and the XML Document Mining Challenge (Denoyer and P. Gallinari, 2006). WikipediaXML has become a standard machine readable form for Wikipedia, suitable for most Computational Linguistics purposes. It makes it easy to identify and read in the text portions of the document, removing or altering html and wiki code that is difficult to process in a standard way. The WikipediaXML standard has (so far) been used to process Wikipedia documents written in English, German, French, Dutch, Spanish, Chinese, Arabic and Japanese.

3.3 The Controversial Wikipedia Corpus

The English Wikipedia corpus is quite large (about 800K articles and growing). Frozen versions of the corpus are periodically available for download. We selected a 5 million word subcorpus which we believed would be good for a wide variety of annotation schemes. In particular, we chose articles listed as being controversial (in the English speaking world) according to the November 28, 2006 version of the following Wikipedia page: http://en.wikipedia.org/wiki/Wikipedia: List_of_controversial_issues. We believed that controversial articles would be more likely than randomly selected articles to: (1) include interesting discourse phenomena and emotive language; and (2) have interesting "talk" pages (indeed, some of Wikipedia pages have no associated talk pages).

3.4 The Multi-linguality of Wikipedia

One of the main good points of Wikipedia is the fact that it is a very large multilingual resource. This provides several advantages over single-language corpora, perhaps the clearest such advantage being the availability of same-genre/same-format text for many languages. Although, Wikipedia in languages other than English do not approach 800K articles in size, there are currently at least 14 languages with over 100K entries.

It should be clear however, that it is definitely not a parallel corpus. Although pages are sometimes translated in their entirety, this is the exception, not the rule. Pages can be partially translated or summarized into the target language. Individually written pages can be linked after they are created if it is believed that they are about the same topic. Also, initially parallel pages can be edited in both languages, causing them to diverge. We therefore decided to do a small small pilot study to attempt to characterize the degree of similarity between English articles in Wikipedia and articles written in other languages that have been linked. There are 476 English Wikipedia articles in the Controversial corpus

Classification	Frequency
Totally Different	2
Same General Topic	3
Overlapping Topics	11
Same Topics	33
Parallel	1

and 384 associated "talk" pages. There are approximately 10,000 articles of various languages that are linked to the English articles. We asked some English/Japanese bilingual speakers to evaluate the degree of similarity of as many of the the 305 Japanese articles that were linked to English controversial articles. As of this date, 50 articles were evaluated with the results summarized as table 3.4.[3] These preliminary results suggest the following:

- Languate-linked Wikipedia would usually be classified as "comparable" corpora as 34 (68%) of the articles were classified as covering the same topics or being parallel.
- It may be possible to extract a parallel corpus for a given pair of languages from Wikipedia. If the above sample is representative, approximately 2% of the articles are parallel. (While the existance of one parallel article does not provide statistically significant evidence that 2% of Wikipedia is parallel, the article's existance is still significant.) Furthermore, additional parallel sentences may be extracted from some of the other comparable articles using techniques along the lines of (Adafre and de Rijke, 2006).

Obviously, a more detailed study would be necessary to gain a more complete understanding of how language-linked articles are related in Wikipedia.[4] Such a study would include characterizations of all linked articles for several languages. This study could lead to some practical applications, e.g., (1) the creation of parallel subcorpora for a number of languages; (2) the selection of an English monolingual subcorpus consisting of articles, each of which is parallel to some article in some other language; etc.; (3) A compilation of parallel sentences extracted from comparable articles. While parallel subcorpora are of maximal utility, finding parallel sentences could still be extremely useful. (Adafre and de Rijke, 2006) reports one attempt to automatically select parallel Dutch/English sentences from language-linked Wikipedia articles with an accuracy of approximately 45%. Even if higher accuracy cannot be achieved, this still suggests that it is possible to create a parallel corpus (of isolated sentences) using a combination of automatic and manual means. A human translator would have to go through proposed parallel sentences and eliminate about one half of them, but would not have to do any manual translation. Selection of corpora for annotation purposes depends on a number of factors including: the type of annotation (e.g., a corpus of isolated sentences would not be appropriate for discourse annotation); and possibly an application the annotation is tuned for (e.g., Machine Translation, Information Extraction, etc.)

It should be noted that the corpus was chosen for the controversialness of its articles in the English-speaking community. It should, however, not be expected that the same articles will be controversial in other languages. More generally, the language-linked Wikipedia articles may have different cultural contexts depending on the language they are written in. This is an additional feature that we could test in a wider study. Furthermore, English pages are somewhat special because they're considered as the common platform and expected to be neutral to any country. But other lanauages somewhat reflects the view of each country where the language is spoken. Indeed, some EN articles are labeled as *USA-centric* (cf. http://en.wikipedia.org/wiki/Category:USA-centric).

Finally, our choice of a corpus based on controversy may have not been the most efficient choice if our goal had been specifically to find parallel corpora. Just as choosing corpora of articles that are controversial (in the English-speaking world) may have helped finding articles interesting to annotate it is possible that some other choice, e.g., technical articles, may have helped select articles likely

[3]According to www.wikipedia.org there are currently over 350K Japanese articles.

[4]Long Wikipedia articles may be split into multiple articles. This can result in N to 1, or even N to N, matches between language-linked articles if a topic is split in one language, but not in another.

to be translated in full[5] Thus further study may be required to choose the right Wikipedia balance for a set of priorities agreed upon by the annotation community.

4 Legal Issues

The American National Corpus has taken great pains to establish that the open subset of the corpus is freely usable by the community. The open license[6] makes it clear that these corpora can be used for any reason and are freely distributable.

In contrast, some aspects of the licensing agreement of corpora derived from Wikipedia are unclear. Wikipedia is governed by the GNU Free Document License which includes a provision that "derived works" are subject to this license as well. While most academic researchers would be uneffected by this provision, the effect of this provision is unclear with respect to commercial products.

Under one view, a machine translation system that uses a statistical model trained on Wikipedia corpora is not derived from these corpora. However, on another view it is derived. We contacted Wikipedia staff by letter asking for clarification on this issue and received the following response from Michelle Kinney on behalf of Wikipedia information team:

> Wikipedia does not offer legal advice, and therefore cannot help you decide how the GNU Free Documentation License (GFDL) or any other free license applies to your particular situation. Please contact a local bar association, law society or similar association of jurists in your legal jurisdiction to obtain a referral to a competent legal professional.
>
> You may also wish to review the full text of the GFDL yourself:
>
> http://en.wikipedia.org/wiki/Wikipedia:Text_of_the_GNU_Free_Documentation_License

While some candidate corpora are completely in the public domain, e.g., political speeches and very old documents, many candidate corpora are under the GFDL or similar "copyleft" licenses. These include other licenses by the GNU organization and several Creative Commons licenses. It is simply unclear how copyleft licenses should be applied to corpora used as data in computational linguistics and we believe that this is an important legal question for the Computational Linguistics community. In addition to Wikipedia, this issue effects a wide variety of corpora (e.g., other wiki corpora, some of the corpora being developed by the American National Corpus, etc.).

However, getting such legal opinions is expensive and has to be done carefully. Hypothetically, suppose NYU's legal department wrote an opinion letter stating that products that were not corpora themselves were not to be considered derived works for purposes of some list of copyleft licensing agreements. Furthermore, let's suppose that several annotation projects relied on this opinion and produced millions of dollars worth of annotation for one such corpus. Large corporations still might not use these corpora unless their own legal departments agreed with NYU's opinion. For the annotation community, this could mean that certain annotation would only be used by academics and not by industry, and most annotation researchers would not be happy with this outcome. It therefore may be worth some effort on the part of whole NLP community to seek some clear determinations on this issue.

5 Concluding Remarks

The working group selected two freely distributable corpora for purposes of annotation. Our goal was to choose texts for annotation by multiple annotation research groups and describe the process and the pitfalls involved in selecting those texts. We, furthermore, aimed to establish a protocol for sharing texts, so that the same texts are annotated with multiple annotation schemes. This protocol cannot be setup carte blanche by this group of researchers. Rather, we believe that our report in combination with the discussion at the upcoming meeting of the Lingustic Annotation Workshop will provide the jumpstart necessary for such a protocol to be put in place.

[5] Informally, we observe that linked Japanese/English pairs of articles about abstract topics (e.g., Adultery, Agnosticsism, Antisemitism, Capitalism, Censorship, Catholicism) are less likely to contain parallel sentences than articles about specific events or people (e.g., Adolf Hitler, Barbara Streisand, The Los Angeles Riots, etc.)

[6] http://projects.ldc.upenn.edu/ANC/ANC_SecondRelease_EndUserLicense_Open.htm

References

Sisay Fissaha Adafre and Maarten de Rijke. 2006. Finding Similar Sentences across Multiple Languages in Wikipedia. In *EACL 2006 Workshop: Wikis and blogs and other dynamic text source*, Trento, Italy.

Razvan Bunescu and Marius Paşca. 2007. Using Encyclopedic Knowledge for Named Entity Disambiguation. In *Proc. of NAACL/HLT 2007.*

D. Ahn and V. Jijkoun and G. Mishne and K. Müller and M. de Rijke and S. Schlobach. 2004. Using Wikipedia at the TREC QA Track. In *Proc. TREC 2004.*

Ludovic Denoyer and Patrick Gallinari. 2006. The Wikipedia XML Corpus. *SIGIR Forum.*

L. Denoyer and A. Vercoustre P. Gallinari. 2006. Report on the XML Mining Track at INEX 2005 and INEX 2006 : Categorization and Clustering of XML Documents. In *Advances in XML Information Retrieval and Evaluation: Fifthth Workshop of the INitiative for the Evaluation of XML Retrieval (INEX'06).*

N. Fuhr, M. Lalmas, and S. Malik. 2006. Advances in XML Information Retrieval and Evaluation. In *5th International Workshop of the Initiative for the Evaluation of XML Retrieval, INEX 2006.*

N. Ide and C. Macleod. 2001. The american national corpus: A standardized resource of american english. In *Proceedings of Corpus Linguistics 2001*, Lancaster, UK.

N. Ide and K. Suderman. 2004. The american national corpus first release. In *Proceedings of LREC 2004*, pages 1681–1684, Lisbon, Portugal.

N. Ide and K. Suderman. 2006. Integrating linguistic resources: The american national corpus model. In *Proceedings of the 6th International Conference on Language Resources and Evaluation*, Genoa, Italy.

D. P.T. Nguyen, Y. Matsuo, and M. Ishizuka. 2007. Subtree Mining for Relation Extraction from Wikipedia. In *Proc. of NAACL/HLT 2007.*

Simone Paolo Ponzetto. 2007. Creating a Knowledge Base From a Collaboratively Generated Encyclopedia. In *Proc. of NAACL/HLT 2007.*

Rüdiger Gleim and Alexander Mehler and Matthias Dehmer. 2007. Web Corpus Mining by instance of Wikipedia. In *Proc. 2nd Web as Corpus Workshop at EACL 2006.*

M. Strube and S. P. Ponzetto. 2006. WikiRelate! Computing semantic relatedness using Wikipedia. In *Proc. of AAAI-06*, pages 1419–1424.

F. M. Suchanek, G. Kasneci, and G.Weikum. 2007. YAGO: A core of semantic knowledge. In *Proc. of WWW-07.*

Antonio Toral and Rafael Mu noz. 2007. A proposal to automatically build and maintain gazetteers for Named Entity Recognition by using Wikipedia. In *Proc. of NAACL/HLT 2007.*

Torsten Zesch and Iryna Gurevych. 2007. Analysis of the Wikipedia Category Graph for NLP Applications. In *Proc of NAACL-HLT 2007 Workshop: TextGraphs-2.*

Panel Session: Discourse Annotation

Manfred Stede
Dept. of Linguistics
University of Potsdam
stede@ling.uni-potsdam.de

Janyce Wiebe
Dept. of Computer Science
University of Pittsburgh
wiebe@cs.pitt.edu

Eva Hajičová
Faculty of Math. and Physics
Charles University
hajicova@ufal.ms.mff.cuni.cz

Brian Reese
Dept. of Linguistics
Univ. of Texas at Austin
bjreese@mail.utexas.edu

Simone Teufel
Computer Laboratory
Univ. of Cambridge
sht25@cl.cam.uk

Bonnie Webber
School of Informatics
Univ. of Edinburgh
bonnie@inf.ed.ac.uk

Theresa Wilson
Dept. of Comp. Science
Univ. of Pittsburgh
twilson@cs.pitt.edu

1 Introduction

The classical "success story" of corpus annotation are the various syntax treebanks that provide structural analyses of sentences and have enabled researchers to develop a range of new and highly successful data-oriented approaches to sentence parsing. In recent years, however, a number of corpora have been constructed that provide annotations on the *discourse* level, i.e. information that reaches beyond the sentence boundaries. Phenomena that have been annotated include coreference links, the scope of connectives, and coherence relations. Many of these are phenomena on whose handling there is not a general agreement in the research community, and therefore the question of "recycling" corpora by other people and for other purposes is often difficult. (To some extent, this is due to the fact that discourse annotation deals "only" with surface reflections of underlying, abstract objects.) At the same time, the efforts needed for building high-quality discourse corpora are considerable, and thus one should be careful in deciding how to invest those efforts. One aspect of providing added-value with annotation projects is that of *shared* corpora: If a variety of annotation efforts is executed on the same primary data, the series of annotation levels can yield insights that the creators of the individual levels had not explicitly planned for. A clear case is the relationship between coherence relations and connective use: When both levels are marked individually and with independent annotation guidelines, then afterwards the correlations between coherence relations, cue usage (and possibly other factors, if annotated) can be studied systematically. This conception of *multi-level* annotation presupposes, of course, that the technical problems of setting annotation levels in correspondence to one another be resolved.

The panel on discourse annotation is organized by Manfred Stede and Janyce Wiebe. It aims at surveying the scene of discourse corpora, exploring chances for synergy, and identifying desiderata for future corpus creation projects. In preparation for the panel, the participants have provided the following short descriptions of the various copora in whose construction they have been involved.

2 Prague Dependency Treebank (Eva Hajičová, Prague)

One of the maxims of the work on the Prague Dependency Treebank is that one should not overlook, disregard and thus lose what the *sentence* structure offers when one attempts to analyze the structure of discourse, thus moving from "the trees" to "the forest". Therefore, we emphasize that discourse annotation should make use of every possible detail the annotation of the component parts of the discourse, namely the sentences, puts at our disposal. This is, of course, not only true for the surface shape of the sentence (i.e., the surface means of expression), but (and most importantly) for the underlying representation of sentences. The panel contribution will introduce the (multilayered) annotation scenario of the Prague Dependency Treebank and illustrate the point using some of the particular features of the underlying structure of sentences that can be made use of in planning the scenario of discourse 'treebanks'.

Proceedings of the Linguistic Annotation Workshop, pages 191–196,
Prague, June 2007.

3 SDRT in Newspaper Text (Brian Reese, Austin)

We are currently working under the auspices of an NSF grant to build and train a discourse parser and codependent anaphora resolution program to test discourse theories empirically. The training requires the construction of a corpus annotated with discourse structure and coreference information. So far, we have annotated the MUC6[1] corpus for discourse structure and are in the process of annotating the ACE2[2] corpus; both corpora are already annotated for coreference. One of the goals of the project is to investigate whether using the right frontier constraint improves the system's performance in resolving anaphors. Here we detail some experiences we have had with the discourse annotation process.

An implementation of the extant SDRT (Asher and Lascarides, 2003) glue logic for building discourse structures is insufficient to deal with open domain text, and we cannot envision an extended version at the present time able to deal with the problem. Thus, we have opted for a machine learning based approach to discourse parsing based on superficial features, like BNL. To build an implementation to test these ideas, we have had to devise a corpus of texts annotated for discourse structure in SDRT.

Each of the 60 texts in the MUC6 corpus, and now 18 of the news stories in ACE2, were annotated by two people familiar with SDRT. The annotators then conferred and agreed upon a gold standard. Our annotation effort took the hierarchical structure of SDRT seriously and built graphs in which the nodes are discourse units and the arcs represent discourse relations between the units. The units could either be simple (elementary discourse units: EDUs) or they could be complex. We assumed that in principle the units were recursively generated and could have an arbitrary though finite degree of complexity.

4 Potsdam Commentary Corpus (Manfred Stede, Potsdam)

Construction of the Potsdam Commentary Corpus (PCC) began in 2003 and is still ongoing. It is a genre-specific corpus of German newspaper commentaries, taken from the daily papers *Märkische Allgemeine Zeitung* and *Tagesspiegel*. One central aim is to provide a tool for studying mechanisms of argumentation and how they are reflected on the linguistic surface. The corpus on the one hand is a collection of "raw" data, which is used for genre-oriented statistical explorations. On the other hand, we have identified two sub-corpora that are subject to a rich multi-level annotation (MLA).

The *PCC176* (Stede, 2004) is a sub-corpus that is available upon request for research purposes. It consists of 176 relatively short commentaries (12-15 sentences), with 33.000 tokens in total. The sentences have been PoS-tagged automatically (and manually checked); sentence syntax was annotated semi-automatically using the TIGER scheme (Brants et al., 2002) and Annotate[3] tool. In addition, we annotated coreference (PoCos (Krasavina and Chiarcos, 2007)) and rhetorical structure according to RST (Mann and Thompson, 1988). Our annotation software architecture consists of a variety of standard, external tools that can be used effectively for the different annotation types. Their XML output is then automatically converted to a generic format (PAULA, (Dipper, 2005)), which is read into the linguistic database ANNIS (Dipper et al., 2004), where the annotations are aligned, so that the data can be viewed and queried across annotation levels.

The *PCC10* is a sub-corpus of 10 commentaries that serves as "testbed" for further developing the annotation levels. On the one hand, we are applying recent guidelines on annotation of information structure (Götze et al., 2007). On the other hand, based on experiences with the RST annotation, we are replacing the rhetorical trees with a set of distinct, simpler annotation layers: thematic structure, conjunctive relations (Martin, 1992), and argumentation structure (Freeman, 1991); these are complemented by the other levels mentioned above for the PCC176. The primary motivation for this step is the high degree of arbitrariness that annotators reported when producing the RST trees (see (Stede, 2007)). By separating the thematic from the intentional information, and accounting for the surface-oriented

[1]The Message Understanding Conference, www-nlpir.nist.gov/related_projects/muc/.

[2]The Automated Content Extraction program, www.nist.gov/speech/tests/ace/.

[3]www.coli.uni-saarland.de/projects/sfb378/negra-corpus/annotate.html

conjunctive relations (which are similar to what is annotated in the PDTB, see Section 6), we hope to

- make annotation easier: handling several "simple" levels individually should be more effective than a single, very complex annotation step;
- end up with less ambiguity in the annotations, since the reasons for specific decisions can be made explicit (by annotations on "simpler" levels);
- be more explicit than a single tree can be: if a discourse fulfills, for example, a function both for thematic development and for the writer's intention, they can both be accounted for;
- provide the central information that a "traditional" rhetorical tree conveys, without loosing essential information.

5 AZ Corpus (Simone Teufel, Cambridge)

The Argumentative Zoning (AZ) annotation scheme (Teufel, 2000; Teufel and Moens, 2002) is concerned with marking argumentation steps in scientific articles. One example for an argumentation step is the description of the research goal, another an overt comparison of the authors' work with rival approaches. In our scheme, these argumentation steps have to be associated with text spans (sentences or sequences of sentences). AZ–Annotation is the labelling of each sentence in the text with one of these labels (7 in the original scheme in (Teufel, 2000)). The AZ labels are seen as relations holding between the meanings of these spans, and the rhetorical act of the entire paper. (Teufel et al., 1999) reports on interannotator agreement studies with this scheme.

There is a strong interrelationship between the argumentation in a paper, and the citations writers use to support their argument. Therefore, a part of the computational linguistics corpus has a second layer of annotation, called CFC (Teufel et al., 2006) or Citation Function Classification. CFC– annotation records for each citation which rhetorical function it plays in the argument. This is following the spirit of research in citation content analysis (e.g., (Moravcsik and Murugesan, 1975)). An example for a citation function would be "motivate that the method used is sound". The annotation scheme contains 12 functions, clustered into "superiority", "neutral comparison/contrast", "praise or usage" and "neutral".

One type of research we hope to do in the future is to study the relationship between these rhetorical phonemena with more traditional discourse phenomena, e.g. anaphoric expressions.

The CmpLg/ACL Anthology corpora consist of 320/9000 papers in computational linguistics. They are partially annotated with AZ and CFC markup. A subcorpus of 80 parallelly annotated papers (AZ and CFF) can be obtained from us for research (12000 sentences, 1756 citations). We are currently porting both schemes to chemistry in the framework of the EPSRC-sponsored project SciBorg. In the course of this work a larger, more general AZ annotation scheme was developed. The SciBorg effort will result in an AZ/CFC–annotated chemistry corpus available to the community in 2009.

In terms of challenges, the most time-consuming aspects of creating this annotated corpus were format conversions on the corpora, and cyclic adaptations of scheme and guidelines. Another problem is the simplification of annotating only full sentences; sometimes, annotators would rather mark a clause or sometimes even just an NP. However, we found these cases to be relatively rare.

6 Penn Discourse Treebank (Bonnie Webber, Edinburgh)

The Penn Discourse TreeBank (Miltsakaki et al., 2004; Prasad et al., 2004; Webber, 2005) annotates *discourse relations* over the Wall Street Journal corpus (Marcus et al., 1993), in terms of *discourse connectives* and their arguments. Following the approach towards discourse structure in (Webber et al., 2003), the PDTB takes a lexicalized approach, treating discourse connectives as the anchors of the relations and thus as discourse-level predicates taking two *Abstract Objects* as their arguments. Annotated are the *text spans* that give rise to these arguments. There are primarily two types of connectives in the PDTB: *explicit* and *implicit*, the latter being *inserted* between adjacent paragraph-internal sentence pairs not related by an explicit connective.

Also annotated in the PDTB is the *attribution* of each discourse relation and of its arguments (Dinesh et al., 2005; Prasad et al., 2007). (Attribution itself is not considered a discourse relation.) A preliminary version of the PDTB was released in April 2006 (PDTB-Group, 2006), and is available for download at http://www.seas.upenn.edu/~pdtb. This release only has implicit connectives annotated in three sections of the corpus. The annotation of all implicit connectives, along with a hierarchical semantic classification of all connectives (Miltsakaki et al., 2005), will appear in the final release of the PDTB in August 2007.

Here I want to mention three of the challenges we have faced in developing the PDTB:

(I) Words and phrases that can function as connectives can also serve other roles. (Eg, *when* can be a relative pronoun, as well as a subordinating conjunction.) It has been difficult to identify all and only those cases where a token functions as a discourse connective, and in many cases, the syntactic analysis in the Penn TreeBank (Marcus et al., 1993) provides no help. For example, is *as though* always a subordinating conjunction (and hence a connective) or do some tokens simply head a manner adverbial (eg, *seems as though ...* versus *seems more rushed as though ...*)? Is *also* sometimes a discourse connective relating two abstract objects and other times, an adverb that presupposes that a particular property holds of some other entity? If so, when one and when the other? In the PDTB, annotation has erred on the side of false positives.

(II) In annotating implicit connectives, we discovered systematic non-lexical indicators of discourse relations. In English, these include cases of marked syntax (eg, *Had I known the Queen would be here, I would have dressed better.*) and cases of sentence-initial PPs and adjuncts with anaphoric or deictic NPs such as *at the other end of the spectrum, adding to that speculation*. These cases labelled ALTLEX, for "alternative lexicalisation" have not been annotated as connectives in the PDTB because they are fully productive (ie, not members of a more easily annotated closed set of tokens). They comprise about 1% of the cases the annotators have considered. Future discourse annotation will benefit from further specifying the types of these cases.

(III) The way in which spans are annotated as arguments to connectives also raises a challenge. First, because the PDTB annotates both structural and anaphoric connectives (Webber et al., 2003), a span can serve as argument to >1 connective. Secondly, unlike in the RST corpus (Carlson et al., 2003) or the Discourse GraphBank (Wolf and Gibson, 2005), discourse segments are not separately annotated, with annotators then identifying what discourse relations hold between them. Instead, in annotating arguments, PDTB annotators have selected the *minimal* clausal text span needed to interpret the relation. This could comprise an embedded, subordinate or coordinate clause, an entire sentence, or a (possibly disjoint) sequence of sentences. As a result, there are fairly complex patterns of spans within and across sentences that serve as arguments to different connectives, and there are parts of sentences that don't appear within the span of *any* connective, explicit or implicit. The result is that the PDTB provides only a partial but complexly-patterned cover of the corpus. Understanding what's going on and what it implies for discourse structure (and possibly syntactic structure as well) is a challenge we're currently trying to address (Lee et al., 2006).

7 MPQA Opinion Corpus (Theresa Wilson, Pittsburgh)

Our opinion annotation scheme (Wiebe et al., 2005) is centered on the notion of *private state*, a general term that covers opinions, beliefs, thoughts, sentiments, emotions, intentions and evaluations. As Quirk et al. (1985) define it, a *private state* is a state that is not open to objective observation or verification. We can further view private states in terms of their functional components — as states of *experiencers* holding *attitudes*, optionally toward *targets*. For example, for the private state expressed in the sentence *John hates Mary*, the experiencer is *John*, the attitude is *hate*, and the target is *Mary*.

We create private state frames for three main types of private state expressions (*subjective expressions*) in text:

- explicit mentions of private states, such as "fears" in "The U.S. fears a spill-over"
- speech events expressing private states, such as "said" in "The report is **full of absurdities**,"

Xirao-Nima said.

- expressive subjective elements, such as "full of absurdities" in the sentence just above.

Frames include the source (experiencer) of the private state, the target, and various properties such as polarity (*positive*, *negative*, or *neutral*) and intensity (*high*, *medium*, or *low*). Sources are *nested*. For example, for the sentence "China criticized the U.S. report's criticism of China's human rights record", the source is ⟨*writer, China, U.S. report*⟩, reflecting the facts that the writer wrote the sentence and the U.S. report's criticism is the target of China's criticism. It is common for multiple frames to be created for a single clause, reflecting various levels of nesting and the type of subjective expression.

The annotation scheme has been applied to a corpus, called the "Multi-Perspective Question Answering (MPQA) Corpus," reflecting its origins in the 2002 NRRC Workshop on Multi-Perspective Question Answering (MPQA) (Wiebe et al., 2003) sponsored by ARDA AQUAINT (it is also called "OpinionBank"). It contains 535 documents and a total of 11,114 sentences. The articles in the corpus are from 187 different foreign and U.S. news sources, dating from June 2001 to May 2002. Please see (Wiebe et al., 2005) and Theresa Wilson's forthcoming PhD dissertation for further information, including the results of inter-coder agreement studies.

References

Nicholas Asher and Alex Lascarides. 2003. *Logics of Conversation*. Cambridge University Press, Cambridge.

Sabine Brants, Stefanie Dipper, Silvia Hansen, Wolfgang Lezius, and George Smith. 2002. The TIGER treebank. In *Proceedings of the Workshop on Treebanks and Linguistic Theories*, Sozopol.

Lynn Carlson, Daniel Marcu, and Mary Ellen Okurowski. 2003. Building a discourse-tagged corpus in the framework of rhetorical structure theory. In J. van Kuppevelt & R. Smith, editor, *Current Directions in Discourse and Dialogue*. Kluwer, New York.

Nikhil Dinesh, Alan Lee, Eleni Miltsakaki, Rashmi Prasad, Aravind Joshi, and Bonnie Webber. 2005. Attribution and the (non-)alignment of syntactic and discourse arguments of connectives. In *ACL Workshop on Frontiers in Corpus Annotation*, Ann Arbor MI.

Stefanie Dipper, Michael Götze, Manfred Stede, and Tillmann Wegst. 2004. Annis: A linguistic database for exploring information structure. In *Interdisciplinary Studies on Information Structure*, ISIS Working papers of the SFB 632 (1), pages 245–279.

Stefanie Dipper. 2005. XML-based stand-off representation and exploitation of multi-level linguistic annotation. In Rainer Eckstein and Robert Tolksdorf, editors, *Proceedings of Berliner XML Tage*, pages 39–50.

James B. Freeman. 1991. *Dialectics and the Macrostructure of Argument*. Foris, Berlin.

Michael Götze, Cornelia Endriss, Stefan Hinterwimmer, Ines Fiedler, Svetlana Petrova, Anne Schwarz, Stavros Skopeteas, Ruben Stoel, and Thomas Weskott. 2007. Information structure. In *Information structure in cross-linguistic corpora: annotation guidelines for morphology, syntax, semantics, and information structure*, volume 7 of *ISIS Working papers of the SFB 632*, pages 145–187.

Olga Krasavina and Christian Chiarcos. 2007. Potsdam Coreference Scheme. In *this volume*.

Alan Lee, Rashmi Prasad, Aravind Joshi, Nikhil Dinesh, and Bonnie Webber. 2006. Complexity of dependencies in discourse. In *Proc. 5th Workshop on Treebanks and Linguistic Theory (TLT'06)*, Prague.

William Mann and Sandra Thompson. 1988. Rhetorical structure theory: Towards a functional theory of text organization. *TEXT*, 8:243–281.

Mitchell Marcus, Beatrice Santorini, and Mary Ann Marcinkiewicz. 1993. Building a large scale annotated corpus of English: The Penn TreeBank. *Computational Linguistics*, 19:313–330.

James R. Martin. 1992. *English text: system and structure*. John Benjamins, Philadelphia/Amsterdam.

Eleni Miltsakaki, Rashmi Prasad, Aravind Joshi, and Bonnie Webber. 2004. Annotating discourse connectives and their arguments. In *NAACL/HLT Workshop on Frontiers in Corpus Annotation*, Boston.

Eleni Miltsakaki, Nikhil Dinesh, Rashmi Prasad, Aravind Joshi, and Bonnie Webber. 2005. Experiments on sense annotation and sense disambiguation of discourse connectives. In *4^{t} Workshop on Treebanks and Linguistic Theory (TLT'05)*, Barcelona, Spain.

Michael J. Moravcsik and Poovanalingan Murugesan. 1975. Some results on the function and quality of citations. *Soc. Stud. Sci.*, 5:88–91.

The PDTB-Group. 2006. The Penn Discourse TreeBank 1.0 annotation manual. Technical Report IRCS 06-01, University of Pennsylvania.

Rashmi Prasad, Eleni Miltsakaki, Aravind Joshi, and Bonnie Webber. 2004. Annotation and data mining of the Penn Discourse TreeBank. In *ACL Workshop on Discourse Annotation*, Barcelona, Spain, July.

Rashmi Prasad, Nikhil Dinesh, Alan Lee, Aravind Joshi, and Bonnie Webber. 2007. Attribution and its annotation in the Penn Discourse TreeBank. *TAL (Traitement Automatique des Langues*.

Randolph Quirk, Sidney Greenbaum, Geoffry Leech, and Jan Svartvik. 1985. *A Comprehensive Grammar of the English Language.* Longman, New York.

Manfred Stede. 2004. The Potsdam commentary corpus. In *Proceedings of the ACL Workshop on Discourse Annotation*, pages 96–102, Barcelona.

Manfred Stede. 2007. RST revisited: disentangling nuclearity. In Cathrine Fabricius-Hansen and Wiebke Ramm, editors, *'Subordination' versus 'coordination' in sentence and text – from a cross-linguistic perspective.* John Benjamins, Amsterdam. (to appear).

Simone Teufel and Marc Moens. 2002. Summarising scientific articles — experiments with relevance and rhetorical status. *Computational Linguistics*, 28(4):409–446.

Simone Teufel, Jean Carletta, and Marc Moens. 1999. An annotation scheme for discourse-level argumentation in research articles. In *Proceedings of the 9th European Conference of the ACL (EACL-99)*, pages 110–117, Bergen, Norway.

Simone Teufel, Advaith Siddharthan, and Dan Tidhar. 2006. An annotation scheme for citation function. In *Proceedings of SIGDIAL-06*, Sydney, Australia.

Simone Teufel. 2000. *Argumentative Zoning: Information Extraction from Scientific Text.* Ph.D. thesis, School of Cognitive Science, University of Edinburgh, Edinburgh, UK.

Bonnie Webber, Matthew Stone, Aravind Joshi, and Alistair Knott. 2003. Anaphora and discourse structure. *Computational Linguistics*, 29:545–587.

Bonnie Webber. 2005. A short introduction to the Penn Discourse TreeBank. In *Copenhagen Working Papers in Language and Speech Processing*.

Janyce Wiebe, Eric Breck, Chris Buckley, Claire Cardie, Paul Davis, Bruce Fraser, Diane Litman, David Pierce, Ellen Riloff, Theresa Wilson, David Day, and Mark Maybury. 2003. Recognizing and organizing opinions expressed in the world press. In *Working Notes of the AAAI Spring Symposium in New Directions in Question Answering*, pages 12–19, Palo Alto, California.

Janyce Wiebe, Theresa Wilson, and Claire Cardie. 2005. Annotating expressions of opinions and emotions in language. *Language Resources and Evaluation*, 39(2/3):164–210.

Florian Wolf and Edward Gibson. 2005. Representing discourse coherence: A corpus-based study. *Computational Linguistics*, 31:249–287.

Author Index

Association for Computational Linguistics
209 N. Eighth Street
Stroudsburg, Pennsylvania 18360